D0165661

# The United States and China

## DATE DUE

| | |
|---|---|
| | |
| | |
| | |
| | |
| | |
| | |
| | |
| | |
| | |
| | |
| | |
| | |
| | |
| | |
| | |
| | |
| | |
| | |
| | |
| | PRINTED IN U.S.A. |

Uncle Sam — "*Make good use of it, my friend*"

"Uncle Sam and Young China." This cartoon illustrates China's positive response when America decided to use some Boxer Rebellion indemnity money for Chinese students in the United States. "Young China" also shows his willingness to learn from Uncle Sam in appreciation of "a new epoch in the history of the relation between America and China." *Source: The Chinese Students' Monthly 5, no. 3 (January 1910): 145–146.*

# ASIA/PACIFIC/PERSPECTIVES
## Series Editor: Mark Selden

# The United States and China

## *A History from the Eighteenth Century to the Present*

Dong Wang

ROWMAN & LITTLEFIELD PUBLISHERS, INC.
Lanham • Boulder • New York • Toronto • Plymouth, UK

Published by Rowman & Littlefield Publishers, Inc.
A wholly owned subsidary of The Rowman & Littlefield Publishing Group, Inc.
4501 Forbes Boulevard, Suite 200, Lanham, Maryland 20706
www.rowman.com

10 Thornbury Road, Plymouth PL6 7PP, United Kingdom

British Library Cataloguing in Publication Information Available

**Library of Congress Cataloging-in-Publication Data**
Wang, Dong, 1967–
The United States and China : a history from the eighteenth century to the present / Dong Wang.
p. cm. — (Asia/Pacific/perspectives)
Includes bibliographical references and index.
ISBN 978-0-7425-5781-9 (cloth : alk. paper) — ISBN 978-0-7425-5782-6 (pbk. : alk. paper) —
ISBN 978-0-7425-5783-3 (electronic) 1. United States—Foreign relations—China. 2. China—
Foreign relations—United States. I. Title.
E183.8.C5W3416 2013
327.7305109'033—dc23
2012039575

The paper used in this publication meets the minimum requirements of American
National Standard for Information Sciences Permanence of Paper for Printed Library
Materials, ANSI/NISO Z39.48-1992.

Printed in the United States of America

# Contents

# Acknowledgments

While presenting my findings from original research, a historical synthesis such as this book also draws on the work and wisdom of others. Looking back on the six-year preparation of *The United States and China*, I take the keenest pleasure in acknowledging the assistance provided by colleagues, friends, and students across North America, Asia, Europe, and Oceania.

I am beholden to Mark Selden, Charles Hayford, and Flemming Christiansen for counsel, criticism, and editing. Our vigorous exchange of ideas has helped make a better book than it otherwise would have been. This is also the proper place to express my profound gratitude to my long-time editor, Paul Sorrell in New Zealand, who has left an imprint throughout this book.

Susan McEachern, my editor at Rowman & Littlefield, has been instrumental in supporting me to deal with unexpected delays and guiding me through the book production process. I wish to acknowledge, with deep appreciation, her dedication to publishing in the area of China and the United States, as well as the Rowman & Littlefield team of Carolyn Broadwell-Tkach, Janice Braunstein, Matt Evans, and others, for their professionalism.

My participation in events organized by the University of Cologne, the University of Erfurt, the University of Göttingen, and the University of Hamburg has been uniformly rewarding. Karen Shire at the University of Duisburg-Essen in Germany generously invited me to visit the Institute of East Asian Studies under the sponsorship of the German Science Foundation. I am also grateful to Duisburg-Essen's Käte Hamburger Kolleg (the Centre for Global Cooperation Research) funded by the German Federal Ministry of Education and Research. The large, vibrant intellectual community with a social sciences bent in Germany's industrial heartland has helped shape and fine-tune my thinking about U.S.-Chinese relations in global affairs.

My sincere thanks also go to countless individuals for their help. At the risk of leaving out some of their names, I should like to acknowledge the contribution of David Armstrong, Thomas Askew, Daniel H. Bays, Petra Brandt, Chang Li, Anthony Cheung, Paul Cohen, Derek Curtis, John Fitzgerald, Andrea Francioni, Henrietta Harrison, Nancy Hearst, Geir Helgesen, Shirley Houston, Daisy Hu, Juha Janhunen, Jiang Junxin, Jin Guangyao, Kawashima Shin, Samuel Keller, Thoralf Klein, Annamari Leppäniemi, Timothy Mahoney, Susan McHone, Eugenio Menegon, Paul Midford, Rana Mitter, Tak-Wing Ngo, Dave O'Ryan, John Pomfret, Caroline Reeves, Mark Sargent, Timo Soikkanen, Sun Youli, Tang Chi-hua, Tao Feiya, Tao Wenzhao, Gary Tiedemann, William Tsutsui, Wang Jianlang, Wang Xi, Jeffrey Wasserstrom, Susanne Weigelin-Schwiedrzik, Ian Welch, Tom Wells, Tim Wright, Xu Xiaoqun, Xu Yihua, Margherita Zanasi, Zhang Xiaoyan, Zhao Quansheng, and Zhao Suisheng. Some of my new ideas about the roles of China and the United States on the world scene were sparked by conversations with my students from China, Finland, France, Great Britain, Hong Kong, India, Italy, Japan, Russia, Spain, Ukraine, and other countries and places.

Over the years, many institutions have allowed me to utilize their libraries and archival resources. Among them are the Baker Library, the Harvard-Yenching Library, the Law School Library, the Houghton Library, the Widener Library, the Divinity School Library, the Fairbank Center for Chinese Studies Library (all at Harvard University), the Boston Public Library, the Sterling Memorial Library and Divinity School Library at Yale University, the British Library, the British National Archives at Kew, the John Rylands Library at the University of Manchester, the School of Oriental and African Studies Library at London University, Leiden University Libraries, the Finnish National Library, the Nordic Institute of Asian Studies Library, the Institute of Modern History Library at the Chinese Academy of Social Sciences in Beijing, the Academia Historica in Taipei, and the Archives of the Institute of Modern History at the Academia Sinica (Taipei). The main library at the University of Turku in Finland filled many of my interlibrary loans requests. Gordon College (Wenham, Mass.), the University of Turku, the Academy of Finland, and the Toivola Foundation provided financial support for part of the research for this book.

Parts of chapters 7, 10, and 12 have previously appeared in article form as follows: "Portraying Chinese Christianity: The American Press and U.S.-China Relations since the 1920s," *Journal of American-East Asian Relations* 13 (2004–2006, published in November 2008): 81–119; "Circulating American Higher Education: The Case of Lingnan University (1888–1951)," *Journal of American-East Asian Relations* 9, nos. 3–4 (Fall–Winter 2000, published in 2006): 147–167; and "China's Trade Relations with the United States in Perspective," *Journal of Current Chinese Affairs* 39, no. 3 (October 2010): 165–210. I thank the above journals for granting me the right to reprint the material here. Several paragraphs in chapters 2, 4, 5, and 7 are drawn from my books, *China's Unequal Treaties* (Lexington Books, 2005) and *Managing God's Higher Education* (Lexington Books, 2007).

During the last two decades since I left China for the United States in 1993, my family has scattered across the United States, Italy, Germany, Finland, Denmark, and China. Despite the spatial separation, we have remained connected in good and difficult times alike. I am indebted to "the flower"—my daughter—fourteen-year-old Rose, who has lovingly followed her mother to Europe, despite her attachment to her home cities of Boston and Seattle. Rose appreciates the European experience that has enabled an American teenager to learn to speak five different languages within a short time.

Dong Wang
Pikisaari, at the mouth of the Finnish-Swedish archipelago

# Introduction

Combining original research with contemporary scholarship, this book reexamines over two centuries of interaction between the United States and China in a changing world. It explains the foundations and character of their political, economic, military, social, and cultural relations, and shows how they have come to shape the domestic and international affairs of the two countries. But this is not the complete picture. American-Chinese relations have also been affected by national and global forces. Societal interchanges and government-level interactions are dual themes, although the boundaries of these connections are often hard to distinguish. This research survey differs from conventional overviews of United States–China relations in that I give equal consideration to American and Chinese experiences and perspectives, and to the modern (approximately from 1800 to the 1950s) and contemporary (post-1950s) periods.[1]

Since 1784 when the first American ship, the *Empress of China*, landed in Canton, U.S.-Chinese relations have moved from the periphery to the center of strategic attention, for both countries. This transformation has not eroded either American supremacy or Chinese sovereignty, but in the twenty-first century has given rise to a new order of national, bilateral, and supranational institutions that conjoins the two countries.

From a long historical perspective, the relationship between the United States and China has passed through three phases, roughly divided in the mid-nineteenth and mid-twentieth centuries. Relations shifted significantly from the interaction between an empire (Qing China) and a young nation-state (the United States), to the interplay between two nation-states, and then to wide-ranging encounters between a nation-state (the People's Republic of China) and an empire (the United States).

The concept of *empire* in the history of American-Chinese relations has two connotations. When applied to Qing China (1644–1911), it refers to the last of China's dynastic empires—one that still evoked the glory of an ancient civilization but found it hard to understand what nation-states and sovereignty meant until the latter half of the nineteenth century.[2] When used as an epithet for the United States after World War II, *empire* denotes the proselytizing exercise of national power and influence over other peoples—criticized by some as a deviation from the ideals of America's founding fathers, hailed by others as America's proud mission, a duty to make the world a better place for everyone. Some critics have seen the American empire as grounded in the U.S. view of itself as a global state with no boundaries, and a belief that American ideals and institutions ought to be emulated by the rest of the world. In the words of Rosemary Foot, "While at times this [view] has persuaded Americans that they would do better to retreat from the world and be content to act as a beacon to others, the trend over the second half of the twentieth century and into the twenty-first has been to take the lead in attempts to universalize American values so as to guarantee a stable global order."[3]

What issues dominated U.S.-Chinese relations in the past? As William C. Kirby noted in the mid-1990s, many historians of China's foreign relations have shied away from the realist school of international relations, which treats states as primary actors pursuing national interests and rational geopolitics.[4] Three influential conceptual frameworks for understanding the relationship are John K. Fairbank's paradigm—built around the Western impact on and stimulation of China, and China's response; Paul A. Cohen's China-centered (and, more recently, his "China unbound" or human-centered) approach; and William C. Kirby's focus on internationalization. The three political, economic, and cultural propositions considered by the present study validate the perspectives that these different methodologies and viewpoints share more than what separates them.[5]

## PROPOSITION ONE: U.S.-CHINESE RELATIONS CONSTITUTE AN ONGOING CONTEST BETWEEN TWO STATES IN A CHANGING GLOBAL CONTEXT

The American and Chinese states, as the primary shapers of their mutual relationship, have a mandate and an obligation to manage their relations. The forces of nationalism and globalization confront each state with choices in its dealings with the outside world. Each government needs to manage complex trade-offs between domestic welfare and the external environment on a case-by-case basis. The entangling of nationalism and globalization as considerations in decision making complicates the process.

America's early experiences in China (1784–1850s) reveal the dynamic beginnings of American nationalism in the country's transformation from a British colonial frontier to a sovereign state. This historical process had two distinct components, which have received scant attention in scholarly discussions of early U.S.-Chinese relations. The first was America's conscious pursuit of national greatness as an independent country. The second element was the entrepreneurial flexibility and tactical pragmatism shown by the United States.

In 1843, just after China's defeat by Britain in the Opium War (1840–42), U.S. Secretary of State Daniel Webster (1841–43, 1850–52) directed Caleb Cushing, the U.S. commissioner to China, to concentrate on matters of strategic importance to the United States—that is, to avoid contentious issues, to be mindful of American national dignity, and to be respectful of the Chinese:

> It will be no part of your duty to enter into controversies which may exist between China and any European State; nor will you, in your communications, fail to abstain altogether from any sentiment or any expression which might give to other Governments just cause of offence. It will be quite proper, however, that you should, in a proper manner, always keep before the eyes of the Chinese the high character, importance, and power, of the United States. You may speak of the extent of their territory, their great commerce, and the numerous schools and institutions established in them, to teach men knowledge and wisdom. It cannot be wrong for you to make known, where not known, that the United States, once a country subject to England, threw off that subjection years ago, asserted its independence, [s]word in hand, established that independence after a seven years' war, and now meets England upon equal terms upon the ocean and upon the land.[6]

The assertion of national identity and independence was of prime importance to the U.S. secretary of state in the 1840s. What, then, concerned the Qing empire's decision makers? Among other things, they worried about the Americans' request to visit Beijing, China's capital, in order to negotiate directly with the Qing court. European-originated notions of sovereign states and trading terms were incomprehensible to the Qing rulers. In a memorial to the emperor, Qiying—the Qing government representative appointed to negotiate the first treaty with the United States—reported on his meetings with the Americans in June 1844:

> They were polite and very respectful but did not mention going to Peking for an audience and the presentation of their credentials. For

several days in succession Your slave has sent Huang En-t'ung, with various officials, to explain everything clearly, to commend the envoy for having waited in Kwangtung peacefully, and also to tell him that even if he went to Peking he would certainly be ordered back, thus making the trip in vain & Then he [Cushing] presented the précis of a commercial treaty. Although translated into Chinese, it was not clear and the phraseology was uncouth, but the purport was in general like the recently fixed regulations [with Britain]. Moreover, he said that they would not venture to follow the example of the English barbarians in appropriating islands. Your slave examined it carefully and there seemed to be nothing detrimental to the general commercial picture & Your slave considered it reasonable to conclude negotiations.[7]

In the latter half of the nineteenth century, the United States seized the opportunity to further its geopolitical, commercial, religious, and cultural presence in China. The American state strengthened its regional and global power through diverse diplomatic strategies—a policy of noninterference or neutrality in European affairs, the forceful Monroe Doctrine aimed at keeping Europeans out of Latin and South America, and the Open Door principle in China. Rather than following the Europeans and Japanese who scrambled for Chinese territories, concessions, and spheres of influence, the United States championed the Open Door doctrine—free trade and the maintenance of Chinese territorial and administrative integrity.

Meanwhile, Qing China was forced to submit to the global expansion of capitalism and to conform to Western standards of free trade and diplomatic protocol. The treaty system imposed on China (1842–1943) is probably the best example of this submission. Modern Chinese nationalism was forged on the anvil of degradation and decline visited on China by foreign intervention and the economic competition between predatory nation-states. It was also framed by the xenophobic attitude that held the Manchus—the Qing dynasty rulers—responsible for all China's miseries in modern times. A strong, central state was the key to China's national success, but the pathway to modernization remained elusive, frustrating generations of Qing Chinese leaders and elites.

In a public speech in 1899, President Theodore Roosevelt commented on the differences between the Chinese and American attitudes toward national life and global competition:

We cannot, if we would, play the part of China, and be content to rot by inches in ignoble ease within our borders, taking no interest in what goes on beyond them, sunk in a scrambling commercialism; heedless of the higher life, the life of aspiration, of toil and risk, busying ourselves with the wants of our bodies for the day, until suddenly we should find, beyond a shadow of question, what China has already found, that in this world the nation that has trained itself to a career of unwarlike and isolated ease is bound, in the end, to go down before other nations which have not lost the manly and adventurous qualities.[8]

During the first half of the twentieth century, the United States and China developed different national programs and used differing strategies to deal with new global geopolitical and economic challenges. The fall of the Qing empire in 1912 put an end to a dynastic system that had lasted for over 2,000 years. But what would replace imperial rule? American-style republicanism, rather than constitutional monarchy on the British model, attracted many anti-Manchu Chinese. China's ensuing experiment in constitutional government, the first Republic of China (1912–28), was accompanied by political and military disintegration. But it also further opened up China to foreign technologies, science, ideas, and modes of governance. The United States proved to be an important source of inspiration to many Chinese, who were also exposed to Russian, Japanese, German, and other models of development.[9] As a result of all these influences, the first Republic of China tenaciously pursued equitable treatment on the international stage.

In the United States, the end of the Gilded Age (1876–96) witnessed a heightened feeling of national identity and a confidence in the spread of American power around the globe—as befitted an "exemplary" nation endowed with the moral superiority of a capitalist economic system, democratic institutions, and Protestant values. The drive for progressive reform—seen in terms of social justice and political order—continued into the Woodrow Wilson administration (1913–21). Lauded as a supreme hero responding courageously to the gathering storm clouds of a European war, Wilson infused America's mission to the world with a new vigor: the "idea of America is to serve humanity," he declared, and the United States was to strive "for the elevation of the spirit of the human race."[10] His later failures aside, the new paths envisaged by Wilson essentially referred to the need for the United States to set a global agenda in conformity with its emerging economic and political hegemony.

In contrast, during the 1920s China was engulfed by the anti-imperialist, anti-warlord revolution that aimed to unify the nation. As a political and social platform, violent revolution held a growing appeal for many Chinese. The two major political parties—the Guomindang (Nationalist Party, GMD) and the Chinese Communist Party (CCP)—were alike in their nationalistic outlook and Soviet Bolshevik–influenced worldview, but grew apart over the tactics and content of the revolution in 1927. As the Chinese Nationalist government (1928–49) set out to modernize the country, its leader, Chiang Kai-shek, looked to the United States to contain Japan's and Russia's imperial ambitions in China. The United States outflanked other interested parties by being the first to sign a treaty with China in 1928 granting it tariff autonomy, an important step appreciated by the Nanjing authorities. The bilateral relationship was more important to Chiang than to the United States, though, which at the time was more inclined toward Japan. Japan's attack on the United States in 1941 strengthened American-Chinese political and military relations. During World War II, the United States proved helpful to Chiang's attempts to raise China's international status and to eliminate his chief enemy on the home front, Mao Zedong and the Chinese Communist Party. China's quest for treaty revisions and cancellations was realized in 1943 with the aid of the United States.

Rival nationalist leaders—in particular Chiang and Mao—resisted and ultimately upset American and Russian designs for China. America's unwillingness to use military force to intervene in the Chinese Civil War and its failure to abandon the unattainable goal of establishing a progressive, anti-Communist Chiang government led ultimately to disappointment in Washington. The Chinese Communists became the historical agent of change.

Following World War II, the United States assumed global leadership in the anti-Communist crusade and established its long-standing military hold on the Asia-Pacific region. The National Security Act of 1947 placed U.S. military forces on a permanent footing geared toward securing America's global preeminence. The hyperpower of the national security state was, however, both constrained and legitimized by its democratic, representative form of governance.[11] During the 1950s, Mao's new People's Republic of China leaned toward the Soviet bloc. It sought to resist American hegemonic ambitions, circumvent the U.S. isolation of China, and improve relations with America's allies—such as Britain, France, and

Japan—and newly independent Asian and African countries. As the United States drew itself into the conflict across the Taiwan Strait, it found that it could not easily push either Chiang or Mao around. The People's Republic vehemently asserted its sovereign rights to Taiwan, while Chiang defied American efforts to reduce the Nationalists' military presence on the offshore islands.

Against the backdrop of nationalist revolutions and the Cold War, the People's Republic and the United States faced off in the two major conflicts of the postwar era, first in Korea in 1951–53 and then in Indochina in the 1960s, particularly Vietnam. The stalemate in Korea and the U.S. defeat in Vietnam, together with mutual recognition of a Soviet threat, led to the opening of formal relations between the United States and China. But it took the United Nations twenty-three years to admit Mao's China as a member state, and the United States thirty years to officially recognize China, although the two countries held 136 meetings at the ambassadorial level between 1955 and 1970. Internally, the Chinese Communist state was consumed by the Cultural Revolution (1966–76) and missed the opportunity to fully engage in the burgeoning regional economy—unlike its neighbors Japan, South Korea, Taiwan, and Hong Kong.

A new phase in the relationship began in the early 1970s with Nixon's historic visit to China. Rapprochement and the normalization of relations grew out of shared antagonism toward the Soviet Union, America's redefinition of its role in a diverse world, and China's continuing efforts to build a strong and unified nation. The establishment of full diplomatic relations in 1979 helped China reorient its priorities; Deng Xiaoping led the country in rebuilding an economy which had been on the brink of collapse. At this time, industrialization now at last seemed to be within reach for China. If achieved, it would be the only real success experienced by the majority of Chinese in two hundred years of dynastic decline, foreign aggression and national humiliation, and revolutionary upheavals. However, China deferred to most of the American-made rules during this period. In the 1980s, the two countries worked out their differences peacefully, especially on the Taiwan issue. Creating and sustaining a peaceful international environment for economic development became China's national priority in foreign affairs. And in 1985–86 China and the Soviet Union, led by the reform-minded Mikhail Gorbachev, improved their relations.

Subsequently, relations between the United States and China endured some sharp swings, especially during 1989–2001. During this period, the relationship was shaped by many factors: conditions arising from the end of the Cold War, China's rejuvenated reforms, constant political conflicts between the two nations, change of leadership in Taiwan, China's accession to the World Trade Organization, the consequences of the September 11 attacks in the United States, the global financial crisis in 2008, and the national pride and goodwill generated by the 2008 Beijing Olympics and the 2010 Shanghai Expo.

From China's perspective, its diplomatic efforts have largely been in reaction to issues and criticisms initiated by the United States. China's chief priority has been to maintain a sense of national dignity while remaining open to the world. From the American perspective, China has been steadily pushing the United States out of the Asia-Pacific region, and a strong China is seen as a threat to American national and international interests. During the last two decades, China did not seek to openly challenge American global supremacy, but rather to restrict its scope and impact. This approach was met with resistance from some Asian states which perceived China's rise as aggressive and as a threat to the peace and stability of the region.

Both the United States and China have sought to strengthen their positions through nurturing good relationships with other countries, diverting resources to third parties, revitalizing existing regional and global economic and political frameworks, and developing new security structures.[12] In the new millennium, American-Chinese relations have been built within a very different system of bilateral and supranational institutions. These institutions include the U.S.-China Strategic and Economic Dialogue; the U.S.-China Comprehensive Framework for Promoting Strong, Sustainable and Balanced Growth and Economic Cooperation; the East Asia Summit; the Association of Southeast Asian Nations; the Asia-Pacific Economic Cooperation; the Trans-Pacific Partnership; the G20 Summit; the Doha Round negotiations; the International Monetary Fund; the European Union; and the United Nations.

## PROPOSITION TWO: ECONOMICALLY, CHINA HAS BEEN CATCHING UP, CLASHING WITH AMERICA'S CAPABILITY AND DESIRE TO CONTROL CHANGE

The story of intellectual property rights (IPR) reflects an important historical and economic dimension of American-Chinese relations. This is another area of contention between the two countries. The common impression is that China is the main IPR offender in modern and contemporary times. [13] However, among other factors, the real driver for their respective IPR policies and their implementation is the different choices made by the American and Chinese states in order to balance benefits against costs.

In China, most of the laws and regulations regarding intellectual property were issued in the final decade of the Qing dynasty, under foreign pressure and as part of the Qing government's tardy attempts at modernization, known as Xinzheng (the new policy). The Sino-British, Sino-U.S., and Sino-Japanese commercial treaties of 1902 and 1903 represent the earliest international efforts to regulate IPR in China through treaties.

The earliest American attempt to regulate IP matters in China is evidenced in Articles 9 (trademarks), 10 (patents), and 11 (copyrights) of the Treaty as to Commercial Relations between the United States and China concluded in October 1903 and ratified in January 1904. The treaty protected the exclusive use within the United States of trademarks lawfully patented by foreign nationals. And the U.S. government required the Qing state to give full reciprocal protection to American commercial interests in China, irrespective of whether these were represented by individuals or firms. The treaty stated, "The Chinese Government agrees to issue by its proper authorities proclamations, having the force of law, forbidding all subjects of China from infringing on, imitating, colorably imitating, or knowingly passing off an imitation of trade-marks belonging to citizens of the United States." [14] In addition, the Qing government agreed to establish a patent office and give full protection to the American authors, designers, or proprietors of any book, map, print or engraving, or translation into Chinese of any book. In other words, Americans were given exclusive rights to print and sell such material.

These new initiatives were strongly opposed by Chinese negotiators, intellectuals, and political elites. As Zhang Zhidong, the Qing statesman and one of the regime's chief negotiators, commented, "At the moment, China is learning from foreigners how to make machines and is translating foreign books in order to enlighten its own people. If we were to agree to these two clauses, it would be harmful to us. China would lose any hope of becoming strong."[15] The Chinese negotiators were also concerned that "the poor could ill afford the rising book prices" that would result if Americans were given exclusive rights to print and sell these books.

Qing China was not exceptional in resisting the implementation of intellectual property protection for Americans. Economists commonly observe that during the early stages of modernizing development, the regulatory incentives for developing countries to protect foreign IPR are low because they prefer to protect their national economies from global competition. Trade protectionism and free trade worked side by side as, depending on the issue at hand, both were closely linked with nation building and industrialization. The U.S. Copyright Act of 1790, for example, granted copyright protection only to American citizens, while Britain—the first industrialized nation—took the lead in extending reciprocal copyright protection to foreign countries. An essay by the leading American industrialist and philanthropist Andrew Carnegie (1835–1919) sheds light on America's resentment against the British at the time. According to Carnegie, a major source of Anglo-American tensions was industrial competition: "In our day, when every nation of the front rank aspires to manufacture and produce for its own wants, 'Foreign Commerce' and 'Free Trade' do not always make for peace and good will among nations, but the contrary. Nations are disposed to resent industrial invasion, Free-Trade Britain no less than Protective Germany."[16]

In China's Nationalist government era (1928–49), Chiang Kai-shek promoted industrial development through newly formed state-owned enterprises, especially during the Sino-Japanese War (1937–45). A stream of recent scholarship has questioned the long-established view that Chiang's government was hostile to business and industrial entrepreneurship. Characterizing the Guomindang government as an "embryonic developmental state," William C. Kirby argues that Chiang "sought to control China's progress from the center" through bureaucratic superagencies such as the National Reconstruction Commission, the National Economic Council, and the National Resources Commission, all instruments set up to manage the economy.[17]

On the question of Chinese IPR, the Nationalist government was not as motivated to bring about reform as it was in areas of high national priority such as the unequal treaties and China's international status.[18] In September 1932, patent regulations—not formal legislation, but provisional regulations on promoting industrial technology—went into effect in China on the order of the industrial and administrative ministries.

The government documents relating to these measures were unequivocal about the reasoning behind them. First, in light of the "infant state of our country's industrial technology," the Nationalist government decided to "continue adopting a protectionist policy" in its international dealings and to continue "confining the protection of inventions to domestic nationals." Second, the government noted that making the regulations temporary and informal through ministerial order (*buling* 部令) would avoid international "troubles":

> We are using the following expedient to deal with any international protests and request for patent protection. We do not have special national statutes, or registration offices, or membership of international industrial unions; if the proposed regulations pass the legislative council, and if the National Government publicly issues them, there is a real fear that the international community would come to us and complain that the patent law was already promulgated, or that confining protection only to Chinese was in violation of treaty provisions. This would be a nuisance.[19]

In Nationalist China of the 1930s, these measures had predictable consequences, and not only for Chinese nationals. Carl Crow (1884–1945)—a pioneering American advertising agent and author based in Shanghai—responded to the serious issues at stake with disarming humor:

> The Chinese manufacturer is also a graceless and shameless imitator of trade marks. . . . At one time we were advertising a sticky pomade which would keep the hair slicked down and give heads the appearance of having been covered with lacquer. It enjoyed a good sale. . . . In a few weeks there was an imitation brand on the market, and an average of one or more new imitations appeared every month. We finally began collecting them, like new issues of postage stamps. At one time, we had twenty-one varieties.[20]

Since World War II, the United States has been the driving force in constructing the global IPR regime. American control of changes in IPR corresponded to growing U.S. economic might in the twentieth century. In

1900 the United States produced around 30 percent of total world industrial output, in 1913 it produced 36 percent, and by 1926 it produced 42 percent. By the end of World War II, the United States already held two-thirds of the world's gold reserves and produced half of the world's goods. By 1957, American gross national product per capita was over US$2,500,[21] whereas mainland China could muster no more than US$10.

Economic relations between the United States and the People's Republic of China took off after President Nixon's historic visit to China in 1972. Thereafter, China gradually entered the American-dominated world economic order. Over the last four decades, China has become the largest consumer market in the world—but IPR remains one of the main sources of friction between the United States and China. The issue has spawned both conflict and conciliation as the two countries have competed to turn IPR to their own advantage. Besides bilateral negotiations and dialogues, the U.S. government has used the World Trade Organization to compel China to make statutory adjustments. American-initiated changes in China's IPR laws met with a degree of passivity on the Chinese side during the 1980s–90s.

Today, China is seeking to seize back the initiative on this issue. In current scholarly debates over IPR in China, the most notable—but probably most neglected—aspect is the guiding and coordinating role that the Chinese developmental state is undertaking. Intellectual property rights are being treated by the Chinese government as a "strategic resource" (*zhanlüe ziyuan* 战略资源) in China's IPR strategy (*zhishi chanquan zhanlüe* 知识产权战略) for national development.

American-Chinese relations over IPR involve interactions between two different capitalist systems—between a market-based and profit-oriented American system, on the one hand, and a Chinese form of capitalism on the other. The latter includes a three-tiered developmental state, with huge politically integrated corporations at the national level, other large capitalist firms, and vast numbers of small and medium-sized enterprises. Over the last two decades, the Chinese state has worked to develop IPR capability on an unprecedented scale. This has been a deliberate, national strategy similar to Japan's in the 1960s–70s. Thus we have seen an enhanced state ability to invest in advanced and green technology—such as high-speed railways, sulfur dioxide scrubbers, and flue-gas desulfurization facilities—where the state-guided acquisition of IPR, expanding markets, and technology are strategically integrated. The state's strategy has also involved planning and creating IPR frameworks and funding structures and enabling the coordination and transfer of knowledge through superagencies such as the State Intellectual Property Office and the State Development and Reform Commission in China. As the *Wall Street Journal* noted in May 2012, "Most economies can pull two levers to bolster growth—fiscal and monetary. China has a third option: The National Development and Reform Commission can accelerate the flow of investment projects."[22]

For both China and the United States, continuous technological innovation holds the key to controlling their economic futures. The United States has been making its own strategic adjustments. In September 2011, the U.S. Patent Reform Act was signed into law. Together with the Fiscal Year 2010–2015 Strategic Plan of the U.S. Patent and Trademark Office (USPTO), American patent reform is designed to maintain American global dominance in IPR and to aid the creation and growth of American businesses.[23]

## PROPOSITION THREE: WHILE THE UNITED STATES IS AN IMPORTANT MODEL FOR CHINA, AMERICA'S ROLE HAS BEEN CHALLENGED FROM THE BEGINNING

Global power is in large part dominance over ideas and agendas. The U.S. role as one of China's models or tutors is perhaps best symbolized by American missionary endeavors in China from 1830 to 1951 and the massive flow of Chinese students to the United States. Despite the probability that Americans, in the opinion of Werner Levi, were considered as "the best liked and least suspected foreigners" in modern Chinese history, China has challenged America's dominant role from the inception of the relationship.[24]

Beginning in the 1870s, American- and Chinese-sponsored educational efforts cultivated an elite power base in China, along with a belief in American values and influence on China's future and its intellectual elite in particular. Chen Xujing (1903–67), who received a PhD from the University of Illinois in 1928, became the president (1948–52) of Lingnan University, founded in 1888 by an American Presbyterian missionary. He went so far as to champion the total Americanization and Westernization of Chinese education and culture. Chen did not stand alone. The leaders of the National Trade Commission in China—an organization on a par with the National Resources Commission that controlled both public and private trading enterprises in the Nanjing government between 1937 and 1945—personified America's role as China's teacher. Of the ninety-five senior members of the commission, forty-two had received degrees, mostly masters and doctorates, from American universities or from St. John's University in Shanghai, established by an American missionary organization.[25]

Compared with Catholic and British foreign missions, the American Protestant missionary enterprise was a late starter, but was carried out with great energy and a strong social agenda. Besides proselytizing, many U.S. missionaries in China devoted considerable time and resources to help modernize Chinese education, science, technology, medicine, and culture, and society in general. Mostly founded or financed by Americans, the eighteen Chinese Christian colleges and universities were the most visible fruit of these missionary endeavors. But they do not represent the full picture. Between 1860 and 1900, for example, the missionary presence provoked anti-Christian agitation and violence among Chinese elites, officials, and ordinary villagers—incidents that "challenged the most skillful diplomacy of all the nations involved." Qing Chinese leader Li Hongzhang (1823–1901, Li Hung Chang) did not hesitate to voice his opinion that Americans were able to build locomotives and steamships yet still believed in devils and miracles—concepts Li dismissed as "missionary propaganda."[26]

In an interview with *The Independent*, Yuan Shikai (1859–1916), the president of the first Republic of China (1912–28), questioned the efficacy of Christian missionary work—albeit in friendly tones—while affirming the role of Confucianism as China's state religion:

> I could not have proclaimed Christianity with any effect, even had I so desired; for ninety-nine per cent of our people would not have known what it meant. But when I used the name of the wonderful Confucius and called upon the people everywhere to take upon his words, teachings and examples again, there was an immediate response. And a better China is already here. This, in itself, creates a larger and better field for the Christian missionary, for, as the noted Bishop Fabre once said to me, "Confucius is an excellent stepping stone to Christ."[27]

Many Chinese perceived Christianity as a foreign intrusion into their religious and cultural traditions. During 1922–27, the powerful Anti-Christian Movement in China severely shook American missionaries and their supporters. The Chinese intellectuals and students who orchestrated this anti-Western backlash declared that Christianity was "not only unscientific and outdated, but also a major obstacle to China's attainment of national independence." The Restoring Educational Rights Movement in 1924 bore an even stronger nationalistic and anti-imperialist bent, targeting Christian colleges and schools in China. "China is the most difficult field in the world for missionary work," one American newspaper article lamented.[28]

Aside from proselytizing and the pursuit of imperial exceptionalism, American cultural approaches to China were shaped in part by Cold War anti-Communism. To many Americans, the Communist victory in China in 1949 had violated the "law of history."[29] In the words of Harold R. Isaacs,

> Americans assumed responsibility for the minds, bodies, and immortal souls of the Chinese, and the United States assumed responsibility for China's political independence and administrative integrity. . . . It was an experience shared by all the millions who put pennies, dimes, and quarters on collection plates for generations, who contributed to relief funds for the Chinese, and whose tax money made up the vast sums, ultimately billions of dollars, paid out to succor and support China and its people in peace and war. . . . They [the Chinese] ejected Americans from China through that very Door which Americans had striven so long and so valiantly to keep Open. . . . They were, in short, ungrateful wretches.[30]

Ironically, Red China has come close to realizing the vision held until 1949 by many Americans of a stable, biddable China governed by Chiang Kai-shek. Christianity is now an important part of the Chinese spiritual landscape; millions of Chinese have been lifted out of poverty in a much more open, diverse China. The People's Republic has given the United States due credit for helping steer the nation's transition from belief in violent revolution to belief in prosperity through evolution. During the first ten years of the new millennium, nearly a million Chinese students—most of whom are the only child in their families belonging to the post-1980s generation—left home to study in the United States. As the People's Republic became further integrated into the U.S. orbit, America's expectations for a China "made in America's image" have increased accordingly. But China's contemporary resurgence has also sharpened its perception that the American-led global political and financial order is inequitable. Development and peace are "Red" China's theme songs for the twenty-first century; they take their place alongside democracy and freedom, America's most loudly trumpeted values.

## NOTES

1. The term "research survey" derives from Michael H. Hunt, *The Making of a Special Relationship: The United States and China to 1914* (New York: Columbia University Press, 1983), preface. For a historical appraisal, see "Further Reading" following the epilogue.

2. For the debate over nomadic empires, see Peter C. Perdue, *China Marches West: The Qing Conquest of Central Eurasia* (Cambridge, Mass.: Belknap Press of Harvard University Press, 2005). For a discussion of *empire* as a notion applied to the United States, see Michael H. Hunt and Steven I. Levine, *Arc of Empire: America's Wars in Asia from the Philippines to Vietnam* (Chapel Hill, N.C.: University of North Carolina Press, 2012), introduction. Also see Michael Hardt and Antonio Negri, *Empire* (Cambridge, Mass.: Harvard University Press, 2000). For a comparative study of the transition from empire and nation, see Joseph W. Esherick, Hasan Kayali, and Eric Van Young, eds., *Empire to Nation: Historical Perspectives on the Making of the Modern World* (Lanham, Md.: Rowman & Littlefield, 2006).

3. Rosemary Foot, "Strategy, Politics, and World Order Perspectives: Comparing the EU and US Approaches to China's Resurgence," in Robert S. Ross, Øystein Tunsjø, and Zhang Tuosheng, eds., *US-China-EU Relations: Managing the New World Order* (London: Routledge, 2010), pp. 212–232.

4. William C. Kirby, "Chinese-American Relations in Comparative Perspective, 1900–1949," in Warren I. Cohen, ed., *Pacific Passage: The Study of American-East Asian Relations on the Eve of the Twenty-First Century* (New York: Columbia University Press, 1996), pp. 163–189.

5. Ssu-yü Teng and John King Fairbank, *China's Response to the West: A Documentary Survey, 1839–1923* (Cambridge, Mass.: Harvard University Press, 1954; 1982 reprint with a new preface); Paul A. Cohen, *China Unbound: Evolving Perspectives on the Chinese Past* (New York: RoutledgeCurzon, 2003), introduction; William C. Kirby, "The Internationalization of China: Foreign Relations at Home and Abroad in the Republican Era," *China Quarterly* 150 (June 1997): 433–458.

6. Instructions from Daniel Webster on May 8, 1843, in Jules Davids, ed., *American Diplomatic and Public Papers: The United States and China* (Wilmington, Del.: Scholarly Resources, 1973), series I, vol. 1, pp. 150–156.

7. Jules Davids, ed., *American Diplomatic and Public Papers*, series I, vol. 1, pp. 253–254.

8. Theodore Roosevelt, *The Strenuous Life: Essays and Addresses* (New York: Century Co., 1900), p. 6.

9. Wang Gungwu, *Anglo-Chinese Encounters since 1800: War, Trade, Science, and Governance* (Cambridge: Cambridge University Press, 2003), synthesizes a broad range of interactions between the Anglo world—including the United States—and the Chinese. Moving beyond politics and diplomacy, Wang calls for further attention to be paid to the underappreciated impact of the West on China's modernization.

10. Woodrow Wilson, "Annapolis Commencement," June 5, 1914, http://www.presidency.ucsb.edu/ws/?pid=65380 (accessed November 28, 2010).

11. The nature and effectiveness of these checks and balances have fueled the ongoing controversy over the extent of the power exercised by the U.S. government. See William Novak, "The Myth of the 'Weak' American State," *American Historical Review* 113, no. 3 (June 2008): 752–772; Michael Hudson, *Super Imperialism: The Origin and Fundamentals of U.S. World Dominance* (London: Pluto Press, 2003; 1st ed. in 1972). For insights on the strength of the Chinese state and revolution, see Joseph W. Esherick's "Ten Theses on the Chinese Revolution," *Modern China* 21, no. 1 (January 1995): 44–76.

12. In 2011, the U.S. military was spending about US$500 billion per annum, 5 percent of its GDP and over 40 percent of the world's total military expenditure. In the same year, the United States had over 83,000 troops deployed in East Asia and the Pacific. "Roundtable: Turning to the Pacific: U.S. Strategic Rebalancing toward Asia," *Asia Policy*, no. 14 (July 2012): 21–49.

13. Available research correctly ascribes the persistence of counterfeiting in China to the country's political culture, the complex network of bureaucracies, and the lack of state capacity for protecting the three IPR branches—copyright, trademark, and patent—through administrative, civil, and criminal law. Three representative works on this topic are Martin K. Dimitrov, *Piracy and the State: The Politics of Intellectual Property Rights in China* (New York: Cambridge University Press, 2009); Andrew C. Mertha, *The Politics of Piracy: Intellectual Property in Contemporary China* (Ithaca, N.Y.: Cornell University Press, 2005); William P. Alford, *To Steal a Book Is an Elegant Offense: Intellectual Property Law in Chinese Civilization* (Stanford, Calif.: Stanford University Press, 1995).

14. William M. Malloy, comp., *Treaties, Conventions, International Acts, Protocols and Agreements between the United States of America and Other Powers, 1776–1909* (Washington, D.C.: Government Printing Office, 1910), vol. 1, pp. 261–270.

15. Wang Yanwei (王彦威), comp., *Qingji waijiao shiliao* [清季外交史料 Diplomatic sources for the late Qing] (Beijing: Shumu chubanshe, 1987), vol. 3, p. 2722.

16. According to Carnegie, America's anti-British sentiments also drew strength from the Canadian question. Canadians and Americans wrangled over the Irish-American terrorists, tariffs, boundaries, fishing rights, and seal hunting. Andrew Carnegie, "Does America Hate England?" originally published in 1897, in his *The Gospel of Wealth and Other Timely Essays* (Cambridge, Mass.: Harvard College, 1962), pp. 197–210.

17. William C. Kirby, "Engineering China: Birth of the Developmental State, 1928–1937," in Wen-Hsin Yeh, ed., *Becoming Chinese: Passages to Modernity and Beyond* (Berkeley, Calif.: University of California Press, 2000), pp. 137–160.

18. Dong Wang, *China's Unequal Treaties: Narrating National History* (Lanham, Md.: Rowman & Littlefield, 2005).

19. Zhongguo di'er lishi dang'anguan, comp., *Zhonghua minguoshi dang'an ziliao huibian* [中华民国史档案资料汇编 Collected archival sources for the history of the Republic of China] (Nanjing: Jiangsu guji chubanshe, 1994), vol. 5, part 1, caizheng jingji (5), pp. 76–97.

20. Carl Crow, *400 Million Customers: The Experiences—Some Happy, Some Sad—of an American in China and What They Taught Him* (Norwalk, Conn.: EastBridge, 2003; reprint of 1937 ed. by Hamilton in London), pp. 268–269. Crow once worked as an advertising agent for the American government in China.

21. U.S. Bureau of the Census, *Historical Statistics of the United States, Colonial Times to 1957* (Washington, D.C.: Government Printing Office, 1960), p. 139.

22. Tom Orlik, "China Option: Show Me the Stimulus Money," *Wall Street Journal*, May 30, 2012, p. 32.

23. http://www.uspto.gov/about/stratplan/USPTO_2010–2015_Strategic_Plan.pdf (accessed June 4, 2012). Wang Fenyu (王奋宇) and Zhao Jing (赵晶), "Meiguo zhuanli zhidu gaige jiqi dui Zhongguo de yingxiang" [美国专利制度改革及其对中国的影响 American patent reform and its impact on China], *Diaoyan baogao* 1561, no. 14 (February 23, 2012).

24. Werner Levi, *Modern China's Foreign Policy* (Minneapolis, Minn.: University of Minnesota Press, 1953), p. 125.

25. Zheng Huixin (郑会欣), *Guomin zhengfu zhanshi tongzhi jingji yu maoyi yanjiu (1937–1945)* [国民政府战时统制经济与贸易研究 A study of the Nationalist government's controlled wartime economy and trade regime] (Shanghai: Shanghai shehui kexueyuan chubanshe, 2009), pp. 326–340.

26. Sir Hiram Stevens Maxim, comp. and ed., *Li Hung Chang's Scrap-Book* (London: Watts & Co., 1913), foreword.

27. Yuan Shikai, "The Chinese Republic Reports Progress," *The Independent*, July 26, 1915.

28. "Christianity in China," *Los Angeles Times*, April 15, 1927, p. A4.

29. Thomas J. Christensen, "A 'Lost Chance' for What? Rethinking the Origins of U.S.-PRC Confrontation," *Journal of American-East Asian Relations* 4, no. 3 (Fall 1995): 249–278.

30. Harold R. Isaacs, *Scratches on Our Minds: American Images of China and India* (New York: John Day Company, 1958), p. 193.

*Part I*

# The Pacific Frontier and Qing China, 1784–1911

# ONE

# Yankee Merchants and the China Trade

Direct contacts between the United States and China originated in the "old" China trade of 1784–1844. The earliest U.S. foray into China in the eighteenth century proved useful for the newly independent republic, which was in political and financial trouble. It also brought North America into the global network of exchange in the Asia-Pacific region. Private Yankee merchants worked profitably within and around the Chinese cohong and British monopoly systems and consciously took on the European imperial powers in overseas markets. On the Chinese side, however, commercial growth did not translate into prosperity for most of Chinese hong traders, especially in the early nineteenth century. The Qing government failed to capitalize on the lucrative Canton trade as a tool for national development. America's private China trade indicated the systemic gap between the enterprising institutions of a young nation and the threadbare economic organization of a declining empire.

## THE SETTING

Trade between South China and the outside world dates back millennia. Before 500 BCE, a vast web of commercial connections linked South China, India, the eastern Mediterranean, the Pacific, Europe, and East and West Africa. From early history, Canton (Guangzhou), the inland seaport on China's southeast coast, was a hub for both domestic and foreign trade. As the starting point of the maritime Silk Road, Canton had established a trade relationship (in silk) with Rome in 116 CE. Other trading partners were India, Ceylon, Syria, Persia, and Arabia. By the eighth century, China's foreign trade market was regulated through the *Shibosi* (Bureau of Sea Trade). Buddhism and Islam were introduced into Canton at this time with the coming of Indian and Arab merchants. Over the following centuries, the Chinese system of taxation, administration, and regulation of trade was well established. Beginning in the sixteenth century, the arrival of Europeans—impelled by improved naval technology and religious zeal—ushered in a new era of capitalist penetration of China. And the Arabs lost their dominant trading position. New intercontinental sea routes that spanned the globe expanded mercantile networks as well as the range of goods traded. This expansion of trading patterns brought South China into closer contact with Europe, India, Southeast Asia, and the Americas.[1]

Americans were latecomers to the China trade conducted on a regional and global scale. The Portuguese had reached Canton in 1517, followed by the Spaniards in 1575, the Dutch in 1604, the English in 1636, and the French in 1660. Between 1690 and 1842, hundreds of ships of diverse nationalities made long voyages to Canton, the sole port open to foreigners. The China trade in early modern times involved multiple companies, governments, ethnic groups, and trading families (Americans, English, Spanish, Portuguese, Dutch, French, Danes, Swedes, Chinese, Parsees, Moors, Armenians, and others). People traded commodities such as tea, silk, porcelain, opium, lacquerware, furniture, and paintings across locations including Macau, Canton, London, Lisbon, Antwerp, Amsterdam, Batavia, Malacca, Manila, Calcutta, Bombay, New York, Boston, and Philadelphia. The old Canton trade was one of the most important contributors to the rise of global maritime trading networks during the century of 1750–1850.

## AMERICAN, CHINESE, AND GLOBAL FACTORS

Why did Americans travel vast distances to trade with China? Besides the exotic and lucrative aspects, two other factors fueled the new nation's push for overseas trading markets as far away as China. First, following independence, a severe economic depression and Anglo-American rivalry prodded Americans to elbow their way into world markets. Second, Canton—the center of the booming Sino-foreign trade—enticed Yankee merchants as "one of the most flexible places to negotiate business," capable of handling large volumes of goods and offering competitive prices, transactions on credit, and, most important of all, profitable deals.[2] Before the American Revolution, the thirteen colonies in North America had already become acquainted with China because their tea arrived in the British East India Company's ships from Canton by way of Great Britain.

## Economic Challenges and Opportunities in the Post-Revolution Era

As a colony of a hegemonic power, America had been included in the British colonial system. It gained entry to global trading markets, with Britain picking up the major military and administrative costs of the colonies. Britain's North American colonies had to some extent been business enterprises, concerned to yield a profit for their charter sponsors. Alongside the agricultural economy, commerce and trade developed among the thirteen colonies themselves and with the British West Indies, England, continental Europe, and West Africa. North American settlers traded rum, meat, fish, and other agricultural goods for sugar, molasses, and slaves with Caribbean islanders and Africans. Colonial products including furs, timber and American-built ships also had access to markets in England and continental Europe.

The Treaty of Paris, signed in September 1783, brought an end to the war between Great Britain and its American colonies, signifying British recognition of America's independence. However, continuing Anglo-American hostility produced problems at all levels during the postwar period, despite some improvements in their relationship as a result of Jay's Treaty of 1794 and Pinckney's Treaty of 1795. There was a new dimension to trade as well. The British and British West Indian ports and trade routes which Americans had utilized for over a century were now closed to the United States. In addition, France and Spain terminated wartime trading privileges by placing maritime constraints on American commerce. In the early years of the republic, foreign trade and the merchant marine were vital components of its economy and diplomacy. The acquisition of independent commercial rights in world markets and the military power to sustain them were matters of national survival.[3] By the late 1780s, American exports per capita had fallen 30 percent from the 1760s.

These changes to the structure of the Atlantic and Caribbean trade forced—indeed, liberated—Americans to find new channels for wealth. The lure of adventure and the hope of making quick fortunes led young men into overseas enterprises aboard refitted privateers.[4]

*Foreign Trade in Canton*

Although the initiative for doing business with China originated from the American side, it would be misleading to conclude that America's old China trade was a unilateral effort. The bustling international port of Canton and the activities of Chinese merchants were well established and well known, attracting American adventurers to the South China Sea.

When Captain John Green and supercargo Major Samuel Shaw of the *Empress of China* reached Canton in 1784, China was ruled by Emperor Qianlong (r. 1736–96) of the Qing (1644–1912), the last imperial dynasty. Qianlong, whose sixty-year reign was the longest in Chinese history, sought to limit and control foreign trade, but not to eliminate it.

Canton, Macau, and the Pearl River Delta constituted the core of the Sino-foreign trade network.[5] River and sea channels forming an A-shaped gulf forty miles long link Canton to the former British colony of Hong Kong at its right foot, and to the former Portuguese colony of Macau at its left.

In 1684, shortly after Taiwan came under Chinese control, the Qing court lifted its ban on the entry of foreign vessels, thus allowing foreign commercial ships legal access to China. The following year, the Qing government designated Canton, Zhangzhou, Ningbo, and Yuntaishan as foreign trading ports and established maritime customs agencies in Guangdong, Fujian, Zhejiang, and Jiangsu. However, in 1757, to control the activities of foreigners and bar them from entering poorly defended coastal areas, all international trade was limited to Canton. This lasted until 1842 when China was defeated in the Opium War.

The Canton trade was structured by a system that consisted of four key components—the Guangdong Maritime Customs (hereafter "Customs"), the port of Macau, the important anchorage at Whampoa, and the cohong system.[6] It was operated by the Customs—the imperial provincial agency—and overseen by the Manchu Qing court. The Canton foreign trade framework included two tiers of supervision—it was intended to "control the Chinese merchants through the government" (*yiguan zhishang*) and "control foreigners through the Chinese merchants" (*yishang zhiyi*). Working alongside the provincial governors of Guangdong and Guangxi, the Guangdong Maritime Customs was headed by a superintendent known as the hoppo.[7] The Customs enforced customs procedures, supervised the hong merchants, regulated foreign shipping, and collected direct duties on foreign vessels and cargoes at Whampoa—the anchorage twelve miles downstream from Canton City where foreign vessels moored in the Pearl River. Under its jurisdiction, there were thirty-one tollhouses, twenty-two inspection posts, and twenty-two registration stations. In 1834, the tax revenue raised through the Customs was over 1.6 million taels.

Macau, about eighty miles from Canton, was the first "port of entry" and a sort of home base for foreign merchants to retreat to when the trading season was over. Foreigners were not permitted to establish permanent settlements in China.

In 1720, the Qing central government instituted the cohong system which authorized a group of merchants, known as the Thirteen Hongs (or guilds), to regulate and conduct business with foreigners.[8] However, the following year, the system was dismantled as a result of objections by foreign merchants. In 1760, Emperor Qianlong granted a petition for a reorganization of the system and exclusive rights to deal with foreign vessels submitted by nine hongs represented by Pan Zhencheng. In 1771, the cohong was again suspended and then reformed in 1780. It continued in this form until 1842, when the signing of the first opium treaties imposed by Britain marked the beginning of a new era in Sino-foreign trade. The licensed Chinese merchants—many of whom immigrated to the Canton area from Fujian Province—functioned as middlemen working between the government and foreign traders. Their monopolistic position enabled them to acquire fortunes. The precise number of hongs varied at different times. Between 1800 and 1803, for instance, there were eight hongs involved in business transactions as shown in table 1.1.[9]

The last dozen miles between the Whampoa anchorage and Canton were closed to foreign trading vessels. Thus, after ships had passed through the Guangdong maritime customhouse at Whampoa, their cargo was unloaded into Chinese riverboats, "chop boats," or "sampans," and carried to the hongs' storage depot, just outside Canton City, where foreign traders maintained their warehouses.

Under the Canton system, foreigners were normally restricted to three locations—Macau, Whampoa, and a quarter-mile radius around the

**Table 1.1. List of Business Names of Merchants, Merchants, and Hong Names**

| Business Names of Merchants | Merchants | Hong Names |
|---|---|---|
| Puankhequa 潘启官 | Pan Zhencheng 潘振承 (b. 1714–88), Pan Zhixiang 潘致祥 (1755–1820) | Tongwen hang 同文行 |
| Mowqua 卢茂官 | Lu Guanheng 卢观恒 (?–1812) | Guangli hang 广利行 |
| Puiqua (伍佩/沛官) or Howqua (浩官) | Wu Bingjun 伍秉钧 (?–1801), Wu Bingjian 伍秉鉴 (1765–1843) | Yihe hang 怡和行 |
| Yanqua (叶仁官) | Ye Shanglin 叶上林 (b. 1753–1809) | Yicheng hang 义成行 |
| Chunqua (刘章官) | Liu Dezhang 刘德章 (?–1825) | Dongsheng hang 东生行 |
| Pongqua (倪榜官) | Ni Bingfa 倪秉发 (?–1810) | Dacheng hang 达成行 |
| Gnewqua (郑侣官) | Zheng Chongqian 郑崇谦 (?–1813) | Huilong hang 会隆行 |
| Conseequa (潘崑水官) | Pan Changyao 潘长耀 (?–1823) | Liquan hang 丽泉行 |

foreign warehouses, which were known as "factories," "foreign hongs," or simply "hongs."[10] European and American buildings with national flags flying over their sloping roofs stood two or three stories high on the banks of the Pearl River. This was also where foreigners stayed while conducting business in the trading season starting in the spring. The trading season ended with the arrival of winter when all foreigners were expected to leave Canton and return home, or at least go back to Macau.[11] Women, as well as guns, spears, or arms of any kind, were expressly banned. Three times a month, foreign seafarers could make special excursions, in groups no larger than ten, across the Pearl River to visit the flower gardens (Fati) or joss house (Buddhist temple) on Honam Island.[12]

Whatever the inconvenience and restrictions imposed on foreign and Chinese merchants alike under the Canton system, the volume of international business in the port steadily increased from the late seventeenth century. Up till 1842, when the Canton system came to an end, the Chinese government, foreigners, and a few hong merchants benefited handsomely from it. In 1783, forty-five European ships sailed into Canton, sixteen of them English. The following year, the total of thirty-five included nine English ships, four French, five Dutch, three Danish, four Portuguese, and one American. In 1787, sixty-eight foreign vessels called at Canton, including fifty-two English ships and five American ships from New York, Philadelphia, and Salem.[13]

Despite discrepancies in the figures, independent Chinese accounts confirm these trends. Liang Tingnan recorded thirty-six foreign vessels in

1783, forty-six in 1785, seventy-three in 1787, and eighty-three in 1789. [14] In 1790, eighty-three foreign vessels anchored in Canton harbor, bringing tax revenues of 1.1 million taels. Over the next half century the number would increase to two hundred, with 1.8 million taels in customs dues, comprising 60 percent of the Guangdong provincial revenues. [15] Chinese hong merchants also reported being swamped by the burgeoning business conducted between Canton and Macau in 1792. [16] This overall increase in shipping underlines the point made by Paul A. Van Dyke: "If Chinese regulators in Canton were indeed only interested in discouraging and restricting the trade, as is so often the hypothesis of modern histories, how is it that the opposite happened?" [17] In other words, "[t]he increasing number of foreigners going to China and the constant expansion of overall goods being handled in the port" scarcely justify the customary portrayal of the Canton system as a hindrance to foreign commerce. [18] A further explanation for the increase in trade volumes was the English Parliament's sharp reduction of the duty on tea (the Commutation Act of 1784), from about 125 percent to 12.5 percent, in an effort to eradicate smuggling. [19]

The Canton system was by no means a free trade regime. It resembled the bulk of European trade with Asia which was carried out by the English, Dutch, and French East India companies and merchant groups that had secured monopoly trading privileges from their respective governments. [20] Mercantile relations between the Chinese authorities, foreign governments, foreign nationals, and local Chinese were further complicated by the lack of agreed diplomatic and legal procedures. An incident recorded in Samuel Shaw's journal makes this painfully clear:

> By the Chinese [customary] law, blood must answer for blood, and there have been instances where the execution of this law has been enforced. About four years since [in 1780], a Frenchman and a Portuguese, both belonging to the same ship, had a scuffle, in which the latter was killed; whereupon the Chinese demanded that the former should be given up. On being told that what the man had done was agreeable to the law of self-defence, they replied that they understood the matter very well, but that they must examine him before their tribunal, it being indispensable that they should take cognizance of such cases, and that after examination he should be restored unhurt. The poor fellow, upon these assurances, was delivered to the Chinese, who the next morning brought him to the waterside, in the neighborhood of the factories, and there strangled him. [21]

In subsequent decades, as the military power of the Europeans grew and China's Qing dynasty declined, these and more fundamental economic and cultural differences would lead to mounting tensions.

## The Empress of China

On Sunday, February 22, 1784—George Washington's birthday—the 360-ton *Empress of China* (hereafter *Empress*), which had served during the American Revolution, departed New York for Canton. Two groups of New York and Philadelphia merchants, Daniel Parker & Company (John Holker, William Duer, and Daniel Parker) and Robert Morris (one of the major financiers of the American Revolution and superintendent of finance appointed by the Continental Congress between 1781 and 1784), had jointly purchased the refitted privateer. With a cargo representing US$120,000, a huge investment at the time,[22] the ship was loaded with American-produced ginseng, wine and brandy, tar and turpentine, woolen garments, cotton, fur skins, and $20,000 in specie.[23] Among the crew of forty-five were Captain John Green, Second Captain Peter Hodgkinson, Supercargo Samuel Shaw of Boston (a war veteran in charge of the business affairs of the ship), Purser John White Swift, and Surgeon and Mate Robert Johnson and Andrew Caldwell.[24]

After stopping over at the Cape Verde Islands, a Portuguese colony off the coast of Senegal in Africa, the vessel crossed the Cape of Good Hope and set sail for the Indian Ocean. In company with two friendly French ships encountered in the Straits of Sunda near the Java shore, the *Empress* headed across the South China Sea. On August 25, 1784, after over six months of the over-18,000-mile journey, the ship arrived at Macau. Here the *Empress* procured the official permit, a chop or stamp, to enter China, hiring a Chinese pilot to guide the ship up the Pearl River to Canton, as well as a *fiador*, or surety—a leading Chinese merchant; a comprador, who furnished provisions and other necessities; and a linguist who arranged for small boats to transfer the ship's goods.

In December 1784, the *Empress*, loaded with 3,000 piculs of Hyson and Bohea tea, sixty-four tons of porcelain, and other goods from China, headed back to the United States and arrived in New York in May 1785.[25] The net profit of the voyage amounted to around $30,727, an estimated 25 to 30 percent return on the original investment.[26] America's venture into the China market was off to a good start. Its ginseng fared especially well in the China market, the price in 1787 rising from US$140 to $200 a picul.[27] In the early Canton trade, the United States essentially provided raw materials, whereas the Chinese offered sophisticated, processed manufactures such as tea, silk, and porcelain.

The expedition was widely noticed in major American newspapers and by the government. Boston's *American Herald* published an excerpt from a diary kept by "a gentleman on board." It noted that American traders were treated "in all respects, as a free and independent nation; as such, during our stay, we were universally considered. The Chinese themselves were very indulgent towards us, and happy in the contemplation of a new people, opening to view, a fresh source of commerce to their extensive empire."[28] Upon his return from Canton, Samuel Shaw reported to key Federalist Party figures Alexander Hamilton, John Adams, and John Jay (U.S. foreign minister). Shaw was later appointed American consul to Canton.

## TRADING COMMODITIES, FINANCE, AND MECHANISMS

Enjoying considerable flexibility compared to their British competitors who contracted with monopoly enterprises,[29] American private traders infused new life into the Asia market. In licit and illicit trade alike, Americans found innovative ways to operate profitably within and around the Canton and British monopoly systems. Although not comparable to the British China trade, the U.S. trade with China rose to the second largest in volume within ten years, surpassing continental Europeans. The annual average number of American ships docking at Canton grew from 7.4 in 1785–1800 to 23.6 in 1801–11.[30]

The U.S. old China trade can be divided into four periods. The first was the period of beginnings and expansion, 1784–90. Then came a period of further expansion and wars (1791–1814), when the China trade experienced a considerable boost during the European wars in the aftermath of the French Revolution. The United States became the neutral common carrier for Europe, and previous trade barriers were swiftly eliminated. Between 1801 and 1811, between a quarter and a half of European imports of tea were re-exported from the United States.[31] The third period lasted from the close of the War of 1812 with Britain to the outbreak of the conflicts over opium (1815–38); during this phase the China trade expanded, most notably in 1818–19, when forty-seven American vessels were trading in Canton.[32] The fourth and final phase (1839–44) was marked by the First British-Chinese Opium War, culminating in the Treaties of Nanjing and Wanghia. The opium wars and their outcome will be discussed in the next chapter.

Among the Chinese exports—chiefly tea, silk, porcelain, furniture, and lacquerware—tea figured very large. After 1784, over two-thirds of the tea business was carried out by the British East India Company, reflecting the numbers and tonnage of English shipping involved in the China trade. In 1784, tea exports from China to Britain and its dependencies weighed in at 14 million pounds, and for the months of March, May, June, September, and December of 1786, the company's tea sales exceeded 15.6 million pounds by weight, amounting to over 3.3 million pounds sterling in value. In 1787, tea exports carried by English ships were upwards of 21 million net pounds in weight.[33]

Following the successful voyage of the *Empress of China*, however, the American tea trade grew rapidly. American tea exports from Canton were 880,100 pounds in 1785, reaching the 1 million pound mark in 1787, over 3 million in 1790, upwards of 5 million in 1800, 9 million in 1830, and more than 19 million pounds in 1840.[34] As a percentage of total American imports from China, tea increased from 36 percent in 1822 to 65 percent in 1837, and 82 percent in 1840. However, Chinese tea imports declined after this period as a result of the reimposition of tariffs following the American Civil War and increased imports of Japanese tea.[35]

Innovation and flexibility helped Americans succeed in the China market. Ships from Boston, such as the *Columbia*, inaugurated the "triangle" fur trade. After sailing around South America to exchange iron chisels for sea otter fur with the Native Americans on the northwest coast, these Bostonian adventurers set off westward across the Pacific to trade fur for teas, silks, and other goods in Canton. After three years at sea, the *Columbia* returned to Boston with earnings of $90,000.[36] From the 1790s to the 1820s, "[t]o the Indians who knew the English as 'King George men,' the Americans were known as 'Boston men.'"[37] In Canton, Yankee fur traders bartered freely, underselling fine-quality British pelts by up to 20 percent.

In November 1794, Britain granted Americans highly limited trading rights in the British West Indies and India under the Treaty of Amity, Commerce and Navigation (the Jay Treaty). Under the treaty provisions, Americans could export and import goods directly only between the United States and India.[38] This severely limited U.S. participation in the lucrative opium trade with China. With no access to the Patna opium exported from Calcutta in eastern India—the production, inspection, and sales of which had been regulated by the British East India Company since 1773—American merchants began exporting Turkish opium from Smyrna to Canton in a bid to crack the British monopoly on the Chinese opium market. Later, American firms such as Augustine Heard & Co. penetrated the Malwa opium network in central India. The cheap Malwa drug was produced by independent princely states in the Malwa uplands and shipped from Bombay by native Parsee and Hindu merchants operating beyond British jurisdiction.

In 1836 American traders sold $275,921 worth of opium—a large sum, but only 4 percent of the $9 million worth of American goods imported into China that year and less than 10 percent of the size of the Anglo-Indian–Canton drug market, a large source of the revenue of the British imperial state. Although the American opium trade in Canton was operated as a subsidiary means of purchasing and shipping teas and silks, the Americans soon undercut their British rivals who had previously enjoyed a monopoly on opium.

As in the case of the *Empress of China*, aboard the American vessels the supercargoes were initially put in charge of purchases. Later, resident trading firms, which hired resident commission agents to work in Canton or represented American mercantile houses, took their place. Resident commission agents of note included Samuel Shaw (of the firm of Shaw & Randall), Samuel W. Russell, John P. Cushing (commissioned by Thomas H. Perkins & Co. of Boston), B. C. Wilcocks of Philadelphia, and Daniel Stansbury of Baltimore. Russell & Co., Perkins & Co., Olyphant & Co., James Oakford & Co., Archer & Co., T. H. Smith & Co., and Wetmore & Co. ranked among the largest American trading houses in Canton.[39]

Under the merchant security system (known as *baoshang zhidu* 保商制度) inaugurated by the Qing in 1745, every foreign seaman and foreign ship was the personal liability of the hong merchants, who were held accountable by the hoppo for inbound and outbound merchandise, import and export duties, and even the behavior of foreigners. Foreigners were not allowed to communicate directly with the authorities; this could only be done through the hong merchants, who virtually became the securities of foreign traders. American and European merchants were thus forced into close partnerships with their Chinese counterparts.

Over time, the multinational mercantile community in Canton developed a unique form of pidgin English, a commercial patois mixed with loan words from Portuguese, Hindi, Cantonese, and other languages. Words such as *mandarin* (originating from Portuguese *mandar*, "to order"); *comprador* (from Portuguese *comprar*, "to buy"); *bazaar* (from Hindi, "market"); *Schroff* (from Hindi, "moneylender"); and *coolie* (from Hindi, *kuli*, "laborer") have since been adopted into standard English usage.

The hong merchants entertained Americans at their grand residences, offering them delicate foods such as "birds' nest soup, with plover's eggs and Bêche-de-Mer, curiously prepared sharks' fins and roasted snail,"[40] sumptuous dinners often costing more than 100,000 taels. Samuel Shaw noted the lengths to which these wealthy merchants went to landscape their properties:

> [T]he gardens belonging to Chowqua [Chen Yuanquan; hong name, Yuanquan hang] are extensive; much art and labor are used to give them a rural appearance, and in some instances nature is not badly imitated. Forests, artificial rocks, mountains, and cascades, are judiciously executed, and have a pleasing effect in diversifying the scene.[41]

Shaw also praised the hong merchants for their professional standards:

> The knavery of the Chinese, particularly those of the trading class, has become proverbial. . . . It must at the same time be admitted that the merchants of the cohoang [cohong] are as respectable a set of men as are commonly found in other parts of the world. . . . They are intelligent, exact accountants, punctual to their engagements, and though not the worse for being well looked after, value themselves upon maintaining a fair character.[42]

Years later, William C. Hunter, a Russell & Co. partner, likewise spoke highly of his Chinese counterparts:

> As a body of merchants, we found them honourable and reliable in all their dealings, faithful to their contracts, and large-minded. Their private residences, of which we visited several, were on a vast scale, comprising curiously laid-out gardens, with grottoes and lakes, crossed by carved stone bridges, pathways neatly paved with small stones of various colours forming designs of birds, or fish, or flowers.[43]

In return for tea and other Chinese processed manufactures, the Americans traded items such as ginseng, raw cotton, yarn, cotton cloth, kerosene, furs, sandalwood, and opium—goods that were mainly raw materials and were not in great demand in China. How then was the

China trade financed? America's trade deficit was redressed with specie, mostly Spanish silver dollars, as well as with loans from London bankers.

In the early nineteenth century, Spanish bullion—the proceeds from the sale of American products in the Spanish West Indies, South America, Portugal, and Gibraltar—made up approximately 65 percent of annual American exports to China, amounting to over $7 million per year (as in 1819).[44] From the late 1820s on, the bulk of Sino-American trade was financed by bills of exchange drawn on London, through credit arrangements with London banking houses such as Barings and Browns—since paying in bullion had become more expensive than sending bills. "During the years 1827–1833, nearly 9 million dollars worth of English bills were used by the American merchants to pay off their debts at Canton . . . during the period 1871–1894, British credit still accounted for one-third of American payments to China."[45] Up until World War I, in international markets "a bill drawn on London was almost the only kind of bill which the holder could be sure of converting into gold in case of any failure of credit, [and] bills drawn on London were preferred to bills drawn on any other commercial center."[46]

A letter written in Canton in 1832 by John Murray Forbes of Russell & Co. affirms this practice:

> Sir, Mr. A [Augustine] Heard [Forbes' partner] having kindly afforded me a letter of introduction to you and assured me that you would be good enough to transact a little business which I may have in your place. I have been induced to order the proceeds of several shipments to Europe and the U.S. (under certain circumstances, [sic]) to be invested in Bills on Payable and remitted to you for collection for my account. . . . As I am about leaving this country for the U. States I have now to beg you that in care of receive [sic] such remittances you will be good enough to advise Mr. A. H. [Augustine Heard] of the same and to hold the amount when collected subject to his orders. The Bills if sent will be guaranteed by Mr. P. B. [full name unknown] B & C. [Reid Beale & Co., a private English trading house in India and China] of London, and I must really say that in case of non acceptance or nonpayment it will be necessary to have them protested immediately and returned, begging your indulgence for troubling you.[47]

While some Chinese hong merchants stood to make large profits from the American trade, throughout the latter half of the eighteenth and the first half of the nineteenth centuries in particular they also accumulated a large volume of arrears and debts—the other side of the expanded foreign trade in Canton. Before the 1730s, when the value and volume of the China trade in the four designated ports was relatively small, accounts were normally cleared by the season or by the ship. Financing arrangements were small scale and manageable—although instances of hong merchants putting down a security deposit for delivery, delay, or default were just as common as cash advances from foreigners.[48] In the latter two-thirds of the eighteenth century, however, most of the hong merchants found themselves in financial difficulties. Trade growth, coupled with the predominance of chartered joint-stock companies such as the British East India Company, exacerbated their funding and supply problems. "[T]he European trade was expanding rapidly while the Hongists' network of trade and sources of income were shrinking; consequently, they became increasingly dependent on the cash advances of foreigners, credit from up-country suppliers and the delayed payment of imperial duties."[49]

Lacking political power, the hong merchants could not appeal to the government but constantly had to submit to official requests for money and the demands of foreign creditors.[50] The merchant security system of 1745 forced all cohongs still in business to assume the debts left by those that had declared bankruptcy. In 1780, hong merchants Kewshaw (Zhang Tianqiu; hong name Yuyuan hang) and Yngshaw (Yang Shiying, Taihe hang) went into bankruptcy for the nearly 2 million silver taels they owed to British traders. As a result, the Chinese government ordered other merchants such as Puankhequa (Pan Wenyan, Pan Shaoguang) to pay off Kewshaw and Yngshaw's debts over ten years.[51] William C. Hunter noted a similar case where, following default by three hong merchants, Hingtai, Mouqua, and Kingqua, the governor of Guangdong and Guangxi required that other cohongs pay off "the indebtedness of three of their own number to 'outside barbarians.'"[52]

The relations between cohong merchants, foreign traders, and the Chinese government were inextricably enmeshed. In the postscript to a letter to John Perkins Cushing, a partner with Russell & Co., dated April 23, 1833, a senior Chinese hong merchant in Canton, Houqua (or Howqua),[53] wrote,

> As I trust you will always feel an interest in whatever relates to me, it will afford you pleasure to learn that my no. 4 son, in whose name is the Hong[,] has within a few days received from the Emperor the highest evidence of his favor, namely a Peacocks Tail!!! In the last serious

rebellion[,] I made, in the name of my son[,] a voluntary donation of a
sum . . . with which proof of loyalty the Emperor was much pleased
and has bestowed this public honor; the greatest a subject can receive,
and for which I esteem this the happiest circumstance of my life.[54]

Houqua was clearly overjoyed with the recognition he and his son received from the Qing imperial court, something coveted by a merchant
whose social status was inherently humble. In late imperial China, silk
rank badges differentiated by decorative animals indicated a mandarin's
importance; peacock tail feathers served the purpose just as well. Success
in the civil service entrance examinations was the normal pathway for
ordinary men to enter the world of officialdom, with its nine grades. The
conferring of such an extraordinary honor on a businessman like Houqua
was the result of the financial contribution he had made in his son's name
to the government's repression of a peasant rebellion. The letter throws
an intimate light on what—beyond wealth—lay closest to the hong merchant's heart.

A story told by Samuel Shaw, on the other hand, details a strained
relationship in which hong merchants found themselves vulnerable to
the extortionate behavior of government officials such as the hoppo:

> A few years since, Shykinkoa, one of the most respectable merchants of
> the co-hoang [sic], having failed in an engagement to send some teas to
> the English ships, assigned as a reason for it, that he had been disap-
> pointed of seeing the hoppo, who, he said, was drunk when he called at
> his house to take out the chop [stamp, permit for the merchant to visit
> the factory]. Shortly after, another of the co-hoang coming to the Eng-
> lish factory, the chief casually mentioned the disappointment, and the
> reason given for it by Shykinkoa. This man, who was Shykinkoa's ene-
> my, reported the matter to the hoppo, and Shykinkoa was forced to
> make his peace by a present of thirty thousand taels![55]

The following letter illustrates another side of the triangular relationship
between foreign businessmen, hong merchants, and the Chinese government. Acting as broker and guarantor between the government and
foreign traders, hongs established close connections with particular
foreign agents, giving them access to the same ships season after season.
Houqua, for example, known as a *bête noire* among English merchants,
preferred to trade with Americans. On June 15, 1833, Houqua wrote offering counsel to John P. Cushing, his business partner, regarding his
associate, Captain Pearson:

Your open letter by Capt. Pearson was handed me yesterday by himself in whom I was happy to recognize an old acquaintance. It is [an] unfavorable moment now to commence Tea operations to the extent that would be required to fill his large ship, and it appears most advisable that he should return for another load of rice and be here again in the commencement of the ensuing season. . . . Captain Pearson will probably get a fair freight on his Rice, although within the last 15 days the price had fallen nearly a dollar per picul, you may rest assured that I should render him every assistance in my power, in the hopes of hearing from you soon.[56]

## ASSESSMENT OF AMERICA'S EARLY CHINA TRADE

The old China trade came to an end because of the wars between Britain and China in the 1840s. Although it had a limited effect on overall economic life, the first encounter brought the United States into a useful relationship with China. Below are three legacies, both tangible and intangible.

First, many American traders and a few Chinese hong merchants amassed vast fortunes in a very short time. In particular, American merchants, as a special-interest group, left a palpable mark on the U.S. economy, politics, and foreign relations, although the significance of the China market in total American exports to the world was minimal, less than 0.5 percent by the end of the nineteenth century.[57]

Elias Hasket Derby (1739–99) of Salem, Massachusetts, one of the early millionaires in the United States, owed his fortunes to the China trade. Known as "King Derby," he was widely credited with resuscitating Salem's failing economy. Others also made their fortune in the trade. John Murray Forbes of Russell & Co., for instance, made profits of $150,000 in two years. On his return to Boston in 1837, he devoted his funds and energy to ironworks, steamships, and railroads. John P. Cushing returned from Canton to Boston in 1828, at the age of forty-one, with over $600,000. Back home, he invested his China money in railroads, textile mills, and other modern enterprises. Some of the capital Forbes invested in western railroads came directly from Houqua's family.

The founder of Girard College, Stephen Girard of Philadelphia, whose ships were engaged in sending opium to China, helped finance the War of 1812 and subscribed $3 million to the Second Bank of the United States in 1816. John Jacob Astor, known as the "landlord" of New York, made his fortune in the China fur trade and became the richest American in 1834. Among Boston's urban landmarks, Tremont House—best known as the first hotel in the United States with indoor plumbing, toilets, bathrooms, and running water—and the Massachusetts General Hospital, still in use today, were built with the fortune amassed by Thomas Handasyd Perkins, Astor's archrival in the China trade.

A few Chinese merchants were on a fast track to wealth as well. In 1834, Houqua estimated his assets at 26 million silver dollars, worth approximately $US52 million, and more than 6 million pounds sterling in 1882.[58] In China, both American and Chinese traders took the lead in creating new steamship companies. Edward Cunningham, Hsun Jun, and Koofunsing founded and financed the Shanghai Steam Navigation Company in 1862 and the China Merchants' Steam Navigation Company, the first steamship company owned and managed by Chinese.[59] However, without the support and encouragement of the Qing state, the enormous potential of the old China trade remained untapped on the Chinese side. In the late 1830s, the growing disparity between the Chinese economy—with a low level of capital accumulation and underdeveloped domestic industry—and the rapidly industrializing British manufacturing sector eventually brought down the Canton system.

Second, the China trade also helped Americans and Chinese become acquainted with each other. The most substantive early American literary works on China were written by maritime traders who had traveled to China. The China trade helped Americans form their understanding of China—both favorable and unfavorable—through their own firsthand experience. American knowledge was not just a simple duplicate of European thought on China.[60] This direct interaction stimulated an American appetite for luxury goods made in China. The artwork and furnishings acquired through the China trade—especially porcelain, paintings, and furniture—have long been admired by Americans.

Third, America's early experiences in China have lodged in the American psyche and become a symbol of national spirit. In the late eighteenth and early nineteenth centuries, the United States was beset with political divisions and economic difficulties. The Canton trade fed anti-British sentiment at the same time as it boosted American self-assurance.

These were embodied in many of the China trade's chief proponents. Samuel Shaw (1754–94) was the first American consul in Canton in 1786;

he had been an aide to General Henry Knox, commander of artillery of American forces during the American Revolution, and was later first secretary of the War Department of the United States. As supercargo of the *Empress of China*, Shaw pointed to British efforts to thwart American advances into the Canton trade:

> It is true, that the Court of Directors [of the British East India Company], in their instructions to the supercargoes, [at] the present season, enjoined it upon them to use every endeavour to prevent the subjects of Great Britain from assisting or encouraging in any shape the American commerce; but if this prohibition was intended by the directors, or construed by their servants, to extend to the civilities heretofore paid the Americans, it cannot be denied that such conduct was extremely illiberal.[61]

Early economic relations between the United States and China reflected the pre-industrial nature of the American economy, which was yet to produce major manufactures for export. The U.S. debut on the China stage, however, constituted the triumphant entry of a new nation into an expanding international system of politics and trade controlled by then hegemonic Britain and other European powers.[62]

## FURTHER READING[63]

In assessing the early American China trade, recent scholarship emphasizes the complex interactions between competition, profitability, the Chinese way of conducting commerce, foreign notions of free trade, and the changing business environment. See Jonathan Goldstein, *Stephen Girard's Trade with China, 1787–1824: The Norms versus the Profits of Trade* (Portland, Maine: MerwinAsia, 2011). Two interpretative strands—the dependency and modernization models—have shaped the broad contours of scholarly writing in this area. The dependency school contends that the old China trade—the commercial component of a westward Pacific movement by the United States—was intrusive and imperialist, with the United States gaining capital for development at the expense of others. The modernization paradigm, on the other hand, suggests that the American enterprise in China ultimately stimulated China's long-term modernization efforts. See James R. Gibson, *Otter Skins, Boston Ships, and China Goods:The Maritime Fur Trade of the Northwest Coast, 1785–1841* (Seattle, Wash.: University of Washington Press, 1999; 1st ed. 1992); Robert Y. Eng, *Economic Imperialism in China: Silk Production and Exports, 1861–1932* (Berkeley, Calif.: University of California Press, 1986); and Yen-p'ing Hao, *The Commercial Revolution in Nineteenth-Century China: The Rise of Sino-Western Mercantile Capitalism* (Berkeley, Calif.: Institute of East Asian Studies, University of California, 1986).

Works in Chinese covering similar ground include Zhang Kaiyuan (章 开沅) and Zhu Ying (朱英), eds., *Jindai jingji guanxi yu Zhongguo jindaihua* [近代经济关系与中国近代化 Modern economic relations and the modernization of China] (Wuhan: Huazhong chubanshe, 1990), and Wang Jingyu (汪敬虞), *Waiguo ziben zai jindai Zhongguo de jinrong huodong* [外国资本在 近代中国的金融活动 The financial activity of foreign capital in modern China] (Beijing: Renmin chubanshe, 1999).

Philip Chadwick Foster Smith's *The Empress of China* (Philadelphia, Pa.: Philadelphia Maritime Museum, 1984) brings history to life with its vivid treatment of financial scandals and human failings surrounding America's China venture. Concerning the U.S. participation in the opium trade, two books stand out: Jacques M. Downs' *The Golden Ghetto: The American Commercial Community at Canton and the Shaping of American China Policy, 1784–1844* (Bethlehem, Pa.: Lehigh University Press, 1997) is strong on the moral challenges of the opium business confronting American merchants. Combining history and anthropology, Thomas N. Layton unearths the story of an opium clipper *Frolic* in *The Voyage of the "Frolic": New England Merchants and the Opium Trade* (Stanford, Calif.: Stanford University Press, 1997).

On the cultural impact of the China trade and early American images of China, see Alfred Owen Aldridge's *The Dragon and the Eagle: The Presence of China in the American Enlightenment* (Detroit, Mich.: Wayne State University Press, 1993) and John Rogers Haddad, *The Romance of China: Excursions to China in U.S. Culture, 1776–1876* (New York: Columbia University Press, 2008).

## NOTES

1. Takeshi Hamashita, Mark Selden, and Linda Grove, *China, East Asia and the Global Economy: Regional and Historical Perspectives* (New York: Routledge, 2008). Guo Deyan (郭德焱), *Qingdai Guangzhou de Basi shangren* [清代广州的巴斯商人 Parsee merchants in Canton during the Qing period] (Beijing: Zhonghua shuju, 2005). Huang Qichen (黄启臣), *Guangdong haishang sichou zhilu* [广东海上丝绸之路 Guangdong's maritime Silk Road] (Guangzhou: Guangdong jingji chubanshe, 2003).

2. *Chinese Repository* 2, no. 7 (November 1833), p. 289.

3. Bradford Perkins, *The Cambridge History of American Foreign Relations*, vol. 1, *The Creation of a Republican Empire, 1776–1865* (Cambridge: Cambridge University Press, 1995), p. 7.

4. Charles L. Ver Steeg, "Financing and Outfitting of the First U.S. Ship to China," *Pacific Historical Review* 22, no. 1 (February 1953): 1–12.

5. Dong Wang, *Managing God's Higher Learning: U.S.-China Cultural Encounter and Canton Christian College (Lingnan University), 1888–1952* (Lanham, Md.: Rowman & Littlefield, 2007), chapter 1.

6. The terms *hong* and *cohong* are derived from the word for "agent" or "guild," denoting the idea of trading companies.

7. The hoppo's full title was "commissioner of the board of revenue in charge of customs duties for the maritime trade of Guangdong province" (*Duli Guangdong sheng yanhai dengchu maoyi shuwu hubu fensi*).

8. Liang Jiabin (梁嘉彬) et al., *Guangdong shisan hang kao* [广东十三行考 The Thirteen Hongs of Canton], reprint (Guangzhou: Guangdong renmin chubanshe, 1999; 1st ed. 1937), pp. 102–104. Zhongguo diyi lishi dang'anguan (中国第一历史档案馆 No. 1 Chinese Historical Archives) and Guangzhou liwanqu renmin zhengfu (广州荔湾区人民政府), eds., *Qinggong Guangzhou Shisanhang dang'an jingxuan* [清宫广州十三行档案精选 Selected Qing court archives on the Thirteen Hongs] (Guangzhou: Guangdong jingji chubanshe, 2002). Zhongguo diyi lishi dang'anguan, comp., *Qinggong Yuegang'ao shangmao dang'an quanji* [清宫粤港澳商贸档案全集 A complete collection of the Qing court archives on trade in Guangdong, Hong Kong, and Macau], 10 vols. (Beijing: Zhongguo shudian chubanshe, 2002).

9. Yang Guozhen (杨国桢), "Yangshang yu daban: Guangdong Shisanhan wenshu chutan" [洋商与大班:广东十三行文书初探 Foreign merchants and supercargoes: A preliminary study of the correspondence relating to the Thirteen Hongs in Guangdong], *Jindaishi yanjiu*, no. 3 (1996): 1–24.

10. Here the term *factories* refers to the establishments of "factors" or "agents"—not manufactories—the residential and business areas which became interchangeable with hongs.

11. Huang Guoxin (黄国信), Huang Qichen (黄启臣), and Huang Haiyan (黄海妍), *Huozhi huayang de yueshang* [货殖华洋的粤商 The Cantonese merchants—trading goods in China and overseas] (Hangzhou: Zhejiang renmin chubanshe, 1997), pp. 167–181.

12. William C. Hunter, *The "Fan Kwae" at Canton before Treaty Days: 1825–1844* (Taipei: Ch'eng-wen Pub. Co., 1965; reprint of 1882 ed. by Kegan Paul, Trench & Co. in London), pp. 28–29.

13. Samuel Shaw, *The Journals of Major Samuel Shaw, the First American Consul at Canton, with a Life of the Author by Josiah Quincy* (Taipei: Ch'eng-wen Pub. Co., 1968; reprint of Wm. Crosby and H. P. Nichols 1847 ed.), pp. 182, 228.

14. Liang Tingnan (梁廷枏, b. 1796–1861), *Yue haiguan zhi* [粤海关志 Gazetteer of the maritime customs of Guangdong] (Taipei: Cheng'wen Pub. Co., 1968), vol. 24, pp. 1783–1796.

15. Tan Bo (覃波), "Qinggong Guangzhou shisanhang dang'an de zhengui jiazhi" [清宫广州十三行档案的珍贵价值 The significance of the Qing imperial archives on the Thirteen Hongs in Canton], *Lishi dang'an* 4 (2003): 117–123.

16. Fong Lau (刘芳), comp., and Zhang Wenqin (章文钦), proofreader, *Putaoya Dongbota dang'anguan cang Qingdai Aomen zhongwen dang'an huibian* [葡萄牙东波塔档案

馆藏清代澳门中文档案汇编 Collected Qing archival sources in Chinese at the Instituto dos Arquivos Nacionais da Torre do Tombo in Portugal] (Macau: Aomen jijinhui, 1999), p. 633, document no. 1241. Yang Guozhen (杨国桢), "Yangshang yu Aomen: Guangdong Shisanhang wenshu xutan" [洋商与澳门:广东十三行文书续探 Foreign merchants and Macau: A further exploration of the correspondence relating to the Thirteen Hongs in Guangdong], *Zhongguo shehui jingjishi yanjiu*, no. 2 (2001): 43–53.

17. Paul A. Van Dyke, *The Canton Trade: Life and Enterprise on the China Coast, 1700–1845* (Hong Kong: Hong Kong University Press, 2005), introduction.

18. Paul A. Van Dyke, *The Canton Trade*, introduction.

19. Samuel Shaw, *The Journals of Major Samuel Shaw*, p. 229. Kuo-Tung Ch'en, *The Insolvency of the Chinese Hong Merchants, 1760–1843* (Taipei: Institute of Economics, Academia Sinica, 1990), pp. 44–46.

20. The British East India Company's business practices in China underwent some major changes over the years. Hosea Ballou Morse, *The Chronicles of the East India Company Trading to China, 1634 to 1833*, 5 vols. (Oxford: Oxford University Press, 1926–29).

21. Samuel Shaw, *The Journals of Major Samuel Shaw*, p. 186.

22. The inaugural capital of the Massachusetts Bank in Boston, opened in 1784, the year the *Empress of China* sailed, was only about twice that involved in the China expedition. The sum of $120,000 could purchase 24,000 acres of good land then. Clarence L. Ver Steeg, "Financing and Outfitting of the First U.S. Ship to China," *Pacific Historical Review* 22, no. 1 (February 1953): 1–12.

23. With regard to the $20,000 in specie put on board, there was a $2,300 shortage caused by Daniel Parker, the cashier for the *Empress of China*. Litigation over the disputed accounts especially involving Samuel Shaw and Daniel Parker was not settled until 1791.

24. Samuel Shaw, *The Journals of Major Samuel Shaw*, p. 212. Clarence L. Ver Steeg puts the number of crew at forty-six, in Steeg, "Financing and Outfitting of the First U.S. Ship to China." Foster Rhea Dulles, *The Old China Trade* (Cambridge, Mass.: Riverside Press, 1930), p. 7. Alfred Tamarin and Shirley Glubok, *Voyaging to Cathay: Americans in the China Trade* (New York: Viking, 1976).

25. 1 picul = 133.33 pounds.

26. John Austin Stevens, *Progress of New York in a Century, 1776–1876: An Address Delivered before the New York Historical Society on December 7, 1875* (New York: Printed for the Society, 1876), p. 45. H. A. Crosby Forbes, review of *The Empress of China* by Philip Chadwick Foster Smith, *New England Quarterly* 57, no. 4 (December 1984): 602–605.

27. Samuel Shaw, *The Journals of Major Samuel Shaw*, p. 252.

28. *American Herald* 4, no. 187 (May 16, 1785). *Providence Gazette and Country Journal* 22, no. 1117 (May 28, 1785).

29. Richard Harding et al., eds., *British Ships in China Seas: 1700 to the Present Day* (Liverpool: National Museum, 2004).

30. Yen-p'ing Hao, "Chinese Teas to America—A Synopsis," in Ernest May and John Fairbank, eds., *America's China Trade in Historical Perspective* (Cambridge, Mass.: Committee on American-East Asian Relations, Harvard University, 1986), p. 13.

31. Kenneth Scott Latourette, *The History of Early Relations between the United States and China* (New Haven, Conn.: Yale University Press, 1917), p. 29 and introduction.

32. Miriam Butts and Patricia Heard, comps., "The American China Trade: 'Foreign Devils to Canton' 1783–1843" (New York: Grossman Publishers, 1974).

33. Samuel Shaw, *The Journals of Major Samuel Shaw*, p. 298.

34. Yen-p'ing Hao, "Chinese Teas to America—A Synopsis." Foster Rhea Dulles, *The Old China Trade*, p. 210.

35. Timothy Pitkin, *A Statistical View of the Commerce of the United States of America: Including Also an Account of Banks, Manufactures, and Internal Trade and Improvements, Together with That of the Revenues and Expenditures of the General Government, Accompanied with Numerous Tables* (New Haven, Conn.: Durrie & Peck, 1835). Isaac Smith Homans Jr., *A Historical and Statistical Account of the Foreign Commerce of the United States* (New York: Putnam, 1857), pp. 181–182.

36. Alfred Tamarin and Shirley Glubok, *Voyaging to Cathay*, pp. 125–133.

37. Foster Rhea Dulles, *The Old China Trade*, p. 55.

38. Article XIII, Treaty of Amity, Commerce and Navigation, in William M. Malloy, comp., *Treaties, Conventions, International Acts, Protocols and Agreements between the United States of America and Other Powers, 1776–1909* (Washington, D.C.: Government Printing Office, 1910), p. 599.

39. Dorothy Schurman Hawes, *To the Farthest Gulf: The Story of the American China Trade* (Ipswich, Mass.: Ipswich Press, 1990), chapter 9.

40. William C. Hunter, *The "Fan Kwae" at Canton*, p. 40.

41. Samuel Shaw, *The Journals of Major Samuel Shaw*, p. 179.

42. Samuel Shaw, *The Journals of Major Samuel Shaw*, p. 184.

43. William C. Hunter, *The "Fan Kwae" at Canton*, p. 40.

44. Kenneth Scott Latourette, *The History of Early Relations between the United States and China, 1784–1844*, p. 71.

45. Earnest R. May and John Fairbank, eds., *America's China Trade in Historical Perspective*, pp. 21–25.

46. Henry Clay, *Economics: An Introduction for the General Reader* (New York: Macmillan, 1918), p. 209.

47. Letter from J. M. Forbes from Canton, dated December 29, 1832, to Aushootes [? illegible in original letter] Esq. in Calcutta. V. F-5, Forbes Family Collection, Baker Library, Harvard Business School.

48. Zhang Wenqin (章文钦), *Guangdong Shisanhang yu zaoqi Zhongxi guanxi* [广东十三行与早期中西关系 Guangdong's Thirteen Hongs and early Sino-foreign relations] (Guangzhou: Guangdong jingji chubanshe, 2009).

49. Weng Eang Cheong, *The Hong Merchants of Canton: Chinese Merchants in Sino-Western Trade* (Richmond, Surrey: Curzon, 1997), p. 246.

50. Kuo-Tung Ch'en, *The Insolvency of the Chinese Hong Merchants*.

51. Liang Tingnan, *Yue haiguan zhi*, vol. 25. Liang Jiabin, *Guangdong shisan hang kao*, pp. 273–274.

52. William Hunter, *The "Fan Kwae" at Canton*, pp. 46–47.

53. Houqua's business name was Wu Shaorong or Wu Bingjian and his hong name was Yihe hang. Huang Guoxin, Huang Qichen, and Huang Haiyan, *Huozhi huayang de yueshang*, pp. 167–181. Zhang Wenqin (章文钦), "Cong fengjian guanshang dao maiban shangren: Qingdai Guangdong hangshang Wu Yihe jiazu pouxi" [从封建官商到买办商人: 清代广东行商伍怡和家族剖析 From feudal official merchant to comprador: An analysis of Guangdong's hong merchant Yihe Wu clan in the Qing dynasty], *Jindaishi yanjiu*, nos. 3 and 4 (1984): 167–197, 231–253.

54. V. F-5. John Murray Forbes, 1813–1898, Forbes Family Collection, Baker Library, Harvard Business School.

55. Samuel Shaw, *The Journals of Major Samuel Shaw*, p. 184.

56. V. F-5. John Murray Forbes, 1813–1898, Forbes Family Collection, Baker Library, Harvard Business School.

57. 0.3 percent in 1890, less than 1 percent in 1910, and a little over 2 percent in 1930. Michael H. Hunt, "Americans in the China Market: Economic Opportunities and Economic Nationalism, 1890s–1931," *Business History Review* 51, no. 3 (Autumn 1977): 277–307.

58. William C. Hunter, *The "Fan Kwae" at Canton*, p. 48. Liang Jiabin, *Guangdong shisan hang kao*, p. 216. Morse, *The Chronicles of the East India Company*, vol. 4, p. 348.

59. Ernest R. May and John Fairbank, eds., *America's China Trade in Historical Perspective*, pp. 29–31.

60. Besides Samuel Shaw, other examples include André Everard Van Braam Houckgeest, *Voyage de l'Ambassade de la Compagnie des Indes Orientales Hollandaises, vers l'Empereur de la Chine, dans les Années 1794 & 1795* [Voyage of the Embassy of the Dutch East India Company to the emperor of China in the years 1794–1795], 2 vols. (Philadelphia, Pa.: M. L. E. Moreau de Saint-Méry, 1797–1798); Amasa Delano, *Narrative of Voyages and Travels, in the Northern and Southern Hemispheres, Comprising three Voyages round the World; together with a Voyage of Survey and Discovery, in the Pacific Ocean and Oriental Islands* (Boston, Mass.: E. G. House, 1817); Robert Waln Jr., *China: Comprehending a View of the Origin, Antiquity History, Religion, Morals, Government, Laws, Population, Literature, Drama, Festivals, Games, Women, Beggars, Manners, Customs, &c of That Empire* (Philadelphia, Pa.: J. Maxwell, 1823); and Robert B. Forbes, *Remarks on China and the China Trade* (Boston, Mass.: Samuel N. Dickonsen, 1844).

61. Samuel Shaw, *The Journals of Major Samuel Shaw*, pp. 233–234, 250–251.

62. Carl Guarneri, *America in the World: United States History in Global Context* (New York: McGraw-Hill, 2007).

63. The selected references under this heading at the end of each chapter have been chosen to supplement the notes and elaborate the themes throughout the book.

# TWO

## Opium Wars and the Open Door

The defining issues in American-Chinese political relations from the 1840s to the early twentieth century included the Opium Wars, the unequal treaties forced on China by the Western powers, and the development of the "Open Door" doctrine. American policy toward Qing China is one of the most debated topics in both Chinese and English-language scholarship. In 1898 the United States proposed its distinctive Open Door policy, espousing equal commercial opportunity and respect for China's administrative and territorial integrity. Did the United States—as many people today believe—simply follow in Britain's footsteps up until that time, as a "junior partner" or "brother nation" to the European states? The answer must be no.

In the race for global resources, markets, and power, the United States employed an independent and flexible strategy in China that permitted the American state to differentiate itself from the European nations under certain circumstances and to collaborate with them in others. America's rising presence in the East fell within the ambit of its consistent pursuit of national greatness. This strategic stance—pragmatic yet with an eye to the future—validated America's own belief that the United States was set to become a leading world power, although the execution of these ambitions varied depending on whether the national mood veered more toward overseas expansionism or self-absorption. For Qing China, defeat in the two Opium Wars showed that avoiding difficulties and seeking short-term palliatives would be of no use in dealing with foreign countries. Groping for solutions, the Qing state had employed the diplomatic means available to a nation whose material weakness made it susceptible to the machinations of international politics. Obtaining assistance from America and other major powers became part of China's armory of tactics—such as pitting foreign nations against one another, multilateralism, negotiation, and seeking adjustment to the China policies of the foreign powers.

## THE UNITED STATES, THE OPIUM WARS, AND COMMERCIAL TREATIES

*Backdrop*

This section examines the effect of the two Opium Wars between Britain and China (1839–42 and 1856–60) on the relationship between the United States and Qing China. The First Opium War—long viewed as one of the most extraordinary events in modern Chinese history—erupted out of the irritation long brewing on both sides over the opium trade. There were four major factors that prompted Britain to invade China.

First of all, Britain used force in response to the humiliation and business losses inflicted when the Chinese authorities seized and dumped huge quantities of opium, largely owned by British merchants, in Canton. The event that triggered the military conflict was the confiscation of over 20,000 chests of opium in March 1839.[1]

Another herbal stimulant, tea, played an important part in the lead-up to war. Over the course of the eighteenth century, tea had become a national drink in Britain. By 1830, the British East India Company was selling 30 million pounds by weight of Chinese tea per annum, bringing in a net profit of 1 million pounds; at one time the tax on tea provided one-tenth of the British government's entire revenue.[2] Unable to export goods to the Chinese in comparable volume, Britain was forced to pay for the resulting trade deficit in silver bullion. Indian opium, therefore, became a remedy for the trade imbalance, although it was already regarded as contraband in Qing China in 1729, when Emperor Yongzheng (r. 1723–35) issued the first anti-opium edict, holding drug sellers and their local accomplices—rather than opium smokers or cultivators—legally accountable.[3] The push of British Indian supply and the pull of Chinese demand created a powerful web of international business activity outside the legal framework of Anglo-Chinese trade. The importation, cultivation, and consumption of opium were outlawed in China by Emperor Qianlong's (r. 1736–96) edict of 1796. The main vendors—private British merchants—were the "country traders" who shipped opium to China in vast quantities. They worked under license from the East India Company until the abolition of its monopoly on Britain's trade with China in 1833.[4]

Second to this simmering contention over opium, a series of conflicts over Britain's legitimate trade with China contributed to the outbreak of war. Prominent among these was the inglorious end to the mission of Lord William Napier of Meristoun, Britain's chief representative in China. It was a political humiliation that added weight to British arguments for armed intervention.

By the early nineteenth century the gap between the domestic-oriented, self-sufficient Chinese economy and the rapidly developing industrial economy of Britain—with its reliance on foreign trade—made armed collisions inevitable. The results of earlier British attempts to harness Sino-British trade to its own advantage are seen in Sir George Macartney's failed mission to China in 1793 and Lord Amherst's equally unsuccessful mission of 1816. In 1834, one year after the East India Company's trade monopoly had ended, the British foreign secretary Lord Palmerston appointed Lord William Napier, a retired naval officer, as the British government's superintendent of trade in China.[5] Intent on reforming Anglo-Chinese business relations, Napier arrived in Canton in July 1834. His request for a "personal interview" with Lu Kun, the governor-general (or viceroy) of Guangdong and Guangxi provinces, fell on deaf ears.[6] After more than a month's standoff, Lu suspended trade with Britain and ordered Napier to leave Canton. In mid-September a humiliated Napier returned to Macau where he died of malaria the following month. The Napier fiasco effectively sank British attempts to open up China through diplomatic means.[7]

In 1836, Charles Elliot succeeded Napier as superintendent of trade at a time when opium imports to China already exceeded 30,000 chests.[8] In December 1838 Emperor Daoguang dispatched Lin Zexu (1785–1850) as his plenipotentiary commissioner to Canton to put an end to the opium trade.[9] In Canton, Lin targeted foreign opium merchants rather than domestic drug users; he demanded that the merchants forfeit their opium stocks and sign a bond (*jujie* 具结) committing them to desist from the drug trade on penalty of death.[10] According to Robert B. Forbes, a wealthy American trader in Canton, Lin's determination to suppress the opium trade took the foreign community by surprise:

> The merchants supposed that he was coming to make some arrange-ments by which he could keep it out of sight, or to feather his own nest; but he came with an honest intention of doing his duty. . . . He struck directly at the head and front of the offending.[11]

In a similar vein, John Thacker, a British trader, recollected that in expectation of the arrival of Commissioner Lin,

> it was understood by the Chinamen and Europeans that he came to soften matters down from what the Viceroy [Lu] had been doing. . . . It was thought that something would be done to obviate the difficulties that had been thrown in the way by the Viceroy.[12]

Encountering resistance to his demands, Lin imposed an embargo on all trade and ordered Chinese cooks, coolies, and compradors serving foreign merchants in Canton to leave, making the latter virtual prisoners in their own factories. Forbes' eyewitness account of life without servants sparkles with humor:

> Not desiring to starve them, the officers of government, or the Hong merchants, sent in supplies of food in the shape of pigs, fowls, and sheep on the hoof. . . . In the American hong lived Mr. P. W. Snow, United States Consul, Russell & Co., Russell, Sturgies, & Co., and oth-ers. I was called upon to organize the house for work; lots were drawn to settle who should cook, and who play the part of waiters, chamber-men, &c. It fell to me to be chief cook. The first thing to be done was to clean out the kitchen, into which no white man had before entered; all hands went at it, and soon made things fit for my new work. My first effort was fried ham and eggs; when the dish came to table, it was difficult to distinguish between eggs and ham: all bore the color and partook of the consistency of dirty sole-leather. It was immediately voted to depose me, and to put Warren Delano in my place, and I assumed his duties, which were to look after the glass and silver. . . . W. C. Hunter was lamp-trimmer, and all had something to do. The live-stock was driven into the rear, and barricaded . . . pigs, sheep, and fowls all mixed up together, and making day and night hideous with their smell and noises. . . . Bathing being important, and no coolies at hand to carry water to the upper rooms, we rigged whips, and at-tempted to hoist up the big pails into the verandas; but this proved a

failure, the ropes twisted up, and the pails remained suspended in mid air.[13]

In response to these most effective measures, Elliot was forced to call upon his countrymen to surrender their opium stocks to Lin. On June 3, 1839, Lin began destroying over 20,000 chests of opium—then worth around US$10 million (about 9 million Mexican silver dollars) by dissolving them in trenches. Trade was reopened—but only briefly. Rather than continue to wrangle with Lin over the signing of bonds, the British community in China decided to cease trading, vacate Canton, and move to Macau (later to Hong Kong). China was to be punished for its intransigence. At the urging of a group of merchants headed by William Jardine and James Matheson, the British Parliament voted in favor of war against China in early 1840. In May, sixteen British warships (armed with 540 guns), four steamers, one troopship, and twenty-seven transports—carrying about 4,000 foot soldiers led by Charles Elliot and his cousin Admiral George Elliot—left Macau for Canton and the coast of Zhejiang Province. These events marked the outbreak of the First Opium War.

Third, the British business community in China had its own reasons for war. British merchants had never ceased to resent what they saw as the arbitrary trade restrictions and customs fees imposed under the Canton system. Clamoring for access to the China interior market, they advocated armed intervention, believing that it would enable them to force a commercial treaty on China and thus conduct business under military protection and on very favorable terms.[14] The Chinese understood the British motives only too well; the opening sentence of an essay by a Chinese commentator written around 1850 reads, "Cunning were the British barbarians who had long been coveting the inland territories."[15] From this perspective, the war can be understood less as a conflict over drugs and more as a commercial trade war.[16] In the 1830s in particular, there had been lengthy discussions of the opium trade in the *Chinese Courier and Canton Gazette*, the *Chinese Repository*, and the *Canton Register*, English-language newspapers published in Canton and Hong Kong. The evidence clearly shows that the British expatriate community in China virtually drew up plans for military action, as well as for treaty negotiations with the Qing court—provisions which were enacted by the British negotiators after the war.

Finally, British opium traders had a psychological motive for pressing Britain to fight a war with China, because opium smuggling was not a legal, sustainable business. Although the distribution of the drug was mostly handled by Chinese smugglers from a base on Lintin Island—the warehouse of the opium trade about two miles northeast of Macau— British "country traders" such as William Jardine and James Matheson would sometimes service buyers along the Chinese coast themselves. Dealing with drugs contradicted middle-class mores in nineteenth-century England, which opposed addiction whether to rum or opium. Britain banned the domestic importation of opium in 1856. Maurice Stewart Collis (b. 1889–1973), a British colonial administrator and writer, summed up the moral issues at stake:

> To trade in a noxious drug was not characteristic of British commerce. The wares of England had always been noted for the soundness of their workmanship and the excellence of their material; and her merchants for their solidarity, their caution and their honesty. . . . That so reputable a community should in China have fifty per cent of its capital sunk in opium smuggling was a role that did not really suit it.[17]

### The United States, the First Opium War, and the Treaty of Wanghia

As the Anglo-Chinese trade conflict intensified, American expatriates, politicians, and diplomats took up the China question in their own way. American traders in the Canton region responded to the opium crisis with flexibility and pragmatism, and benefited by complying with Commissioner Lin Zexun's demands. At the same time, both businessmen and missionaries exerted pressure on the U.S. government to take a more active role. As a further complication, the American government and public alike were not slow to pass judgment on the moral issues arising from the Opium War.

In contrast to their British colleagues, American merchants continued to trade with China, making profitable journeys up and down the Pearl River between May 1839 and June 1840, when Canton was blockaded by British forces. When in May 1839 Charles Elliot asked Robert B. Forbes (of Russell & Co., the largest American trading house in China) to consider suspending trade so as to bring the "rascal . . . Chinese to terms," Forbes replied jokingly that "we Yankees had no Queen to guarantee our losses." Forbes recalled that Elliot "asked if I was willing to do business with a chain around my neck, and said he would soon make Canton too hot for us. I rejoined that the chain was *imaginary* [emphasis in original], the duty to constituents and the commission account was *real* [ibid.]."[18]

The international ramifications of the opium crisis were the subject of discussion by Americans both at home and abroad. The war between Great Britain and the Qing empire was seen by one newspaper editor as involving "more or less directly a large portion of the human family."[19] Labeling the Opium War as a "conflict between two of the mightiest nations of the globe," John Quincy Adams (1767–1848, president 1825–29)—then representative of the state of Massachusetts and chairman of the Committee of Foreign Affairs—took Britain's part. For Adams, "commercial intercourse between nations" was "among the natural rights and duties of men" under "the Christian law of nations." For him,

> [t]he cause of the war is the pretension on the part of the Chinese, that in all their intercourse with other nations, political or commercial, their superiority must be implicitly acknowledged, and manifested in humiliating forms. . . . It is time that this enormous outrage upon the rights of human nature, and upon the first principle of the rights of nations, should cease.[20]

In his report to Congress on January 24, 1843, Adams continued to insist that

> the war declared by Great Britain against China had originated in the refusal of the Chinese Government to receive ministers of peace appointed by the British sovereign, and by the rejection and expulsion, with insult and indignity, of Lord Napier, a commissioner and plenipotentiary so appointed. . . . The conflict was, in root and substance, for equal rights of independent nations, against the insolent and absurd assumption of despotic supremacy.[21]

In contrast to Adams' views, British moral failure was the target of some American critics. Invoking Christianity as Adams had also done, one editorial attributed the Anglo-Chinese conflict to the "low state of morality, among western nations," and foreign contempt for the Chinese edicts and appeals issued against the introduction of opium.[22] In March 1840, Caleb Cushing was vocal in his disapproval of the British action:

> But God forbid me that I should entertain the idea of cooperating with the British Government in the purpose, if purpose it has, of upholding the base cupidity and violence and high-handed infraction of all law, human and divine, which have characterized the operation of the British, individually and collectively, in the seas of China.[23]

One lengthy article written by a lawyer for *Hunt's Merchants' Magazine* called the British the "invader."

> [Although the] bearing of the Chinese government was preposterous,
> and the aspect of Chinese institutions, to a stranger, ludicrous in the
> extreme. . . . China has as perfect a right to regulate the character of her
> imports, as either of the countries with whom she trades; and we can
> imagine no more glaring violation of the law of nations, than the suc-
> cessful attempt which has been made to cram down her throat, by
> force, an article which she had deliberately refused to receive.[24]

The growing tensions between Britain and Qing China and the increasing
efforts of the United States to promote commerce as well as to further its
political influence led to greater American involvement in China. In its
rapid rise on the world stage, the United States—despite its expressed
sympathies and rapport with the Chinese hong merchants—often found
itself more on the side of the European powers.

Pressure for federal government intervention was finally translated
into action. At the request of American traders and missionaries in China,
President John Tyler dispatched Lawrence Kearny, the commander of the
U.S. East India Squadron, to China to protect American lives and property. The "squadron" that set sail comprised two vessels, the flagship *Constellation* and the *Boston*. On arrival in Macau in March 1842, Kearny, in
response to a report in the *Hong Kong Gazette*, took a hard line against the
opium trade. He informed both the Chinese and the international community that "the government of the United States does not sanction 'the
smuggling of opium' on this coast, under the American flag, in violation
of the laws of China. Difficulty arising therefrom in respect to the seizure
of any vessel by the Chinese, the claimants certainly will not, under my
instructions, find support or any interposition, on my part, after the publication of this notice."[25] Kearny was specifically instructed by the State
Department to inquire into allegations that Robert B. Forbes, American
consul in Canton, had links with a company engaged in the opium
trade.[26]

In June 1840, British warships—after successfully blockading Can-
ton—seized the island of Zhoushan on the Chinese Zhejiang coast. Qing
Emperor Daoguang removed Commissioner Lin Zexu and appointed Qi-
shan to negotiate with Charles Elliot, but the result ultimately satisfied
neither party. The war resumed when Elliot was replaced by Sir Henry
Pottinger in August 1841. Sixty British ships were deployed along the
Zhejiang coast, an important communications center and entry to the
Grand Canal, the artery through which rice from southern China reached

the northern capital. The First Opium War ended in July 1840 with the fall of Zhenjiang, an important city on the Yangzi River. The Qing court authorized Qiying, a prominent official, to make peace, but with no clear objectives other than the withdrawal of British troops. The Treaty of Nanjing—known as the first of the "Unequal Treaties"—comprising thirteen articles, was signed on August 29, 1842, on the British flagship *Cornwallis* by Qiying, Yilibu, and Henry Pottinger.[27]

Progress on the Treaty of Nanjing was closely watched by Americans. Learning of British successes in securing legal and trade rights in China, Kearny jockeyed with the British for a favorable "postwar settlement." In a letter to the governor of Canton, Kearny wrote that he

> learns with deep interest [that] the high Imperial commissioners [Qiying and Yilibu] deputed to arrange commercial affairs with the British are expected in a short time to arrive at Canton, and that a commercial treaty is to be negotiated to operate in favor of "British merchants" exclusively. . . . The undersigned is desirous that the attention of the Imperial government might be called with respect to the commercial interest of the United States, and their citizens, in that matter, be placed upon the same footing as the merchants of the nation most favored.[28]

At the urging of President Tyler, Caleb Cushing, and other China lobbyists such as Peter Parker, the Committee on Foreign Affairs, following several years of debate on the China issue, proposed an appropriation of $40,000 to fund a mission to China in January 1843. Four months later, while Congress was in recess, President Tyler appointed Cushing as the American commissioner to China.[29] Cushing arrived in Macau in February 1844.

American missionaries Peter Parker and Elijah C. Bridgman were made joint Chinese secretaries to the legation in the United States dealing with the Chinese government. Diplomatically, the American legation attempted to steal a march on the British by making it known that the United States was "the most disinterested and the most valuable of the friends of China."[30] To the disquiet of the Qing court, however, Cushing expressed the hope that the new American envoy might travel north to the imperial capital of Beijing and be officially welcomed there. In April 1844, the Qing emperor appointed Qiying as imperial commissioner with orders to hasten to Canton to mollify Cushing and restrain the American legation from undertaking the long journey to Beijing.[31] At the end of

May, Qiying arrived and commenced negotiations with Cushing in Macau.

In the negotiations, the primary concern of the Qing court was Cushing's planned trip to Beijing in North China, rather than trade regulations—the terms of which were mostly incomprehensible to the Chinese. So having been assured that the United States would not follow Britain to take Chinese islands away, Qiying reached a speedy conclusion to negotiations with Cushing in Wanghia Village near Macau in South China on July 3, 1844.

Fuller and more coherent than the Treaty of Nanjing, the Treaty of Wanghia between the United States and the Qing was considered "superior" to the British treaty by early American commentators.[32] Primarily owing to the efforts of Cushing, a Massachusetts lawyer, the new treaty would "give to American commercial interests in China the best possible opportunities for the prosecution of their growing trade in the face of British competition."[33] As a "basis for the conduct of trade," it proved to be a "model treaty" for other nations, in particular the French, Norwegians, and Swedes. The American treaty was ratified by Congress in December 1845.

A clause specifying the details of most-favored-nation (MFN) status was added to Article 8 of the Supplementary Treaty at the last minute. Privileges and immunities granted by Qing China to the citizens of one country would be extended to all other foreign nationals, but Chinese subjects overseas would not enjoy reciprocal treatment. Article 21 introduced consular jurisdiction (extraterritoriality), whereby American citizens in China were subject to U.S. law.

Missing from the British treaty, the issue of opium is addressed in Article 33 of the Treaty of Wanghia, confirming America's opposition to illegal opium trafficking. It stands in stark contrast to the provisions cited above for most-favored-nation status and consular jurisdiction.

> Citizens of the United States, who shall attempt to trade clandestinely with such of the ports of China as are not open to foreign commerce, or who shall trade in opium or any other contraband article of merchandise, shall be subject to be dealt with by the Chinese Government, without being entitled to any countenance or protection from that of the United States; and the United States will take measures to prevent their flag from being abused by the subjects of other nations, as a cover for the violation of the laws of the Empire.[34]

With foresight and a cautious confidence, the United States had posi-
tioned itself advantageously in China. In certain moods, America talked
up its destiny as a future world power. As William H. Seward (senator
from New York, 1849–61; secretary of state, 1861–69) pronounced in 1846,
"Our population is destined to roll its resistless waves to the icy barriers
of the North, and to encounter oriental civilization on the shores of the
Pacific."[35]

### The United States, the Second Opium War, and the Treaty of Tianjin

The outbreak of the Second Opium War in 1856 was rooted in China's
continued trade imbalance and ongoing friction between the trading
powers, mainly Britain and China but also, increasingly, the United
States and China. By the mid-1850s, Qing China had become Britain's
third-largest importer, following the United States and France. Between
1853 and 1881, Chinese imports (£323 million), principally tea and silk,
totaled more than two and a half times the value of British exports to
China (£121 million).[36] Britain's trade deficit with China, about £4 million
per annum on average, continued to be covered by income derived from
opium. However, opium was still an illegal drug in China—the Treaty of
Nanjing contained no reference to it. It took another war and a set of
treaties for Britain to square off with the self-consumed Qing empire.
This conflict, known as the Second Opium War, resulted in the signing of
the Treaty of Tianjin and the conditional legalization of opium as an
import.

The ostensible cause of the war was the dispute between Britain and
China over whether the Treaty of Nanjing had given British subjects the
right of trade and residence within the walls of Canton—and, if so, when
they would be allowed to exercise those rights. After 1844, when Henry
Pottinger was replaced as the governor of Hong Kong by J. F. Davis,
relations between Britain and China began to deteriorate. In 1847, Davis
ordered the capture of the forts guarding the approaches to Guangzhou.
Qiying was forced to promise the British entry into Canton City in spring
1849. In 1848, Emperor Daoguang (r. 1821–50) dismissed Qiying and appointed Xu Guangjin as governor-general of Guangdong and Guangxi
and commissioner for foreign affairs. Both Xu and Ye Mingchen—
governor of Guangdong and later governor-general of Guangdong and
Guangxi—disliked dealing (and especially compromising) with foreigners. As April 1849—the agreed date for British entry into Canton—ap-

proached, Xu encouraged local gentry to use their militia to oppose any occupation. He then forged an imperial edict ordering him to "respect the will of the people." Sir George Bonham, the newly appointed governor of Hong Kong, accepted a further postponement of British entry—a concession which was greeted by the Chinese as a victory and marked by the granting of imperial honors to Xu and Ye. The whole affair was deeply resented by the local British community.

Another continuing irritant was the question of treaty revisions. As far as the Americans were concerned, the legal basis for the treaty revisions that fell due in 1856 lay in Article 34 of the Treaty of Wanghia:

> When the present Convention shall have been definitively concluded, it shall be obligatory on both powers, and its provisions shall be not be altered without grave cause; but, in as much as the circumstances of the several ports of China open to foreign commerce are different, experience may show that inconsiderable modifications are requisite in those parts which relate to commerce and navigation; in which case the two governments will, at the expiration of twelve years from the date of said Convention, treat amicably concerning the same, by the means of suitable persons appointed to conduct such negotiation.[37]

For the American side, revising the Treaty of Wanghia was necessary on two counts. First, owing to the disruption caused by the Taiping Rebellion (see chapter 4), the treaty was in abeyance in Shanghai where the Qing government was unable to fulfill its obligation to protect American citizens. The unstable situation in China had severely damaged American commercial interests as well, although the United States was committed to aiding China in quelling the Taiping rebels.[38] Second, inconsistent internal taxes (transit dues, *likin*), applied to foreign as well as Chinese goods by local authorities, interfered with the expansion of American influence and trade with China. American commissioner Robert McLane struck a typically pragmatic note: "As a consideration for such enlargement of the *protectorate* [sic] character of the existing treaty, the interior should be opened to us, where we would extend the moral power of our civilization, and the material power necessary to protect the lives and property of our people."[39]

Although the British handling of its entry into Canton was perceived as an aggressive act by some Americans in China including James Biddle and Peter Parker, the United States acted in alliance with Britain, France, and Russia in formulating treaty revisions in the 1850s while maintaining its opposition to opium. This time, the American government also used military force against China in concert with other powers.

In 1856, two events—the *Arrow* Incident and the murder in Guangxi of Abbé Auguste Chapdelaine (1814–56), a French priest—became convenient pretexts for foreign military intervention. This action was directed at commercial reform—abolishing the limits on trade and the irregular transit fees levied on foreign goods—as well as punishing the Qing government for its lack of cooperation in revising existing treaties. On October 8, 1856, the Qing Canton naval force arrested twelve Chinese crewmen aboard the *Arrow*, a Chinese-owned lorcha (small boat) with an expired registration with the British authority in Hong Kong, on suspicion of piracy. The Chinese boarding party allegedly tore down the British flag flying from the ship's mast. The British consul in Canton, Harry S. Parkes, pressed Ye Mingchen, viceroy of Guangdong and Guangxi, to release the crewmen and apologize for the disrespect shown for the British flag, but without satisfaction. To punish the recalcitrant Ye, John Bowring, British plenipotentiary and chief superintendent of trade in China, ordered an attack on Canton.

After the news reached London, Lord Palmerston, now prime minister, decided to send an expeditionary force, headed by the Earl of Elgin, to seek further redress. The British forces were joined by a French task force. On December 29, 1857, the combined British and French forces, commanded by the new British plenipotentiary Lord Elgin and French representative Baron Gros, seized Canton and soon afterward demanded revisions to the existing treaties. Having exhausted his military resources, on May 29, 1858, Emperor Xianfeng appointed Guiliang and Huashana as his representatives with full powers to negotiate with Britain, France, the United States, and Russia, who were then all occupying Tianjin near Beijing.

The resulting Sino-British Treaty of Tianjin and the agreement containing Rules of Trade and Tariff involved little negotiation. Less than a month elapsed between Emperor Xianfeng's authorizing of negotiations on May 29 and the conclusion of the fifty-six-article treaty on June 25, 1858. In the case of the Rules of Trade and Tariff, the negotiations in Shanghai lasted only twenty-four days. For the Qing dynasty, the signing of the Treaty of Tianjin was merely an expedient to get the foreigners to withdraw their troops threatening Beijing.

Central to the negotiations was the issue of permanent residence for the British representative in Beijing, a demand which Emperor Xianfeng personally resented the most. British diplomats were permitted residence in Beijing under Article 2, "Appointment of Ambassadors," and Article 3, "Residence of [the] British Representative at Peking." In addition, three other contentious clauses dealt with rights of travel in the interior, trade on the Yangzi River, and the issue of indemnity for foreign powers.[40] Although the emperor approved the Treaty of Tianjin with Britain, he continued to harbor a strong desire to have these unpalatable clauses deleted.

After the close of negotiations over the Rules of Trade, Britain, France, and the United States resumed their military campaign and marched toward Beijing with the intention of subduing the Qing court. China had insisted that the ratification of the Treaty of Tianjin should not take place in the imperial capital. In June 1859, foreign diplomats returned to Tianjin to ratify the treaty. When they attempted to pass the Dagu forts, Chinese forces opened fire, killing more than four hundred British seamen and sinking four ships. On September 21, 1860, the 10,500-strong British Expeditionary Force, assisted by more than 6,000 French soldiers, defeated an army of 30,000 of the Qing empire's crack troops in the suburbs of Beijing. The following day Emperor Xianfeng fled to his summer retreat at Rehe, about one hundred miles from Beijing, leaving it to his brother, Prince Gong (Yixin), to deal with the approaching foreign forces. Beijing fell on October 13. Eleven days later, Prince Gong signed the peace treaty known as the Sino-British Convention of Beijing—establishing once and for all the right of foreign diplomatic representation in China's capital—presented by Lord Elgin, with France, Russia, and the United States following suit shortly afterward. Thus, the protracted disputes over treaty revisions came to a halt.[41]

During the 1850s–60s, the United States seized the opportunity to further develop its mercantile, religious, and geopolitical involvement in China. Despite reservations and disagreements, the American government decided to put its weight behind the European powers in conflict with Qing China. As part of the imperialism of free trade, the unequal treaty system institutionalized the conduct of both the Americans and Europeans in China. On the commercial front, the United States was confronted with a moral dilemma, the opium question, and ultimately championed the criminalization of the drug trade in the first quarter of the twentieth century. In combination with the anti-opium movements in other countries, this led to the dismantling of the lucrative trade centered on the triangle of Britain, British India, and China. The U.S. push for the international suppression of the opium trade was closely linked with the attitudes and moral judgments which Americans had developed in their earlier contacts with China.

## EXERCISING "SOFT POWER" IN CHINA: THE OPEN DOOR DOCTRINE

This section examines the context, meaning, and significance of what became known as America's Open Door policy toward China. It can be seen as but one permutation of nineteenth-century U.S. foreign policy in China, sitting alongside other positions such as neutrality, noninterference and nonentanglement, expansionism, and the Monroe Doctrine— various policy stances adopted simultaneously or at different times by the United States.

In 1895, for example, President Grover Cleveland and his secretary of state, Richard Olney, picked a quarrel with Great Britain over the essentially trivial question of the boundary between Venezuela and British Guiana when gold was discovered in the disputed area.[42] In this case, America's nonentanglement policy was stopped dead in the water. In a dispatch dated June 20, 1895, Richard Olney declared to Lord Salisbury, the British foreign minister, that "Today . . . the United States is practically sovereign on this continent, and its fiat is law upon the subject to which it confines its interposition." Britain accepted American demands and agreed to a treaty of arbitration with Venezuela that satisfied the United States.[43]

The Open Door doctrine gave expression and form to America's consistent pursuit of its national interests, independence, and perceived distinctiveness since its first contact with China in 1784. In the real world, the application of the Open Door, as a policy and a principle, varied greatly depending on the particular historical moment and the individual actors involved. Notions identical to the Open Door can be found in British commercial practices and in the Berlin Conference of 1885 that was intended to keep the balance of power in the European scramble for territories in Africa.

The so-called Open Door notes, drawn up with measured caution by two China hands—William W. Rockhill of the United States (1853–1914, minister to China, 1905–10) and Alfred E. Hippisley of Britain (1842–1940)—recognized the limits of American power in China at a time when the United States was on the cusp of national greatness. Rather than emulating the European and Japanese way—as exhibited in the contest for concessions and territory in China at the turn of the twentieth century—the Open Door was a reasoned policy designed to exert American soft, persuasion power in an American manner. The Open Door doctrine was the corollary of U.S. strategic operations in other parts of the world.

Japan's rapid victory over China in the Sino-Japanese War of 1894–95, which was fought for influence over Korea, precipitated an international race among Europeans and Japanese to carve China into spheres of influence for control of China's port cities, railroads, and mines. In the United States, where a severe economic depression had begun in 1893, political and economic leaders were concerned about the consequences of being squeezed out of China. In January 1898, a group of business leaders in New York founded a lobby group, the Committee on American Interests in China—later renamed the American Asiatic Association—to pressure the State Department to oppose the possible partition of China.

Through its close contacts with John Hay, secretary of state in the William McKinley and Theodore Roosevelt administrations (1897–1905), the association effectively pushed its mission to "foster and safeguard the trade and commercial interests of the citizens of the United States, and others associated therewith, in the Empires of China, Japan, and Korea, and in the Philippine Islands, and elsewhere in Asia or Oceania."[44] As a result, the government was increasingly swayed to protect the American business community in China.

During the final years of the nineteenth century, the United States was exercising its regional and global clout in various ways—gearing up to challenge Spain in Cuba, the Philippine Islands, Guam, and Puerto Rico, while reaching the brink of war with Germany over the tiny island of Samoa in the Pacific and quarreling with Britain over the boundary between Venezuela and British Guiana.[45] The outbreak of the Spanish-American-Cuban-Filipino war in April 1898 thrust the United States into playing a more active role throughout the Asia-Pacific region.

It was against this complex background that the Open Door principle was announced. America's "'open-door' policy"—to cite the expression used by John Hay—was officially declared in two sets of nonbinding circular letters sent on September 6, 1899, and July 3, 1900, to the governments of France, Germany, Britain, Italy, Japan, and Russia, requesting them to "make a formal declaration" of such a principle "in the territories held by them in China."[46] The first of these diplomatic notes is documented in *Papers Relating to the Foreign Relations of the United States, with the Annual Message of the President Transmitted to Congress December 5, 1899*, under the heading of "Correspondence Concerning American Commercial Rights in China."[47]

William Rockhill, who was commissioned by Hay to draw up the Open Door notes in 1899, addressed the American Asiatic Association at its fourth annual dinner in 1902. For Rockhill, trade and support for administrative reform in China—rather than change of regime—and assistance in safeguarding China's territorial integrity and political independence were integral to the U.S. Open Door principle.[48] Later, Rockhill wrote, "The whole of our policy since Mr Hay's time has been based on a proper recognition of the interrelation of commerce, finance and politics."[49] For Rockhill, serving American trade and financial interests, protecting American citizens, preserving China's territorial and administrative integrity, and competing with international rivals in China were all interconnected issues, and together lay at the heart of the Open Door policy.

In 1899, by way of Andrew D. White, American minister to Germany, John Hay asked the German government to give formal assurances that the treaty rights and privileges of American citizens would not be jeopardized in the port of Jiaozhou and the adjacent territory, newly leased by Germany, in China's Shandong Province. In addition, the United States urged Germany to "lend its cooperation in securing like assurances from the other interested powers."[50] In his note to Britain, John Hay clarified the Open Door principle further—not only did it include retaining the open market in the foreign spheres of influence such as the British-leased territory of Weihaiwei in Shandong, but Hay also pushed for political reforms to maintain China's territorial integrity.[51] Since the U.S. proposals encountered no clear objections, foreign assent was considered "final and definitive."[52]

In 1900, the "China problem"—the result of the Boxer Uprising (see chapter 4), directed against foreigners in China—became a most noticeable issue in American foreign affairs circles, as explained by President McKinley in his annual message to Congress.[53] Emerging in northwest and southwest Shandong, the Boxers referred to those poverty-stricken villagers practicing martial arts with the belief that, possessed by spirits, they had a magical invulnerability to weapons. In spring 1900 the Boxer Movement gained strength; its followers attacked foreigners, destroyed property and railways, killed Christian converts, and ended up besieging the foreign legations in Beijing until a joint international relief force reached the city. Viewing the Boxer Uprising as a dangerous anarchy, on July 3, 1900, John Hay circulated a second note to the powers, reiterating that the policy of the United States "is to seek a solution which may bring about permanent safety and peace to China, preserve Chinese territorial and administrative entity [*sic*], protect all rights guaranteed to friendly powers by treaty and international law, and safeguard for the world the principle of equal and impartial trade with all parts of the Chinese Empire."[54]

Apart from stabilizing China in the race for territories and in the face of the Boxer threat, American business and missionary interest groups lobbied the McKinley administration to do more in China. They presented China as a vast market for American business interests, a fertile ground for Christian missions, and a political "sleeping giant" whose reawakening largely depended on the stance taken by the United States.[55]

The Chinese had their takes on the Open Door principle. To some reformers at the end of the nineteenth century, "the carving up of China and the scramble for spheres of influence equate to political aggression as a tactic in power competition; talk of preserving China's integrity and the opening up of China are common means of economic aggression employed by all the powers."[56] Liang Qichao—a prominent political activist and essayist at the turn of the twentieth century—labeled the Open Door as "the new way to exterminate China" (*mieguo xinfa* 灭国新法) devised by the imperialists, an example of "intangible partition" (*wuxing guafen* 无形瓜分):

> Those who claim to preserve China's integrity seek to do so by adopting the Open Door. The literal rendering of "Open Door" means opening up the whole country as treaty ports. Great Britain is, in essence, an

open-door country, but unlike China it does not yield extraterritorial rights to foreigners. The so-called territorial concessions in Shanghai and Hankou are nothing more than colonies. Opening up the whole of China as trade ports would be the same as turning the whole of China into a colony. . . . The Western policy of "preserving China's integrity" will in reality spell the end for China—like fish rotting from the inside.[57]

Taking a different tack, the Qing leaders, such as Zhang Zhidong, had their own version of the Open Door, parallel to the American policy. Formulated and partially implemented in the latter half of the nineteenth century, the Chinese policy involved playing the powers off against one another—keeping the balance of power by opening the Chinese market to all parties and giving each of them an interest in curbing monopoly privileges.[58] Manchuria became the testing ground for these various "open door" principles. In 1900, Russian troops moved into Manchuria in Northeast China on the pretext of protecting the Chinese Eastern Railway from the Boxer disturbances. Diplomatic talks between China and Russia over the withdrawal of Russian forces dragged on. Russia's intention to exercise exclusive control over Manchuria expedited the conclusion of the Anglo-Japanese alliance against Russia in 1902. To counter Russia, the United States asked that new ports be opened in Manchuria to Americans and other foreigners. The Russo-Japanese War of 1904–5 enabled Japan to consolidate its already strong hold on South Manchuria, and prompted China to step up its efforts to open up the region (as well as other territories) to American diplomatic and business interests under the William Howard Taft administration (1909–13). In the end, however, Taft's secretary of state Philander C. Knox (1909–13) was forced to opt for a cooperative policy—in tandem with Britain, Germany, France, Japan, and Russia—attempting to float three major loan projects to finance China's currency reform, and economic development and reorganization, in addition to the construction of the Huguang Railways.[59]

## CONCLUDING THOUGHTS

The 1899 Open Door policy has often been perceived as a watershed, demarcating a shift in America's China policy from a de facto "follower" of British diplomacy—allowing the United States to jointly reap political, religious, and commercial gains from China—to an "independent" player. As one scholar puts it, "[u]ntil 1899, the United States simply deferred to Great Britain on most China policy matters."[60] This tendency to characterize early U.S. policy in China as following the lead of Great Britain has been challenged in recent years.[61]

At the end of the nineteenth century, the nationalistic bent came increasingly to the fore in American politics. A group of influential figures including Theodore Roosevelt and Henry Cabot Lodge, the Massachusetts senator, were lobbying President McKinley over the direction of U.S. foreign policy.[62] Roosevelt and Lodge were trumpeting expansionist foreign policies, in their view important to "our national well-being." In an essay, Lodge wrote,

> England has studded the West Indies with strong places which are a standing menace to our Atlantic seaboard. We should have among those islands at least one strong naval station. . . . The modern movement is all toward the concentration of people and territory into great nations and large dominions. . . . It is a movement which makes for civilization and the advancement of the race. As one of the great nations of the world, the United States must not fall out of the line of march.[63]

In a confidential letter, Roosevelt revealed that his circle had been keeping up the pressure on President McKinley:

> I earnestly hope we can make the President look at things our way. Last Saturday night Lodge pressed his views upon him with all his strength. I have been getting matters in shape on the Pacific coast just as fast as I have been allowed. . . . I do not fear England; Canada is a hostage for her good behavior; but I do fear some of the other powers.[64]

Fiercely critical of America's self-righteous war in Vietnam in the 1960s, John K. Fairbank argued that American imperialist behavior ought to be dated back to its first endeavors in Asia rather than to the 1898 Open Door. Disputing the notion of America's "virtue" and "innocence" in the Far East during the nineteenth century, Fairbank said of American involvement that we cannot "overlook its genetic unity as a foreign intrusion upon Asian societies," or ignore the "conflict between the Atlantic and the East Asian civilizations."[65] He even went so far as to claim that "[t]he most basic decisions affecting American activity in China were made in London." On the other hand, Fairbank was clearly aware of Anglo-American tensions during this early period, the "nation-state rivalries in Asia," the so-called "dynamic mechanism of Europe's expansion." Nevertheless, "Americans were still inveighing against British imperialism while using British facilities like Hong Kong in order to rival Britain in the trade of these Chinese and Japanese treaty ports."[66]

While Fairbank's characterization of U.S. activity in China as unalloyed imperialism is certainly plausible, it underestimates the paradoxical complexity of American nation building in the nineteenth century. As a latecomer on the international scene, the United States had the will to dismantle the obstacles to entering a geopolitical arena dominated by Great Britain. American involvement in China had a quintessentially American flavor, the American Way. Commenting on the French mission led by M. de Lagrenée following the First Opium War, Caleb Cushing was assertive about the American instinct for competition: "Whatever additional concessions either English or French force may extort from China, none of them can be exclusive; and, in equal circumstances, the enterprise of our merchants and the skill and courage of our navigators may be safely trusted to the chances of all fair commercial competition in China."[67] Subsequently, it was not a question of the United States either following the European powers or sitting on its hands; rather America acted pragmatically, sometimes undermining the other powers' efforts in China, and at other times encouraging or collaborating with other nations including Great Britain, France, Germany, Russia, and Japan.

## FURTHER READING

Michael Hunt's *The Making of a Special Relationship: The United States and China to 1914* (New York: Columbia University, 1983) is an incisive diplomatic and cultural study of the Open Door constituency—businessmen, missionaries, and diplomats—in the seminal phase of United States–China relations. The First Opium War is treated in Hsin-Pao Chang, *Commissioner Lin and the Opium War* (Cambridge, Mass.: Harvard University Press, 1964); Peter Ward Fay, *The Opium War, 1840–1842: Barbarians in the Celestial Empire in the Early Part of the Nineteenth Century and the War by Which They Forced Her Gates Ajar* (Chapel Hill, N.C.: University of North Carolina Press, 1997; reprint of 1975 ed.); and Julia Lovell, *The Opium War: Drugs, Dreams and the Making of China* (London: Picador, 2011). In Chinese, the best single-volume monographs on the mismatched military maneuvers and discrepant perceptions of treaty negotiations that marked the two opium wars are Mao Haijian (茅海建), *Tian-chao de bengkui: Yapian zhanzheng zai yanjiu* [天朝的崩溃:鸦片战争再研究 The fall of the celestial kingdom: A re-examination of the Opium War] (Beijing: Sanlian shudian, 1995) and Mao Haijian, *Jindai de chidu: Liangci Yapian Zhanzheng junshi yu waijiao* [近代的尺度:两次鸦片战争军事与外交 Military and diplomatic aspects of the two opium wars: A modern assessment] (Shanghai: Sanlian shudian, 1998).

For the creation of the unequal treaty system, see John King Fairbank, *Trade and Diplomacy on the China Coast: The Opening of the Treaty Ports, 1842–1854* (Stanford, Calif.: Stanford University Press, 1969; 1st ed. 1953 by Harvard University Press). A documentary collection that can usefully be consulted alongside Fairbank's study is Earl Swisher, *China's Management of the American Barbarians: A Study of Sino-American Relations, 1841–1861, with Documents* (New Haven, Conn.: Far Eastern Publications for the Far Eastern Association, 1951). In *Bargaining with the State from Afar: American Citizenship in Treaty Port China, 1844–1942* (New York: Columbia University Press, 2001), Eileen P. Scully argues that the relationship between the American government and U.S. expatriates in China was more about exercising jurisdiction over its sojourning citizens than protecting them. Curtis T. Henson, *Commissioners and Commodores: The East India Squadron and American Diplomacy in China* (University, Ala.: University of Alabama Press, 1982), explores the introduction and role of American naval power in China. For the roles of individual American policy makers, see David L. Anderson, *Imperialism and Idealism: American Diplomats in China, 1861–1898* (Bloomington, Ind.: Indiana University Press, 1985).

On the Open Door policy, Marilyn B. Young's *The Rhetoric of Empire: American China Policy, 1895–1901* (Cambridge, Mass.: Harvard University Press, 1968) sheds light on the contributions of commercial and missionary groups to the changing climate of public opinion that gave rise to the policy. Two further contributions on this subject, Jerry Israel, *Progressivism and the Open Door: America and China, 1905–1921* (Pittsburgh, Pa.: University of Pittsburgh Press, 1971) and Paul A. Varg, *Open Door Diplomat: The Life of W. W. Rockhill* (Urbana, Ill.: University of Illinois, 1952), should be read along with Alfred Whitney Griswold, *The Far Eastern Policy of the United States* (New Haven, Conn.: Yale University Press, 1966; 1st ed. 1938 by Harcourt, Brace). Four publications in Chinese reflect changing trends in research on the Open Door over the last three decades: Wang Xi (汪熙), "Lüelun Zhongmei guanxishi de jige wenti" [略论中美关系史的几个问题 A brief discussion of several issues in Sino-American relations], *Shijie lishi*, no. 3 (1979): 12–19; Ding Mingnan (丁名楠) et al., eds., *Diguo zhuyi qinhuashi* [帝国主义侵华史 A history of imperialist aggression in China] (Beijing: Renmin chubanshe, 1986), vol. 1; Niu Dayong (牛大勇), "Yingguo yu duihua Menhu kaifang zhengce de qiyuan" [英国与对华门户开放政策的起源 Great Britain and the origins of the Open Door policy], *Lishi yanjiu*, no. 4 (1990): 21–35; Wang Wei (王玮) and Dai Chaowu (戴超武), *Meiguo waijiao sixiangshi (1775–2005)* [美国外交思想史 A history of American diplomatic thought] (Beijing: Renmin chubanshe, 2007).

## NOTES

1. One chest weighed about 63.5 kilograms, and the average cost of Indian Malwa opium was 539.76 Mexican silver dollars per chest, exclusive of interest and commission. Timothy Brook and Bob Tadashi Wakabayashi, eds., *Opium Regimes: China, Britain, and Japan, 1939–1952* (Berkeley, Calif.: University of California Press, 2000), pp. 6–7.

2. Jack Beeching, *The Chinese Opium Wars* (San Diego, Calif.: A Harvest/HBJ Book, 1975), p. 29.

3. Li Gui (李圭, b. 1842–1903), *Yapian shilüe* [鸦片事略 A sketch of the opium question], in Xuxiu siku quanshu bianzuan weiyuanhui [续修四库全书编纂委员会], comp., *Xuxiu siku quanshu* [续修四库全书 A Sequel of the Complete Library of the Four Treasuries] (Shanghai: Shanghai guji chubanshe, 1995–99), pp. 308–310.

4. Tripta Desai, *The East India Company: A Brief Survey from 1599 to 1857* (Amherst, N.Y.: Prometheus Books, 1985).

5. Viscount Palmerston to Lord Napier, January 25, 1934, *Correspondence relating to China, no. 1, Correspondence, Orders in Council, and Reports Relative to the Opium War in China, 1840: British Parliamentary Papers*, vol. 30 (Shannon, Ireland: Irish University Press, 1971), p. 239.

6. Lord Napier to Viscount Palmerston, August 9, 1834 (received January 31, 1835), Correspondence relating to China, no. 6, *Correspondence, Orders in Council, and Reports Relative to the Opium War in China, 1840: British Parliamentary Papers*, vol. 30, pp. 245–249.

7. Frederic Wakeman Jr., "The Canton Trade and the Opium War," in Denis Twitchett and John K. Fairbank, eds., *The Cambridge History of China* (Cambridge: Cambridge University Press, 1978), vol. 10, part I, pp. 163–212.

8. "Report from the Select Committee on Trade with China; Together with the Minutes of Evidence, Taken before Them. And An Appendix, and Index, Ordered by the House of Commons, to be Printed, June 5, 1840," Captain John Thacker's testimony, in *Correspondence, Orders in Council, and Reports Relative to the Opium War in China, 1840: British Parliamentary Papers*, vol. 30, pp. 60–77.

9. For the Chinese imperial court's debates on opium, see Liang Tingnan (梁廷枏, b. 1796–1861), *Yifen wenji* [夷氛闻记 Records of things heard in the company of barbar-

ians], reprint of 1959 annotated ed. (Beijing: Zhonghua shuju, 1997; originally publ. circa 1850), vol. 1, pp. 8–17.

10. Liang Tingnan, *Yifen wenji*, p. 18.

11. Robert E. Forbes, *Personal Reminiscences*, 2nd ed. (Boston, Mass.: Little, Brown, 1882, 1st ed. in 1876), p. 145.

12. *Correspondence, Orders in Council, and Reports Relative to the Opium War in China, 1840*, p. 60.

13. Robert E. Forbes, *Personal Reminiscences*, pp. 145–147.

14. Wu Yixiong (吴义雄), "Yapian zhanzheng qian zaihua xiren yu duihua zhanzheng yulun de xingcheng" [鸦片战争前在华西人与对华战争舆论的形成 The moulding of public opinion in support of war with China among Westerners in China prior to the Opium War], *Jindaishi yanjiu* 179, no. 2 (March 2009): 23–43.

15. Liang Tingnan, *Yifen wenji*, vol. 1, p. 1.

16. Liu Cunkuan (刘存宽), "Shilun yingguo fadong diyici Yapian zhanzheng de shuangchong dongyin" [试论英国发动第一次鸦片战争的双重动因 On the dual motives of the British in the First Opium War], in Liu Cunkuan, *Xianggang shi luncong* [香港史论丛 Essays on the history of Hong Kong] (Hong Kong: Qilin shuye youxian gongsi, 1998), pp. 1–24.

17. Maurice Stewart Collis, *Foreign Mud: Being an Account of the Opium Imbroglio at Canton in the 1830s and the Anglo-Chinese War That Followed* (New York: New Directions, 2002; reprint of 1946 Faber and Faber ed.), p. 183.

18. Robert B. Forbes, *Personal Reminiscences*, pp. 149–150. *Letters from China: The Canton-Boston Correspondence of Robert Bennet Forbes, 1838–1840*, compiled and edited, and with background essays, by Phyllis Forbes Kerr (Mystic, Conn.: Mystic Seaport Museum, 1996).

19. Editorial article, "Retrospection, or a Review of Public Occurrences in China during the Last Ten Years, from January 1st, 1832, to December 31st, 1841," *Chinese Repository* 11, no. 5 (May 1842), 241.

20. John Quincy Adams, "Lecture on the War with China, Delivered before the Massachusetts Historical Society, December 1841," *Chinese Repository* 11, no. 5 (May 1842): 274–288.

21. John Quincy Adams, "China and Sandwich Islands," 27th Congress, 3rd Session, January 24, 1843, in Jules Davids, ed., *American Diplomatic and Public Papers: The United States and China* (Wilmington, Del.: Scholarly Resources Inc., 1973), series I, vol. 1, p. 148.

22. "Remarks on the present crisis in the opium traffic, with inquiries respecting its causes, and the best course to be pursued by those now connected with it," *Chinese Repository* 8, no. 1 (May 1839): 1–8. Michael C. Lazich, "American Missionaries and the Opium Trade in Nineteenth-Century China," *Journal of World History* 17, no. 2 (June 2006): 197–223.

23. Tyler Dennett, *Americans in East Asia: A Critical Study of United States Policy in the Far East in the Nineteenth Century* (New York: Barnes & Noble, 1963; reprint of 1922 Macmillan ed.), pp. 104–105.

24. Francis Wharton, "China and the Chinese Peace," *Hunt's Merchants' Magazine and Commercial Review* 8, no. 3 (March 1843): 205–226.

25. Lawrence Kearny, letters sent from U.S. Ship *Constellation*, Macao Roads, March 31, 1842, and April 22, 1843, in Jules Davids, *American Diplomatic and Public Papers: The United States and China*, series I, vol. 1, pp. 5, 13.

26. H. S. Legare of Department of State, letter on June 12, 1843, in Jules Davids, *American Diplomatic and Public Papers: The United States and China*, series I, vol. 1, p. 17.

27. The origins of what are today understood in China as the "Unequal Treaties" can be found in the treaties, conventions, and agreements concluded between China and various foreign states during the nineteenth century. The most important treaty rights ceded to foreign interests in China were low fixed tariffs, extraterritoriality, concessions and settlements, leased territories, and the nonreciprocal most-favored-nation clause. The Treaty of Nanjing was the first of two formative instruments that shaped the "Unequal Treaties" in China—particularly in its two annexes, the General Regulations for Trade and Tariff of 1843 and the Supplementary Treaty (also known as the Treaty of the Bogue) of 1843. The second was the Sino-British Treaty of Tianjin of 1858. Seventeen countries benefited from these inequitable treaty relations with China. They were Britain (from 1842), the United States (1844), France (1844), Sweden/Norway (1847), Russia (1851), Prussia (1861), Portugal (1862), Denmark (1863), the Netherlands (1863), Spain (1864), Belgium (1865), Italy (1866), Austria (1869), Japan (1871), Brazil (1881), Mexico (1899), and Switzerland (1918). Tariff autonomy was restored to China in 1930, but extraterritoriality was not revoked until 1943. Dong Wang, *China's Unequal Treaties: Narrating National History* (Lanham, Md.: Rowman & Littlefield, 2005), chapter 1.

28. Lawrence Kearny, letter to the governor of Canton on October 8, 1842, in Jules Davids, *American Diplomatic and Public Papers: The United States and China*, series I, vol. 1, p. 64.

29. John Adams, report on January 24, 1843, "China and Sandwich Islands," to accompany bills H.R. nos. 720 and 721, House of Representatives, Rep. no. 93, 27th Congress, 3rd Session, in Jules Davids, *American Diplomatic and Public Papers: The United States and China*, series I, vol. 1, p. 147.

30. United States legation, dispatch, Macao, April 24, 1844, in Jules Davids, *American Diplomatic and Public Papers: The United States and China*, series I, vol. 1, pp. 213.

31. Wen Qing (文庆) et al., eds., *Chouban yiwu shimo* [筹办夷务始末 A complete account of the management of barbarian affairs], Daoguang chao [Daoguang's reign] (Beijing: Zhonghua shuju, 1964), vol. 6, pp. 2812–2815.

32. Kenneth Scott Latourette, *The History of Early Relations between the United States and China, 1784–1844* (New Haven, Conn.: Yale University Press, 1917), p. 140.

33. Tyler Dennett, *Americans in Eastern Asia*, pp. 159–160.

34. William Frederick Mayers, ed., *Treaties between the Empire of China and Foreign Powers, Together with the Regulations for the Conduct of Foreign Trade* (Taipei: Ch'eng-wen Publishing Company, 1966; reprint of 1877 J. Broadhurst Tootal, "North China Herald" Office, ed. in Shanghai), p. 83.

35. William H. Seward, *The Works of William H. Seward* (New York: Redfield, 1884), vol. 3, p. 409.

36. Freda Harcourt, "Black Gold: P&O and the Opium Trade, 1847–1914," *International Journal of Maritime History* 6, no. 1 (June 1994): 1–83.

37. William M. Malloy, comp., *Treaties, Conventions, International Acts, Protocols and Agreements between the United States of America and Other Powers, 1776–1909* (Washington, D.C.: Government Printing Office, 1910), vol. 1, pp. 205–206.

38. "Meishi Mailian zhi Liangjiang Zongdu Yiliang zhaohui" [美使麦莲致两江总督怡良照会 American commissioner Robert McLane's note to the governor of Jiangnan and Jiangxi, Yiliang], dated June 22, 1854, Zhongyang yanjiuyuan jindaishi yanjiusuo

(中央研究院近代史研究所), comp., *Zhongmei guanxi shiliao: Jiaqing, Daoguang, Xianfeng chao* [中美关系史料:嘉庆,道光,咸丰朝 Sources on Sino-American relations: The reigns of Jiaqing, Daoguang, and Xianfeng] (Taipei: Zhongyang yanjiuyuan jindaishi yanjiusuo, 1968), document no. 235, p. 165.

39. U.S. Congressional Printed Documents, *Robert M. McLane Correspondence*, Senate Document no. 22, Serial no. 734, 33rd Congress, June 14, 1854, p. 54.

40. Qi Sihe (齐思和) et al., eds., *Di'erci Yapian Zhanzheng* [第二次鸦片战争 The second Opium War] (Shanghai: Shanghai renmin chubanshe, 1978–79), vol. 3, p. 544.

41. This material draws on Dong Wang, *China's Unequal Treaties*, chapter 1.

42. Anders Stephanson, "Global Competition and Manifest Destiny on the Cusp of the Twentieth Century," in Elizabeth Cobbs Hoffman and Jon Gjerde, eds., *Major Problems in American History: Documents and Essays, vol. 2, Since 1865* (Boston, Mass.: Houghton Mifflin, 2007), pp. 103–109.

43. Judith Ewell, *Venezuela and the United States: From Monroe's Hemisphere to Petroleum's Empire* (Athens, Ga.: Georgia University Press, 1996).

44. John Eperjesi, "The American Asiatic Association and the Imperialist Imaginary of the American Public," *Boundary 2*, vol. 28, no. 1 (Spring 2001): 195–219.

45. Anders Stephanson, "Global Competition and Manifest Destiny on the Cusp of the Twentieth Century," in Elizabeth Cobbs Hoffman and Jon Gjerde, eds., *Major Problems in American History: Documents and Essays, vol. 2, Since 1865*, pp. 103–109.

46. John Hay to Mr. Vignaud, September 6, 1899, United States Department of State, *Papers Relating to the Foreign Relations of the United States, with the Annual Message of the President Transmitted to Congress December 5, 1899* (Washington, D.C.: U.S. Government Printing Office, 1899), p. 128. Arguably there was a "third" set of diplomatic notes: during the negotiations among foreign powers for the restoration of order in China, John Hay reaffirmed the American policy regarding "impartial trade and the integrity of the Chinese Empire" in his notes of October 29, 1900, addressed to the British and German governments. United States Department of State, *Papers Relating to the Foreign Relations of the United States, with the Annual Message of the President Transmitted to Congress December 3, 1900* (Washington, D.C.: Government Printing Office, 1902), p. 355.

47. United States Department of State, *Papers Relating to the Foreign Relations of the United States*, 1899, pp. 128–143.

48. William Rockhill, "Response by Hon. William W. Rockhill," *Journal of the American Asiatic Association* 2, no. 5 (June 1902): 112–114. For Rockhill, the gradual, peaceful reform of the Chinese administrative system was the more sustainable option: "To try to change the present regime [the Qing government] and substitute something more in conformity with Western ideas would be folly and entail responsibilities which no nation could afford to assume. The Powers have also realized that administrative reform in China can only result from constant and general pressure from without, and that sudden change must inevitably bring revolution and be followed by years of chaos."

49. William W. Rockhill to John V. A. MacMurray, April 11, 1913, William Woodville Rockhill papers, 1854–1914, Letters, 1912–1913, bMS Am 2121 (2155)–(2174), folder 1, file no. 2172, Houghton Library, Harvard University.

50. John Hay to Andrew D. White, September 6, 1899, United States Department of State, *Papers Relating to the Foreign Relations of the United States, 1899*, p. 129.

51. John Hay to Joseph H. Choate (b. 1832–1917, American ambassador to the Court of St. James's in England, 1899–1905), September 6, 1899, United States Department of State, *Papers Relating to the Foreign Relations of the United States, 1899*, p. 131.

52. John Hay, instructions sent mutatis mutandis to the U.S. ambassadors at London, Paris, Berlin, St. Petersburg, and Rome, and to the U.S. minister at Tokyo, March 20, 1900, United States Department of State, *Papers Relating to the Foreign Relations of the United States, 1899*, p. 142.

53. United States Department of State, *Papers Relating to the Foreign Relations of the United States, 1900*, p. vii.

54. United States Department of State, *Papers Relating to the Foreign Relations of the United States, 1900*, pp. xiv, 299.

55. James Lorence, *The American Asiatic Association, 1898–1925: Organized Business and the Myth of the China Market*, PhD dissertation, University of Wisconsin, 1970.

56. Yu Zichen (雨子臣), "Lun shijie jingji jingzheng zhi dashi" [论世界经济竞争之大势 On trends in international economic competition], in Zhang Nan (张枏) and Wang Renzhi (王忍之), eds., *Xinhai geming qian shinianjian shilun xuanji* [辛亥革命前十年间时论选集 A selection of political essays from the decade before the Xinhai Revolution] (Beijing: Sanlian shudian, 1960), series 1, vol. 1, pp. 202–203. Zhang Xiaolu (张小路), "Zhongguo yu Menhu kaifang zhengce" [中国与"门户开放"政策(1899–1911) China and the Open Door policy], in Gu Yunshen (顾云深), Shi Yuanhua (石源华), and Jin Guangyao (金光耀), *Jianzhi wanglai: Bainian Zhongmei jingji guanxi de huigu yu qianzhan* [鉴知往来: 百年来中美经济关系的回顾与前瞻 Looking backward and forward: A century of Sino-American economic relations] (Shanghai: Fuda daxue chubanshe, 1999), pp. 189–211.

57. Liang Qichao (梁启超), "Guafen weiyan" [瓜分危言 Warnings about the carve-up], written in 1898, in Liang Qichao, *Yinbingshi heji* [饮冰室合集 Collected essays by Liang Qichao] (Beijing: Zhonghua shuju, 1989), Yinbingshi wenji, no. 4, pp. 36–39. "Mieguo xinfa lun" [灭国新法论 A new method of exterminating a nation-state employed by Western countries], written in 1901, in Liang Qichao, *Yinbingshi heji*, Yinbingshi wenji, no. 6, pp. 32–47.

58. Yang Tianhong (杨天宏), "Wanqing 'Junshi' waijiao yu 'Menhu kaifang,'" [晚清"均势"外交与"门户开放" The diplomacy of "the balance of power" in the late Qing and the "Open Door"], *Shehui kexue yanjiu*, no. 6 (2008): 146–153.

59. Michael H. Hunt, *Frontier Defense and the Open Door: Manchuria in Chinese-American Relations, 1895–1911* (New Haven, Conn.: Yale University Press, 1973).

60. Michael Schaller, *The United States and China: Into the Twenty-First Century* (Oxford: Oxford University Press, 2001), p. 26.

61. Macabe Keliher, "Anglo-American Rivalry and the Origins of U.S. China Policy," *Diplomatic History* 31, no. 2 (April 2007): 227–258; Macabe Keliher, "Americans in Eastern Asia, Revisited: Anglo-American Rivalry and the China Market," MA thesis, George Washington University, 2007.

62. When Theodore Roosevelt came to office, he retained McKinley's cabinet including John Hay as secretary of state, and Elihu Root as secretary of war.

63. Henry Cabot Lodge, "The Business World vs. the Politicians" (1895), *Documents in United States History* (Upper Saddle River, N.J.: Prentice Hall, 2006), CD-ROM, Part 20: America around the Globe.

64. Theodore Roosevelt's letter to Alfred Thayer Mahan, May 3, 1897, in Elting E. Morison, ed., *The Letters of Theodore Roosevelt* (Cambridge, Mass.: Harvard University Press, 1951), vol. 1, pp. 607–608.

65. John K. Fairbank, "'American China Policy' to 1898: A Misconception," *Pacific Historical Review* 39, no. 4 (November 1970): 409–420.

66. John K. Fairbank, "'American China Policy' to 1898: A Misconception."

67. Caleb Cushing to Hon. John C. Calhoun (secretary of state), Macao, August 16, 1844, in Jules Davids, ed., *American Diplomatic and Public Papers: The United States and China*, series I, vol. 2, p. 271.

# THREE

# Chinese Immigration: Roots in the United States?

Chinese immigration has been an important aspect of the relationship since the mid-nineteenth century. It illuminates both nations' approaches to "global" issues and throws light on the pattern of Chinese settlement in the United States. Three main lines of inquiry are pursued in this chapter.

First, over the course of the century 1848–1943, U.S. congressional legislation targeted Chinese immigrants with the deliberate aim of restricting their numbers and influence. The federal government exercised and expanded its power through regulating immigration and depriving resident Chinese of their citizenship and other constitutional rights. Second, I question the perception that Chinese in America were merely "silent sojourners, passive victims, and the model minority," keeping a low profile under unfavorable circumstances. As some scholars have pointed out, this view undervalues the extent of social activism among the Chinese diaspora in the United States.[1] Indeed, resistance, protest, and a level of defiance permissible in the American legal and political system were often part of the story of Chinese immigration to the United States. Third, the checks and balances inherent in the American political system often produced favorable judicial decisions for Chinese petitioners, decisions which—unpopular as they were—overrode the judgments of local bureaucrats.

## MIGRATION BETWEEN CHINA AND THE UNITED STATES: AN OVERVIEW

The majority of Chinese immigrant workers in the United States hailed from the Pearl River Delta, the fertile alluvial area of Guangdong Province where the Pearl River flows into the South China Sea. As discussed in the preceding chapters of this book, from early times, the Pearl River region has been a major hub of domestic and international trade. Economically, it is still the most dynamic region in China. Over time, much of its population emigrated to Southeast Asia, and later to North and South America, as well as to other places, forging significant links between the region, overseas Chinese, and the outside world.

In common with labor migration to other parts of the globe, the influx of Chinese to the United States was primarily driven by economic factors. It was a widely held belief that the mass of Chinese immigrants to the United States in the nineteenth century were coolies, no better than indentured slaves. In the mid-nineteenth century, the flourishing Asian coolie trade took the place of the African slave trade to make up labor shortages on South American and Caribbean plantations. Chinese coastal cities such as Amoy, Macau, Hong Kong, Canton, and Shantou served as major ports where laborers were bought, sold, and shipped out.[2] In 1866, in view of the abuses done to coolies who were "abducted by malignant people to go abroad," the Qing government attempted to regulate the labor market and sought an agreement with the United States.[3] Six years later, admitting its failure to enforce these regulations at the local level, the Zongli Yamen, the Qing government's foreign office, again expressed its desire to collaborate with the United States.

The Chinese who came to America were far from being a faceless collection of laborers. Chinese villagers of the second half of the nineteenth century had to deal with overpopulation, rebellions, ethnic feuds, natural disasters, and a host of other pressures. To them, the United States represented the prospect of economic advancement and employment in mining, railways, and agriculture, especially after gold was discovered at Sutter's Mill in California in 1848. Of the half a million or so Chinese who eventually came to the United States, more than half were from a single county, today's Taishan, in Guangdong Province.

The first three Chinese, two men and one woman, arrived in San Francisco in the autumn of 1848.[4] Chinese immigration to the United

States rapidly reached a peak in 1852, and the registered number of immigrants that year was 18,434, among whom only 50 were women. For the remainder of the nineteenth century, Chinese immigration displayed a severe gender imbalance, with a male-female ratio of 27:1 in 1890.

During the twenty years of 1848–68, over 100,000 Chinese arrived in the United States, more than 45,000 of whom eventually returned to their homeland as a result of the hostility they experienced in California. From 1869 until 1882 when the Chinese Exclusion Act was signed into law, 200,000 Chinese entered the United States. Lured by the promise of making a quick fortune on the gold fields, over 70 percent settled in California, constituting about 8 percent of the state's population.[5]

The coming of Chinese immigrants was closely linked with the benefits as well as the downside of America's rapid industrialization. Although over 80 percent of Chinese migrant workers were engaged in mining in early years, a substantial number labored on the railways. As an important industrial force for mass production and marketing, railroad construction—the pioneers of big business—received support from federal and state governments with public land grants. In 1862, the Central Pacific Railroad Corporation and the Union Pacific were chosen to build the first transcontinental railroad in the United States. Hailed at the time as a triumph of American technological know-how, the transcontinental railroad shrank the time it took to cross the United States from between four and six months to only six days. Faced with a labor shortage, the Central Pacific took on over 12,000 Chinese navvies to construct the 690-mile railway through the Sierra Nevada Mountains and across Nevada to Utah.

The flow of Chinese workers across the Pacific was a two-way traffic, which fluctuated dramatically according to political, economic, and legal conditions in both China and the United States. In the United States, anti-Chinese agitation and discrimination showed its hand at an early stage. The sharp fall in Chinese migrant labor from 18,434 in 1852 to a mere 4,316 in 1853 was the direct result of repeated calls for legislation against Chinese miners. These included a "special message" from the governor of California, John Bigler, which urged the legislature to stem the inflow of "Asiatic" immigrants, particularly Chinese coolies, by imposing heavy taxes on immigration and foreign mining ventures.[6] In May 1852 the California legislature passed two discriminatory bills: the first authorized a foreign miners' license tax of US$3 per month to discourage mining by the Chinese, and the second enacted a commutation tax of approximately US$5 on each new Chinese migrant. Combined, these taxes accounted for 25 percent of the state's entire revenue until the miners' tax was repealed in 1870. Further discriminatory measures followed. In 1853 the California State Supreme Court ruled that Chinese as a class were not eligible to vote in California, testify in court, or become U.S. citizens.[7] This provoked the widespread appropriation of Chinese mining sites. Although the West Coast, and California in particular, was the stronghold of anti-Chinese sentiment, antagonism toward Chinese was not institutionalized on a national scale until the 1870s and 1880s. Intensified by worsening unemployment and the failure of financial markets, anti-Chinese violence broke out widely across the western states and territories, as we will see below. The most vocal proponent of this racist agitation was the Irish-born labor leader Denis Kearney and the Workingman's Party he led in the 1870s.

The changing political landscape, the economy, and the state of the bilateral relationship all contributed to the flow of immigrants to America. After the repeal of the Chinese exclusion laws on December 17, 1943—an enactment known as the Magnuson Act—Chinese elites and refugee émigrés escaping the Chinese Communist takeover of China began arriving via Hong Kong and Taiwan. Other measures swelled the flow. A combination of the War Brides Act of 1945, the Alien Wives Act of 1946, and various refugee acts doubled the growth of the Chinese diaspora between 1950 and 1960 from over 110,000 to more than 230,000.[8] As a result of the Civil Rights Act of 1964, the Immigration Act of 1965 (the Hart-Celler Act), and the establishment of diplomatic relations between the United States and the People's Republic of China, the Chinese population increased rapidly, from 430,000 in 1970 to about 3 million at the beginning of the twenty-first century.[9]

## WIELDING AND CONTESTING THE POWER OF THE STATE

This section begins with an outline of the pertinent Sino-American treaties and the American domestic legislation relating to Chinese immigration (intended to channel social discontent against the Chinese and thereby strengthen the federal government), followed by an analysis of the various efforts at the state and federal levels to control the flow of immigrants. These treaties and laws are key to understanding the nature of

**Table 3.1. Chinese Immigration and Emigration, 1848–68**

| Year | Male | Female | Immigration Total | Emigration Total | Excess over Immigration |
|------|------|--------|-------------------|------------------|-------------------------|
| 1848 | 2 | 1 | 3 | 0 | 0 |
| 1849 | 323 | 0 | 323 | 0 | 0 |
| 1850 | 447 | 0 | 447 | 0 | 0 |
| 1851 | 2,716 | 0 | 2,716 | 261 | 0 |
| 1852 | 18,384 | 50 | 18,434 | 2,056 | 0 |
| 1853 | 3,917 | 399 | 4,316 | 4,405 | 89 |
| 1854 | 14,450 | 513 | 15,063 | 2,386 | 0 |
| 1855 | 3,188 | 24 | 3,212 | 3,328 | 116 |
| 1856* | 4,935 | 95 | 5,030 | 2,675 | 0 |
| 1857* | 5,383 | 423 | 5,806 | 2,675 | 0 |
| 1858* | 5,358 | 323 | 5,681 | 2,675 | 0 |
| 1859 | 3,100 | 427 | 3,527 | 2,907 | 0 |
| 1860 | 7,312 | 308 | 7,620 | 2,079 | 0 |
| 1861 | 5,997 | 510 | 6,507 | 2,151 | 0 |
| 1862 | 5,583 | 442 | 6,025 | 3,001 | 0 |
| 1863 | 7,149 | 32 | 7,181 | 2,510 | 0 |
| 1864 | 2,756 | 175 | 2,931 | 3,086 | 155 |
| 1865 | 2,375 | 0 | 2,375 | 1,945 | 0 |
| 1866 | 2,350 | 1 | 2,351 | 3,015 | 664 |
| 1867 | 3,779 | 27 | 3,806 | 4,167 | 361 |
| 1868 (to July 1) | 5,101 | 16 | 5,117 | 565 | 0 |
| Total | 104,705 | 3,766 | 108,471 | 45,887 | 1,387 |

*Source:* The statistical data, with adjustments by the present author, are taken from the letter by Daniel Cleveland of San Francisco to J. Ross Brown, American minister to China, dated July 27, 1868, in Jules Davids, ed., *American Diplomatic and Public Papers: The United States and China*, p. 1.

*Figures from 1856 to 1858 are estimates.

Chinese immigration to the United States. Popular familiarity with the issues usually ends at the discriminatory legislation and the injustices visited upon Chinese immigrants. Two important (and related) questions have been sketchily handled in many previous accounts: How did the U.S. government seek to align its constitution and domestic laws with international law and treaties in the case of the "China problem"? And

**Table 3.2. Chinese Immigration to the United States, 1869–1943**

| Year | Immigration | Year | Immigration | Year | Immigration |
|------|------------|------|------------|------|------------|
| 1869 | 12,874 | 1894 | 1,170 | 1919 | 1,964 |
| 1870 | 15,740 | 1895 | 539 | 1920 | 2,330 |
| 1871 | 7,135 | 1896 | 1,441 | 1921 | 4,009 |
| 1872 | 7,788 | 1897 | 3,363 | 1922 | 4,406 |
| 1873 | 20,292 | 1898 | 2,071 | 1923 | 4,986 |
| 1874 | 13,776 | 1899 | 1,660 | 1924 | 6,992 |
| 1875 | 16,437 | 1900 | 1,247 | 1925 | 1,937 |
| 1876 | 22,781 | 1901 | 2,459 | 1926 | 1,750 |
| 1877 | 10,594 | 1902 | 1,649 | 1927 | 1,471 |
| 1878 | 8,992 | 1903 | 2,209 | 1928 | 1,320 |
| 1879 | 9,604 | 1904 | 4,309 | 1929 | 1,446 |
| 1880 | 5,802 | 1905 | 2,166 | 1930 | 1,589 |
| 1881 | 11,890 | 1906 | 1,544 | 1931 | 1,150 |
| 1882 | 39,579 | 1907 | 961 | 1932 | 750 |
| 1883 | 8,031 | 1908 | 1,397 | 1933 | 148 |
| 1884 | 279 | 1909 | 1,943 | 1934 | 187 |
| 1885 | 22 | 1910 | 1,968 | 1935 | 229 |
| 1886 | 40 | 1911 | 1,460 | 1936 | 273 |
| 1887 | 10 | 1912 | 1,765 | 1937 | 293 |
| 1888 | 26 | 1913 | 2,105 | 1938 | 613 |
| 1889 | 118 | 1914 | 2,502 | 1939 | 642 |
| 1890 | 1,716 | 1915 | 2,660 | 1940 | 643 |
| 1891 | 2,836 | 1916 | 2,460 | 1941 | 1,003 |
| 1892 | 0 | 1917 | 2,237 | 1942 | 179 |
| 1893 | 472 | 1918 | 1,795 | 1943 | 65 |

*Source:* Helen Chen, "Chinese Immigration into the United States: An Analysis of Changes in Immigration Policies," PhD dissertation, Brandeis University, 1980, p. 174.

how did Chinese migrants survive and ultimately thrive by making use of American political and legal institutions?

## The Burlingame Treaty of 1868

The first legal instruments to deal with immigration were the additional articles to the treaty between the United States and China of June

18, 1858, known as the Burlingame Treaty. This treaty was signed in Washington on July 28, 1868, by Secretary of State William H. Seward for the United States, and by Anson Burlingame (1822–70)—a retired American minister to China who had been appointed by the Chinese emperor as "ambassador from China to all the treaty powers" (*banli geguo zhongwai jiaoshe shiwu dachen* 办理各国中外交涉事务大臣)—and two further Chinese representatives, Zhigang and Sun Jiagu. Burlingame, Zhigang, and Sun constituted the first-ever Qing diplomatic envoy to Europe and the United States.[10] Opposing forced immigration, Article 5 of the Burlingame Treaty states unequivocally the principle of free migration and immigration between the two countries as "the inherent and inalienable right of man to change his home and allegiance." In recognition of the "mutual advantage" of migration, Article 6 states that Americans resident in China

> enjoyed the same privileges, immunities, or exemptions in respect to travel or residence, as may there be enjoyed by the citizens or subjects of the most favored nation. And, reciprocally, Chinese subjects visiting or residing in the United States, shall enjoy the same privileges, immunities, and exemptions in respect to travel or residence as may there be enjoyed by the citizens or subjects of the most favored nation.[11]

One day before the signing of the Burlingame Treaty, the 40th U.S. Congress, Session 2, declared in the same spirit that "the right of expatriation is a natural and inherent right of all people, indispensable to the enjoyment of the rights of life, liberty, and the pursuit of happiness; and . . . in the recognition of this principle this government has freely received emigrants from all nations, and invested them with the rights of citizenship."[12]

### The Amended Treaty of 1880

Under pressure from anti-Chinese agitators, most notably labor unions on the Pacific West Coast, the U.S. government soon sought to abrogate the 1868 Burlingame Treaty, much to the chagrin of the Qing government. The government expressed the opinion that both the influx of Chinese laborers and resident Chinese in America threatened the national interests and order of the United States. In the end, the Chinese government gave way and in 1880 signed an amended treaty permitting the American government to regulate, limit, or suspend immigration—but it "may not absolutely prohibit it." This provision was applicable only to Chinese laborers, not to teachers, students, merchants, or tourists. Article 2 of the revised treaty stipulated that the United States accorded to Chinese already residing in the United States "all the rights, privileges, immunities, and exceptions which are accorded to the citizens and subjects of the most favored nation."[13] Resident Chinese "shall be allowed to go and come of their own free will." Although not providing for total exclusion, this amended treaty set the direction for the more thoroughgoing exclusionary immigration policy that would soon be put in place.

*The Chinese Exclusion Act of 1882, Its 1888 Supplement, the Geary Act of 1892, and the 1904 Act*

Contradicting its previous acts and proclamations, Congress for the first time put restrictions on voluntary, free immigration through the Chinese Exclusion Act of 1882, which was signed into law on May 6, 1882, by President Chester Arthur. It was the first law to bar immigration of a particular racial group into the United States. Asserting that the influx of Chinese laborers endangered the "good order of certain localities within the territory," the 1882 Exclusion Act (also known as the Scott Act) ordered that the admission to the United States of Chinese laborers, both skilled and unskilled, be suspended for ten years; that no courts should admit Chinese to citizenship; and, further, that a certificate authorized by either the U.S. or the Chinese government identifying Chinese laborers or "Chinese other than laborers" should be retained for inspection by immigration officers on arrival, departure, or return. The act stipulated further, "No Chinese person shall be permitted to enter the United States by land without producing to the proper office of customs the certificate in this act required of Chinese persons seeking to land from a vessel."[14]

Since the 1882 Exclusion Act was vague on whether Chinese laborers could be allowed to stay on in America or return to America after a short visit overseas, on October 1, 1888, Congress attempted to correct alleged abuses of the law and passed a new act explicitly barring Chinese laborers from returning to, or remaining in, the United States without authorization.[15] In May 1892, the Geary Act passed in Congress, going further than any previous legislation in discriminating against Chinese. This new law not only continued all previous legislation excluding Chinese from the United States for a further ten years, but also mandated all legal

Chinese residents or persons of Chinese descent to apply for a certificate of residency to avoid arrest and deportation.[16] Twelve years later, in 1904, Congress consolidated all its legislative efforts to close the door to all would-be Chinese immigrants, "without modification, limitation, or condition."[17]

*The 1894 Treaty Regulating Chinese Immigration*

In step with these congressional acts, the 1894 treaty between the United States and China reaffirmed that Chinese laborers were "absolutely prohibited" from immigrating to the United States. "[I]n view of the antagonism and much deprecated serious disorders to which the presence of Chinese laborers has given rise in certain parts of the United States," the Chinese government bowed to the wishes of the American government, expressing its desire "to prohibit the emigration of such laborers from China to the United States."[18] However, the treaty was terminated on December 7, 1904, following notice given by the Chinese government that its provisions were disadvantageous to China.

Two major conclusions emerge from this body of legislation and treaty making. First, in line with its evolving policies of racial exclusion, the executive branch of the U.S. government kept up the pressure on the Chinese government to sign new bilateral treaties which were intended to keep pace with American domestic laws. Second, excluding Chinese laborers through legislation had become a congressional priority; Congress refused to surrender control over immigration to bilateral treaties and thus increased the capacity of the federal government in this area. Implementing the Chinese exclusion laws involved a massive effort—the first of its kind—by the federal government to provide customs collectors and to expand the Immigration Bureau established in 1891 in the Treasury Department.[19] Taking cognizance of international treaties, the U.S. Supreme Court was firm that control over immigration was indispensable to the sovereignty of an independent state such as the United States. In concert with the federal government, the Court had the disposition to subject international law to the U.S. Constitution and American congressional acts on matters of enforcement, modification, or repeal. "The power of the legislative department of the government to exclude aliens from the United States is an incident of sovereignty which cannot be surrendered by the treaty making power."[20] And again, the Court affirmed,

"This government could never give up the right of excluding foreigners whose presence it might deem a source of danger to the United States."

CONTROLLING IMMIGRATION AND SURVIVING EXCLUSION

Two points are helpful in gauging the extent of American "legal imperialism" aimed at controlling immigration and the Chinese countertactics directed at surviving exclusion.

First, American legal imperialism in the case of Chinese immigration was exhibited at several levels. As the highest court in the land and the sole interpreter of the Constitution, the Supreme Court had the last word on immigration issues at the federal level. At the same time, spokesmen for state and local government (such as in California) urged the federal government to take measures to prevent further immigration by Chinese.[21] Nevertheless, responsibility for enforcing and interpreting the exclusion regulations mostly devolved upon customs collectors and court judges, especially in San Francisco.

Second, some setbacks were experienced by exclusionists, in particular those who advocated empowering the federal government in the area of immigration. The American political and legal system allowed for resident Chinese to seek redress for their grievances through the courts. The Chinese legation in the United States repeatedly lobbied the State Department, protesting the losses, injuries, and hardships suffered by resident Chinese and demanding that bilateral treaty obligations be observed. In a variety of ways, Chinese supporters argued that it was unconstitutional, illiberal, and detrimental to the interests of the United States and California to exclude Chinese immigration.

Since it was agreed that a sovereign state like the United States could not give away its rights to exclude foreigners deemed dangerous to national interests, promises made to the Chinese through bilateral treaties were deemed to be inferior to the American Constitution. This principle was upheld time after time in the courts. In 1889, the Supreme Court in an 8–0 decision ruled against Chae Chan Ping, a Chinese laborer in San Francisco who was refused reentry to the United States after a four-month visit to China.[22] Chae contended that this denial was in violation of existing treaties such as the Burlingame Treaty between China and the United States. Although the Court conceded that the congressional act of 1888 "is in contravention of express stipulations of the treaty of 1868 and of the supplemental treaty of 1880," it also insisted that a treaty made by the United States with any foreign nation was "subject to such acts as Congress may pass for its enforcement, modification, or repeal."[23] Sometimes judgment was made in favor of the Chinese plaintiff. In 1898, a case was brought by Wong Kim Ark—a twenty-one-year-old born in the United States to Chinese parents living in San Francisco—who was likewise denied entry after a visit to China. Having been issued a writ of habeas corpus, Wong argued that he had been "restrained of his liberty" by the collector of customs, and by the general manager of the steamship company involved, in violation of the Constitution and laws of the United States, solely upon the pretense that he was not a citizen of the United States.[24] In a 6–2 decision in favor of Wong, the Supreme Court gave its opinion that the fundamental rule of citizenship by birth included all children of resident aliens born in the United States. Wong was a citizen since he was born in the United States, and therefore the Chinese exclusion acts did not apply to him.[25]

The decisions arrived at in Chinese exclusion cases helped establish the superiority of the Constitution and the Supreme Court's preference for a legal recourse based on the principles of liberty and natural rights. The Court also did not bar Congress from enacting laws which were inconsistent with the international obligations of the U.S. government. In other words, the treaty violation argument—adopted by some Chinese immigrants, their supporters, and the Chinese government—did not prevail in the courts.

But that did not stop the federal government from seeking international solutions to the "China problem." Archival records show that during the latter half of the nineteenth century the U.S. government launched inquiries into the coolie trade and pressed the Qing, British, Canadian, and Mexican governments to stop the flow of Chinese laborers. It became clear to the American government that the source of the problem lay in the British and American steamship companies which facilitated human trafficking in Hong Kong, Macau, Nassau, and Havana. On March 7, 1884, in a memorandum to Frederick T. Frelinghuysen (secretary of state, 1881–85), John Russell Young, American minister to China (1882–85), summarized the issue:

> [W]hile the cause of the evil is in Hongkong or Macao, we have no treaty with China to prevent Chinamen going from Canton to these ports; that once at Hongkong or Macao, ports within a few hours of sail

of Canton, the Chinese are outside of the jurisdiction of the emperor, and under the control of Great Britain or Portugal, that it is not within the power of Prince Kung to give us a remedy![26]

To counter the problem, the U.S. government proposed negotiating with the British and Mexican governments to help enforce the Chinese Exclusion Act. Young commented that

the [U.S.] Government will never reach the root of this trouble, until you have an understanding with Great Britain so far as Hongkong is concerned, and with Portugal in regard to Macao. . . . For it stands to reason that if Chinese subjects can pass in a few hours from Canton to Macao and Hongkong, and can there purchase from any knavish firm fraudulent certificates entitling them to land in the United States, the trade will not only be a flourishing one, but a trade that this government cannot suppress. . . . China might as well ask us to prevent emigration from Nassau or Havana, or to punish our people who choose to lead evil lives there.[27]

The results of the U.S. requests to Great Britain, Mexico, and Canada were negative. Mexico confirmed that its refusal was based on its constitutional provisions, which made it impossible to "carry out any plan for enforcing legislation against the entry from Mexico into the United States of Chinese laborers."[28] The Canadian government reached a similar conclusion:

There is no Canadian law by virtue of which restrictions could be placed on Chinese residents in Canada to fetter their freedom of movement any more than any other foreign resident. . . . The Dominions are therefore of the opinion that no practical way exists by which effect could be given to the request embodied in the resolution of the Senate and House of Representatives of the United States above referred to.[29]

Over the years, the series of congressional laws restricting Chinese immigration and their enforcement by federal officials prompted Chinese to contest the power of the state through the courts. Individual Chinese placed thousands of writs of habeas corpus before federal district and circuit courts, a process which—together with America's treaty obligations to protect the rights of Chinese already residing in the United States—scotched the popular assumption that the Exclusion Act would end Chinese immigration for good.

As a staunch opponent of Chinese immigration, the Californian customs collector, John S. Hager, implemented the Exclusion Act in the strictest terms by regularly refusing to allow intending Chinese immigrants to land. Like anyone else, however, Chinese were entitled to challenge the detention imposed by the collector through a procedural recourse to habeas corpus by claiming to have been unlawfully restrained of their liberty. As a result, in California's northern district, between June 27, 1882, and December 1, 1890, individual Chinese filed 7,080 writ petitions in Judge Ogden Hoffman's docket, leaving the courts with little time to conduct regular judicial business.[30] Judge Hoffman, along with Judge Lorenzo Sawyer, often rendered unpopular decisions in favor of Chinese petitioners. On January 25, 1888, the *Alta California* reported that, five years after the passage of the Chinese Exclusion Act, 87 percent of the nearly 4,000 Chinese migrants seeking writs of habeas corpus from the federal courts had succeeded and landed in San Francisco. Similarly, Mary Roberts Coolidge's research reveals that the number of merchants' wives and children debarred from entering the United States fell dramatically over a two-year period, from 25 percent in 1904 to 8 percent in 1906, while at the same time the total number of Chinese applying for admission had almost doubled.[31]

The nature of the American judicial system forced a case-by-case appraisal of Chinese petitioners, each of whom had the right to present evidence or argument in favor of their case. This process often differed from the administrative procedures adopted by the executive branch that systematically excluded Chinese.[32]

Anti-Chinese violence was at an apex in the 1880s in more than ten states in the United States, and there were over 200 "roundups" or "pogroms" ridding communities of Chinese in California.[33] On October 31, 1880, Chinatown in Denver, Colorado (with 450 Chinese residents), was destroyed by a mob, killing one Chinese, Look Young, and allegedly causing $20,000 to $30,000 losses in property damage. The Chinese legation complained about the incompetence of the local authorities and demanded the punishment of those responsible. In response, William M. Evarts, secretary of state (1877–81), insisted that the federal government—limited by the Constitution—could not interfere in the administration of the municipal laws of an individual state. Both Evarts and his successor, James G. Blaine, refused to make indemnity to the Chinese residents of Denver, labeling it a "misconception" to regard international treaties as part of the supreme law of the United States.[34]

The Rock Springs Massacre of 1885 in Rock Springs, Wyoming, was the most extreme example of racial violence directed against Chinese immigrants in American history. Its origins lay in a labor dispute over better wages between the Union Pacific Railroad and white immigrant Irish, Cornish, Welsh, and Swedish/Finnish miners. Chinese miners were often used as strikebreakers when white miners went on strike, and this was the case at Rock Springs. In the early morning of September 2, 1885, a dozen or so white miners stormed a coal pit and injured three Chinese miners. That afternoon around 150 armed white immigrants went on a rampage, killing at least twenty-eight Chinese, injuring fifteen, and burning and looting over seven hundred Chinese residences. Later, Chinese miners were found burned alive, scalped, mutilated, branded, decapitated, and hanged. Federal troops were called in to suppress the continuing violence. Under pressure, the U.S. government agreed to indemnify the Chinese government the sum of US$147,748.74. Nevertheless, a grand jury in Wyoming refused to indict any suspects.[35]

Stressing the importance of harmonious relations with Qing China, in his first annual message President Grover Cleveland (presidency 1885–89) admitted that the "condition of the China question" was "far from satisfactory," and that "individual cases of hardship" had occurred which called for judicial determination since they were beyond the power of his office to redress. While attributing the Rock Springs Massacre to "race prejudice" and the "lawlessness" of men "not citizens of the United States engaged in competition with Chinese laborers," Cleveland was also firm on the "admitted right" of the American government to "prevent the influx of elements hostile to its internal peace and security." According to him, the United States did no worse than Canada in legalizing Chinese exclusion.[36]

In the face of the strengthening anti-Chinese crusade, the Chinese also defended their rights through the American establishment, using the same language of liberty and equality as ordinary Americans. In 1852, in reaction to California governor Bigler's anti-Asian message, businessman Sang Yuen appealed to Bigler by openly invoking the U.S. Constitution and Declaration of Independence:

> I am a Chinaman, a republican, and a lover of free institutions; am much attached to the principles of the Government [sic] of the United States, and therefore take the liberty of addressing you as the chief of the Government of this State. . . . I am not much acquainted with your

logic, that by excluding population from this State you enhance its wealth. . . . You are deeply convinced you say "that to enhance the prosperity and preserve the tranquility of this State, Asiatic immigration must be checked." This, your Excellency, is but one step towards a retrograde movement of the Government . . . immigration made *you what you are* [emphasis in original]—your nation what it is. . . . The declaration of your independence, and all the acts of your government, your people, and your history, are all against you.[37]

Individual Chinese and Chinese community associations, including the Chinese Six Companies (the Chinese Consolidated Benevolent Association), articulated their grievances and solicited the support of Caucasian lawyers, large business owners, commissioners of immigrants, Christian missionaries, and the China lobby to denounce the policy of excluding Chinese immigration as unconstitutional and detrimental to the best interests of the nation.[38] In a letter dated July 27, 1868, to J. Ross Brown, American minister to China, attorney Daniel Cleveland stated unequivocally, "The Chinese constitute a large and important element in our society. . . . Their sudden removal . . . would cause a great and lasting injury to our State. . . . It would cause a diminution in our State revenue of at least one-fourth, and would be regarded as an inconvenience by almost every citizen."[39]

The status of resident Chinese was also tenuous. On March 24, 1894, Henry D. Paul—the lawyer retained by Sam Moy, Hip Lung, and other prominent Chinese residents—wrote to Walter Q. Gresham, secretary of state (1893–95), seeking a legal remedy to the disabilities suffered by Chinese, including those lawfully resident in the United States. He called Gresham's attention to "features of our Chinese exclusion laws and administrative questions likely to cause trouble to Chinamen of the exempt classes." At the time, there was no detailed provision for the registration and certification of any Chinese migrants except laborers. Yet, at the same time, there were stringent provisions for the arrest and deportation of all Chinese who had not registered or could not produce certification "to the satisfaction of the justice, judge or commissioner before whom they may be taken for hearing at the instance of any meddlesome or interested person choosing to set the law in motion." Characterizing the problems he had identified as "infamous instances of our administration of the Chinese exclusion acts," Henry Paul continued,

> The Chinese government is not in a position to know the status of its
> non-resident subjects nor of their children born here who are not Chi-
> nese subjects but American citizens, consequently can give no certifica-
> tion of value except to persons directly within its knowledge and juris-
> diction who are about to depart for America. Chinamen long resident
> here (for instance, Sam Moy came here when seven years old and has
> been here twenty eight years) have no Chinese acquaintances nor inter-
> ests, [sic] this government is the only one which could give them or
> their children born here any certificate upon knowledge.[40]

As an organization that desired to "maintain the best possible relations"
with China, the American Asiatic Association spoke out against the illib-
erality of the Chinese exclusion laws and the "brutality with which they
have been administered." In connection with the visit of the Qing Chinese imperial commission led by Dai Hongci and Duanfang, the association commented on the exclusion acts that "the business and professional
men of the United States are as much disgusted with this chapter of our
legislation as the most critical of Chinamen can possibly be."[41] In face of
strong opposition in Congress and the mass media, the association also
joined the unpopular effort to moderate the exclusion laws so as to nar-
row the definition of the excluded class of Chinese.

The Chinese in America also received support from China. A boycott
of American goods broke out in Chinese cities such as Shanghai, Canton,
and Xiamen from May 1905 to October 1906.[42] Although unsuccessful in
forcing the U.S. government to abandon its exclusion laws, the anti-
American boycott, as a social movement, raised awareness among mainland Chinese of the exclusionary legislation, the mistreatment of immigrant Chinese, and the new treaty negotiations under way between the
United States and Qing China.

The Chinese government and its U.S. legation repeatedly urged the
U.S. government to protect the rights of Chinese living in the United
States according to existing treaty stipulations. In 1880 Yung Wing—the
first Chinese student to graduate from an American university (Yale College)—lodged a protest with the U.S. secretary of state over the mistreatment of Chinese in violation of bilateral treaties.[43] At times the critics
went further and challenged the validity of the exclusionary laws. Following the Chinese line of argument, Wu Tingfang, the Chinese minister
to the United States, protested that "the continuation of the exclusion of
Chinese laborers and the restrictions placed upon Chinese merchants and
others seeking admission to the United States are not only without inter-

national authority but in violation of treaty stipulations."[44] Wu asked for the formation of a joint commission to settle the issues at stake to the satisfaction of both China and the United States.

But the federal government remained adamant. Blaming the European press in China for alerting the Chinese to the mistreatment of Chinese in the United States, the executive offices of the U.S. government regularly rejected these Chinese requests on the grounds of the priority of the Constitution over international treaties.

## CONCLUSION

Between the 1860s and the 1910s—the periods known as the Gilded Age and the Progressive Era in American history—over 40 million immigrants from Europe, Asia, and Latin America had contributed to the rapid urbanization of the United States and provided much-needed labor for the transformation of the country from an agrarian to an industrialized society. By 1910, the United States produced over one-third of the world's manufacturing products. Chinese immigration became part of the accompanying political and social problems, and, more importantly, part of the movements that promoted social justice and liberty, on the one hand, and order and efficacy on the other.[45]

The application of different legal frameworks to different races was a principle espoused by some prominent figures in the United States and was publicly practiced, not only in the domestic context but also in the American government's dealings with the Qing government over anti-missionary violence in China, as discussed in the next chapter. In his speech on the Opium War, President John Quincy Adams (1767–1848) spelled out his position on employing different laws for different nations:

> There is also a Law of Nations between *Christian* [emphasis in original] communities, which prevails between the Europeans and their descendants throughout the globe. . . . But we have a separate and different Law of Nations for the regulation of our intercourse with the Indian tribes of our own Continent; another Law of Nations between us and the woolly headed natives of Africa; another with the Barbary Powers and the Sultan of the Ottoman Empire . . . and lastly a Law of Nations with the flowery Land, the celestial Empire, the Mantchoo Tartar Dynasty of Despotism.[46]

Despite criticisms of its efficacy and contradictions, during the late nineteenth century the strengthening of U.S. state power was implemented vertically and horizontally through institutional infrastructure such as the legislative, executive, and judicial offices and organizations (both public and private) at the federal, state, and local levels. At the same time, resident Chinese refused to be driven out, defying immigration policies and rallying support for their constitutional rights in the United States. Thus the pro-Chinese lobby was able to draw on these same mechanisms of governance to accomplish their objectives. Although fifteen congressional Chinese exclusion acts were passed between 1882 and 1913, the Chinese diaspora took root with tenacity and resilience; by 1940 the population had reached over 77,000, with a dramatically rebalanced male-female ratio of 2.9:1.[47] As Adam McKeown argues, immigration procedures and exclusion laws were in effect "an exercise in force, a demonstration" that the U.S. government could obstruct the desires of individual Chinese, classify them, detain them, and treat them like animals.[48] On the other hand, ostensibly at least, immigration administration and procedures were instituted as a "vehicle of justice, rule of law, fair play, and modern efficiency." The checks and balances built into the American system did not always produce straightforward results, nor total victory for any party.

## FURTHER READING

Chinese immigration and diaspora are the subject of a flourishing scholarly literature. Current research has moved beyond two well-versed story lines: one focusing on the push-pull factors driving Chinese emigrants to a strange land, the other exploring the racist and sinophobic treatment they encountered in their new homes. In addition to those cited above, the following works are recommended.

Alexander Saxton, *The Indispensable Enemy: Labor and the Anti-Chinese Movement in California* (Berkeley, Calif.: University of California Press, 1971); James W. Loewen, *The Mississippi Chinese: Between Black and White*, 2nd ed. (Prospects Heights, Ill.: Waveland Press, 1988; 1st ed. 1971 by Harvard University Press); Delber L. McKee, *Chinese Exclusion versus the Open Door Policy, 1900–1906: Clashes over China Policy in the Roosevelt Era* (Detroit, Mich.: Wayne State University Press, 1977); Sucheng Chan, *This Bittersweet Soil: The Chinese in California Agriculture, 1860–1910* (Berkeley,

Calif.: University of California Press, 1987); Sucheng Chan, ed., *Entry Denied: Exclusion and the Chinese Community in America, 1882–1943* (Philadelphia, Pa.: Temple University Press, 1991); Madeline Y. Hsu, *Dreaming of Gold, Dreaming of Home: Transnationalism and Migration between the United States and South China, 1881–1943* (Stanford, Calif.: Stanford University Press, 2000); Peter H. Koehn and Xiao-huang Yin, eds., *The Expanding Roles of Chinese Americans in U.S.-China Relations: Transnational Networks and Transpacific Interactions* (Armonk, N.Y.: M. E. Sharpe, 2002); Flemming Christiansen, *Chinatown, Europe: An Exploration of Overseas Chinese Identity in the 1990s* (London: RoutledgeCurzon, 2003); Mary Ting Yi Lui, *The Chinatown Trunk Mystery: Murder, Miscegenation, and Other Dangerous Encounters in Turn-of-the-Century New York City* (Princeton, N.J.: Princeton University Press, 2005); Gregor Benton, *Chinese Migrants and Internationalism: Forgotten Histories, 1917–1945* (New York: Routledge, 2007); Ian Welch, "'Our Neighbors but Not Our Countrymen': Christianity and the Chinese in Nineteenth-Century Victoria (Australia) and California," in Dong Wang, ed., *Christianity in the History of U.S.-China Relations*, a special volume of the *Journal of American-East Asian Relations* 13 (November 2008): 149–183; Philip A. Kuhn, *Chinese among Others: Emigration in Modern Times* (Lanham, Md.: Rowman & Littlefield, 2008); Sucheng Chan and Madeline Yuan-yin Hsu, eds., *Chinese Americans and the Politics of Race and Culture* (Philadelphia, Pa.: Temple University Press, 2008); Sascha Auerbach, *Race, Law, and "The Chinese Puzzle" in Imperial Britain* (New York: Palgrave Macmillan, 2009); Gregory R. Nokes, *Massacred for Gold: The Chinese in Hells Canyon* (Corvallis, Oreg.: Oregon State University Press, 2009); Him Mark Lai, *Chinese American Transnational Politics*, ed. Madeline Y. Hsu (Urbana, Ill.: University of Illinois Press, 2010).

## NOTES

1. Judy Yung, Gordon H. Chang, and Him Mark Lai, comps. and eds., *Chinese American Voices: From the Gold Rush to the Present* (Berkeley, Calif.: University of California, 2006), preface.

2. Robert W. Irick, *Ch'ing Policy toward the Coolie Trade, 1847–1878* (Taipei: Chinese Materials Center, 1982); Yen Ching-hwang, *Coolies and Mandarins: China's Protection of Overseas Chinese during the Late Ch'ing Period (1851–1911)* (Singapore: Singapore University Press, 1985).

3. Zhongyang yanjiuyuan jindaishi yanjiusuo (中央研究院近代史研究所), comp., *Zhongmei guanxi shiliao: Tongzhi chao* [中美关系史料,同治朝 Sources on Sino-American

relations: The reign of Tongzhi] (Taipei: Zhongyang yanjiuyuan jindaishi yanjiusuo, 1968), vol. 1, document no. 381, p. 311, and vol. 2, document no. 994, p. 887.

4. Daniel Cleveland of San Francisco's letter to J. Ross Brown, American minister to China, on July 27, 1868, in Jules Davids, ed., *American Diplomatic and Public Papers: The United States and China* (Wilmington, Del.: Scholarly Resources, 1979), series II, vol. 13, pp. 1–11.

5. Mary Roberts Coolidge, *Chinese Immigration* (New York: Henry Holt, 1909), preface.

6. See table 3.1. "Governor's Special Message," *Daily Alta California* 3, no. 115 (April 25, 1852), p. 2.

7. Charles J. McClain, *In Search of Equality: The Chinese Struggle against Discrimination in Nineteenth-Century America* (Berkeley, Calif.: University of California Press, 1994).

8. Judy Yung et al., *Chinese American Voices*, pp. 225–227.

9. Yen Ching-hwang, *The Chinese in Southeast Asia and Beyond: Socioeconomic and Political Dimensions* (Singapore: World Scientific Publishing, 2008).

10. The Burlingame Mission of 1868–70 represented the first voluntary diplomatic initiative on the part of the Qing government. In addition to Burlingame, Zhigang, and Sun, the mission had an international mix consisting of J. McLeavy Brown, Chinese secretary of the British legation; E. de Champs, a French official attached to the Chinese imperial Maritime Customs Service; and a few minor Chinese officials and attachés. Countries the mission visited included the United States, Britain, France, Belgium, Sweden, Prussia, Denmark, the Netherlands, Russia, and Spain. Burlingame was an important Republican and an abolitionist who stood for liberal racial and cultural ideals which were defeated in the late nineteenth century. The Qing government considered Burlingame "even-tempered" and "knowledgeable about the Chinese and world affairs." Zhongyang yanjiuyuan jindaishi yanjiusuo, comp., *Zhongmei guanxi shiliao: Tongzhi chao*, vol. 1, document no. 540, p. 478.

11. U.S. Congress, *The Statutes at Large, Treaties and Proclamations of the United States of America* (Boston, Mass.: Little, Brown, 1863–69), vol. 16, pp. 739–741.

12. "An Act concerning the Rights of American Citizens in Foreign States," U.S. Congress, *The Statutes at Large, Treaties and Proclamations of the United States of America* (Boston, Mass.: Little, Brown, 1863–69), vol. 15, pp. 223–224.

13. William Malloy, ed., *Treaties, Conventions, International Acts, Protocols and Agreements between the United States of America and Other Powers, 1776–1909* (Washington, D.C.: Government Printing Office, 1910), vol. 1, p. 238.

14. U.S. Congress, "An Act to Execute Certain Treaty Stipulations Relating to Chinese," 47th Congress, Session 1, Ch. 126, May 6, 1882, *U.S. Statutes at Large* (Washington, D.C.: Government Printing Office, 1883), vol. 22, pp. 58–60.

15. U.S. Congress, "An Act Supplement to an Act Entitled 'An Act to Execute Certain Treaty Stipulations Relating to Chinese,' Approved on the Sixth Day of May Eighteen Hundred and Eighty-Two," 52nd Congress, Session 1, Ch. 1064, October 1, 1888, *U.S. Statutes at Large* (Washington, D.C.: Government Printing Office, 1889), vol. 25, pp. 504.

16. U.S. Congress, "An Act to Prohibit the Coming of Chinese Persons into the United States," 52nd Congress, Session 1, Ch. 60, May 5, 1892, *U.S. Statutes at Large* (Washington, D.C.: Government Printing Office, 1893), vol. 27, pp. 25–26.

17. U.S. Congress, "An Act Making Appropriations to Supply Deficiencies in the Appropriations for the Fiscal Year Ending June Thirtieth, Nineteen Hundred and

Four, and for Prior Years, and for Other Purposes," 58th Congress, Session 2, Ch. 1630, April 27, 1904, *U.S. Statutes at Large* (Washington, D.C.: Government Printing Office, 1905), vol. 33, part I, p. 428.

18. John V. A. MacMurray, comp. and ed., *Treaties and Agreements with and Concerning China, 1894–1919* (New York: Oxford University Press, 1921), pp. 9–11.

19. Kitty Calavita, "The Paradoxes of Race, Class, Identity, and 'Passing': Enforcing the Chinese Exclusion Acts, 1882–1910," *Law and Social Inquiry* 25, no. 1 (Winter 2000): 1–40. Samuel Keller, "Congressional Legislation and the Plight of Immigrant Chinese during the Era of Exclusion 1882–1943," manuscript written in May 2007.

20. The Chinese Exclusion Case (*Chae Chan Ping v. U.S.*), 130 U.S. 581 (1889), http://supreme.justia.com/us/130/581/case.html (accessed July 31, 2010).

21. The Chinese Exclusion Case, 130 U.S. 581 (1889), http://supreme.justia.com/us/130/581/case.html (accessed July 31, 2010). Louis Henkin, "The Constitution and United States Sovereignty: A Century of 'Chinese Exclusion' and Its Progeny," *Harvard Law Review* 100, no. 4 (February 1987): 853–886.

22. Teemu Ruskola, "Canton Is Not Boston: The Invention of American Imperial Sovereignty," *American Quarterly* 57, no. 3 (September 2005): 859–884.

23. *Chae Chan Ping v. U.S.*, 130 U.S. 581 (1889).

24. Habeas corpus refers here to a writ (a written court order) that may be issued to bring one party before a court or judge to grant or deny the release of that party from unlawful restraint.

25. *U.S. vs. Wong Kim Ark*, 169 U.S. 649 (1898).

26. William Woodville Rockhill (1854–1914) papers, Houghton Library, Harvard University, bMS Am 2122 (66), Chinese immigration treaty: Letters, notes and memoranda, 1884–1894, folder 1 of 4, no. 376.

27. Letter from John Russell Young to Frederick T. Frelinghuysen, no. 481, July 21, 1884. William Woodville Rockhill (1854–1914) papers, Houghton Library, Harvard University, bMS Am 2122 (66), Chinese immigration treaty: Letters, notes and memoranda, 1884–1894, folder 1 of 4.

28. Letter from Mr. Dougherty to James Blaine, no. 537, January 1891. William Woodville Rockhill (1854–1914) papers, Houghton Library, Harvard University, bMS Am 2122 (66), Chinese immigration treaty.

29. Report of a Committee of the Privy Council, April 15, 1891. William Woodville Rockhill (1854–1914) papers, Houghton Library, Harvard University, bMS Am 2122 (66), Chinese immigration treaty.

30. Christian G. Fritz, "A Nineteenth Century 'Habeas Corpus Mill': The Chinese before the Federal Courts in California," *American Journal of Legal History* 32, no. 4 (October 1988): 347–372.

31. Mary Roberts Coolidge, *Chinese Immigration*, p. 305.

32. Christian G. Fritz, "A Nineteenth Century 'Habeas Corpus Mill': The Chinese before the Federal Courts in California."

33. Ian Welch, comp., "Anti-Chinese Riots in North America in the 19th Century," manuscript, April 2010; Jean Pfaelzer, *Driven Out: The Forgotten War against Chinese Americans* (New York: Random House, 2007). For the economic, political, and racial arguments used against the Chinese in the nineteenth century, see Diana L. Ahmad, *The Opium Debate and Chinese Exclusion Laws in the Nineteenth-Century American West* (Reno, Nev.: University of Nevada Press, 2007).

34. [Doc. No. 25], no. 187, Chen Lan Pin of the Chinese legation in Washington to Mr. Evarts, on November 10, 1880; [Doc. No. 26], enclosure 1, Report of F. A. Bee,

Chinese consul in San Francisco, on December 8, 1880; [Doc. No. 27], no. 188, W. M. Evarts to Chen Lan Pin, Dec. 30, 1880; [Doc. No. 28], no. 190, Chen Lan Pin to Mr. Evarts, January 21, 1881; [Doc. No. 29], no. 192, James G. Blaine to Chen Lan Pin, March 25, 1881. Jules Davids, ed., *American Diplomatic and Public Papers: The United States and China, 1861–1893*, series II, *The United States, China, and Imperial Rivalries, 1861–1893*, vol. 12, *The Coolie Trade and Outrages against the Chinese* (Wilmington, Del.: Scholarly Resources, 1979), pp. 163–170.

35. See telegraphs, letters, and memorials of Zheng Zaoru (郑藻如) and Zhang Yin-huan (张荫桓), Chinese ministers in the United States, to the Zongli Yamen (Chinese foreign ministry) in 1885 in Chen Hansheng (陈翰笙), ed., *Huagong chuguo shiliao hui-bian* [华工出国史料汇编 A comprehensive collection of historical sources on overseas Chinese laborers] (Beijing: Zhonghua shuju, 1980–85), series 1, vol. 4, pp. 1333–1360. See also Cheng-tsu Wu, ed., *Chink! A Documentary History of Anti-Chinese Prejudice in America* (New York: World Publishing, 1972), pp. 152–164; Craig Storti, *Incident at Bitter Creek: The Story of the Rock Springs Massacre* (Ames, Iowa: Iowa State University Press, 1991).

36. Grover Cleveland, "First Annual Message," December 8, 1885, http://www.presidency.uscb.edu/ws/?pid=29526 (accessed December 25, 2011).

37. Norman Asing (Sang Yuen), "To His Excellency Gov. Bigler," *Daily Alta California*, May 5, 1852, p. 2.

38. Charles J. McClain Jr., "The Chinese Struggle for Civil Rights in Nineteenth Century America: The First Phase, 1850–1870," *California Law Review* 72, no. 4 (July 1984): 529–568; Yucheng Qin, *The Diplomacy of Nationalism: The Six Companies and China's Policy toward Exclusion* (Honolulu, Hawaii: University of Hawai'i Press, 2009).

39. Letter from Daniel Cleveland of San Francisco to J. Ross Brown, American Minister to China, dated July 27, 1868, in Jules Davids, ed., *American Diplomatic and Public Papers: The United States and China* (Wilmington, Del.: Scholarly Resources Inc., 1979), series II, vol. 13, p. 1.

40. Letter from Henry D. Paul to W. Q. Gresham on March 24, 1894. William Woodville Rockhill (1854–1914) papers, Houghton Library, Harvard University, bMS Am 2122 (66), Chinese immigration treaty: Letters, notes and memoranda, 1884–1894, folder 1 of 4.

41. Current Comment, *Journal of the American Asiatic Association* 6, no. 1 (February 1906), p. 1. The Qing imperial commission was a part of the Qing government's tardy attempts at modernization, *Xinzheng* (the new policy), during the last years of its life. The Qing court under the Empress Dowager dispatched a group of five princes and officials to Japan, the United States, Britain, France, Germany, Russia, and Italy to study their political systems. Douglas R. Reynold, *China, 1898–1912, the Xinzheng Revolution and Japan* (Cambridge, Mass.: Harvard University Press, 1993).

42. Zhou Mingqi (周明绮), *Yijiu lingwu nian de fanmei aiguo yundong* [1905年的反美爱国运动 The anti-American patriotic movement of 1905] (Beijing: Zhonghua shuju, 1962); A Ying (阿英), *Fanmei huagong jinyue wenxueji* [反美华工禁约文学集 A collection of writings on the opposition to the American exclusion acts directed against Chinese laborers] (Beijing: Zhonghua shuju, 1960); Yang Guobiao (杨国标), *Meiguo huaqiaoshi* [美国华侨史 A history of Chinese Americans] (Guangzhou: Guangdong gaodeng jiaoyu chubanshe, 1989); Zhang Qingsong (张庆松), *Meiguo bainian paihua neimu* [美国百年排华内幕 The inside story of a hundred years of American exclusion of the Chinese] (Shanghai: Shanghai renmin chubanshe, 1998).

43. Yung Wing (Rong Hong, b. 1828–1912), "Shimei Rong Hong zhi Meiguo Waiwu dachen qing zhaoyue bude kedai huaren zhaohui" [使美容闳致美国外务大臣请照约不得苛待华人照会 A diplomatic note from Yung Wing, Chinese deputy minister to the United States, to the American secretary of state urging the United States not to mistreat Chinese in accordance with the treaties], in Chen Hansheng, ed., *Huagong chuguo shiliao huibian*, series 1, vol. 4, p. 1330.

44. Tingfang Wu (b. 1842–1922, Chinese minister to the United States, Spain, Peru, Mexico, and Cuba), *America through the Spectacles of an Oriental Diplomat*, reprint (Charleston, S.C.: BiblioBazaar, 2007; 1st ed. 1914), pp. 37–41. Yen Ching-Hwang, *Coolies and Mandarins*; Yen Ching-Hwang (颜清湟), *Haiwai huarenshi yanjiu* [海外华人史研究 A study of the history of the overseas Chinese] (Singapore: Xinjiapo yazhou yanjiu xuehui, 1992).

45. Charles W. Calhoun, ed., *The Gilded Age: Essays on the Origins of Modern America* (Wilmington, Del.: Scholarly Resources, 1996); Allen F. Davis, *Spearheads for Reform: The Social Settlements and the Progressive Movement, 1890–1914* (Oxford: Oxford University Press, 1967). For influential treatments by contemporaries of these issues, see Edward Bellamy, *Looking Backward, 2000–1887* (New York: Random House, 1951; 1st ed. 1887 by Ticknor and Comp.); Frances A. Kellor's *Out of Work: A Study of Unemployment* (New York: Putnam, 1915). Allen F. Davis, *Spearheads for Reform: The Social Settlements and the Progressive Movement, 1890–1914* (Oxford: Oxford University Press, 1967).

46. John Quincy Adams, "J. Q. Adams on the Opium War," *Proceedings of the Massachusetts Historical Society* 43 (February 1910): 295–325.

47. Judy Yung, Gordon H. Change, and Him Mark Lai, *Chinese American Voices*, p. 104.

48. Adam McKeown, "Ritualization of Regulation: The Enforcement of Chinese Exclusion in the United States and China," *American Historical Review* 108, no. 2 (April 2003): 377–403.

# FOUR

# American Protestantism: Roots in China?

While riding the Beijing-Tianjin high-speed train on December 27, 2009, I was drawn to a brochure in back of the seat in front: it listed Christmas services for all the Christian churches in Tianjin and Beijing. Two days earlier, a photograph in the official newspaper, *Beijing qingnian bao*—captioned "600-year old Qianmen Street celebrates the 'foreign festival' for the first time"—offered readers a snapshot of this new situation.[1] As a fast-growing wing of the worldwide evangelical movement over the last three decades, Christianity has formed an important part of the Chinese spiritual landscape. How did Christianity—a foreign religion in origin—take root in China? What kind of impact did the emergent forms of Chinese Christianity have on China, the United States, and the peoples? The early encounters between American Protestantism and China hold some answers from history.

## AMERICAN CHRISTIANITY IN CHINA: THE BACKDROP

Beginning with the earliest plantings of Christian faith in Chinese soil, this section covers the international and domestic context of the American missionary movement and its broad impact on Qing China.

The first known contact between the Chinese and Christianity occurred at the beginning of the Tang dynasty (618–960) when Nestorian missionaries from Persian Mesopotamia settled in China. In the thirteenth century, two Catholic religious orders, the Franciscans and Dominicans, dispatched John of Montecorvino to Beijing, then ruled by the Yuan Mongols (1279–1368). A new wave of Roman Catholic missions arrived in the sixteenth century, part of the Jesuit promulgation of Christianity in Asia and Ming China (1368–1644). Over 450 Jesuits, including the Italian missionary Matteo Ricci (1552–1610), labored in China until the dissolution of the Society of Jesus in 1773. The worldwide Catholic missionary movement was overseen by a special Vatican agency established in the seventeenth century, the Congregation for the Propagation of the Faith, giving Christianity a truly global reach. In China, the Congregation operated through administrative divisions known as vicariates apostolic, each headed by a vicar apostolic who held the rank of bishop in the Church's hierarchy. The vicariate apostolic was based on provincial boundaries, and each vicariate was entrusted to a particular religious order. [2]

By the early nineteenth century, the total number of Catholics in China was around 200,000 to 250,000. This was the time when a resurgence of interest in Catholic missions took place in Europe, marked by the revival of established religious orders as well as the establishment of new congregations and societies. One noted example was the Society for the Propagation of the Faith, founded in France in 1822 in order to stimulate support for global missions. In 1839 there were 57 foreign Catholic priests working in China, 114 native priests, and an estimated 303,000 converts. [3]

Hard on the heels of their Catholic counterparts, Protestant missionaries in Britain and later in the United States were infusing new zeal into the international evangelical movement that had arisen from the Evangelical Revival and the First and Second Great Awakenings at the close of the eighteenth century. These movements bore fruit in the founding of new Protestant denominations and transnational institutions, including the Methodist Church, the Salvation Army (founded in 1865), the YMCA (founded in 1844 in London), the YWCA (1855), the London Missionary Society (1795), the Church Missionary Society (1799), and the British and Foreign Bible Society (1804). All were clamoring for overseas missions.

The arrival in China of Robert Morrison (1782–1834) of the London Missionary Society in 1807 signified the official beginnings of the Protestant enterprise in China. The founder of the Anglo-Chinese College in Malacca in 1818, Morrison translated the Old and New Testaments (with the aid of William Milne) and compiled the first Chinese–English dictionary.

As elsewhere in the nineteenth century, the rapid growth of Protestant faith in the United States went hand in hand with industrialization and the growth of the nation-state. This desire to spread the gospel of individual salvation through foreign missions was a significant aspect of social development in America, particularly in the northeastern United States. Five mission boards played a key role in the development of foreign missions: the Philadelphia Bible Society (1808), the American Board of Commissioners for Foreign Missions (1810), the American Baptist Board of Foreign Missions (1814), and the Episcopal and Methodist missions (both founded in 1820). In addition, the Student Volunteer Movement for Foreign Missions—based on a millenarian revivalism that stressed the urgent need to evangelize the world before the Second Coming of Christ—energized college graduates for missionary work overseas.[4] Unlike Hawaii, the Mediterranean, the Near and Middle East, and South Asia, China did not become a priority for missionary endeavor until the 1890s. Nevertheless, the American missionary movement in China was played out on an international scale—comparable to the evangelical revival in other parts of the world.

In contrast with the entrance into China of first Catholic and then British missionaries, the American Protestant undertaking was a late starter—beginning with the arrival of Elijah C. Bridgman (1801–61) in Canton in February 1830—but was carried out with considerable energy. Bridgman, a Congregationalist and a graduate of Amherst College and the Andover Theological Seminary, was appointed by the American Board of Commissioners for Foreign Missions to proselytize in China. Until 1847, he was the editor of *The Chinese Repository* (1832–51), a monthly English-language magazine published in Canton and a valuable source of information for contemporary researchers.[5] American Catholicism arrived even later, not making an entry into China until the First World War. The American missionary movement in China came to an end when the United States and China clashed with each other in the Korean War in 1951. Chinese Christianity, however, persisted and increasingly took on an indigenous flavor.

## "FLAWED BUT SINCERE SOWERS OF THE SEED"[6]: AMERICAN MISSIONS AND TREATY RIGHTS

In China, as elsewhere in the nineteenth century, the Bible followed the flag. The way was opened for a considerable expansion of Christian activities in China by the opium treaties of 1842–44 (including the Sino-British Treaty of Nanjing and the Treaty of Wanghia between the United States and China) and the 1858 Sino-French Treaty of Tianjin.

Although the opium treaties contained no explicit provisions on proselytizing, missionaries were entitled to take up residence, like other foreigners, in the five treaty ports of Guangzhou (Canton), Xiamen (Amoy), Fuzhou (Foochow), Ningbo (Ningpo), and Shanghai. Here they enjoyed immunity from Chinese law under treaty stipulations dealing with extraterritoriality and most-favored-nation status. Foreign residents continued to lobby and pressure the Chinese and their own governments for increased protection. However, such conspicuous political favoritism proved to be a liability for missionaries, particularly in the 1920s when Chinese nationalism was reaching a peak.

In the 1840s, military conflicts between the Qing and foreign governments often put American missionaries on the spot and pointed up the contradictions inherent in the relationship between politics, diplomacy, and missionary endeavor. The gathering storm of the Opium War confronted American missionaries with a moral dilemma, as illustrated in an editorial by Elijah Bridgman in *The Chinese Repository*. To Bridgman, the coming Sino-British clash was a "trial for supremacy," as "[m]odern improvements, in sciences and arts, have greatly changed the relations of states and empires." Blaming the Qing government for refusing to change and for rejecting British overtures, Bridgman asserted, "The time has come when CHINA MUST BEND or BREAK [emphasis in original]." It was the will of Providence that the restrictions on foreign contact and the dissemination of Christianity imposed by China be removed. Although it was right that the Chinese government should strive to prevent opium—"the deadly charm"—from entering China, the means it employed were unacceptable. In the end, Bridgman's position left him ambivalent, recognizing Chinese autonomy but seeking a minimal level of intervention from Great Britain when required: "The British government, we are unwilling to believe, will seek for anything beyond what is just and right. Accordingly we conclude that, *simple redress* for injuries sustained, with *ample securities* for the future [emphasis in original], will be the two grand objects aimed at."[7]

In a newspaper article published in 1900, Charles Denby, former U.S. minister to China, described the protection secured for missionaries under the treaties China had signed with Britain, the United States, France, and Russia in 1842–44 and 1858–60 as "toleration clauses." "The toleration clauses in these treaties allow missionaries to reside at all open ports, and to prosecute their religious and charitable work. They may also travel in every province."[8]

Several articles in the Sino-French Treaty of Tianjin and the Beijing Convention signed in 1858 and 1860 addressed the issue of Catholic missions and extended benefits to Protestant endeavors due to the most-favored-nation provisions. Signed by Baron Gros for France, and Guiliang and Huashana, Article 13 of the Treaty of Tianjin specifically extended permission to Catholic missionaries to preach in the interior and mandated protection for Chinese converts. All previous anti-Christian documents were renounced. In the Chinese text of the 1860 Beijing Convention—but not in the French text of the same treaty—it was permitted to French priests "to rent and purchase land in all the provinces, and to erect buildings thereon at their pleasure."[9]

Most American missionaries supported these treaties, which imposed on China responsibility for ensuring freedom of religion and its promulgation. Elijah Bridgman and Peter Parker (1804–88), for example, assisted Caleb Cushing in various treaty negotiations, as did the Presbyterian William Alexander Parsons Martin in the talks over the Tianjin Treaty. Parker, a medical missionary, rendered his first services to the U.S. government in his role as Chinese secretary and advisor to the Cushing-led mission in 1844. "My most sanguine hopes have been exceeded in the results of these negotiations, by which a treaty of peace, amity, and commerce has been concluded between America and China on terms the most honorable and advantageous to both nations."[10]

With the protection afforded by the treaties, both Catholic and Protestant missionary movements experienced unprecedented growth after 1860—although their respective governing bodies did not often see eye to eye.[11] By 1870, there were roughly 250 European Catholic priests active in China. Fifteen years later, this figure had jumped to 488, and by 1900 it stood at 886.

Differing in numerous respects from centrally organized Catholicism, by the end of 1851 the Protestant churches had eighteen independent denominational societies, with a total of 150 missionaries deployed in Hong Kong, Macau, Malacca, Bangkok, Singapore, Canton, Fuzhou, Amoy, Shanghai, Ningbo, and other centers in Asia. The missions involved included the London Missionary Society, the American Board of Commissioners for Foreign Missions, the American Baptist Missionary Union, the Board of Foreign Missions of the Presbyterian Church of the United States, and the Methodist Missionary Society of USA, to name only some of the major players.

The five treaty ports and China's coastal cities became Protestant strongholds from the beginning. American missionaries outnumbered their British counterparts. Of the 150 missionaries mentioned above, 88 were Americans and 47 British, the rest coming from the European continent. In China proper, 44 were from the United States and 23 from Britain.[12] The number of American missionaries neared the 100 mark around 1860.[13] By 1870, 200 American missionaries were stationed in China. The growth of foreign missions was startling. In 1900 there were 61 missionary societies active in China, and by 1920 the number had increased to 130. By 1907, among 3,445 Protestant missionaries, 37 percent were from the United States and 52 percent from Britain (a move back in Britain's favor). By 1920, there were more than 6,500 Protestant missionaries in China, with close to 350,000 converts in nineteen provinces. On the Catholic side, it was claimed that in 1920 the Church had over 2 million believers in the country.[14]

Despite attempts to push into the interior and into the countryside, by the early 1920s Protestantism was pretty much a coastal and urban phenomenon. Two-thirds of the missionaries and a third of all Chinese Christian workers lived in cities of over 50,000 inhabitants. However these cities constituted only 6 percent of China's total population of 440 million.[15]

## THE TAIPING REBELLION AND AMERICAN CHRISTIANITY

The Taiping Rebellion, in the words of historian Daniel Bays, was "China's first indigenous Christian movement," a distinct religious phenomenon that piqued the interest of European and American Protestant missionaries in China.[16] In July 1851, *The Chinese Repository* gave notice of an anti-Qing insurgency that went under the name of Taiping: "There is a very general impression in Canton and its vicinity that they are somehow connected with foreigners and with Christianity, and the term *Shangti Hwui* [the God-Worshipper's Society] is often applied to them."[17] In August 1853, *The Independent*, a Boston-based newspaper, gave a further glimpse of Taiping—a "very extraordinary movement"—and of its leaders, who were professing Christians.[18] Treating the alleged Christian character of the movement with a pinch of salt, *The Independent* correspondent nevertheless accurately observed that "strong religious as well as anti-Tartar [Manchu] feelings prevailed" among the rebels.

Continuing for thirteen years, from 1851 to 1864, and causing enormous devastation, the Taiping Rebellion originated in a poor region of Guangxi Province in South China. The rebellion—a civil war—was responsible for the destruction of around 20 million lives and over six hundred cities. It was led by Hong Xiuquan from Huaxian, a village about thirty miles from Canton.[19]

After three failed attempts to pass the civil service examinations in 1837, Hong had experienced a nervous breakdown. Bedridden for over a month, the hallucinating Hong believed that he had ascended into heaven where he met an awe-inspiring elderly figure—God in his later interpretation—who bestowed on him a sword and a seal tied with a ribbon (signifying power) to subdue devils and teach people to do good deeds. In his dream, Hong also encountered an "older brother," whom he identified as Jesus, to assist him in slaying demons, which he interpreted to mean the Qing regime. Hong's personal disillusion with the Qing system, as well as his exposure to the teachings of the American Baptist missionary Issachar Roberts and Christian tracts in Chinese—including *Quanshi liangyan* (Good Words to Admonish the World), compiled by Liang Afa (Fa), Robert Morrison's first Chinese convert—kindled a revolutionary resolve in him. In this way a religious, militant movement, Bai Shangdi Hui (the God-Worshippers Society), came to be formed among the economically and socially disadvantaged villagers and miners of Guangxi Province, neighboring Guangdong.

Numbering 1 to 2 million, in early 1851 the Taiping rebels established their own government in Jintian, Guangxi, calling it Taiping Tianguo (the Heavenly Kingdom of Great Peace) and declaring Hong as their king. In March 1853 the Taipings took over Nanjing on the Yangzi River as their capital. With the Bible as their testament and hostile to Manchu rule and imperial institutions, Taiping beliefs were a dynamic blend of Anglo-American Protestantism with anti-government ideas and Chinese popular religion. To many missionaries and other foreigners, this heterodox mix originated from their "monstrous misapprehension" of the Old Testament, which left them "no better than Mormons or Mohammedans."[20] As American medical missionary Charles Taylor noted, "[T]he Old Testament is much more in favor than the new and hence, while the ten commandments [sic] are the established rule of life, polygamy is lawful and prevalent: and to destroy enemies is not only lawful, but a religious obligation."[21] Despite these deviations in doctrine and practice, the Taipings proved fascinating to foreigners, particularly the missionaries—who disagreed among themselves over Sabbatarianism, methods of immersion in the rite of baptism, and whether the correct term for "God" in Chinese was *Shangdi, Shen,* or *Tianzhu.*

Initially, the movement enjoyed some diplomatic credibility. The British governor of Hong Kong, Sir George Bonham, was the first diplomat to visit the Taiping rebels in Nanjing in April 1853, followed in 1854 by Robert McLane, American minister to China.

American missionaries were often sympathetic to the insurgents and made serious attempts to visit them, despite the physical and legal risks involved. The legal obstacle was the passing by the U.S. Congress on August 11, 1848, of an act explicitly outlawing Americans' involvement in anti-Chinese government activities: "That murder and insurrection, or rebellion against the Chinese government, with intent to subvert the same, shall be capital offences, punishable with death."[22] In a clear violation of the American government's neutrality, Charles Taylor made two trips to the Taiping camp in June 1853. He was the first missionary to do so, and later wrote an account of his adventures. The Qing government deployed strong forces to besiege the insurgents on land and blockade them on the water. With the aid of a Chinese guide, Taylor at one point passed the government fleet in the dark.

> We were hailed several times and threatened with being fired upon. I had enjoined perfect silence; but my boatmen, who were very much alarmed, wished to comply with the command to "come to," and go up alongside. I, however, positively forbade it, and said, "let them fire—they are poor marksmen at best, for it is seldom they can hit an object in the daytime, and it is not likely they can hit us in this dark night![23]

In the end, however, the forces arrayed against the Taiping rebels proved too powerful. These included internal strife and conflicting claims to enjoying direct access to God among the Taiping leaders, and the emergence of a new type of Qing army—known as Xiangjun (the Hunan Army, originally a local militia) and Huaijun (the Anhui Army). These twin forces were led respectively by two great statesmen, Zeng Guofan and Li Hongzhang, who were loyalists of the imperial Manchu court and staunch defenders of the Confucian moral order. Their support, together with the intervention of the "Ever-Victorious Army" under the command of the American Frederick Ward and the British Charles Gordon, brought the Taiping Rebellion to an end in 1864.

The Taipings provided a foretaste of the Chinese version of Christian salvation as a mass social movement, although American missionaries for the most part came to reject this early indigenous "fruit" of their labor on Chinese soil. Historian Kenneth S. Latourette expressed the Western consensus when he described the Taipings as "a Chinese sect, displaying some interesting results of contact with Christianity, but drawing most of its beliefs and characteristics from its Chinese environment and the erratic genius of its leaders."[24]

## AMERICAN CHRISTIANITY AS BOTH A FOREIGN AND CHINESE INSTITUTION

### Anti-Christian Violence

The varied, often contradictory experience of Christianity in China involved both conflict and accommodation.[25] From its beginnings in China, the missionary movement provoked a countermovement—at times a violent one—among Chinese elites, officials, and ordinary people. During the seven decades from 1840 to 1910, there were probably more than 1,500 violent anti-Christian incidents (*jiao'an* 教案), disturbances, or riots directed against missionaries, church property, and Chinese converts.[26]

At its heart, the American "missionary problem" had two main causes. First, Christianity did not (and does not) operate in a spiritual vacuum in China. Its major rivals were (and still are) traditional Confucianism, Daoism, Buddhism, Islam, and folk beliefs.[27] Long before the entry of Protestantism into China, a series of works by elite scholars portrayed Christianity as a heterodox sect which threatened the moral, political, and social stability of China.[28] To many, Christianity was in league with the subversive White Lotus and Taiping rebels. Anti-Christian agitation and scandalmongering fed off these established cultural and psychological associations. In June 1870, rumors mushroomed among the people of Tianjin that French Catholic priests—sponsored by the Oeuvre de la Sainte-Enfance (Society of the Holy Childhood)—were kidnapping young children and putting them in orphanages. Here, allegedly, their eyes were gouged out, and their hearts and other body parts were removed to make grisly medicine. The resulting popular outburst of anti-Christian feeling led to the deaths of twenty foreigners in the city, including the French consul, two priests, and ten nuns.[29]

Other incidents were sparked by foreign clergy insisting on building their mission stations, churches, and Bible schools at sites considered sacred by local Chinese or linked with feng shui, prescribing the destiny of the town or village concerned.[30] The Fuzhou (Foochow, a treaty port) missionary incident was a typical example. In August 1878, despite repeated peaceful displays of opposition from locals, the Reverend John R. Wolfe of the Church Missionary Society went ahead with the construction of a new school on a site known as Wushi shan (Black Boulder Hill), a sacred hill in Fuzhou. Angry residents from all social classes burned the offending building to the ground, although with no serious injury or loss of life. Although Wolfe was proficient in both written and spoken Chinese—according to Sir Thomas Wade, British minister to China—he possessed "an indifference to popular feeling."

The second barrier for foreign missions was linked to their privileged position. Since the 1840s, relations between the missionaries and the Chinese had developed within the legal framework of nonreciprocal treaty rights and obligations contracted between various foreign countries and China. This situation had created an inequitable political, socioeconomic, and cultural environment that had the potential to ignite popular antipathy to the privileged missionaries and their converts in local communities. In response to acts of violence against the missions and opposition from Chinese officials, American missionaries demanded that military force be used to protect them. In May 1895, anti-missionary riots broke out in Chengdu, the capital of Sichuan Province, resulting in damage to American, British, Canadian, and French mission property. Charles Denby, American minister to China (1885–98), along with the French and British ministers, had warships rushed to the Yangzi region and ultimately forced the Qing government to remove Governor Liu Bingzhang and punish other officials involved.[31]

There were also incidents in which Chinese believers in dispute with non-Christian Chinese resorted for support to Christian clergy who were ready to demand—and usually succeeded in obtaining—protection, intervention, and redress for their people from their diplomatic ministers and consuls in China.[32] The study by Joseph Tse-Hei Lee shows how "missionary trouble" was compounded by competition for Chinese converts. One such incident took place in Kuxi, a village near Canton, and involved Protestant (the American Baptist Missionary Society) and Catholic (the Paris Foreign Missions) missionaries. Preexisting communal feuds between clans and within lineages were translated into violent conflicts between the Baptist and Catholic village communities. The clergy took sides with their own converts and persuaded their own governments and the Chinese government to intervene in village politics.[33]

Chinese living in the United States, on the other hand, enjoyed no treaty protections. As we have seen in the preceding chapter, while insisting on the supremacy of the U.S. Constitution over its treaty obligations toward China, American courts and executive officers were inclined to reject the argument—made by the Chinese government and some Chinese residents and their supporters in the United States—that the American Chinese exclusion laws were in violation of its treaties with China. At the same time, when American missionaries were subjected to violence, the U.S. government demanded that China fulfill its treaty obligations. In June 1869, J. Ross Browne, American minister to China (March 1868–July 1869), broached the missionary troubles in a dispatch to Hamilton Fish, secretary of state:

> I would simply say, in reference to this question, that either the missionaries should be protected, in their rights as citizens, or the provision of treaty which guarantees that protection to them should be annulled. . . . Where is the amelioration to come from? My own belief is that it will come from foreign war, or the shock of revolution. Retrogression must end sooner or later. No Government [Chinese government] can persistently evade its obligations to the world at large, without final sacrifice of its sovereign power. These outrages upon missionaries, I have no doubt, will continue till force is interposed to arrest them.[34]

*The Boxer Uprising of 1899–1900*

The Boxer Uprising was a violent, and ultimately tragic, mass movement directed against Christians and foreigners and widely supported by impoverished peasants during the late nineteenth century. The revolt was sparked by a potent mix of misery and resentment resulting from natural disasters, ongoing foreign domination, and hostility between Christians and non-Christians in southwest and northwest Shandong.[35]

In 1898, the Yellow River flooded over 2,000 villages in Shandong followed by severe drought. The suffering and displacement of the rural population that resulted from natural disasters provided fertile soil for social discontent. The escalation in acts of violence directed against Christians in Shandong also contributed to the explosive growth of the Boxer Movement in spring 1900. In the Liyuantun Incident of 1897, for instance, the Plum Flower Boxers—one of the main organizations involved in the Boxer Uprising—and their followers attacked a Catholic church and killed one local believer in Liyuantun, Guan County. The incident originated from long-standing friction between missionaries, Christian converts, and non-Christian villagers led by the local gentry over the erection of a Catholic church on the site of a village temple in the 1880s.

Another event that exacerbated anti-foreign sentiment in the region was the Juye Incident: in November 1897, Richard Henle and Francis Xavier Nies, two German Catholic missionaries of the Society of the Divine Word, were murdered by bandits. The Big Sword Society, another key organization in the Boxer Uprising, was allegedly behind the killings. Under pressure from the German government, the Qing government sentenced two main suspects to death; fired or demoted local officials including Li Bingheng, governor of Shandong; rebuilt churches; and compensated the church for property damage. Germany exploited the opportunity further and forced the Chinese government into leasing it the coveted Jiaozhou Bay and port of Qingdao on the Shandong Peninsula. This triggered a scramble for concessions and spheres of influence among the foreign powers in China and prompted the circulation of the American Open Door notes, as discussed in chapter 2.

Lacking a unified leadership and believing in supernatural interventions such as spirit possession and invulnerability to weapons, the Boxers, also known as the Society of Righteousness and Harmony (*Yihetuan*), promoted the practice of martial arts among their followers. Encouraged by conservative members of the Qing court, displaced Chinese from rural areas began indiscriminately targeting local Christians and destroying symbols of foreign influence such as railways and telegraph lines. In summer 1900, swarms of poor peasants marched on Tianjin and Beijing, launching attacks on foreigners and mission stations in North China. They besieged the foreign legations in Beijing for fifty-five days (June 20–August 14) and killed foreigners, including the German minister, Baron von Ketteler. In the province of Shanxi alone, 159 foreign missionaries lost their lives amid the violence—over 80 percent of foreign missionaries killed that year in the whole of China.[36] In mid-August 1900, a 20,000-strong relief force—half of them Japanese and the rest Russians, British Indians, French, Germans, Americans, Italians, and Austrians—arrived in Beijing and crushed the Boxers. The "liberation" of Beijing was followed by a military occupation and accompanied by a reign of terror and plunder. President William McKinley sent about 3,500 American troops under the command of Adna Chaffe from the Philippines to join the coalition.[37]

China was to pay a high price for the uprising. On September 7, 1901, the Boxer Protocol, consisting of twelve articles, was signed by Li Hongzhang and representatives of eleven nations (Germany, Great Britain, Austria-Hungary, Belgium, France, Italy, Japan, the Netherlands, Spain, Russia, and the United States). First, the Qing government agreed to erect monuments to the memory of the German minister and the over two hundred other Westerners who had been killed. Second, China was to execute those high officials who had supported the Boxers. Third, China was to pay an indemnity of 450 million taels (the Qing government's annual revenue was only 250 million taels). Fourth, the importation of arms was forbidden. Fifth, the foreign legation quarters were to be strengthened with fortified garrisons. Sixth, the Zongli Yamen (the Office of General Management of Foreign Affairs, founded in 1861) was to become the Ministry of Foreign Affairs. This was to raise the status of the Ministry of Foreign Affairs, which had been low in rank compared with other government ministries in China. Seventh, China agreed to carry out thoroughgoing domestic reforms including reform of its laws.

The Boxer Uprising and its revengeful suppression sparked mixed reactions in the United States. In 1900, in his annual message to Congress, after crowing over America's prosperity, especially the almost $80 million surplus revenue for the fiscal year, President William McKinley described the Boxer Uprising as "the dominant question" in American foreign relations. To him the Boxer trouble lay "deep in the character of the Chinese races and in the traditions of their Government."[38] However, the same events were perceived quite differently by some other Americans. In an article published in the *Los Angeles Times* in 1901, the anonymous author expressed strong criticism of the Western powers:

> While attending the coronation the other day—I beg pardon, the inauguration—of President McKinley, I asked a member of the Committee on Foreign Affairs what he thought of the position in China. "Barbarians don't interest me," he replied. He there voiced the opinion of millions, both in America and Europe. This is their mental attitude toward one of the most interesting crises in modern history. . . . The murder of Baron Von Ketteler and the attack on the legations were absolutely inexcusable. . . . But the attack on the legations, horrible as it was, has been avenged ten-fold. The conduct of a great portion of the allied troops has been so utterly disgraceful to Western civilization that it is a most disagreeable task to a historian to refer to it, and it is absolutely impossible to go into a description of details. To an impartial observer, if the term "barbarian" was to be applied to either side, it might just as fittingly be applied to the invaders as to the invaded.[39]

These sentiments echoed the attitudes of some Chinese contemporaries of the Boxers, who saw the Boxer Movement as motivated by patriotism—albeit in backward, xenophobic dress—directed against foreign domination. In 1901, Liang Qichao commented,

> The Boxer Movement was essentially driven by patriotic sentiments, for the sake of empowering China and resisting foreigners. The movement simply erupted at the time, lacking any particular men of genius or advanced military technology. Despite being totally defeated, the movement had its own legitimacy. People from all over responded. From now on, the spirit it embodied will surely strike root in the hearts of the people and spread its influence to the whole country.[40]

### Changing China: The American Social Gospel

Despite their severity at particular moments and in particular places, instances of violent confrontation and anti-missionary agitation should not be taken as representing the full Christian experience in China. Collaboration, appreciation, and localization (in the sense of the indigenization of the Christian Gospel) were also integral to the interaction between American Protestantism and Chinese society.

Quite a few American missionaries adjusted themselves to their new environment. They concerned themselves not only with saving souls, but with modernizing China by propagating the American way of life, disseminating science and technology, pursuing education and medical reform, and involvement in disaster relief work. In support of the Self-Strengthening Movement of the 1860s under Emperor Tongzhi (reigned 1861–75), Protestant missionaries including John Fryer assisted Qing statesmen Zeng Guofang, Li Hongzhang, and Zuo Zongtang in building modern arsenals at Jiangnan and Fuzhou, and shipyards, textile mills, coal mines, iron factories, railroads, and telegraph and electric companies. The impact of American missionaries on Chinese modernization efforts reached a peak during the Hundred Days' Reform of 1898.

The missionaries also created their own development institutions. Founded in 1894 by Reverend Gilbert Reid (1857–1927), the Mission among the Higher Classes of China exerted a significant influence on reform-oriented elites in Beijing.[41] Insofar as it was a modernizing and progressive cultural force, the American Social Gospel found a warm reception in local Chinese communities.

A further significant contribution by American Protestant missionaries was made in the sphere of publishing. In addition to translating and publishing Christian literature in Chinese, they produced books on Western culture and learning as well as publications for foreign and Chinese readers about China, the United States, and the world at large. These influential publications and translations included *The Chinese Repository*, edited by Elijah C. Bridgman; Bridgman's *Meilige guo zhilüe* (A Brief Account of the United States of America) published in 1838; *Wanguo gongfa*, published in 1864 in Beijing; W. A. P. Martin's translation of Henry Wheaton's *Elements of International Law*; and *Jiaohui xinbao* (The Church Newspaper), a weekly magazine by Young John Allen (1836–1907).[42]

In the field of medicine, Peter Parker, a Yale graduate, was the first American medical missionary dispatched to China. Parker opened the Canton Hospital in 1835, one of the first hospitals in China, and founded the Medical Missionary Society in China in 1838. Over the forty-four years from 1855 to 1899, as head of the Canton Hospital, John G. Kerr (1824–1901) of the American Presbyterian Mission treated 740,000 patients and performed 49,000 operations.[43] By 1920, Protestant missions had established over 326 hospitals in 237 Chinese cities. Fujian Province took the lead in the number of missionary residential centers with thirty-one Christian hospitals, followed by Guangdong (twenty-seven), Shandong (twenty), Sichuan (twenty), and Manchuria (twenty).[44] American Protestant missionaries were also involved in medical education, training some of China's first modern physicians such as Ho Kai and Sun Yat-sen.

Toleration was a social fact embedded in the interaction between some missionaries and the local communities they served. Edward Bliss, a medical missionary, was stationed from 1892 to 1932 in Shaowu—a remote town 250 miles from Fuzhou—under the auspices of the American Board of Commissioners for Foreign Missions. His years in China transformed him. Writing to his relatives in Newbury, Massachusetts, he said, "[N]ever since I came here have I seen any indication that the people don't want us here."[45]

> They [the Chinese] taught him [Bliss] moderation, and they taught him understanding. In letters he stopped referring to "the heathen." It was not that he no longer cared about whether China became a Christian nation. . . . It was, rather, that he had acquired so much respect for the Chinese that he could no longer call them heathen. The term stuck in his throat. They became, instead, Taoist, Buddhist, or Mohammedan. He had respect for them, first of all, as individuals. He healed them, delivered their babies—or lost them—one at a time. Each Chinese colleague is referred to in his letters as So-and-so Xian, or Mr. So-and-so. He simply could have used their surnames. He never did.[46]

Education was considered the "responsibility of the Christian Church," and was not limited to its communicant membership. The American Protestant missions believed that "through the Christian school it is possible to make distinct contributions not only to the religious training of the younger generation, but also to the social, economic, and physical welfare of society in general."[47] By 1920, the total number of lower primary schools run by missions was 5,637, compared with 956 higher primary schools, and 291 middle schools; the students enrolled in Protestant primary and middle schools totaled almost 200,000.[48]

In the realm of higher education, American Protestantism with its strong social agenda took the lead, outshining their Protestant peers from other countries and the Catholic missions. Before 1952, there were eighteen Christian colleges and universities, the majority of which were either founded or mainly financed by Americans. Those institutions run by Protestant missions were Canton Christian College (Lingnan University, Lingnan daxue), Fujian Christian University (Fujian xiehe daxue), Ginling College (Jinling nü wenli xueyuan), Hangchou University (Zhejiang daxue), Hsiang-Ya Medical College (Xiangya yixueyuan, also Yale-in-China, in Changsha), Huachung University (Huazhong daxue), Hwa Nan College (Huanan nü wenli xueyuan), Shangtung University (Qilu daxue), St. John's University (Sheng yuehan daxue), Soochow University (Dongwu daxue), the University of Nanking (Jinling daxue), the University of Shanghai (Hujiang daxue), the Women's Christian Medical College (Shanghai nüzi yixueyuan), West China Union University (Huaxi xiehe daxue Chengdu, founded in 1911), and Yenching University (Yanjing daxue). The Catholic institutions were Aurora University (Zhendan daxue), the Catholic University (Furen daxue), and Tsinku University (Jingu daxue, in Tianjin).

There was no greater index of the changes brought about by American Protestantism than the increase in the numbers of educated Christian Chinese women. Established in 1888 by Andrew Happer, an American Presbyterian missionary, and operating until 1952, Canton Christian College (Lingnan University) spearheaded coeducation and higher education for women in China. It was the first Christian college to admit girls to the secondary grades, in 1903, and the first to open its collegiate courses to females, from 1908 on. Education for women at Lingnan was developed through a combination of its increasing public profile, especially in the media, and a pragmatism with roots in both American and Southern Chinese culture. In church newspapers such as *Wanguo gongbao*, extensive coverage of women's rights and education for women in countries such as Japan, the United States, Germany, India, Switzerland, Russia, Persia, Turkey, England, Mexico, France, Sweden, and New Zealand prepared the ground for the advent of women's education in China. [49]

What advantages did modern education hold for Chinese women? Liu Fung Hin, a former Lingnan student (she was also a graduate of Wellesley College and the Teachers College at Columbia University), argued that higher education would equip Chinese women to better follow their vocation as bridge builders and peacemakers:

> The task that the modern woman has before her is not the copying of the West here and the East there, but rather of creating a new thing through a deeper appreciation of what is best in both. . . . The woman of China in her eagerness to follow her western sisters must not forget the legacy that has been handed down to her. Her duty is to make music and harmony out of the world of strife. . . . It is the task of the

modern woman to extend this influence throughout society and to fill the whole world with the melody of calm and peace.[50]

## CONCLUSION: AN ADAPTED VERSION OF AMERICAN CHRISTIANITY

The early history of American Christianity in China was full of contradictions. The widespread anti-Christian agitation discussed in this chapter tells a tale of confrontation, protest, and resistance. The other, parallel, story was one of appreciation, accommodation, and collaboration. More importantly, what emerged from the transfer of Christianity to Qing China was an adapted version of American Protestantism that was in competition with other religions and beliefs in China for souls and allegiance.

I can find no single example that offers a more nuanced account of the Christian experience in China than that of John Livingstone Nevius (1829–93), an influential American missiologist and Presbyterian missionary who lived in China for forty years.

John Nevius went to China with his wife in 1853, and was first dispatched to Ningbo. In 1860, the couple moved north to Chefoo (Yantai) and later Tungchow (Dengzhou), where he died in 1893. Nevius was remembered for introducing American fruits and vegetables to Shandong. He brought back from California and New York hundreds of pear, orange, and apple trees and successfully acclimatized them to their new environment. Nevertheless, for him, improving material life for Chinese came second to spreading the Gospel. For four decades, Nevius devoted the first four or five months of each year to making his pastoral rounds in rural Shandong, counseling native evangelists, establishing mission stations, appointing elders and teachers, teaching the catechism, and baptizing converts. From June to late August, the Neviuses would open up their home to train thirty to fifty Chinese communicants in theology and Bible studies. Then, for the remainder of the year, Nevius returned to his sixty mission stations to preach.

Between 1885 and 1886, he published eight letters in the *Chinese Recorder* describing his localized version of mission work,[51] which I have elsewhere named the Nevius model. The key components of the Nevius model were the principles of self-support, self-propagation, and self-government for the local Chinese church. All the chapels under his guidance were erected and sustained by local believers, and all evangelistic groups were led by unpaid workers; native pastors were not to be financed by foreign funds. Nevius explained his understanding of the contextualization of Christianity in typically down-to-earth terms:

> The purpose of our mission is to save people who are lost. Yet not all people are alike; the differences between them are great. Some are rich and some poor. Some have great wisdom, whereas others are not so wise and understanding. . . . Some are learned scholars, while others are common peasants. Some are happy folks, others worry a great deal. . . . Therefore, when we seek to do the work of evangelism we must take note of the situation and particular context in which we find each separate people and adapt a method which will suit the particular opportunity they represent.[52]

## FURTHER READING

Useful bibliographical references include Charles W. Hayford, *American China Missions: An Introductory Bibliography* (April 23, 2003), http://www.library.yale.edu/div/MissionsResources.htm (accessed December 31, 2011); Xiaoxin Wu, ed., *Christianity in China: A Scholars' Guide to Resources in the Libraries and Archives of the United States* (Armonk, N.Y.: M. E. Sharpe, 2008); R. Gary Tiedemann, *Reference Guide to Christian Missionary Societies in China: From the Sixteenth to the Twentieth Century* (Armonk, N.Y.: M. E. Sharpe, 2008); R. Gary Tiedemann, ed. *Handbook of Christianity in China* (Leiden: Brill, 2009), vol. 2.

The most authoritative general study of the subject is Daniel H. Bays, *A New History of Christianity in China* (Malden, Mass.: Wiley-Blackwell, 2012). For individual portraits of some important American missionaries, see Jonathan D. Spence, *To Change China: Western Advisers in China, 1620–1960* (reprint New York: Penguin, 2002; 1st ed. 1969). Other recommended studies include Larry Clinton Thompson, *William Scott Ament and the Boxer Rebellion: Heroism, Hubris and the "Ideal Missionary"* (Jefferson, N.C.: McFarland, 2009); Alvyn Austin, *China's Millions: The China Inland Mission and Late Qing Society, 1832–1905* (Grand Rapids, Mich.: William B. Eerdmans, 2007); Lawrence D. Kessler, *The Jiangyin Mission Station: An American Missionary Community in China, 1895–1951* (Chapel Hill, N.C.: University of North Carolina Press, 1996); Charles Ewing and Bessie Ewing, *Death Throes of a Dynasty: Letters and Diaries of Charles and Bessie Ewing, Missionaries to China*, ed. E. G. Ruoff (Kent, Ohio: Kent State

University Press, 1990); Eva Jane Price, *China Journal 1889–1900: An American Missionary Family during the Boxer Rebellion: With the Letters and Diaries of Eva Jane Price and Her Family* (New York: Scribner, 1989); William R. Hutchison, *Errand to the World: American Protestant Thought and Foreign Missions* (Chicago, Ill.: University of Chicago Press, 1987); Charles W. Hayford, "Chinese and American Characteristics: Arthur H. Smith and the Respectable Middle Class View of China," in Suzanne W. Barnett and John K. Fairbank, eds., *Christianity in China: Early Protestant Missionary Writings* (Cambridge, Mass.: East Asian Research Center, Harvard University Press, 1985), pp. 153–207; Irwin T. Hyatt Jr., *Our Ordered Lives Confess: Three Nineteenth-Century American Missionaries in East Shantung* (Cambridge, Mass.: Harvard University Press, 1976).

## NOTES

1. Yang Xiaoxue (杨晓雪), "Liubai sui Qianmen dajie shouguo 'yangjie,'" [六百岁前门大街首过"洋节" 600-year old Qianmen Street celebrates the "foreign festival" for the first time], *Beijing qingnian bao*, December 25, 2009, p. 1.

2. Nicolas Standaert, ed., *Handbook of Christianity in China: 635–1800* (Leiden: Brill, 2001), vol. 1; Samuel Hugh Moffett, *A History of Christianity in Asia* (Maryknoll, N.Y.: Orbis Books, 1998), 2 vols.

3. Charles Denby, "Toleration in China," *The Independent*, September 27, 1900.

4. Nathan D. Showalter, *The End of a Crusade: The Student Volunteer Movement for Foreign Missions and the Great War* (Lanham, Md.: Scarecrow Press, 1998). Murray A. Rubinstein, *The Origins of the Anglo-American Missionary Enterprise in China, 1807–1840* (Lanham, Md.: Scarecrow Press, 1996).

5. Fred W. Drake, "Protestant Geography in China: E. C. Bridgman's Portrayal of the West," in Susan Wilson Barnett and John K. Fairbank, eds., *Christianity in China: Early Protestant Writings* (Cambridge, Mass.: Harvard University Press, 1985), pp. 89–106; Michael C. Lazich, *E. C. Bridgman (1801–1861): America's First Missionary to China* (Lewiston, N.Y.: Edwin Mellen Press, 2000).

6. Daniel H. Bays, "From Foreign Mission to Chinese Church," *Christian History & Biography*, no. 98 (Spring 2008): 6–13.

7. Elijah C. Bridgman, "Foreign Relations with China: Retrospect of the Past: Questions at Issue; Further Prospects and Desiderata," *Chinese Repository* 9, no. 1 (May 1840): 1–9. Murray A. Rubinstein, "The Wars They Wanted: American Missionaries' Use of *The Chinese Repository* before the Opium War," *American Neptune* 48, no. 4 (Fall 1988): 271–282. Stuart Creighton Miller, "Ends and Means: Missionary Justification of Force in Nineteenth Century China," in John K. Fairbank, ed., *The Missionary Enterprise in China and America* (Cambridge, Mass.: Harvard University Press, 1974), pp. 249–282.

8. Charles Denby, "Toleration in China," *The Independent*, September 27, 1900.

9. For the Chinese and French versions of the treaty, see Wang Tieya, *Zhongwai jiu yuezhang huibian* [Compilation of former treaties and conventions between China and foreign countries 中外旧约章汇编] (Beijing: Sanlian shudian, 1982; 1st ed. 1957), vol. 1,

pp. 146–148, and William Frederick Mayers, *Treaties between the Empires of China and Foreign Powers*, reprint (Taipei: Ch'eng-wen Publishing, 1966; 1st ed. 1877 in Shanghai ed. by J. Broadhurst Tootal), pp. 72–75.

10. George B. Stevens, *The Life, Letters, and Journals of the Rev. and Hon. Peter Parker, M.D.: Missionary, Physician, Diplomatist, the Father of Medical Missions and Founder of the Ophthalmic Hospital in Canton* (Boston, Mass.: Congregational Sunday-School and Publishing Society, 1896), p. 252. See also Edward Vose Gulick, *Peter Parker and the Opening of China* (Cambridge, Mass.: Harvard University Press, 1973). Obviously, Parker's view of the first treaty between the United States and China as favorable to both countries was not shared by the Chinese.

11. Bob Whyte, *Unfinished Encounter: China and Christianity* (London: Fount Paperbacks, 1988).

12. Article I, "List of Protestant Missionaries to the Chinese, with the Present Position of Those Now among Them," *Chinese Repository* 20, nos. 8–12 (August–December 1851): 514–545.

13. John B. Littell, "Missionaries and Politics in China—the Taiping Rebellion," *Political Science Quarterly* 43, no. 4 (December 1928): 566–599.

14. China Continuation Committee, *The Christian Occupation of China: A General Survey of the Numerical Strength and Geographical Distribution of the Christian Forces in China* (Shanghai: China Continuation Committee, 1922), pp. 307, 403.

15. China Continuation Committee, *The Christian Occupation of China*, pp. 33–35.

16. Daniel H. Bays, *A New History of Christianity in China* (Malden, Mass.: Wiley-Blackwell, 2012), p. 53.

17. Article 11, *Chinese Repository*, vol. 20, no. 7 (July 1851): 497–498.

18. Agricola, "The Civil War and 'Christianity' in China," *The Independent*, August 5, 1853.

19. Xia Chuntao (夏春涛), *Taiping tianguo zongjiao* [太平天国宗教 The Taiping religion] (Nanjing: Nanjing daxue chubanshe, 1992); Mao Jiaqi (茅家琦), *Taiping tianguo duiwai guanxi shi* [太平天国对外关系史 The foreign relations of the Taiping Heavenly Kingdom] (Beijing: Renmin chubanshe, 1984); Zhongguo shehui kexueyuan jindaishi yanjiusuo, comp., *Taipingjun beifa xiliao xuanbian* [太平军北伐资料选编 Selected material on the northern expedition of the Taipings] (Jinan: Qilu shushe, 1984); Thomas H. Reilly, *The Taiping Heavenly Kingdom: Rebellion and the Blasphemy of Empire* (Seattle, Wash.: University of Washington Press, 2004); Jonathan Spence, *God's Chinese Son: The Taiping Heavenly Kingdom of Hong Xiuquan* (New York: Norton, 1996); Paul A. Cohen, "Christian Missions and Their Impact to 1900," in Denis Twitchett and John K. Fairbank, eds., *The Cambridge History of China* (Cambridge: Cambridge University Press, 1978), vol. 10, pp. 543–90.

20. Robert McLane's (American minister to China) report in Prescott Clarke and J. S. Gregory, comps., *Western Reports on the Taiping: A Selection of Documents* (Honolulu, Hawaii: University Press of Hawaii, 1982), pp. 131–137. Eugene P. Boardman, "Christian Influence upon the Ideology of the Taiping Rebellion," *Far Eastern Quarterly* 10, no. 2 (February 1951): 115–124. In a narrative of a visit to the Taipings in the company of Robert McLane in 1854, Reverend M. S. Culbertson concluded, "The chief difference between the old [Qing imperial government] and the new [Taiping] doctrine appears to be this, that the old Emperor claimed supremacy as the 'Son of Heaven'; the new Ruler, as the 'Brother of Jesus,'" in Prescott Clarke and J. S. Gregory, comps., *Western Reports on the Taiping*, p. 140.

21. *Christian Advocate*, vol. 28 (September 22, 1853), p. 151. John B. Littell, "Missionaries and Politics in China—the Taiping Rebellion." The *Christian Advocate* was published by the Methodist Episcopal Church starting in 1826.

22. George Minot, ed., *Statutes at Large and Treaties of the United States of America from December 1, 1845, to March 3, 1851* (Boston, Mass.: Charles C. Little and James Brown, 1851), vol. 9, pp. 276–278. Later on December 5, 1854, participation in rebellion against the Chinese government was made a "high misdemeanor," punishable by a fine of no more than US$10,000 or imprisonment for no more than three years.

23. Charles Taylor, *Five Years in China with an Account of the Great Rebellion, and a Description of St. Helena* (New York: Derby & Jackson, 1860), chapter 26, p. 335.

24. Kenneth S. Latourette, *A History of Christian Missions in China* (New York: Macmillan, 1929), p. 298.

25. Daniel H. Bays, ed., *Christianity in China: From the Eighteenth Century to the Present* (Stanford, Calif.: Stanford University Press, 1996); Dong Wang, *Managing God's Higher Learning: U.S.-China Cultural Encounter and Canton Christian College (Lingnan University), 1888–1952* (Lanham, Md.: Rowman & Littlefield, 2007); Eugenio Menegon, *Ancestors, Virgins, and Friars: Christianity as a Local Religion in Late Imperial China* (Cambridge, Mass.: Harvard University Asia Center, 2010).

26. Some scholars put the number of anti-missionary incidents at over four hundred. Gu Weimin (顾为民), *Jidujiao yu jindai Zhongguao shehui* [基督教与近代中国社会 Christianity and modern Chinese society] (Shanghai: Shanghai renmin chubanshe, 1996), p. 192.

27. North China Herald, *The Anti-foreign Riots in China in 1891, with an Appendix* (Shanghai: North China Herald, 1892). Also see the Chinese translation of part 1 by Wang Dong (王栋), "Menggu shijian" [蒙古事件 The Mongolian Incident], *Jindaishi ziliao* 82 (November 1992): 159–171.

28. Examples are found in *Poxie ji* [破邪集 An anthology of writings aimed at rooting out heterodoxy], with a preface dated 1640; it comprises about sixty essays and other pieces that question Christian teaching. In 1724, Emperor Yongzhen listed Christianity as a forbidden sect. Paul A. Cohen, "The Anti-Christian Tradition in China," *Journal of Asian Studies* 20, no. 2 (February 1961): 169–180; Paul A. Cohen, *China and Christianity: The Missionary Movement and the Growth of Chinese Antiforeignism, 1860–1870* (Cambridge, Mass.: Harvard University, 1963); Wang Dong, "Daoxian jingshi pai Jidujiao guan shuping" [道咸经世派基督教观述评 The anti-Christian sentiments of the Statecraft Scholars during the Daoxian period], *Beifang luncong* 2 (1990): 91–94.

29. Henrietta Harrison, "'A Penny for the Little Chinese': The French Holy Childhood Association in China, 1843–1951," *American Historical Review* 113, no. 1 (February 2008): 72–92; Liu Haiyan (刘海岩), "Youguan Tianjin jiao'an de jige wenti" [有关天津教案的几个问题 A few questions about the Tianjin missionary incident], in Sichuan sheng zhexue shehui kexue lianhehui and Sichuan sheng jindai jiao'an shi yanjiuhui, *Jindai Zhongguo jiao'an yanjiu* [近代中国教案研究 A study of missionary incidents in modern China] (Chengdu: Sichuansheng shehui kexueyuan chubanshe, 1987), pp. 224–236; John K. Fairbank, "Patterns behind the Tientsin Massacre," *Harvard Journal of Asiatic Studies* 20, nos. 3–4 (December 1957): 480–511.

30. James E. Kirby Jr., "The Foochow Anti-missionary Riot—August 30, 1878," *Journal of Asian Studies* 25, no. 4 (August 1966): 665–678; Shen Chunsheng (申春生), "Fuzhou Wushi shan jiao'an" [福州乌石山教案 The Fuzhou missionary incident], in Qi Qizhang and Wang Ruhui, eds., *Wanqing jiao'an jishi*, pp. 142–148.

31. Wang Ruhui (王如绘), "Chengdu jiao'an" [成都教案 The Chengdu missionary incident], in Qi Qizhang and Wang Ruhui, eds., *Wanqing jiao'an jishi*, pp. 249–257; George E. Paulsen, "The Szechwan Riots of 1895 and American 'Missionary Diplomacy,'" *Journal of Asian Studies* 28, no. 2 (February 1969): 285–298.

32. R. Gary Tiedemann, "Protestant 'Missionary Cases' (jiao'an) in Shandong Province, 1860–1900," *Ching Feng* 8, nos. 1–2 (2007): 153–195; Wang Dong, MA thesis, "Lun shijiu shiji xia banye Jidujiao (Xinjiao) zai Shandong de chuanbo" [论十九世纪下半叶基督教(新教)在山东的传播 On the spread of Christianity (Protestantism) in Shandong in the latter half of the 19th century], Shandong University, 1987.

33. Joseph Tse-Hei Lee, "The Lord of Heaven versus Jesus Christ: Christian Sectarian Violence in Late-Nineteenth-Century South China," *Positions* 8, no. 1 (Spring 2000): 77–99; R. Gary Tiedemann, ed., *Handbook of Christianity in China* (Leiden: Brill, 2009), vol. 2, pp. 302–337.

34. J. Ross Browne to Hamilton Fish, June 15, 1869, document no. 1, in Jules Davids, ed., *American Diplomatic and Public Papers: The United States and China*, series II, *The United States, China, and Imperial Rivalries, 1861–1893*, vol. 14, *Antiforeignism in China*, pp. 3–8.

35. Robert Bickers and R. G. Tiedemann, eds., *The Boxers, China, and the World* (Lanham, Md.: Rowman & Littlefield, 2007); Diana Preston, *Besieged in Peking: The Story of the 1900 Boxer Rising* (London: Constable, 1999); Paul A. Cohen, *History in Three Keys: The Boxers as Event, Experience, and Myth* (New York: Columbia University Press, 1997); Joseph W. Esherick, *The Origins of the Boxer Uprising* (Berkeley, Calif.: University of California Press, 1987); Xu Xudian (徐绪典), ed., *Yihetuan yundong shi yanjiu luncong* [义和团运动史研究论丛 Essays on the history of the Boxer Movement] (Jinan: Shandong daxue lishixi, 1982); Lu Yao (路遥) and Cheng Xiao (程歗), *Yihetuan yundong shi yanjiu* [A study of the history of the Boxer Movement] (Jinan: Qilu shushe, 1988); Su Weizhi (苏位智) and Liu Tianlu (刘天路), eds., *Yihetuan yanjiu yibainian* [义和团研究一百年 One hundred years of Boxer studies] (Jinan: Qilu shushe, 2000); Su Weizhi and Liu Tianlu, eds., *Yihetuan yundong yibai zhounian guoji xueshu taolunhui lunwenji* [义和团运动一百周年国际学术讨论会论文集 Collected essays presented at the international symposium on the centennial of the Boxer Movement] (Jinan: Shandong daxue, 2002).

36. This resulted largely from the support given the Boxers by Yuxian, the antiforeign governor of Shanxi. R. G. Tiedemann, "Baptism of Fire: China's Christians and the Boxer Uprising of 1900," *International Bulletin of Missionary Research* (January 2000): 7–12.

37. Michael H. Hunt, "The Forgotten Occupation: Peking, 1900–1901," *Pacific Historical Review* 48, no. 4 (1979): 501–529.

38. Message of the president, *Papers Relating to the Foreign Relations of the United States with the Annual Message of the President, Transmitted to Congress December 3, 1900* (Washington, D.C.: Government Printing Office, 1902), vii–li.

39. Author unknown, "The War of the Civilizations in the Far East," *Los Angeles Times*, April 21, 1901.

40. Liang Qichao, *Yinbingshi heji* [饮冰室合集 Collected works of Liang Qichao] (Beijing: Zhonghua shuju, 1989), Yinbingshi wenji, no. 6, "Mieguo xinfa lun" [灭国新法论 A new way of extirpating a nation-state employed by Western countries], pp. 32–47.

41. Tsou Mingteh, "Christian Missionary as Confucian Intellectual: Gilbert Reid (1857–1927) and the Reform Movement in the Late Qing," in Daniel H. Bays, ed.,

*Christianity in China: From the Eighteenth Century to the Present* (Stanford, Calif.: Stanford University Press, 1996), pp. 73–90.

42. *Jiaohui xinbao* (教会新报) was later known successively as *Wanguo gongbao, The Global Magazine*, 1875–83, and *Review of the Times*, 1889–1907. Adrian A. Bennett and Kwang-Ching Liu, "Christianity in Chinese Idiom: Young J. Allen and the Early Chiao-hui hsin-pao, 1860–1870," in Susan Wilson Barnett and John K. Fairbank, eds., *Christianity in China*, pp. 159–196.

43. Gu Weimin, *Jidujiao yu jindai Zhongguo shehui*, p. 249.

44. China Continuation Committee, *The Christian Occupation of China*, p. 305.

45. Edward Bliss Jr., *Beyond the Stone Arches: An American Missionary Doctor in China, 1892–1932* (New York: Wiley, 2001), p. 73. For the latest research on the mutual appreciation experienced between medical missionaries and Chinese, see Hu Cheng (胡成), "Heyi xinxi: Zhongguo Jidujiao yiliao chuanjiaoshi yu difang shehui (1835–1911)" [何以心系:中国基督教医疗传教士与地方社会 (1835–1911) I left my heart in China: Chinese Protestant medical missionaries and local society], *Jindaishi yanjiu* 178, no. 4 (July 2010): 16–33.

46. Edward Bliss Jr., *Beyond the Stone Arches: An American Missionary Doctor in China, 1892–1932*, p. 68.

47. China Continuation Committee, *The Christian Occupation of China*, p. 301.

48. China Continuation Committee, *The Christian Occupation of China*, p. 302.

49. Material in this section is drawn from Dong Wang, *Managing God's Higher Learning*, chapter 4. For other relevant studies of women and Christian education in China, see Jane Hunter, *The Gospel of Gentility: American Women Missionaries in Turn-of-the-Century China* (New Haven, Conn.: Yale University Press, 1984); Pui-lan Kwok, *Chinese Women and Christianity, 1860–1927* (Atlanta, Ga.: Scholars Press, 1992); Gael Graham, *Gender, Culture, and Christianity: American Protestant Mission Schools in China, 1880–1930* (New York: Peter Lang, 1995).

50. Liu Fung Ling, "The Epic Woman of China," *Ling Naam: The News Bulletin of Canton Christian College* 1, no. 1 (August 1924).

51. John Nevius, "Principles and Methods Applicable to Station Work," *Chinese Recorder* 16, nos. 10 and 11 (November and December 1885): 421–424, 461–467; "Methods of Mission Work," 17, nos. 1–3, no. 5, nos. 7–8 (January–March, May, July–August 1886): 24–31, 55–64, 102–112, 165–178, 252–260, 297–305. Wang Dong, "Ni Weisi chuanjiao fangfa" [倪维思传教方法 Nevius' missionary approach], *Shijie zongjiao ziliao* 2 (1991): 15–21.

52. Ni Weisi (John Nevius), *Xuanjiao zhigui* [宣教指规 Manual of evangelization] (Shanghai: Meihua shuju, 1862). Samuel H. Chao, "John L. Nevius (1829–1893) and the Contextualization of the Gospel in 19th Century China: A Case Study," *Asia Journal of Theology* 2, no. 2 (1988): 294–311.

*Part II*

# The United States and China in the Era of World Wars and Revolutions, 1912–1970

# FIVE

# Revolutions, Nationalism, and Internationalization

During the early twentieth century, the United States and China embarked on different national programs and used differing strategies to cope with new world situations. Although their relationship became strategically important, it was neither a partnership nor a rivalry. A web of attitudinal, legal, and cultural ties have also left their imprint to the present day. American-Chinese relations were tested and transformed in the turmoil of World War I, the Great Depression, and World War II. Japan, a cooperative member of the international community in the 1920s, became an expansionist rival of the United States and invaded China, starting with the seizure of Manchuria in 1931 and culminating in full-scale aggression in 1937. In response, the United States offered China no more than moral support until the Japanese bombing of America's Pearl Harbor in December 1941.

Three developments are key to understanding the Sino-American relationship between World War I and 1931. The first was China's pursuit of equitable treatment as an equal nation-state on the world stage in the era of revolutions and nationalism. The continuing demand for treaty revisions and cancellations was an integral part of this quest. Second, the voice of America was increasingly felt in Chinese affairs, set against the influence of Japan, Russia, Germany, Britain, and other European powers. Progressive and revolutionary Chinese thus found themselves in a position to assess competing foreign models of modernization. The third development was the increased visibility of China on the U.S. domestic political horizon. I will leave the discussion of this last aspect to a later chapter.


THE UNITED STATES AND THE BEIJING GOVERNMENT (1912–28)

American-Chinese relations were strengthened in the tumultuous years of wars, revolutions, nationalism, anti-imperialism, and internationalization between 1912 and 1928. Paradoxically, the two countries were brought closer as a result of their divergent stages of national development as well as through the adoption of particular geopolitical strategies. Abhorrent of violent revolutions, the United States became involved in Chinese politics with caution. The Beijing government (1912–28, the first Republic of China) conducted its foreign relations within the strictures of the established treaty regime. It also worked to enhance China's international status and set its relations with foreign nations on an equal footing by seeking legal justification for revising and abolishing the unequal treaties through diplomatic means. The American government's promotion of the United States as the guardian of world peace and democracy, in place of the "colonial and imperialist diplomacy" of the European powers, had given many Chinese leaders hope that such ideals could be implemented.[1]

The lessons learned from the experience of the first Republic of China in parliamentary government have important implications for the history of American-Chinese relations and also for advocates of democracy and civil society in China today. In 1911 a revolution toppled Manchu rule, marking the demise of the Chinese dynastic system (since 221 BCE) and ushering in the ultimately failed experiment in republican government and constitutional monarchy.[2] On October 10, a mutiny initiated by a group of anti-Manchu, revolution-minded New Army officers broke out in Wuchang (modern Wuhan) in Hubei Province on the Yangzi River. With the support of the provincial assembly, rebels seized the city, declaring Hubei Province independent of the Qing monarchy. By the end of the year, a number of provinces in central and south China had endorsed the view that China should become a republic under the provisional presidency of Sun Yat-sen (1866–1925), founder of the Nationalist Party (Guomindang). The Qing Manchu court in Beijing appealed to Yuan Shi-kai (1859–1916), a leading Qing politician and general.[3] Sun's provisional government opened negotiations with Yuan—who was favored by the

United States, Britain, and other foreign powers after a period of cautious neutrality. Expressing his opposition to this "prolonged" period of neutrality, William J. Calhoun—American minister to China (1909–13)—asserted, "If the Powers had supported Yuan when first suggested I believe he would have ended revolution by this time. Continued neutrality only encourages disorder."[4]

Opposition to the regime did not fade away. Yuan agreed to make the Qing emperor, a young boy, abdicate in February 1912 on condition that he, Yuan, become president of the new Republic of China. In March, Yuan took office in Beijing, and he was formally reelected in 1913. Yuan was respected by some foreigners—especially Frank J. Goodnow, Yuan's American advisor; William W. Rockhill, the mastermind of the U.S. Open Door doctrine; and Sir John Jordan, the British minister to Beijing—as a progressive, realistic, and skillful politician. Between 1912 and 1916, Yuan ruled China, first as president and then as emperor. However, his death in 1916 threatened China once again with disintegration. Until 1928 the Beijing administration was the sole government recognized by the foreign powers, but it exercised only symbolic authority. Real power rested in the hands of warlords and two modern political parties, Sun Yat-sen's Nationalist Party (GMD) and the Chinese Communist Party (CCP). In the course of the sixteen years of its life, the Beijing government—the first republic—produced seven heads of state and forty-six cabinets riven by various political and military factions and challenged by the GMD and GMD-CCP governments in Canton (Guangzhou). The GMD and CCP forged an ephemeral alliance in 1924, but this broke up abruptly three years later. In 1928 GMD Nationalist forces occupied Beijing, and the first Chinese experience with constitutional government came to an end. Between 1928 and 1937, the GMD continued to maintain the Republic of China in Nanjing, while at the same time attempting to root out its rivals—in particular the CCP—and appealed to the United States and other powers for interference in the face of Japanese aggression.

The GMD and CCP were responsible for shaping the Chinese political landscape from the early twentieth century. Both parties espoused the nationalistic view of history in relation to moving China into the modern world, but differed over tactics, intellectual and cultural allegiances, and, last but not least, over the leadership and beneficiaries of the revolution. The Nationalist Party grew out of anti-Manchu revolutionary organiza-

tions including the United League created by Sun Yat-sen and his followers in 1905 in Tokyo. The Nationalists aimed to overthrow the Manchu
Qing regime and to restore Han leadership by establishing a republic,
freeing China from foreign encroachment, and equalizing land ownership.[5] In 1912 Sun transformed the party into the Guomindang, an organization wielding considerable political clout and posing a threat in the
Parliament to Yuan. In contrast, the Chinese Communist Party was
formed under the influence of Soviet Russia. The first CCP Congress was
organized in secret on July 1, 1921, in Shanghai by a small group of
young nationalistic intellectuals—including Li Dazhao, Chen Duxiu, and
Mao Zedong—convinced by Marxist and Leninist ideology and rhetoric
about the world Communist revolution, class struggle, and anti-imperialism.[6]

In the United States, the domestic and international conditions proved
to be a source of inspiration to many Chinese who were exposed to the
other models (Russian, Japanese, German, British, etc.) of development as
well. The end of the Gilded Age (1876–96, from the presidency of Ruther-
ford B. Hayes to that of Benjamin Harrison) brought about an increased
consciousness of national identity and a confidence in the projection of
the American system around the globe. Opulence, urbanization, technological advances, mass participation, immigration, poverty, labor unrest,
the unequal distribution of wealth, and pressure for social reform and
state intervention all became integral parts of the national development
mix in the United States. William McKinley's election in 1897 marked not
only the end of the economic depression that had begun in 1893—dogged
by a 20 percent unemployment rate—but also the birth of the modern
American presidency, characterized by presidents who played an active
and potent role in domestic life and foreign affairs. Progressivism aiming
at social justice through government actions continued into the Woodrow
Wilson administration (1913–21). The national development that had tak-
en root in the United States during the preceding decades was consolidated under Wilson's leadership, confirming the nation's position as a major
world manufacturer and global power. The United States produced over
one-third of the total world industrial output in 1913, and 42 percent by
1926, illustrating its growing economic might.[7]

In China, American support was much coveted by competing political
forces,[8] and Yuan Shikai's new regime in Beijing was especially "cha-
grined by the failure of the United States to recognize their new Govern-

ment."[9] The American legation in Beijing suggested that the United States might harm its own interests if it continued to withhold recognition of the Republic of China until the other powers (including Great Britain) all agreed. The delay in recognition would "merely promote the aggressive designs" of other nations (such as Japan and Russia) who had territorial, economic, and judicial ambitions in China. Additional grounds for recognition were also provided to the State Department. First, although the Chinese people "are too ignorant to understand the meaning of the word 'republic' . . . [they] are making no resistance to the new order." Second, there was no rival contending with the Republic of China for the governance of China. Finally, in April 1914, President Wilson guardedly recognized Yuan Shikai's Republic of China.[10]

In 1915, an editorial note in *The Independent*, an American newspaper, offered a glimpse of the Chinese leader as optimistically portrayed by the American press:

> As an actual ruler of over three hundred millions of people at a time when the country is passing thru the most critical period in its history, President Yuan Shih-K'ai occupies a position of responsibility rarely if ever equaled in the history of the world. He had carried thru the delicate transition from an autocratic to a republican form of government; he has met the peril of domestic rebellion and a threatened foreign war with a tact and firmness that has aroused the admiration even of his enemies.[11]

On the basis of an interview with a journalist, William Francis Mannix, given at 1 a.m. in Yuan's private quarters in the Forbidden City in Beijing, *The Independent* commented wryly that "Chinese officialdom clings tenaciously to the night for the transaction of most affairs." At pains to present the Chinese president in a favorable light, the editorial went on to report that, when Yuan was shown a copy of *The Independent* containing his picture, "he inspected it closely and smiled so broadly that his unmistakably Rooseveltian teeth could be accurately counted."[12] Yuan told Mannix that China welcomed foreign merchants and traders, who "will be given fullest protection in the prosecution of all their legitimate enterprises." Yuan expressed a measured view of the United States, asserting that "while America was the only country of the world which denied admittance to our countrymen, it was also the only nation which stood like the Great Wall between China and dismemberment."

As events turned out, World War I stimulated relations between China and the United States. In June 1914, Archduke Franz Ferdinand, heir to the Austrian and Hungarian thrones, and his wife, Sophie, were assassinated by ultranationalist Serbian revolutionaries during a state visit to the Bosnian capital of Sarajevo. Austria declared war on Serbia. Soon Germany, Austria's ally among the Central Powers, turned the war on the Balkans into the Great War by attacking its enemies, Belgium and France, which were in a military alliance with Russia and Britain (the Allies). Both the Beijing government and the Woodrow Wilson administration made an effort to preserve their neutral status in the European conflict and in the Far East. In August 1914, the Chinese legation in Washington sent a memo of neutrality to the U.S. government, which—as a neutral country too—was in broad agreement that the neutralization of Chinese treaty ports, respect for China's neutrality, and the preservation of the status quo in China were "most important to American interests." [13]

However, events were soon to force the United States to revise its neutral stance. In February 1917, Germany resumed its policy of unrestricted submarine warfare, sinking a total of ten American commercial liners as they approached Britain and European countries controlled by the enemies of Germany. In April, the U.S. Congress voted in support of President Wilson to declare war on Germany and the other Central Powers, for the first time breaking the "Great Rule" laid down by George Washington mandating nonentanglement in European affairs. [14]

Wilson injected a new vision into America's mission to the world. In his words, the "idea of America is to serve humanity," and the United States was to strive "for the elevation of the spirit of the human race,"

> For that is the only distinction that America has. Other nations have been strong, other nations have piled wealth as high as the sky, but they have come into disgrace because they used their force and their wealth for the oppression of mankind and their own aggrandizement; and America will not bring glory to herself, but disgrace, by following the beaten paths of history. We must strike out upon new paths. [15]

Despite later failures, the "new paths" envisaged by Wilson essentially referred to the need for the United States to set a global agenda as an emerging world leader. On January 8, 1918, Wilson addressed a joint session of Congress on the conditions of a peace that would make the world "fit and safe to live in," a peace program widely promoted as the

Fourteen Points.[16] Denouncing the use of force and self-serving aggression, Wilson espoused the principles of self-determination, equality among nations, open diplomacy (no secret treaties), and the creation of an international organization (the League of Nations) as the "new things" essential to the transformation of world politics.

Wilson's crusading sentiments electrified Chinese elites and senior government officials. In part, they resonated with the predilection for Western democracy and science among many educated Chinese at the time. In part also, they were an aspect of the American government's propaganda campaign for Wilsonian democracy and self-determination in China and around the globe.[17] Chen Duxiu—one of the nation's most prolific public essayists and the founding leader of the Chinese Communist Party—called President Wilson "the first good person in today's world."[18] Wellington Koo, then Chinese minister to the United States, telegraphed Beijing urging it to go to war against the Central Powers, a step China indeed took in August 1917.[19] Internal discord over China's entry into the war, however, exacerbated tensions between President Li Yuanhong, the Parliament (where an anti-war clique was led by the Nationalist Party), the cabinet (with a pro-war faction headed by Premier/General Duan Qirui), and the *dujuns*—military governors or warlords who denounced Li for yielding to the Parliament and dismissing Duan. In June 1917, under intense pressure from the warlords, Li decided to dissolve the Parliament. The Nationalist Party MPs fled to Canton and set up an autonomous military government which challenged the legitimacy of the Beijing government. The open rift that opened up between North and South China and the continuous warfare among the warlords in the North became a source of embarrassment and uncertainty for China. These political developments were closely documented by Paul S. Reinsch, American minister to China.[20] On November 11, 1918, the Allied and German delegates signed an armistice on terms established by the Allies, paving the way for the "Big Four"—Prime Minister David Lloyd George of Britain, Prime Minister Vittorio Orlando of Italy, Premier Georges Clemenceau of France, and President Woodrow Wilson of the United States—to make a peace settlement. The Chinese Beijing government was invited to participate in the Paris Peace Conference as one of the victorious powers.

The Chinese representatives included some young, rising diplomats and politicians such as Sao-ke Alfred Sze (1876–1958), W. W. Yen

(1876–1950), C. T. Wang (1882–1961), and Wellington Koo (1888–1985), all four of whom graduated from American universities before serving in ministerial and ambassadorial posts, first for the Beijing government (1912–28) and then the Nationalist government (1928–49). This phenomenon pointed to the changing tempo of America's influence in its competition with other powers for allegiance among Chinese leaders and elites.

In Versailles, the Chinese delegates took the opportunity to apply principles of international law to China's grievances about two major issues. First and foremost was the Shandong question: China demanded the restoration of territory leased to Germany and the rights it held in Shandong Province, which was as important to China as Alsace-Lorraine to France.[21] In addition, China requested the termination of the treaties and agreements which had allowed Japan to acquire all of Germany's former privileges in Shandong. Second, the so-called "Questions for Readjustment" (also known as the "Seven Aspirations") were submitted by China to the conference. The seven questions included the renunciation of spheres of influence by foreign powers in China, the withdrawal of foreign troops and police, the dismantling of foreign post and telegraph offices, the abolition of consular jurisdiction, the relinquishment of leased territories, and the restitution of tariff autonomy.

In contrast to China's expectations, it was the League of Nations that lay at the heart of the American agenda in Paris. Ignoring most of Wilson's peace aspirations, the Treaty of Versailles did however include a covenant mandating the League of Nations in exchange for Wilson's acquiescence in the colonial claims of other Allied powers. The peace treaty was signed by all the negotiating countries with the single exception of China, which protested against the arbitrary settlement of the Shandong question. The Chinese delegation had received 7,000 telegrams calling on them not to put their signatures on the treaty. Japan, too, felt aggrieved as a result of its failed attempt to insert a racial equality clause into the peace settlement. On the other hand, Japan succeeded in pressing the Allied powers to recognize its wartime seizure of Shandong and its claim to special rights in China on the basis of a number of secret agreements—the "Twenty-One Demands" of 1915 and the exchange of diplomatic notes between China and Japan in September 1918. As far as China's "Questions for Readjustment" were concerned, they were deemed important but beyond the scope of the conference. The ending of the war failed to solve the problems which had led to it—the breakdown of the nineteenth-century diplomacy of imperialism and the absence of a new world order to replace the old system.

The U.S. Senate, led by Republican senator Henry Cabot Lodge, declined to ratify the Treaty of Versailles; many lawmakers feared that the League of the Nations would restrict the United States from taking independent action in international matters. Intense disappointment and resentment toward Wilson was felt among the Chinese, the British, and the Japanese, for example, as well as at home, but for very different reasons. Paul S. Reinsch, American minister to China from 1913 to 1919 and strongly pro-China, was candidly critical of Wilson's compliance with Japan:

> President Wilson tried to make himself and others believe that with the acceptance of the Treaty and Convenant, the Shantung [Shandong] question would be solved through fulfillment by Japan of its promise "to restore Shantung Peninsula to China with full sovereignty," reserving only economic rights. This was his primary misconception. The ownership by a foreign government of a trunk railway reaching from a first-class port [Qingdao] to the heart of China could not be correctly termed an economic right.[22]

Reinsch rejected Wilson's fear that "Japanese delegates might follow the lead of the Italians and leave the Conference," and his belief that sacrifices must be made to accommodate them, as "unfounded." "I had seen indications enough, of which I had told the Government, that . . . She [Japan] would never forgo the first-class status bestowed by the arrangements of the Peace Conference." Chen Duxiu, who had earlier praised President Wilson as the savior of an unjust world (see above), denounced power politics in disillusionment on receiving the news from Paris. "Every country focuses on its own national rights. So much for universal principles, perpetual peace, President Wilson's Fourteen Points—they all became worthless, empty words!"[23] To some extent, the "Wilson blame" was engendered by Wilson's political enemies in the United States. The American failure to ratify the peace treaty largely reflected the considerable disagreement between and within the executive and legislative branches of the U.S. government. As was so often the case, what the American president had promised overseas or to foreign governments would not necessarily receive endorsement on the home front.

Back in China, when news of the Versailles decision reached Beijing, 3,000 students took to the streets on May 4, 1919—an anti-Japanese protest that rapidly turned into a nationwide campaign, the May 4th Movement, provoking a fiery outburst of anti-imperialist and nationalist agitation that continued well into the 1920s. Chinese leaders and elites continued to weigh the merits of different roads to national wealth and strength, and the Russian Bolshevik model of violent revolution was considered alongside American-style democracy and personal freedom.

## THE NATIONALIST REVOLUTION AND AMERICAN PATRONAGE

In the decade following the Paris Peace Conference, American-Chinese relations were dominated by Chinese domestic politics and Japan's ambitions in East Asia. America's recognition of the Nationalist government in Nanjing, led by Chiang Kai-shek, which replaced the Beijing government in 1928, symbolized the measured American involvement in China—now outstripping Britain and in competition with the Soviet Union and Japan. The alignment of the United States with one political party in particular, the Nationalist Party (Guomindang, GMD), has left an enduring legacy to this day.

China's grievances about its international position were again presented at the Washington Conference of 1921–22. The conference was intended to establish a new world order and constituted a meaningful step forward from the unpopular Versailles Treaty of 1919. Although it never joined the League of Nations created by its own president, and although many Americans wanted to avoid foreign entanglements and stay focused on domestic issues, the United States remained engaged and in fact increased its cooperation with many international agencies and conferences (including those run by the League). In 1921, for instance, President Warren G. Harding (presidency 1921–23) and Secretary of State (1921–25) Charles E. Hughes initiated an international conference calling on the major naval powers of Britain, France, Italy, and Japan, and other interested nations (Belgium, China, the Netherlands, and Portugal, but not the Soviet Union) to address the issues of multinational cooperation, arms reduction, and security issues in the Asia-Pacific region. At the Washington Conference on Naval Disarmament of 1921–22, two separate committees were formed—one the Committee on the Limitation of Armament, the other handling "Pacific and Far Eastern Questions." The conference produced a series of treaties and agreements that instituted the "Washington Conference system," the first international cooperative framework of its kind. The Four-Power Pact signed in 1921 dissolved the Anglo-Japanese alliance of 1902, committing the United States, Britain, Japan, and France to consultation in the case of any crisis in East Asia. Under the Five-Power Pact, the signatories agreed, for the first time in history, to reduce the tonnage of new battleships to a fixed ratio of 5 for the United States and Britain, 3 for Japan, and 1.67 for France and Italy. A mixture of war weariness, fears of another arms race, faltering economies, parsimonious electorates, constraints on military spending, and other factors led the three major players, the United States, Britain, and Japan, to accept this rebalancing of international power in a cooperative spirit.

Adopting an approach similar to their stance at the Paris Conference, the Chinese representatives at the Washington Conference, Sao-ke Alfred Sze, Wellington Koo, and Wang Chonghui, described the old treaty regime as unjust, imposed by the strong upon the weak. Sze presented a statement which set out ten general principles to be followed in determining questions relating to China—respect for its territorial integrity; removal of existing limitations on China's political, jurisdictional, and administrative freedoms; application of the Open Door policy to the whole of China; and the establishment of procedures for the peaceful settlement of international disputes in the Pacific and Far East regions.[24] On the other hand, the Chinese representatives offered to make the abolition of the existing treaty system conditional on assurances of political stability and juridical reform. Approving these principles in the Nine-Power Treaty signed in February 1922, the United States, Belgium, Britain, China, France, Italy, Japan, the Netherlands, and Portugal all agreed to support policies to "stabilize conditions in the Far East, to safeguard the rights and interests of China, and to promote intercourse between China and the other Powers upon the basis of equality of opportunity."[25]

This collective commitment to the peace and stability of the Asia-Pacific region came at a time when China was spiraling down into internal political disarray and military conflict. From the end of 1921 to 1922, the Beijing government had ten cabinets in office, the longest of which did not last more than three months, and the war between the military Zhili clique (led by Cao Kun) and the Fengtian group (headed by Zhang Zuolin) was still in progress. The issue of Chinese tariff autonomy was left for a future international meeting, the Special Conference on Tariffs, to resolve. China and Japan settled the Shandong dispute in Washington through the mediation of Charles Hughes and Arthur Balfour, the head of the British delegation. Japan agreed to return the former German-leased territory in Shandong Province that it had taken over during World War I.[26]

In October 1925, the Special Conference on Tariffs opened in Beijing, with the original nine powers at the Washington Conference and the four adhering powers of Denmark, Norway, Spain, and Sweden in attendance. The American delegation, in tune with their counterparts, recognized the principle that, as a sovereign state, China had the inherent right to tariff autonomy and that this should be embedded in a formal treaty.[27] Nevertheless, although tariff autonomy was a theoretical desideratum, China's internal divisions and anti-imperialist rhetoric hindered its realization. Hostilities between the warlord alliances of Wu Peifu and Zhang Zuolin, on the one hand, and Feng Yuxiang on the other escalated in the Beijing area. In a cable to the U.S. secretary of state, John MacMurray, American minister to China (1925–29), commented on the "unreal world" of the conference table:

> You cannot imagine the curious adaption of one's mind that is necessary, in order to discuss at one meeting [the Special Conference on Tariffs] the business of realizing for China its national aspirations toward tariff autonomy and unrestricted sovereignty, and ten minutes later having to discuss whether or not we should telegraph the latest phase of the military situation [in China] which seems to make it impossible that the administration with which we are dealing can continue for more than a few weeks or even a few days.[28]

In many ways a parallel to the politicization of the ratification of the Versailles Treaty in the United States, the unequal treaty issues came into focus at a time of intense anti-imperialist and pro-nationalist sentiment when many Chinese—long oppressed by foreign powers—sought ways to vent their anger. Ventures involving foreign countries or Chinese nationals working with foreigners were often the targets of large-scale outbursts of violence. In protest over America's collaboration with the Beijing government, Eugene Chen—the acting minister for foreign affairs of the Nationalist authority in Canton—charged that the American government was "moved to apply its 'evolutionary' policy to the revolutionary facts of the Chinese situation."[29] However, the rapid pace of developments within the nationalist camp during 1925–27 ultimately produced conciliation and cooperation between the United States and the National-ist regime founded in Nanjing in 1928.

Between 1924 and 1927, the GMD and the Chinese Communist Party, acting out of strategic mutual needs, forged the United Front alliance which agreed to pursue a twofold revolution—anti-warlordism (national unification) and anti-imperialism (abolition of the unequal treaties)—through class struggle and violent action. These developments were di-rectly linked to the activities of the radical Soviet Bolsheviks who had seized power in Russia in October 1917.[30]

Vladimir Lenin, the Soviet leader, urged that China liberate itself from the shackles of Western exploitation and become a part of the world Communist revolution. In order to achieve independence and freedom, semi-colonial and "backward" countries must "oust the imperialist pow-ers and smash their own ruling class which compromises with those powers."[31] For radicals of all stamps, Lenin's theories of a worldwide revolution, nationalist agitation, and the formation of united political fronts provided sound diagnoses of—and political solutions to—the problems facing China. In his eulogy of Lenin, Sun Yat-sen called him a "National Friend and People's Mentor."[32] In the words of Chiang Kai-shek, the appeal of the Soviet Bolsheviks to China, "where a sub-colonial state had resulted from a series of unequal treaties imposed upon her," lay in their promise of "a short cut to Utopia by a world revolution of the masses [against imperialism and capitalism]."[33]

Guided by Soviet Russia and its ideologically based tactics, the Chi-nese nationalist revolution found its full expression in mass mobilization. To further its own interests and stimulate revolution overseas, Soviet Russia and the Comintern—the Communist International, 1919–43, led by the Soviet Union—dispatched young cadres to make contact with and finance various political groups in China, including the CCP, Sun Yat-sen's Nationalist Party, the Feng Yuxiang army, and the Beijing govern-ment. Comintern advisors, such as Hendricus Sneevliet (known under the pseudonym Maring) and Michael Borodin, offered political, financial, and military support to Sun Yat-sen and his Canton military government, which was embroiled with other military forces in South China.

At the same time, the Russians proposed that the minuscule CCP (which had only 432 members in 1923 and was far outnumbered by the GMD, which allegedly had over 200,000 members) should ally itself to the GMD without relinquishing its own separate membership. Thus the reorganized GMD brought peasants and laborers into the nationalist revolution. The Bolshevik advisors' chief contribution to the Chinese Nationalist Party was to teach GMD politicians how to secure mass support.[34] The Communist members of the GMD began to propagandize actively among the peasantry in the countryside. Mao Zedong, later to become the CCP's leader, was the head of the party's Propaganda Bureau. In July 1926, Guomindang and Communist forces launched their joint Northern Expedition, declaring their intent to eliminate the warlords in North China and to do away with the unequal treaties as soon as possible, in studied opposition to the Beijing government's policy of gradualism and diplomacy. The GMD-CCP coalition—the United Front—was strained and precarious at best. The radical (i.e., GMD leftists, Communists, and Borodin's clique against Chiang Kai-shek) and conservative (GMD rightists, Chiang's faction) wings of the nationalist revolution clashed over issues of power and control, military strategy, and the use of violent labor organizations to seize foreign concessions in Wuhan and Shanghai. In April 1927, Chiang and his supporters, notably the underworld Green Gang, carried out a bloody purge of labor activists and Communists in Shanghai—an event that turned the CCP into a fugitive party.

Having disposed of the GMD-CCP alliance, Chiang continued military unification, and at the end of 1928, Manchurian warlord Zhang Xueliang pledged allegiance to the Nationalist regime. The unequal treaties issue was central to the agenda of the new Chiang government inaugurated in Nanjing in April 1927. Beginning in mid-1927, Chiang reversed his anti-negotiation, anti-revision, and anti-gradualist stance to one of negotiation and cooperation with the powers, especially the United States, Britain, and Japan, on the issues of tariff autonomy and abolition of the unequal treaties—a policy pursued by the Beijing government that had been derided by the GMD only a short time before. Chiang's change of approach to foreign powers indicated that he was now willing to pursue a more "moderate" course than his Communist rivals.

Along with his other strategic moves toward Japan and the United States, Chiang's handling of the "Nanjing Incident" indicated that he was the Chinese leader the United States could work with best. On March 24, 1927, Nationalist troops entered Nanjing. Foreign consulates and residences were attacked in the accompanying looting allegedly committed by retreating Shandong and Zhili warlord soldiers. Three Britons and one resident each of American, French, Italian, and Japanese citizenship were killed. In retaliation, the British and American naval ships *Noa* and *Preston* shelled Nationalist soldiers attempting to storm the Standard Oil compound where over fifty British and Americans were sheltering. Exploiting his diplomatic links, especially with Japan, Chiang Kai-shek convinced Frank B. Kellogg, secretary of state (1925–29) under President Calvin Coolidge (presidency 1923–29), that he "was strongly opposed to these outrages . . . and that he [Chiang] believed that the outrages at Nanking [Nanjing] were caused by the radicals among the Cantonese who were trying to discredit Chiang Kai-shek."[35] John MacMurray's proposal to threaten the Nanjing regime with sanctions was met with disapproval by Kellogg: "It would weaken the moderate leaders if demands were pressed at this time and would perhaps drive them to the side of the extremists. . . . We should not be hurried into action . . . which may not be effective in any event, as it is doubtful whether the Kuomintang [Guomindang] leaders could, divided as they are, meet the demands even if they were disposed to do so."[36] Anxious to settle the matter, the Nanjing government accepted full responsibility for the incident, expressed its profound regret, and offered compensation for injuries and property damages incurred by foreign residents. By the end of 1927, the U.S. government had accepted the settlement and also made it clear that it would be prepared to take up the question of treaty revision.

In a statement made on June 15, 1928, the Nanjing government announced that China was at last unified and that the civil wars were over. The time was ripe for taking immediate steps "in accordance with legitimate and diplomatic procedures, to negotiate new treaties with friendly countries on the basis of equality and mutual respect."[37] The United States was the first to proceed with a new treaty. On June 11, having still not formally recognized the new government, Frank Kellogg agreed to discuss the question of tariffs with Wu Chaoshu, the GMD minister to Washington. Shortly afterward, Kellogg pressed MacMurray to commence negotiations with the Nationalist authorities for revision of the tariff provisions in treaties between the United States and China: "Undoubtedly we are now in *de facto* relationship with the Nanking Government and negotiating with them for a treaty would at least be recognition of that status."[38] After a few days of meetings between MacMurray and T. V. Soong, the finance minister of the Nanjing government, a new treaty was agreed on July 25, 1928. It contained two articles only, virtual recognition of the Nanjing regime as the sole government of China accorded by the United States. The United States recognized China's right of tariff autonomy on condition that it would continue to enjoy most-favored-nation status (guaranteeing America the same treatment accorded to other countries by China). Eleven nations followed suit with similar treaties; they included Germany (August 1928), Norway (November 1928), the Netherlands (November 1928), Sweden (December 1928), Britain (December 1928), France (December 1928), and Japan (May 1930). The question of the relinquishment of extraterritorial rights was left unsettled until 1943.

## CONCLUSION

As the 1920s drew to a close, U.S.-Chinese relations had weathered the storms of revolution, nationalism, anti-imperialism, and regime change. The collapse of the dynastic system in 1912 and the introduction of a new form of government ushered in two decades of political fluidity and instability in China that nevertheless offered opportunities for new international contacts and alliances. Limited American patronage was obtained by both the Beijing and Nanjing governments, which set their respective sights on improving China's international position, especially in relation to the cancellation of the "old" treaty rights and privileges in China granted to foreign powers. In this, the Beijing and Nanjing governments enjoyed a measure of success. In both the United States and China, administrations sought less confrontational pathways within new domestic and international environments. Representing a country politically divided and militarily and economically disadvantaged, the diplomats of the Beijing government continued to lay China's grievances before international conferences and organizations, notably the Paris Peace Conference, the Washington Conference, and the Special Tariff Conference. Their commitment to legal gradualism—at odds with the violent radicalism of the Chinese Communist Party and the Nationalist Party—emphasized collaboration with the United States and other contractual powers. Although the regime change in China brought about in 1928 by Chiang Kai-shek—newly married to Madame Soong Mayling, a Methodist and a Wellesley graduate—fell in America's favor, Chiang was not swayed by the U.S. model of democratic governance. Despite his heavy-handedness in foreign relations, Chiang appointed many of the former Beijing government's key diplomats such as Wellington Koo, Chonghui Wang, W. W. Yen, and Sao-ke Alfred Sze, who all had American ties. To some degree, these appointments suggest that the new regime was keen to make friendly overtures to the United States.

In keeping with its increased but measured involvement in Chinese and world affairs, the United States assumed a cautious, independent role in cooperating with other countries to reduce international conflicts and "keep China from becoming a hostile agent of Soviet Russia against western powers, including the United States."[39] In response to the growing nationalist movement and Russian and Japanese influence in China, the United States outflanked other interested parties by being the first to sign a treaty with China in 1928 granting China tariff autonomy, an important step appreciated by the Nanjing authorities. This strategic move laid the foundations—legal, attitudinal, and cultural—for the friendly relationship between the United States and Nationalist China in the years ahead.

## FURTHER READING

Dorothy Borg's *American Policy and the Chinese Revolution, 1925–1928* (New York: Macmillan, 1947) is a classic study of U.S. policy toward China in the age of revolution and nationalism; Shinkichi Etō's chapter, "China's International Relations 1911–1931," in *The Cambridge History of China*, vol. 13, part 2, ed. John King Fairbank and Albert Feuerwerker (Cambridge: Cambridge University Press, 1986), pp. 74–115, focuses on major diplomatic events and developments, particularly Japan's and the Soviet Union's influence in a divided China from the fall of the Qing to the Nationalist revolution; Akira Iriye's chapter—"Japanese Aggression and China's International Position 1931–1949"—in the volume above (pp. 492–546), delineates Japan's rise, the collapse of international cooperation, and power configurations in the Sino-Japanese and Pacific Wars. William C. Kirby's *Germany and Republican China* (Stanford, Calif.: Stanford University Press, 1984) is a rich study of the political, military, economic, and ideological interaction between Germany and Republican China from 1927 to 1937. Kirby suggests that substantial economic ties, military planning, national reconstruction, and Chinese admiration for the German way of life and governance contributed to an equal partnership between the two countries. *The Generalissimo: Chiang Kai-shek and the Struggle for Modern China* (Cambridge, Mass.: Belknap Press, 2009) by Jay

Taylor offers an absorbing account of Chiang Kai-shek and Republican China's international relations.

For different viewpoints on Wilsonianism, China, and World War I, see Russell H. Fifield, *Woodrow Wilson and the Far East: The Diplomacy of the Shantung Question* (New York: Crowell, 1952); George W. Egerton, "Britain and the 'Great Betrayal': Anglo-American Relations and the Struggle for United States Ratification of the Treaty of Versailles, 1919–1920," *Historical Journal* 21, no. 4 (December 1978): 885–911; David Steigerwald, "The Reclamation of Woodrow Wilson," *Diplomatic History* 23, no. 1 (Winter 1999): 79–99; Bruce A. Elleman, *Wilson and China: A Revised History of the Shandong Question* (Armonk, N.Y.: M. E. Sharpe, 2002); and Guoqi Xu, *China and the Great War: China's Pursuit of a New National Identity and Internationalization* (New York: Cambridge University Press, 2005). A widely consulted book on the May 4th Movement is Tse-tsung Chow's *The May Fourth Movement: Intellectual Revolution in Modern China* (Cambridge, Mass.: Harvard University Press, 1960).

On the Washington Conference, as well as the bilateral relationship in the 1920s, see chapters by Harumi Goto-Shibata and Joseph A. Maiolo in Antony Best, ed., *The International History of East Asia, 1900–1968: Trade, Ideology and the Quest for Order* (London: Routledge, 2010), pp. 57–80; Rodger Dingman, *Power in the Pacific: The Origins of Naval Arms Control* (Chicago, Ill.: University of Chicago Press, 1976); Erik Goldstein and John H. Maurer, *The Washington Conference, 1921–22: Naval Rivalry, East Asian Stability and the Road to Pearl Harbor* (London: Frank Cass, 1994); and Akira Iriye, *After Imperialism: The Search for a New Order in the Far East, 1921–1931*, reprint (Chicago, Ill.: Imprint Publications, 1990; 1st ed. in 1965 by Harvard University Press).

## NOTES

1. Hans Schmidt, "Democracy for China: American Propaganda and the May Fourth Movement," *Diplomatic History* 22, no. 1 (December 1998): 1–28.

2. Zhongguo renmin zhengzhi xieshang huiyi quanguo weiyuanhui wenshi ziliao weiuanhui [中国人民政治协商会议全国委员会文史资料委员会], ed., *Xinhai geming qinli ji* [辛亥革命亲历记 Firsthand accounts of the 1911 Revolution] (Beijing: Zhongguo wenshi chubanshe, 2001); James E. Sheridan, *China in Disintegration: The Republican Era in Chinese History, 1912–1949* (New York: Free Press, 1975); Hsi-sheng Ch'i, *Warlord Politics in China, 1916–1928* (Stanford, Calif.: Stanford University Press, 1976); Edward McCord, *The Power of the Gun: The Emergence of Modern Chinese Warlords* (Berkeley,

Calif.: University of California Press, 1993); Peter Zarrow, *China in War and Revolution 1895–1949* (London: Routledge, 2005), chapters 2–4.

3. After a rapid rise to power, Yuan became indispensable to the Qing court. In 1901 he succeeded the powerful Li Hongzhang as viceroy of Zhili, a crucial post in north China at the time. From 1903, Yuan presided over the formation of a modern Chinese army, which reinforced his position in the Qing regime. Ernest P. Young, *The Presidency of Yuan Shih-k'ai* (Ann Arbor, Mich.: University of Michigan Press, 1977).

4. See William J. Calhoun's various telegrams to the Department of State between November 1911 and January 1912, *Records of the Department of State Relating to International Affairs of China, 1910–1929*, microfilm no. 329, roll 7, 893.00 Political Affairs, vols. 1–2, 893.00/351 1/2-633, National Archives.

5. In the late nineteenth century, the Manchus—as ruling, non-Han Chinese ethnic minorities—were fervently blamed for all the illnesses of China where the majority of the population were Han Chinese. According to Sun's revolutionary platform, the first revolutionary stage would be a military dictatorship, which would be followed by a period of single-party rule, or "political tutelage," and eventually by the introduction of democracy.

6. Wang Qisheng (王奇生), *Geming yu fan geming: Shehui wenhua shiye xia de Minguo zhengzhi* [革命与反革命:社会文化视野下的民国政治 Revolution and counterrevolution: Politics in the first Republic of China from the viewpoint of society and culture] (Beijing: Shehui kexue wenxian chubanshe, 2010); Chen Yung-fa (陈永发), *Zhongguo gongchan geming qishinian* [中国共产革命七十年 The seventy years of the Chinese Communist revolution], revised ed. (Taipei: Lianjing, 2001), chapter 1; Yang Kuisong (杨奎松), *Zhonggong yu Mosike de guanxi (1920–1960)* [中共与莫斯科的关系 The Chinese Communist Party's relations with Moscow] (Hong Kong: Haixiao chuban shiye youxian gongsi, 1997).

7. Douglas Steeple and David O. Whitten, *Democracy in Desperation: The Depression of 1893* (Westport, Conn.: Greenwood Press, 1998); Michael McGerr, *A Fierce Discontent: The Rise and Fall of the Progressive Movement in America, 1870–1920* (New York: Free Press, 2003); David A. Moss, *When All Else Fails: Government as the Ultimate Risk Manager* (Cambridge, Mass.: Harvard University Press, 2002); Shelton Stromquist, *Re-inventing "The People": The Progressive Movement, the Class Problem, and the Origins of Modern Liberalism* (Champaign, Ill.: University of Illinois Press, 2006).

8. While in the United States, Sun Yat-sen requested a secret meeting with Philander C. Knox, secretary of state (1909–13), in Washington but was met with a firm refusal.

9. The American chargé d'affaires (E. T. Williams) to the secretary of state, March 18, 1913, in U.S. Department of State, *Papers Relating to the Foreign Relations of the United States with the Address of the President to Congress December 2, 1913* [*FRUS* hereafter] (Washington, D.C.: Government Printing Office, 1913), p. 98. Tao Wenzhao, "The United States and the Chinese Revolution," in Priscilla Roberts, ed., *Sino-American Relations since 1900* (Hong Kong: Centre of Asian Studies, University of Hong Kong Press, 1991), pp. 205–219.

10. The American chargé d'affaires (E. T. Williams) to the secretary of state, March 18, 1913, in *FRUS, 1913*, pp. 96–98, 116–118.

11. Yuan Shih-K'ai, "The Chinese Republic Reports Progress," *The Independent*, July 26, 1915.

12. Yuan Shih-K'ai, "The Chinese Republic Reports Progress."

13. U.S. Department of State, *Papers Relating to the Foreign Relations of the United States: The Lansing Papers, 1914–1920* (Washington, D.C.: Government Printing Office, 1939), vol. 1, p. 3.

14. Walter A. McDougall, *Promised Land, Crusader State* (Boston, Mass.: Houghton Mifflin, 1997); Robert A. Pastor, ed., *A Century's Journey: How the Great Powers Shape the World* (New York: Basic Books, 1999).

15. Woodrow Wilson, "Annapolis Commencement," June 5, 1914, http://www.presidency.ucsb.edu/ws/?pid=65380 (accessed November 28, 2010).

16. Woodrow Wilson, "Address to a Joint Session of Congress on the Conditions of Peace," January 8, 1918, http://www.presidency.ucsb.edu/ws/?pid=65405 (accessed November 28, 2010). David Steigerwald, *Wilsonian Idealism in America* (Ithaca, N.Y.: Cornell University Press, 1994); Erez Manela, *The Wilsonian Moment: Self-Determination and the International Origins of Anticolonial Nationalism* (Oxford: Oxford University Press, 2007).

17. George Creel, *How We Advertised America: The First Telling of the Amazing Story of the Committee on Public Information That Carried the Gospel of Americanism to Every Corner of the Globe* (New York: Harper & Brothers, 1920).

18. Zhi Yan (Chen Duxiu's alias), *Meizhou pinglun*, no. 1 (December 22, 1918), foreword to the first issue.

19. Wellington Koo, The Wellington Koo Memoir, the Chinese Oral History Project, part II, microfilm reel 1, "The Paris Conference."

20. Paul S. Reinsch to secretary of state, May 30, 1917, file no. 893.00/2579; June 2, 1917, file no. 893.00/2581, *Records of the Department of State Relating to International Affairs of China, 1910–1929*, microfilm no. 329.

21. Margaret MacMillan, *Paris 1919: Six Months That Changed the World* (New York: Random House, 2002), chapter 24. The dispute over Shandong grew directly out of the European war. Shortly after the outbreak of World War I, the Beijing government proclaimed its neutrality on August 14, 1914. Two weeks afterward, Japan informed the Chinese government that Japan had gone to war with Germany and demanded the withdrawal of German forces and equipment from Chinese and Japanese waters and the handover, no later than September 15, of the entire leased territory of Jiaozhou to the Japanese government. In early September 1914, about 20,000 Japanese troops landed at Longkou, a port 150 miles north of Qingdao. By the end of September, the Japanese forces had occupied Jiaozhou Bay and Qingdao.

22. Paul S. Reinsch, *An American Diplomat in China* (Garden City, N.Y.: Doubleday, Page & Comp., 1922), Part IV.

23. Chen Duxiu, "Liangge hehui dou wuyong" [两个和会都无用 The two peace conferences have proved equally useless], *Meizhou pinglun*, no. 20 (May 4, 1919).

24. Zhongguo shehuikexueyuan jindaishisuo (中国社会科学院近代史所), comp. and ed., *Miji lucun* [秘笈录存 Compilation of telegrams between the Beijing government and the Chinese delegates at the Paris Peace Conference and Washington Conference] (Beijing: Zhongguo shehui kexue chubanshe, 1984); Wang Yunsheng (王芸生), *Liushi nianlai Zhongguo yu Riben* [六十年来中国与日本 China and Japan over the past sixty years] (Beijing: Sanlian chubanshe, 1981), vols. 6 and 7; Beijing zhengfu waijiaobu (北京政府外交部), *Waijiao wendu: Huashengdun huiyi an* [外交文牍:华盛顿会议案 Diplomatic correspondence: The Washington Conference] (Beijing: Waijiaobu, 1923).

25. Treaty between the United States of America, the British Empire, China, France, Italy, Japan, the Netherlands, and Portugal, http://avalon.law.yale.edu/20th_century/tr22-01.asp (accessed December 1, 2010).

26. Sadao Asada, "Japan's Special Interests and the Washington Conference, 1921–1922," *American Historical Review* 67, no. 1 (October 1961): 62–70.

27. Yi Ming (佚名), ed., *Guanshui tebie huiyi yishi lu* [关税特别会议议事录 Proceedings of the Special Conference on Tariffs], reprint (Taipei: Wenhai chubanshe, 1970); Stanley F. Wright, *China's Struggle for Tariff Autonomy: 1843–1938* (Shanghai: Kelly & Walsh, 1938).

28. John MacMurray's telegram to the U.S. secretary of state on August 1, 1925, *Records of the Department of State Relating to Political Relations between China and other States, 1910–1929*, no. 793.00/114, microfilm no. 341, roll 1, National Archives.

29. Henry George W. Woodhead, ed., *The China Year Book, 1926–1927* (Tianjin: Tientsin Press, 1928–29), p. 1146.

30. Dong Wang, "Redeeming 'A Century of National Ignominy': Nationalism and Party Rivalry over the Unequal Treaties, 1928–1947," *Twentieth-Century China* 30, no. 2 (April 2005): 72–100; Dong Wang, "The Discourse of Unequal Treaties in Modern China," *Pacific Affairs* 76, no. 3 (November 2003): 399–425. To counter the Russian Bolshevik Revolution, the United States cooperated with British, French, and Japanese forces in an anti-Bolshevik campaign in Russia. Wilson dispatched two American expeditions totaling some 15,000 troops to Russia to stem the growth of Bolshevism, but without success. Victor M. Fic, *The Collapse of American Policy in Russia and Siberia, 1918* (New York: Columbia University Press, 1995); Donald E. Davis and Eugene P. Trani, *The First Cold War: The Legacy of Woodrow Wilson in U.S.-Soviet Relations* (Columbia, Mo.: University of Missouri Press, 2002).

31. Zhongguo shehui kexueyuan (中国社会科学院), transl., *Gongchan guoji youguan zhongguo geming de wenxian, 1919–1928* [共产国际有关中国革命的文献, 1919–1928 The Comintern documents on the Chinese revolution] (Beijing: Zhongguo shehuikexue chubanshe, 1980), vol. 1, pp. 15–32.

32. Guangdong shehui kexueyuan et al., eds., *Sun Zhongshan quanji* [孙中山全集 Collected works of Sun Zhongshan] (Beijing: Zhonghua shuju, 1986), vol. 9, p. 509.

33. Chiang Kai-shek, *Soviet Russia in China: A Summing-up at Seventy* (New York: Farrar, Straus & Cudahy, 1957), p. 5.

34. For Soviet relations with China during the 1920s, see Huang Xiurong (黄修荣), *Gongchan guoji he Zhongguo geming guanxishi* [共产国际和中国革命关系史 The history of the Comintern and the Chinese revolution], 2 vols. (Beijing: Zhonggong zhongyang dangxiao chubanshe, 1989); Yang Yunruo (杨云若) and Yang Kuisong (杨奎松), *Gongchan guoji he Zhongguo geming* [共产国际和中国革命 Comintern and the Chinese revolution] (Shanghai: Shanghai renmin chubanshe, 1988); C. Martin Wilbur, *The Nationalist Revolution in China, 1923–1928* (Cambridge: Cambridge University Press, 1984); C. Martin Wilbur and Julie Lien-ying How, *Missionaries of Revolution: Soviet Advisers and Nationalist China, 1920–1927* (Cambridge, Mass.: Harvard University Press, 1989); Daniel N. Jacobs, *Borodin: Stalin's Man in China* (Cambridge, Mass.: Harvard University Press, 1981); Alexander Pantsov, *The Bolsheviks and the Chinese Revolution, 1919–1927* (Honolulu, Hawaii: University of Hawaii Press, 2000).

35. Telegram from Charles MacVeagh, American ambassador to Japan, to John MacMurray on March 28, 1927, in *FRUS, 1927*, vol. 2, p. 164.

36. Telegraph from Frank Kellogg to John MacMurray on April 20, 1927, in *FRUS, 1927*, vol. 2, pp. 203–204.

37. "Guomin zhengfu feichu jiuyue xuanyan" [国民政府废除旧约宣言 The Nationalist government's manifesto on the nullification of treaties], Di'er lishi dang'anguan (第二历史档案馆), comp., *Zhonghua minguoshi dang'an ziliao huibian* [中华民国史档案资

料汇编 Collected archival sources on the history of the Republic of China] (Nanjing: Jiangsu guji chubanshe, 1991), vol. 5, part 1, waijiao, pp. 33–34.

38. Frank Kellogg's telegram to John MacMurray, June 23, 1928, no. 711.933/13, National Archives, *Records of the Department of State Relating to Political Relations between China and Other States, 1910–1929*, microfilm no. 339, roll 1.

39. John MacMurray's telegram to Frank Kellogg on March 29, 1927, in *FRUS, 1927*, vol. 2, pp. 167–168.

# SIX

# The Pacific War and Red China

Two overarching changes in the geopolitical climate shaped American-Chinese relations in the 1930s and 1940s. The first was the ascendency of Japan which was challenged by the rise of Chinese nationalism. In 1931, the Japanese military conducted a coup in Manchuria, northeast China, leading to the establishment of the Japanese puppet state of Manchukuo and mounting tensions between the United States and Japan, the two competing imperial powers in the region. The outbreak of the Second Sino-Japanese War in 1937, which the United States watched with concern but refused to join, paved the way for the Pacific War. The Japanese attack on Pearl Harbor in 1941 sealed the alliance between the United States and China. The fall of Japan in 1945 compounded the nationalist movement and the Cold War in Asia. The second significant change was the success of the Chinese Communist Party (CCP) under Mao Zedong. Although the United States sided with the Guomindang (GMD, the Nationalist Party) government against the CCP, the Japanese invasion of China opened the door for Mao's Communists to eventually take power by appealing to nationalism and encouraging social revolution.

Some previous studies have approached America's "loss of China" to the Communists by focusing on American attitudes and policies and debating who was to blame, without taking into account the limited alternatives available at the time and the lessons learned by each side. While helpful up to a point, the traditional approach downplays the positive achievements of this period, such as the unprecedented cooperation between Nationalist China and the United States on the diplomatic, eco-

145

nomic, military, and cultural levels. While these decades reveal the roots of the conflict that divided the United States and the People's Republic of China after 1949, when viewed in a long-term perspective they also indicate that their embattled relationship drew them closer together.[1]

## THE MANCHURIAN INCIDENT, THE PACIFIC WAR, AND THE SINO-AMERICAN ALLIANCE

*The Geopolitical Clash between Japan and the United States and Attempts at Reconciliation*

Suspicion of Japan's political penetration of China was a constant element in American strategic thinking in the early twentieth century. U.S.-Japanese relations in the East Asian region were largely determined by a tangled web of cooperation and conflict surrounding China.[2] The United States and Japan were competitors for China's intellectual and economic resources, and vested interests were at stake. For instance, in 1922, China had over half a billion dollars of debt either unsecured or inadequately secured—the two nations most affected by China's "virtual bankruptcy" were Japan and the United States.[3] The direct tensions between the United States and Japan, on the other hand, were concentrated on two issues: Would Japan extend its Manchurian "enterprise" to other parts of China? And would the United States acquiesce in Japan's dominance in China and accept Japan as the hegemon in the Asia-Pacific?[4]

Japan's aggressive behavior in East Asia originated in a number of factors, operating both inside and outside the region. Within a single generation, efforts at modernization undertaken during the reign of Emperor Meiji (1868–1912) had transformed Japan into the only industrialized nation in Asia—a superpower in today's terms. The independence from China of neighboring Korea, Taiwan, Manchuria, and Mongolia was considered essential to Japan's national security—the rationale argued by Japan for the Russo-Japanese War of 1905 and the Sino-Japanese War of 1937–45. Japan was also smarting at the failures of the Western powers to treat it as an equal on issues important to Japan, a slight summed up by the omission of a racial equality clause in the Paris peace settlement following World War I. Both the Japanese army and navy felt frustrated by international treaties that they considered left them at a disadvantage and by the conciliatory noninterference policy of their foreign minister, Shidehara Kijūrō (1924–27, 1929–31), toward China and the Soviet Union. In the United States, overt discrimination against Japanese and other Asians, such as checks on immigration and naturalization, the prohibition of landholding, racial segregation in schools, and personal violence against Japanese in California, also fostered resentment. In America, anti-Asian immigration sentiment culminated in the Immigration Act of 1924 which denied Asians the right to enter the United States and become citizens.

From America's perspective, Japan's territorial ambitions lay at the root of the troubled relations between the two nations. However, the Roosevelt (1901–9) and Taft (1909–13) administrations at times favored Japan over China, resulting in several attempts at formal reconciliation. In November 1908, Takahira Kogorō, Japanese ambassador to the United States, exchanged a series of notes—known as the Root-Takahira Agreement—with Secretary of State Elihu Root (1905–9). Both sides agreed to respect the other's sphere of influence in the Asia-Pacific, especially with regard to China:

> The policy of both governments, uninfluenced by any aggressive tendencies, is directed to the maintenance of the existing *status quo* in the region above mentioned and to the defense of the principle of equal opportunity for commerce and industry in China. . . . They are accordingly firmly resolved reciprocally to respect the territorial possessions belonging to each other in said region. . . . They are also determined to preserve the common interests of all powers in China by supporting by all pacific means at their disposal the independence and integrity of China and the principles of equal opportunity for commerce and industry of all nations in that Empire.[5]

The undefined nature of the "status quo" in the Pacific in the Root-Takahira Agreement was further obscured in the Lansing-Ishii Agreement concluded by Robert Lansing, President Woodrow Wilson's secretary of state (1915–20), and Ishii Kikujirō, ambassador extraordinary and plenipotentiary of Japan on special mission, on November 2, 1917, in Washington. Touted at the time by some as the "augury for the peace of the world," this agreement was full of ambiguous and contradictory terms, for which Japan and the United States had their own separate interpretations.[6] On the one hand, the United States recognized that Japan had "special interests in China," particularly in Manchuria. On the other hand, both countries declared that they would always "adhere to the principle of the so-called 'open door' or equal opportunity for commerce and industry in China." However, Japan's belief that "the survival of the Japanese Empire, and ultimately of the Japanese people, depended on their special interests in Manchuria and Mongolia" was as firm as ever. The United States later discovered that many Japanese understood "equal opportunity" to mean throwing open China's resources for exploitation by Japan alone, rather than being shared among all the national interests in China—in contradiction to America's understanding of the same phrase. The dissolution of the Anglo-Japanese alliance, Japan's adherence to the 1922 Nine-Power Treaty, and its participation in the League of Nations and other international organizations were also conditional on respect for Japan's larger interests, particularly in Manchuria and Inner Mongolia.[7]

## *Japanese Aggression in China and the Sino-American Alliance*

At the end of the 1920s, there was a widespread belief in Japan that the nation's security depended on two key measures: countering the Russian threat and mitigating Japan's economic difficulties. As a result of the Great Depression, Japanese exports to the United States and China dropped between 40 and 50 percent in 1929–30. The world economic cataclysm shook Japan's confidence in the Western powers and the collective commitment to regional stability established by the Washington Conference system. Economic turmoil exacerbated domestic unrest and violence directed against politicians and industrialists in Japan. Manchuria was linked to the survival of Japan. The Japanese army became apprehensive over an upsurge in Chinese nationalism as Nationalist leader Chiang Kai-shek embarked on unifying China and gained the allegiance of Zhang Xueliang, a powerful Manchurian warlord.

At home, jingoism and militarism worked together to undermine Japan's civilian government. The agenda was set by the Japanese Kwantung Army stationed in south Manchuria, which constantly ratcheted up expectations that the civilian government was powerless to quash. The upshot of this agitation was the Mukden Incident, the result of a plot hatched by Ishiwara Kanji and Itagaki Seishirō, two officers of the Kwantung Army. On the night of September 18, 1931, Japanese soldiers blew up a section of the line in the South Manchurian Railway zone near Liutiaohu Village north of Mukden, a trophy from the 1905 Russo-Japanese War controlled by the Kwantung Army. Nelson T. Johnson,

American minister to China (1929–41), reported that at 10 p.m. that night, "a squad of Japanese soldiers, having left Japanese barracks and gone southeast of Mukden City, were firing with rifles at the east camp, arsenal and city and with artillery at the rate of one shell a minute. . . . Japanese soldiers had apparently run amuck, Japanese consular authorities being powerless."[8] Despite lacking approval from its own government, the Japanese army used this incident to create a pretext for military operations. By the end of 1931, Japanese troops had completed the occupation of South Manchuria and in March 1932 established the territory of Manchukuo, a self-proclaimed independent state lying outside Chinese sovereignty. On May 15, 1932, Japanese prime minister and foreign minister Inukai Tsuyoshi, the moderate successor to Shidehara Kijūrō who was viewed by the radical faction as "soft" on China, was assassinated by chauvinistic nationalists for his attempts to curb the growing power of the army. Following this outrage, Japan's civilian leadership eventually succumbed to the militarists.[9]

Two days after the Mukden Incident, Chiang Kai-shek's Nationalist government—preoccupied with extermination campaigns against the Chinese Communists and thus largely ineffectual against the Japanese invaders—lodged a complaint against Japan with the League of Nations, seeking intervention. The response of the United States was cautious and noncommittal, leaving China and the League of Nations holding the baby[10]: the United States referred the matter back to the League while maintaining its neutrality and a posture of nonrecognition of Japan's annexation of the territory. In early January 1932, Henry L. Stimson, secretary of state (1929–33) under President Herbert C. Hoover (1929–33), offered the Chinese minister "our entire sympathy with the general objective of the League, while not running any risk of crossing wires with their work."[11] At the same time, concerned by Japan's intensified military operations in China, Stimson sent a diplomatic note to all governments with interests in Manchuria, confirming, "The American Government continues confident that the work of the neutral commission recently authorized by the Council of the League of Nations will facilitate an ultimate solution of the difficulties now existing between China and Japan." In stronger terms, the United States declared that it

> cannot admit the legality of any situation *de facto* nor does it intend to recognize any treaty or agreement entered into between those Governments, or agents thereof, which may impair the treaty rights of the

United States or its citizens in China, including those which relate to the sovereignty, the independence, or the territorial and administrative integrity of the Republic of China, or to the international policy relative to China, commonly known as the open door policy.[12]

In October 1931 a draft resolution of the League of Nations called on Japan to withdraw its forces to the South Manchurian Railway zone and for China to make arrangements for taking back the territory. In defiance of the League's call, the Japanese advanced on Shanghai on January 28, 1932. Despite the League's prevarication in appointing a commission—headed by the Earl of Lytton—to investigate the dispute (in which the United States and Russia refused to participate), the resulting Lytton Report found that the Japanese military actions during and after the "Mukden Incident" of 1931 had not been taken in self-defense and that the creation of Manchukuo—a Japanese puppet state—did not reflect a genuine movement for independence. However, the report satisfied neither China nor Japan. The Japanese (Matsuoka Yosuke) and Chinese representatives (Wellington Koo) on the League each defended their own positions. In February 1933, the international body approved the Lytton Report, declaring nonrecognition of Manchukuo and condemning Japanese military operations, but without imposing sanctions or taking action against Japan. In protest, Japan withdrew from the League. On the other side, Chiang Kai-shek's hopes for the intervention of the Western powers in halting Japan's hegemonic ambitions received a major check. The Hoover-Stimson approach involving a collective solution to the Sino-Japanese conflict failed to work. This policy direction was virtually abandoned during the rest of the decade under the presidency of Franklin Roosevelt (1933–45), although in April 1934, Secretary of State Cordell Hull (1933–44) issued a vague, timid statement asserting that relations between the three powers were still governed by multilateral treaties and obligations in force since the Washington Conference of 1921–22.

After Manchuria, Japan slipped gradually into the quagmire of a war in China that was neither anticipated nor rationally planned, nor indeed winnable. In the three years between 1933 and 1936, Japan sent its forces south and west, taking control of China's Rehe Province and Eastern Chahar in Inner Mongolia and demanding the independence of five provinces (Hebei, Shandong, Shanxi, Chahar, and Suiyuan) in north China from the Nationalist government. Japanese aggression provoked fervent anti-Japanese boycotts, demonstrations, and strikes in Shanghai,

Beijing, and other cities. Domestic pressure and external threats drew Chiang into a series of responses that fluctuated between negotiation, resistance to Japan, and suppression of internal opposition. The Tanggu Truce of 1933 and the He Yingqin-Umezu Yoshijirō Agreement of 1935 between China and Japan gave de facto recognition to Manchukuo and Japan's control of parts of north China.[13] These agreements were met with violent outrage from the masses toward Japan and the Nationalist government.

Chiang's attempts at appeasement could only buy off the Japanese temporarily. On July 7, 1937, another clash—the Marco Polo Bridge Incident—touched off a full-scale conflict, the Sino-Japanese War, known to the Chinese as the War of Resistance (1937–45).[14] On December 13, 1937, Japanese forces overran Nanjing, the Chinese capital, forcing the Nationalist government to relocate to Chongqing. In Nanjing, Japanese soldiers indiscriminately slaughtered tens of thousands of Chinese civilians, an atrocity known to history as the Nanjing Massacre.

By the end of 1938, however, even the fall of major cities such as Nanjing, Wuhan, and Canton, and Japanese control of the railway network, had failed to force Chiang to surrender or to bring the war to a speedy end, as Japan assumed would happen. Rather, Japan had become mired in a war ranging over vast land areas that it had no ability to exit. Despite this, some historians have criticized China for its alleged limited military response to Japanese aggression. Some downplay the fact that Chinese forces pinned down a million Japanese troops and argue that Japan was defeated only because of American intervention. Others have argued that, since the primary aim of both Chiang Kai-shek and Communist leader Mao Zedong was to eliminate the other, both were at pains to keep their best forces away from the Japanese army.[15]

For its part, the United States did not approve Japan's attempts to establish the Greater East Asian Co-prosperity Sphere, a new Asia-Pacific order, in violation of the Open Door principle, but neither did it take effective steps to deter it throughout the 1930s. Roosevelt's first administration allowed circumstances and unfolding events to determine the course of American action and reaction on an ad hoc basis. Roosevelt, however, did move cautiously to strengthen the American navy by doubling funds for new vessels including two aircraft carriers. Between 1938 and 1941, the United States gradually abrogated the trade treaty with Japan and banned the sale of war supplies—aircraft, metal alloys, fuel oil, and scrap iron—to Japan while still engaging in high-level talks. By the end of 1941, military confrontation between the United States and Japan had become inevitable. To the United States, Japan's expansion into Southeast Asia seeking raw materials was a direct threat to its long-standing national interests in the region; to Japan, asking it to pull its troops out of China was ludicrous.

Chiang Kai-shek's anti-Communist stance and the exigencies of wartime, spurred by Japan's sudden attack on Pearl Harbor in December 1941, made the United States and China allies. Nevertheless, Roosevelt still followed a "Europe First" policy, and while he acknowledged China as a "great power" (*daguo* 大国), it was largely a symbolic gesture. On the other hand, the United States helped China achieve its long-sought goal of abolishing extraterritoriality, an act with enormous significance for the Chinese to the present day. On January 11, 1943, the Sino-American Treaty for the Relinquishment of Extraterritorial Rights in China and the Regulation of Related Matters was concluded in Washington by Wei Daoming, Chinese ambassador to the United States, and Cordell Hull. On the same day, in Chongqing, T. V. Soong, Chinese foreign minister, and Horace J. Seymour, British ambassador to China, signed a corresponding treaty.

American support for China's enhanced international status was exhibited by two further events in 1943. The Roosevelt administration insisted that China be a signatory, along with Britain, the Soviet Union, and the United States, of the Declaration of Four Nations on General Security signed in Moscow on October 30, 1943—an instrument which eventually led to China's permanent seat on the Security Council of the United Nations. At the Cairo Conference held at the end of 1943, Chiang, along with his wife Madame Soong, met with Roosevelt and Winston Churchill, the British prime minister. Roosevelt and Chiang agreed on postwar decolonization and a unified, reformed Chinese government that would include the Communists. The resulting Cairo Declaration stated that Japanese-held Manchuria, Formosa (Taiwan), and the Pescadores should all be restored to China.[16] Chiang was euphoric about his Cairo "victory" and being treated as an "equal" by Roosevelt. Roosevelt, however, quickly reverted to the Europe First strategy, which both Stalin and Churchill demanded.

The Sino-American alliance created different implications and expectations for both sides. Whereas the United States intended to use China as a bulwark against Japan's ambitions in Asia, Chiang Kai-shek was more interested in translating America's declared abhorrence of Communism into military and economic aid to use against Mao's forces. The United States was faced with an intricate geopolitical and moral dilemma, poised between supporting the inefficient, unpopular Nationalist government and making overtures to the ascendant Chinese Communist Party. To compound the already strained relationship, the Nationalists' military failures, particularly during the major 1944 campaign known as Operation Ichigo, weakened Chiang's prestige in American eyes. In July 1944, President Roosevelt issued Chiang an ultimatum that General Joseph W. Stilwell be placed in overall command of Chinese and American forces in China. From the Chinese perspective, the U.S. demand was high-handed, and Chiang resisted it in defense of Chinese sovereignty. In October, however, Chiang and Stilwell found each other irreconcilable, and Stilwell was recalled at Chiang's insistence.

## THE "RED STAR OVER CHINA" AND THE "LOSS OF CHINA"

By the end of the 1940s, attempts to forestall the demise of the Nationalist Party were widely seen as futile. For a "can-do" nation like the United States, America's "loss of China" and China's corresponding "loss of America" in the final showdown between the GMD and CCP produced a ripple effect of shock, denial, and finally some recognition of the United States' own limits.

### Mao Zedong and Chiang Kai-shek: The Struggle between the Chinese Communist Party and the Nationalist Party

The Chinese Communist revolution has been a "story in progress" for over ninety years—a rocky progression from "seizing power through revolution," to "continuing revolution," to "farewell, revolution."[17] What irresistible force was responsible for drawing millions of Chinese into the Communist orbit and, in the process, alienating the U.S. government?

As we saw in the last chapter, Chiang Kai-shek's coup of April 12, 1927, ended his collaboration with the Chinese Communist Party, marking his rejection of the principles of class struggle and wealth redistribution—a platform that the CCP continued to uphold well into the twentieth century. Between 1930 and 1935, Chiang waged five military campaigns aimed at suppressing the Communists. He almost succeeded. In 1934–35, CCP troops were forced to flee for about 6,000 miles across China from their rural Soviet bases in Jiangxi to Shaanxi in northwest China—giving rise to the legend of the "Long March"—where they established their headquarters in Yan'an (Yenan). However, Japanese aggression was to change the fate of both Nationalists and Communists. As Secretary of State Henry Stimson observed in March 1932, "the trend of events in China was proceeding in the direction of eliminating Communism until these recent difficulties with Japan. The present occupation in China by Japanese troops, however, renewed the danger of anarchy in China."[18]

The Japanese invasion was also responsible for forging the second GMD-CCP alliance or United Front. The Xi'an Incident of 1936 acted as a kind of catalyst. On December 12, 1936, Chiang Kai-shek was put under house arrest during a visit to Xi'an, the capital of Shaanxi Province, by one of his own generals, Zhang Xueliang, who was in secret contact with the CCP. Opposed to Chiang's strategy of ridding China of the Communists as a preliminary to ousting Japanese forces, Zhang had decided to kidnap his leader in order to force him to collaborate with the Communists—although secret peace talks between the GMD, CCP, and Stalin's agent in China were already under way without Zhang's knowledge.[19]

While the progressive elements of Chiang's nationalism had since gained some prominence, Chiang sat on the fence when it came to deciding issues of resistance to Japan, on the one hand, or peace negotiations and diplomatic appeasement on the other. Secret contacts and negotiations with the Japanese were pursued intermittently, although Chiang stood his ground and did not surrender to Japan until he was sure that his allies were coming to the rescue.[20] It seems that Chiang was in a no-win situation: "When, after 1937, Chiang's troops did most of the fighting against the Japanese, they were blamed for defeat. When Communist guerrillas engaged the enemy with far less effect, they were lauded by public opinion as heroes."[21]

Mao successfully exploited differences between himself and his Nationalist rival. During the Sino-Japanese War, Mao had discredited Chiang as an "old-timer" and a traitor—the man who had sold out China to Japan—even though Chiang portrayed himself as the heir to the unfinished mission of Sun Yat-sen, the father of the Republic of China. Although Chiang was no demagogue, "improvement of the people's livelihood" was, in his own words, "of prime importance." And the "foundation of the people's livelihood is economic reconstruction, which is a prerequisite for all the other phases of reconstruction."[22] Chiang respected evolution, private property rights, and traditional customs, a stance which held little appeal to radical revolutionaries.

In contrast, Mao developed the concept—later characterized as Maoist Thought—that the people were the real force of history. He held that China's peasant class, forming 70 percent of the population, were oppressed by the landowners—only 10 percent—who charged the peasants high interest rates and taxes, and by imperialists who exploited the peasants through unfair trading practices. Hence, the need for social revolution was pressing. Mao's radical social theories made sense to the poor and were successfully applied, with pragmatic elasticity, to land redistribution (granting all peasants a small plot of land), reductions in rent and interest, and the national "democratic" movement.

Following Japan's defeat in the world war, the tables were turned in favor of the Communists. The CCP's swift and unexpected conquest of China within three momentous years (1946–49) was, to a great extent, attributed to Mao Zedong (1893–1976), the paramount leader and theorist of the Communist revolution. In the initial stages of the Civil War (April 1946–June 1947), the strategy adopted by Mao's People's Liberation Army (PLA) was characterized as "buying time in exchange for territory." Mao traded space for time with the Nationalists by surrendering territory—including his revolutionary base in Yan'an in March 1947—but kept the resistance going and launched selective attacks on Chiang's troops. Within a year, Mao took the offensive, and the war shifted in the PLA's favor. Beginning in autumn 1948, the CCP successfully launched three military campaigns in Manchuria and in northern and central China, and mobilized over 5 million farmers and militia to provide military supplies and services. The CCP eliminated about 1.5 million Nationalist troops who were better equipped and had initially enjoyed a 3:1 superiority in numbers. In April 1949, Mao's army entered Nanjing, the Nationalist capital, forcing Chiang to flee south to Taiwan.[23]

Some American observers were keenly aware of the historical legitimacy of the Communists. In 1946, two journalists from *Time*, Theodore H. White and Annalee Jacoby, gave their own eyewitness analysis of the Civil War and its outcome:

When Chiang tried to fight the Japanese and preserve the old fabric at the same time, he was not only unable to defeat the Japanese but powerless to preserve his own authority. His historic enemy, the Communists, grew from an army of 85,000 to an army of a million, from the governors of 1,500,000 peasants to the masters of 90,000,000. The Communists used no magic; they knew the changes the people wanted, and they sponsored these changes. Both parties lied, cheated, and broke agreements; but the Communists had the people with them, and with the people they made their own new justice.[24]

## The "China Mud" (1941–45)

Economic bankruptcy and ineffectual efforts to resist Japanese forces left the Nationalist government vulnerable to criticism. As World War II came to an end in China, the CCP was in a stronger position than before. The United States embarked on an impossible mission of mediation between the two political rivals, Chiang and Mao. The few impossible options doomed the mediation: the United States withdrew its support for Chiang; Chiang carried out reforms to enhance his standing with the Chinese people; the United States sided with the Communists; and, finally, the American government disengaged from the China Theater. An echelon of American advisors in China—including Joseph W. Stilwell, Patrick Hurley, George C. Marshall, Albert C. Wedemeyer, and John Leighton Stuart—personified the endeavor as well as the limits of American influence in China in the midst of a domestic Chinese revolution.[25]

In the aftermath of Pearl Harbor, the Roosevelt administration increased its military aid to China and dispatched General Joseph W. Stilwell and Claire Chennault's American Volunteer Group ("Flying Tigers") to advise Chiang's infantry forces and operate clandestine air strikes against Japan.[26] In directing Allied operations in China, Stilwell clashed with Chiang over military and political matters. On his arrival in China in 1942, Stilwell's objectives were twofold. First, he believed the infantry should be given priority over other forces because ground tactics were the most likely to be effective in combating the Japanese and keeping Allied supply lines open through Southeast Asia. Second, Stilwell favored training and outfitting Communist troops to create a large and efficient coalition army. For his part, Chiang preferred the air assault strategy of Claire Chennault and neglected the Burma theater while maintaining full control over GMD forces.

Based on a study of Chiang's diary in the Hoover Institution of Stanford University (available since 2006), Wang Jianlang has charted the loss of mutual trust between Chiang and the United States on a number of fronts: the Chiang-Stilwell feud; the Anglo-American war strategy of "Europe First and Asia Second"; Chiang's suspicion of Sun Ke—Sun Yat-sen's son—as his successor, favored by the United States and Britain; and the decisions about a new world order made at the 1943 Cairo Conference and the Yalta Conference of 1945. It has also been argued that Chiang successfully resisted American influence and maintained China's independence while seizing the opportunity to transform China into a global political power.[27]

Assessments of Stilwell's role have, as expected, been various. Barbara Tuchman's acclaimed biography portrayed the general as a true American hero charged with combating the Japanese in China, whose efforts were undermined by an underhanded autocrat with self-seeking motives. By contrast, Chin-tung Liang (a refugee from Communist China and a professor at St. John's University) blamed Stilwell for being subversive and obstructive and for working only for American and British interests.[28]

On the other hand, Mao consciously made peace overtures to the United States, Russia, and even Chiang, in order to weaken his rival and limit American aid to the Nationalist government.[29] The Dixie Mission (July 1944–March 1947), staffed by the U.S. Army Observation Group, was an American undertaking—the fruit of efforts by both Mao and the U.S. side to establish relations—aimed at observing the political and military scope of the Communist movement in their own territory. Led by Colonel David D. Barrett, the mission team consisted of eighteen American military and diplomatic officers, many of whom, including John S. Service (1909–99) and John P. Davies (1908–99), were accused of having Communist sympathies during the McCarthyist witch hunts of the early 1950s.

The Communists treated the Dixie Mission with strategic pragmatism. The party recognized the significance of this visit from American military personnel and foreign reporters as the "beginnings of real external interaction with our new democratic China," which would do a "service" for the party. A communiqué from the party's Central Committee stated, "Therefore we should not treat their visit and observations as something merely ordinary. Rather, we should view it as aiding our international publicity efforts and as the start of our diplomatic work."[30] This aspect of the party's activities was admittedly only in its infancy: "Diplomatic efforts are the most unfamiliar dimension of our work. Our comrades, especially high-level cadres, should give attention to and study this task."[31]

This favorable exposure to the American media, the State Department, and U.S. academics had won the sympathy of influential young Americans such as Edgar Snow, John S. Service, and Theodore White. They were convinced that the Communists were the wave of the future in China, although they were critical of the CCP's governance skills, an assessment which was to prove disastrously prophetic. According to White, "Their [the CCP leaders'] ignorance of the outside world was sometimes shocking. They knew little of high finance, protocol, or Western administration; their understanding of industry, Western engineering, and international commerce was primitive."[32]

The failed efforts to arrive at a peaceful settlement in China by General Patrick J. Hurley (ambassador to China, November 1944–November 1945) heightened America's inability to control both the form and content of its relationship with warring Chinese political forces on its own geopolitical terms. Hurley arrived in Chongqing, Guomindang's wartime capital, in September 1944, initially as the personal representative of the president to China. Negotiations had been under way between the GMD and CCP for the consolidation of all Chinese military forces and the formation of a coalition government. Hurley took the initiative by flying to Yan'an for talks with Mao Zedong and helped formulate a five-point draft agreement whereby the Communists would not hand over command of their troops to the Nationalists before the GMD's one-party rule was abolished and a reorganized government was formed which would represent all parties. Rejecting this offer and alleging that the CCP's real purpose was to overthrow the Nationalist Party and establish its own form of single-party rule, the Nationalist government proposed a counter three-point plan for peace.

In the ensuing months, Hurley brought together rival party leaders, including Mao Zedong and Zhou Enlai representing the CCP and Chiang Kai-shek and Wang Shijie for the GMD, for settlement negotiations. However, Hurley, who sided with Chiang in the Stilwell-Chiang dispute, pushed for a coalition government under Nationalist control. Both the Communists and State Department personnel in China saw him as biased toward Chiang. Hurley's critics at the American embassy in Chongqing continued to argue for military and political cooperation with the CCP. Furious and frustrated, Hurley tendered his resignation to President Harry Truman (1945–53) in November 1945, setting off a politically charged debate in the United States. In his resignation letter, Hurley openly accused his subordinates of Communist leanings:

> Our professional diplomats continuously advised the Communists that my efforts in preventing the collapse of the National Government did not represent the policy of the United States. These same professionals openly advised the Communist armed party to decline unification of the Chinese Communist Army with the National Army unless the Chinese Communists were given control.[33]

### China in the Balance (1945–49)

As the China question was debated and politicized in Congress, a new mission led by General of the Army George C. Marshall—President Truman's special representative in China with the personal rank of ambassador—was announced in December 1945. The Marshall mission was hobbled from the outset by its contradictory objectives, as the government's instructions to him show. The United States must side with Chiang, even if he proved obdurate, lest a disintegrating China and Soviet dominance in Manchuria thwart the "major purpose of our war in the Pacific." "The existence of autonomous armies such as that of the Communist army is inconsistent with, and actually makes impossible, political unity in China." It was in the United States' interests that Chiang end the conflict with the Communists, democratize his government, and maintain peace and unity—by broadening "the bases of that Government . . . to include other political elements in the country"—because the United States could not support Chiang by "military intervention in an internecine struggle." "With the institution of a broadly representative government, autonomous armies should be eliminated as such and all armed forces in China integrated effectively into the Chinese National army."[34] Unlike Hurley, Marshall was involved in extensive discussions with Truman, James F. Byrnes (secretary of state, 1945–47), the State Department, and high-level army, navy, and air force commanders to try and develop a clear American policy toward China.

Compounding the contradictions inherent in the U.S. position, the deep-seated divisions between the Nationalist and Communist parties, as well as the Russians, all hindered the mediation efforts of Marshall, who personally believed that the "Communist group will block all progress in negotiations as far as they can, as the delay is to their advantage."[35] A cease-fire between the GMD and the CCP was reached in January 1946 and lasted intermittently for barely a year. The parties were unable to agree on the composition of even small committees to discuss the reorganization of the State Council to form a joint government that would end the GMD's one-party rule. In November 1946, the Nationalist-dominated National Assembly was convened, and the Communists immediately demanded its dissolution.

In early December 1946, the CCP broke off all negotiations. However, Marshall still held out some hope for a political solution. He believed that the liberals in the Nationalist government and in the minority parties could unite and work under Chiang. He was "anxious to get started on something different."[36] This was not to happen. In January 1947, President Truman recalled Marshall and shortly afterward appointed him as secretary of state.

Meanwhile, the Nationalist and Communist parties turned their attention to Manchuria, both eager to exploit a power vacuum created by the withdrawal of Japanese forces following Japan's surrender on August 15, 1945. Viewing Manchuria as part of its own sphere of influence, as determined in the peace settlements at the Yalta Conference, the Soviet Union was irritated by the GMD's use of American warships and airplanes to transfer its troops to Manchurian ports to reestablish a military and civilian administration in the territory. Fearing American influence in Manchuria, in October 1945 the Russians refused permission to land in Port Arthur and Dalian to Nationalist forces arriving from remote southwestern China. When Chiang's army was permitted to enter the cities of Yingkou and Hulu Dao in Liaoning Province, they found themselves besieged by CCP forces that had spent the war years in Manchuria. Finally, the Nationalist troops were forced to reroute to Qinhuang Dao and enter the Three Northeastern Provinces overland. As a result of a lack of cooperation from the Soviets, GMD forces lost four to five valuable weeks in the race to take over former Japanese-occupied territory. This delay gave the CCP a crucial edge as it rushed its cadres and troops to Manchuria to develop base areas.[37] On June 25, 1947, the Guomindang Foreign Ministry reported that Port Arthur and Dalian were still not under the control of the Nationalist government, and demanded that Russia fulfill its obligations under the 1945 Sino-Russian Treaty of Friendship and Alliance.[38]

In seeking a resolution to China's political fate, John Leighton Stuart (ambassador to China, 1946–49) found himself caught on the horns of the same dilemma as Marshall. While Stuart was pro-Chiang, he supported a democratic, united government inclusive of all Chinese.

> I greatly desired to see him [Chiang] lead the party in a revival of the original revolutionary reform when its leaders really had a high patriotic motive and were heroic in exposing themselves to danger with no thought of self in their desire to establish Chinese independence with a democratic form of government. . . . The reform movement should be inward in correcting the flagrant abuses which were destroying confidence both in China and abroad, and positive in creating socialized legislation that would bring economic benefits to the common people.[39]

The Nationalists were increasingly frustrated with Marshall and Stuart, both for insisting on democratic reforms and for failing to give them unlimited supplies of American aid, while the Communists were outraged by the massive quantities of American aid granted to Chiang in the midst of their mediation efforts. On August 7, 1946, Stuart wrote to Secretary of State Byrnes about his conversations with Chiang Kai-shek and the Communists' chief negotiator, Zhou Enlai, that "we at least know how irreconcilable are the attitudes of the two parties."[40] On July 4, 1947, the State Council dominated by the Nationalists proclaimed the CCP to be in open rebellion against the government, and the GMD was henceforth determined to devote considerable resources to suppressing the Communist insurgents.

But Chiang's administration was in crisis. By spring 1947, runaway inflation, spreading student demonstrations, rice riots, and labor strikes were widespread across China—all manifestations of Chiang's loss of control. The Guomindang's response to the money shortage was to print more banknotes. From September 1945 to February 1947, wholesale prices increased thirtyfold, and then from September 1948 to February 1949, they shot up more than 385 times. A 171-pound of rice sold for 6.7 million Chinese yuan in June 1948 had escalated to 63 million yuan two months later.

In July 1947, Truman sent Lieutenant General Albert C. Wedemeyer to China on a fact-finding tour. Following a month of interviews with (and the collation of written submissions from) Chinese and foreigners living in Nanjing, Shanghai, Beijing, Tianjin, Shenyang (Mukden), Guangzhou (Canton), and Hankou, Wedemeyer made some very frank observations on the shortcomings of the Nationalist government, words which reportedly made the president of the Examination Yuan (the body that oversaw the civil service), Dai Jitao, weep on one occasion. Wedemeyer recommended that the China quagmire should be removed from American mediation and referred to the United Nations. In his report to Truman, Wedemeyer summed up the dilemma faced by the United States:

> On one side is the Kuomintang [Guomindang], whose reactionary leadership, repression and corruption have caused a loss of popular faith in the Government [Nationalists]. On the other side, bound ideologically to the Soviet Union, are the Chinese Communists, whose eventual aim is admittedly a Communist state in China . . . inimical to the interests of the United States, in view of their openly expressed hostility and active opposition to those principles which the United States regards as vital to the peace of the world.[41]

However, the situation was taken out of everyone's hands when the Nationalist regime was decisively defeated in its civil war with the Communists during 1946–49.[42] Manchuria had been the first major battleground as the two factions struggled for dominance following the end of the Second World War. Both sides were well prepared for armed combat. Adapting to new developments and learning valuable strategic lessons from internal problems, setbacks, and defeats, the Communist People's Liberation Army shifted their operational strategy from a guerrilla struggle in rural areas to an effective combination of mobile and base warfare, concentrating on cities and railways while consolidating their Manchurian rural base areas.[43]

As we have seen, by fall 1948 the Communists were poised to launch strategic offensives in Manchuria and in north and central China, known as the Three Military Campaigns (*Liaoshen*, *Huaihai*, and *Pingjin*). Lin Biao, the commander of the Communist army in Manchuria, carried out several decisive attacks and took control of major cities including Changchun and Mukden (Shenyang). Within fifty days or so, Lin's forces had eliminated around 470,000 Nationalist troops and reversed the Nationalist advance. In Henan and Jiangsu provinces, Deng Xiaoping, Liu Bocheng, and Su Yu waged a number of offensives from November 1948 to January 1949 which succeeded in wiping out a Guomindang army of over half a million men. Within two months, key cities including Tianjin and Beijing fell to the Communists, with an additional 520,000 GMD troops defeated. On April 24, 1949, the Communists crossed the Yangzi and swept into Nanjing; the following morning, soldiers broke into Ambassador Stuart's bedroom in the American embassy. The remnants of the beaten Guomindang retreated to Taiwan. On October 1, 1949, in Beijing, Mao Zedong announced the birth of the People's Republic of China.

In this chapter, I have outlined the various American attempts at handling the delicate, unfolding situation in China during these two volatile decades. On the CCP side, the need to learn the fundamentals of diplomatic engagement with the United States and other "imperialists," in both overt and covert ways, determined the direction of the party's foreign policy, especially from 1946 onward.[44] Diplomatic niceties, however, were not always observed. In November 1948 Angus I. Ward, American consul-general, and his staff in Mukden refused to follow the Communist authorities' order to turn in their radio transmitters. They were detained in isolation, put on trial on spy charges, and finally deported in December 1949.[45]

A reading of American diplomats' dispatches from the field suggests the indifferent, uncooperative attitude shown by their international counterparts toward the indignities to which the United States was subjected, as in the Ward Incident. In January 1949, Stuart sent the following notes to the secretary of state:

> While expressing sympathy and concern British and French Ambassadors [Sir Ralph Stevenson and Jacques Meyrier] still refuse to cooperate in joint statement which we believe occasion warrants. It is apparent that these local representatives are quite content to ride along on the coattails of US without appearing to take any positive action which might compromise future dealings themselves or their nationals in CCP-occupied China.
>
> . . .
>
> In our opinion attitude adopted by Chinese Communists toward American Consulate General in Mukden, not to speak of more neutral British and French Consulate Generals there, is little short of blackmail. It is among most convincing evidence yet that Chinese Communist leaders are basically British [sic] bigots out of Bolshevik mold.[46]

Nine months later, the American consul-general in Shanghai, Walter McConaughy, confirmed Stuart's views. From casual conversations with Nanjing diplomats about to embark on British evacuation ships he had gained the impression that, despite their experiences, they would "rec-ommend unreservedly to their Government that recognition be accorded [to Communist China] in the not distant future." Regarding the ongoing difficulties experienced by American consulates in China, McConaughy commented, "It was disturbing to note their casual and even cavalier attitude toward indignities we have suffered at hands of Communists, particularly detention of our consular staff at Mukden." [47]

Despite this diplomatic friction, the Communists arguably left the door open for political and diplomatic contacts with the United States. During his remaining time in China in May–July 1949, Stuart reported on the initiatives the Communists were taking to gain recognition by the United States. According to Stuart's notes, Huang Hua—chief of the Ali-ens Affairs Office, Nanking Military Control Council, an alumnus of Yenching University (Stuart was Yenching's former president) and a classmate of Philip Fugh (Stuart's secretary)—approached Stuart and re-marked amiably that "it would be up to USA, when time came, to make first move in establishment relations with People's Democratic Govern-ment . . . on terms of equality and mutual benefit." [48] Huang Hua let it be known that Mao Zedong and Zhou Enlai would personally welcome Stuart to Beijing if he wished to visit Yenching University. The U.S. government rejected the offer, and Stuart left China for good on August 2, 1949. [49]

## CONCLUSION

During the 1930s and 1940s, American-Chinese relations developed under four broad rubrics. First, during these two decades the political landscape in China was dominated by a complex series of interactions— first between the independent warlords, the Nationalist and Chinese Communist parties, and foreign powers (chiefly Japan, the United States, Germany, Britain, and the Soviet Union), and later between the National-ists, the Communists, the World War II Allies, and the major Cold War rivals, the United States and the Soviet Union.

Second, revolution, nationalism, and anti-imperialism were at work as major forces of change in China and Asia. As the relationship between the United States and Nationalist China continued to strengthen and evolve, the Chinese Communists became the historical agent of change.

Third, American foreign policy was aimed at maintaining a regional and global balance of power that suited its own interests in the Asia-Pacific. The strength of U.S. influence in China rested on its ability to control the bilateral relationship so that China continued to serve the American interests in the region. This was the contingent process behind America's "gain of China." Never before had the United States wielded so much power in China. Rival nationalist leaders—in particular Chiang and Mao—resisted, ignored, and ultimately upset American designs for China. However, America's unwillingness to use military force to intervene in the Chinese Civil War and its inability to abandon the unattainable goal of establishing a progressive, anti-Communist Chiang government led ultimately to the disappointment of the United States.

Fourth, the political rhetoric surrounding the question of "how China was lost"—or the "China question" in broader terms—dominated Sino-American relations and has become a permanent feature of American politics that ebbs and flows in response to the political climate.[50] The politicization of the China issue intensified following the open rift between Patrick Hurley and the American Foreign Service staff in China. Republican senators including Styles Bridges of New Hampshire and Arthur Vandenberg of Michigan fell into line with Hurley, forming the so-called conservative "China lobby." They pressed for increased aid and support for Chiang against the threat of Communism. Democrats such as Tom Connally of Texas—a supporter of a quiet disassociation from Chiang—battled with Republicans at congressional hearings. Espionage charges were made against Judith Coplon of the Justice Department, allegedly a Communist, and German physicist Klaus Fuchs, who had confessed to atomic espionage on behalf of the Soviet Union, as well as China specialists such as John Carter Vincent, John S. Service, and John P. Davies. These indictments laid the groundwork for the rise of McCarthyism in the 1950s.[51]

The impassioned reactions to the publication of the China White Paper in August 1949 were another instance of the Rashomon effect regarding China. Dean Acheson, Truman's secretary of state (1949–53), blamed Chiang and the Chinese themselves for the "ominous result of the civil war in China" since it was "beyond the control of the government of the United States."[52] Furious critics responded that "America's misguided or calculated failure to give Chiang Kai-shek the help he needed to beat the Chinese Communists was leading to Russian control of Asia."[53]

America's entanglement with China during these two decades and the heated debates and rhetoric it produced could also be accounted for by increased cultural, social, religious, and economic encounters between the two countries—a theme to be explored further in the following chapter.

## FURTHER READING

Dorothy Borg and Shumpei Okamoto, eds., *Pearl Harbor as History* (New York: Columbia University Press, 1973) is an important study of U.S.-East Asian relations in the 1930s. Tsou Tang's *America's Failure in China, 1941–50* (Chicago, Ill.: University of Chicago Press, 1963) is a classic account of America's wartime diplomacy in China. John Van Antwerp MacMurray, *How the Peace Was Lost: The 1935 Memorandum "Developments Affecting American Policy in the Far East,"* ed. Arthur Waldron (Stanford, Calif.: Hoover Institution, 1992) illuminates former American minister to China John MacMurray's perspective on the Sino-Japanese conflict. MacMurray saw Bolshevism and the USSR as greater dangers than Japan and advocated a lenient policy toward Japanese involvement in China. Other useful works include Sun Youli, *China and the Origins of the Pacific War, 1931–1941* (New York: St. Martin's, 1993) and Parks M. Coble, *Facing Japan: Chinese Politics and Japanese Imperialism, 1931–1937* (Cambridge, Mass.: Harvard University Press, 1991).

For Chinese, Japanese, Russian, British, and American involvement in and views on the war in Asia, see Akira Iriye and Warren Cohen, eds., *American, Chinese, and Japanese Perspectives on Wartime Asia, 1931–1949* (Wilmington, Del.: SR Books, 1990); Anthony Best, *British Intelligence and the Japanese Challenge in Asia, 1911–1941* (New York: Macmillan, 2002); John Garver, *Chinese-Soviet Relations 1937–1945: The Diplomacy of Chinese Nationalism* (New York: Oxford University Press, 1988); and Odd Arne Westad, *Cold War and Revolution: Soviet-American Rivalry and the Origins of the Chinese Civil War, 1944–1946* (New York: Columbia University Press, 1993).

Japanese-occupied Manchuria and competing Chinese and Japanese nationalisms are studied in Prasenjit Duara, *Sovereignty and Authenticity: Manchukuo and the East Asian Modern* (Lanham, Md.: Rowman & Littlefield, 2003); and Rana Mitter, *The Manchurian Myth: Nationalism, Resistance, and Collaboration in Modern China* (Berkeley, Calif.: University of California Press, 2000). Joshua Fogel, ed., *The Nanjing Massacre in History and Historiography* (Berkeley, Calif.: University of California Press, 2000) examines the Nanjing Massacre as an event and the various interpretations it has elicited.

Lynne Joiner's *The Honorable Survivor: Mao's China, McCarthy's America, and the Persecution of John S. Service* (Annapolis, Md.: Naval Institute Press, 2009) tells a moving story of John S. Service, a wartime foreign service officer in China who advocated establishing ties with the Chinese Communists. John Paton Davies Jr., *China Hand: An Autobiography* (Philadelphia, Pa.: University of Pennsylvania Press, 2012) is a gripping personal account of Chinese history and American diplomacy from the 1930s to the 1950s by an American diplomat and a victim of the McCarthy hysteria. For a biography of Madame Chiang Kai-shek, a major promoter of Nationalist China in the United States, see Laura Tyson Li, *Madame Chiang Kai-Shek: China's Eternal First Lady* (New York: Atlantic Monthly Press, 2006).

Works in Chinese on the victory of the Chinese Communists in 1949 are abundant. Among the most useful are Wang Chaoguang (汪朝光), *1945–1949: Guogong zhengzheng yu Zhongguo mingyun* [1945–1949: 国共政争与中国命运 The political conflict between the GMD and CCP and China's destiny] (Beijing: Shehui kexue wenxian chubanshe, 2010); Yang Kuisong (杨奎松), *Shiqu de jihui? Kangzhan qianhou Guogong tanpan shilu* [失去的机会? 抗战前后国共谈判实录 A lost opportunity? A true account of the negotiations between the GMD and CCP before and after the War of Resistance] (Beijing: Xinxing chubanshe, 2010); Yang Kuisong, *"Zhongjian didai" de geming: Guoji da beijing xia kan Zhonggong chenggong zhidao* ["中间地带"的革命: 国际大背景下看中共成功之道 The "mid-zone" revolution: Tracing the CCP's path to success within a broad international context] (Taiyuan: Shanxi renmin chubanshe, 2010).

## NOTES

1. Nancy Tucker, "Continuing Controversies in the Literature of U.S.-China Relations since 1945," in Warren I. Cohen, ed., *Pacific Passage: The Study of American-East Asian Relations on the Eve of the Twenty-First Century* (New York: Columbia University Press, 1996), pp. 213–246.

2. Walter LaFeber, *The Clash: U.S.-Japanese Relations throughout History* (New York: Norton, 1997); Michael H. Hunt, *Frontier Defense and the Open Door: Manchuria in Chinese-American Relations, 1895–1911* (New Haven, Conn.: Yale University Press, 1973).

3. Interview with Charles Hodges, "China's Salvation at Stake, He Says," *New York Times*, October 1, 1922, p. 45.

4. These questions were much debated at the time; see Paul S. Reinsch, *An American Diplomat in China* (Garden City, N.Y.: Doubleday, Page & Comp., 1922), pp. 307–316.

5. The Root-Takahira Exchange of Notes, 1908, Carnegie Endowment for International Peace, *The Imperial Japanese Mission 1917: A Record of the Reception throughout the United States of the Special Mission Headed by Viscount Ishii* (Washington, D.C.: Carnegie Endowment for International Peace, 1918), publication no. 15, appendix A.

6. The Lansing-Ishii Exchange of Notes, 1917, Carnegie Endowment for International Peace, *The Imperial Japanese Mission 1917*, publication no. 15, Appendix B.

7. Thomas W. Burkman, *Japan and the League of Nations: Empire and World Order, 1914–1938* (Honolulu, Hawaii: University of Hawaii Press, 2007).

8. The minister in China (Johnson) to the secretary of state, September 19, 1931, in U.S. Department of State, *Papers Relating to the Foreign Relations of the United States* [*FRUS* hereafter], *Japan: 1931–1941* (Washington, D.C.: Government Printing Office, 1943), vol. 1, p. 1.

9. Louis Young, *Japan's Total Empire: Manchuria and the Culture of Wartime Imperialism* (Berkeley, Calif.: University of California Press, 1998); Dorothy Borg, *The United States and the Far Eastern Crisis of 1933–1938: From the Manchurian Incident through the Initial Stage of the Undeclared Sino-Japanese War* (Cambridge, Mass.: Harvard University Press, 1964); James B. Crowley, *Japan's Quest for Autonomy: National Security and Foreign Policy, 1930–1938* (Princeton, N.J.: Princeton University Press, 1966).

10. Memorandum by the secretary of state, September 22, 1931; the minister in China (Johnson) to the secretary of state, September 19, 1931, in *FRUS, Japan: 1931–1941*, vol. 1, pp. 5–9.

11. "Dongsheng shibian" [东省事变 The Manchurian Incident], November 1932–February 1933, Waijiaobu dang'an [外交部档案 Archives of the Foreign Ministry], file no. 020-010112-0020, deposited at Academia Historica in Taipei.

12. Telegram, the secretary of state to the consul-general at Nanking (Peck), and memorandum by the secretary of state, both dated January 7, 1932, U.S. Department of State, *FRUS, 1932: The Far East* (Washington, D.C.: Government Printing Office, 1932), vol. 3, pp. 7–9.

13. He Yingqin (1890–1987) was the acting chairman of the Beiping (Beijing) Military Council, and Umezu Yoshijirō (1882–1949) was a commander of the Japanese army.

14. The Marco Polo Bridge is located in Wanping County, south of Beijing.

15. Edward L. Dreyer, *China at War, 1901–1949* (London: Longman, 1995). For different assessments of Chinese and Japanese military performance, see Ger Teitler and Kurt W. Radtke, eds., *A Dutch Spy in China: Reports on the First Phase of the Sino-Japanese War (1937–1939)* (Leiden: Brill, 1999); Hans van de Ven, ed., *Warfare in Chinese History* (Leiden: Brill, 2000); Dick Wilson, *When Tigers Fight: The Story of the Sino-Japanese War, 1937–1945* (New York: Viking, 1982).

16. U.S. Department of State, *United States Relations with China with Special Reference to the Period 1944–1949* (Washington, D.C.: Department of State, 1949), p. 37.

17. Chen Yung-fa (陈永发), *Zhongguo gongchan geming qishinian* [中国共产革命七十年 Seventy years of the Chinese Communist revolution], revised ed. (Taipei: Lianjing, 2001), xvi.

18. Memorandum by the secretary of state, March 11, 1932, in *FRUS, 1932: The Far East* (Washington, D.C.: Government Printing Office, 1932), vol. 3, pp. 566–567.

19. Jay Taylor, *The Generalissimo Chiang Kai-shek and the Struggle for Modern China* (Cambridge, Mass.: Belknap Press, 2009), chapter 3.

20. David P. Barrett and Lawrence N. Shyu, eds., *Chinese Collaboration with Japan, 1932–1945: The Limits of Accommodation* (Stanford, Calif.: Stanford University Press, 2001); So Wai Chor, "The Making of the Guomindang's Japan Policy, 1932–1937: The Roles of Chiang Kai-Shek and Wang Jingwei," *Modern China* 28, no. 2 (April 2002): 213–252; Wu Jingping (吴景平), "1938 nian Guomindang dui Ri hezhan taidu shuping: Yi Jiang Jieshi riji wei zhongxin de kaocha" [1938年国民党对日和战态度述评—以蒋介石日记为中心的考察 An assessment of the Nationalist Party's dual stance of appeasement and resistance to Japan in 1938, based on the diary of Chiang Kai-shek], *Minguo dang'an* (民国档案), no. 3 (2010): 114–126; Shen Yu (沈予), "Lun Kangri zhanzheng shiqi Rijiang de 'heping' jiaoshe" [论抗日战争时期日蒋的"和平"交涉 On the "peace" negotiations between Japan and Chiang during the War of Resistance], *Lishi yanjiu*, no. 2 (1993): 108–127.

21. David M. Gordon, "Historiographical Essay: The China-Japan War, 1931–1945," *Journal of Military History* 70, no. 1 (January 2006): 137–182.

22. Chiang Kai-shek, *Zhongguo zhi mingyun* [中国之命运 China's destiny] (Chongqing: Zhengzhong shuju, 1943), chapters 5 and 6.

23. Timothy Cheek, ed., *A Critical Introduction to Mao* (Cambridge: Cambridge University Press, 2010); Timothy Cheek, *Mao Zedong and China's Revolution: A Brief History with Documents* (Boston: Bedford, 2002); Ross Terrill, *Mao: A Biography* (Stanford, Calif.: Stanford University Press, 1999; 1st ed. 1980 by Harper & Row); Jonathan Spence, *Mao Zedong* (New York: Penguin, 1999).

24. Theodore H. White and Annalee Jacoby, *Thunder out of China* (New York: William Sloane Associates, 1946), introduction.

25. Barbara W. Tuchman, *Stilwell and the American Experience in China, 1911–45* (New York: Bantam, 1972; 1st ed. in 1971 by Macmillan), foreword.

26. For the tensions between Stilwell, Chennault, Roosevelt, and Chiang, see Edward Fisher, *The Chancy War: Winning in China, Burma, and India in World War Two* (New York: Orion Books, 1991); Guangqiu Xu, "The Issue of U.S. Air Support for China during the Second World War, 1942–1945," *Journal of Contemporary History* 36 (July 2001): 459–484.

27. Tao Wenzhao (陶文钊), *Zhongmei guanxishi* (1911–1949) [中美关系史 Sino-American relations] (Shanghai: Shanghai renmin chubanshe, 2004), vol. 1, chapter 6; Wang Jianlang (王建朗), "Xinren de liushi: Cong Jiang Jieshi riji kan Kangzhan houqi de Zhongmei guanxi" [信任的流失：从蒋介石日记看抗日后期的中美关系 The loss of trust: Sino-American relations in the later phases of the Anti-Japanese War as seen through the diary of Chiang Kai-shek], *Jindaishi yanjiu*, no. 3 (2009): 49–62; Wang Jianlang, "Daguo yishi yu daguo zuowei: Kangzhan houqi de Zhongguo guoji jiaose dingwei yu waijiao nuli" [大国意识与大国作为：抗战后期的中国国际角色定位与外交努力 Great power awareness and actions: The establishment of China's international status and diplomatic efforts in the later phases of the War of Resistance], *Lishi yanjiu*, no. 6 (2008): 124–137.

28. Barbara W. Tuchman, *Stilwell and the American Experience in China, 1911–45*; Chin-tung Liang, *General Stilwell in China, 1942–1945: The Full Story* (New York: St. John's University Press, 1972); Hans van de Ven, "Stilwell in the Stocks: The Chinese Nationalists and the Allied Powers in the Second World War," *Asian Affairs* 34, no. 3 (November 2003): 243–259.

29. Mao Zedong, "He Meiguo jizhe An'na Luyisi Sitelang de tanhua" [和美国记者安娜.路易斯.斯特朗的谈话 An interview with American journalist Anna Louise Strong in August 1946], in *Mao Zedong xuanji* (Beijing: Renmin chubanshe, 1966), vol. 4, pp. 1135–1140.

30. "Zhonggong zhongyang guanyu waijiao gongzuo de zhishi," (dated August 18, 1944) [中共中央关于外交工作的指示 Directives of the Central Committee of the Chinese Communist Party relating to diplomatic matters] in Zhongyang dang'anguan (中央档案馆), ed., *Zhonggong zhongyang wenjian xuanji* [中共中央文件选集 Selected documents of the Central Committee of the Chinese Communist Party] (Beijing: Zhonggong zhongyang dangxiao chubanshe, 1989–1992), vol. 14, http://cpc.people.com.cn/GB/64184/64186/66645/index.html (accessed February 20, 2011); John S. Service, *The Ameriasia Papers: Problems in the History of U.S.-China Relations* (Berkeley, Calif.: Center for Chinese Studies, University of California, 1971); David D. Barrett, *Dixie Mission: The United States Army Observer Group in Yenan, 1944* (Berkeley, Calif.: Center for Chinese Studies, University of California, 1979); Joseph W. Esherick, *Lost Chance in China: The World War II Dispatches of John S. Service* (New York: Random House, 1974); Zi Zhongyun (资中筠), *Meiguo duihua zhengce de yuanqi he fazhan (1945–1950)* [美国对华政策的缘起和发展 The origins and development of American policy toward China] (Chongqing: Chongqing chubanshe, 1987).

31. "Zhonggong zhongyang guanyu waijiao gongzuo de zhishi."

32. Theodore H. White and Annalee Jacoby, *Thunder out of China*, p. 229; Edgar Snow, *Red Star over China*, 1st revised and enlarged ed. (New York: Grove Press, 1973); S. Bernard Thomas, *Season of High Adventure: Edgar Snow in China* (Berkeley, Calif.: University of California Press, 1996).

33. "The Ambassador to China (Hurley) to President Truman," in the U.S. Department of State, ed., *United States Relations with China with Special Reference to the Period 1944–1949*, pp. 581–584.

34. " The Marshall Mission: Instructions to General of the Army George C. Marshall regarding United States Policy toward China; First Conferences in China," in *FRUS, Diplomatic Papers, 1945; The Far East, China* (Washington, D.C.: Government Printing Office, 1945), vol. 7, pp. 745–828.

35. " Memorandum by General of the Army George C. Marshall to Fleet Admiral William D. Leahy, Chief of Staff to the Commander in Chief of the Army and Navy," November 30, 1945, in *FRUS, Diplomatic Papers, 1945; The Far East, China*, p. 748.

36. Roger B. Jeans, ed., *The Marshall Mission to China, 1945–1947: The Letters and Diary of Colonel John Hart Caughey* (Lanham, Md.: Rowman & Littlefield, 2011 ), p. 35.

37. At Yalta in the Crimea, Roosevelt, Churchill, and Stalin reached secret agreements. In return for its entry into the Asian theater within three months after the war in Europe was over, the Soviets were granted the Kurile Islands, the southern half of Sakhalin, and railroads and port facilities in North Korea, Manchuria, and Outer Mongolia. Suzanne Pepper, "The KMT-CCP Conflict 1945–1949," in Denis Twitchett and John K. Fairbank, eds., *The Cambridge History of China: Republican China 1912–1949* (Cambridge: Cambridge University Press, 1986), vol. 13, pp. 723–729; Zhongguo lishi di'er dang'anguan, ed., *Zhonghua minguoshi dang'an ziliao huibian*, vol. 5, part 3, wai-

jiao, pp. 698, 706–708; Dong Wang, "Redeeming 'A Century of National Ignominy': Nationalism and Party Rivalry over the Unequal Treaties, 1928–1947," *Twentieth-Century China* 30, no. 2 (April 2005): 72–100.

38. For secret negotiations in Moscow between Nationalist China and the Soviet Union, see Xiaoyuan Liu, *A Partnership for Disorder: China, the United States, and Their Policies for the Postwar Disposition of the Japanese Empire, 1941–1945* (Cambridge: Cambridge University Press, 1996). Liu argues that the Yalta-Moscow system provided American and Russian support for the Nationalist regime to continue to rule China, but modified the Cairo decisions by "reducing China's territories and external sovereignty" (p. 285).

39. Stuart to the secretary of state (James F. Byrnes), 893.00/3-347, March 3, 1947; Stuart to the secretary of state about his conversations with Chiang at Kuling Mountain, 893.00/7-2146, July 21, 1946, in Kenneth W. Rea and John C. Brewer, eds., *The Forgotten Ambassador: The Reports of John Leighton Stuart, 1946–1949* (Boulder, Colo.: Westview Press, 1981), pp. 2–6, 65. John Leighton Stuart, *Fifty Years in China: The Memoirs of John Leighton Stuart, Missionary and Ambassador* (New York: Random House, 1954). *FRUS, 1946*, vol. 10, pp. 1, 205, 537, 580.

40. Stuart to the secretary of state, 893.00/8-746, August 7, 1946; 893.00/8-3046, August 30, 1946; 893.00/11-1346, November 13, 1946, in Kenneth W. Rea and John C. Brewer, eds., *The Forgotten Ambassador*, pp. 7–13, 38.

41. Report to President Truman by Lieutenant General Albert C. Wedemeyer, U.S. Army, September 17, 1947, pp. 764–814.

42. Both Chiang and Stuart underestimated the military prowess of the CCP, as did Mao himself. In September–October 1948, Mao predicted that "it will probably take us five years (counting from July 1946) to wipe out the GMD." Mao's telegraph to Lin Biao and Luo Ronghuan, "Guanyu Liaoshen zhanyi de zuozhan fangzhen" [关于辽沈战役的作战方针 On the operational tactics used in the Liaoshen campaign], *Mao Zedong xuanji*, vol. 4, p. 1277.

43. Victor Shiu Chiang Cheng, "Imaging China's Madrid in Manchuria: The Communist Military Strategy at the Onset of the Chinese Civil War, 1945–1946," *Modern China* 31, no. 1 (January 2005): 72–114; Harold M. Tanner, "Guerrilla, Mobile, and Base Warfare in Communist Military Operations in Manchuria, 1945–1947," *Journal of Military History* 67, no. 4 (October 2003): 1177–1222; Steven I. Levine, *Anvil of Victory: The Communist Revolution in Manchuria, 1945–1948* (New York: Columbia University Press, 1987); Donald G. Gillin and Ramon H. Myers, eds., *Last Chance in Manchuria: The Diary of Chang Kia-ngau* (Stanford, Calif.: Hoover Institution Press, 1989); Xu Yan (徐焰), *Kangri zhanzheng shengli qianxi zhi shengli hou wodang zhanlüe fangzhen de zhuanbian* [抗日战争胜利前夕至胜利后我党战略方针的转变 The transformation of CCP strategy from the eve to the aftermath of victory in the War of Resistance], in Zhongguo geming bowuguan dangshi yanjiushi (中国革命博物馆党史研究室), ed., *Dangshi yanjiu ziliao* (Chengdu: Sichuan renmin chubanshe, 1987), vol. 7.

44. See Mao Zedong's report on March 5, 1949, at the 2nd meeting of the 7th plenary session of the Central Committee in Xibaipo. The CCP regarded this meeting as a key component of its strategy in the lead-up to its final victory in October 1949. *Mao Zedong xuanji*, vol. 4, pp. 1362–1377.

45. Chen Jian, "The Ward Case and the Emergence of Sino-American Confrontation, 1948–1950," *Australian Journal of Chinese Affairs*, no. 30 (July 1993): 149–170; Chen Jian, *Mao's China and the Cold War* (Chapel Hill, N.C.: University of North Carolina Press, 2001), chapter 2; "National Affairs: The Frontiersman," *Time*, vol. 67, no. 14

(April 2, 1956). For detailed reports, see *FRUS, 1948 and 1949, The Far East: China*, 2 vols. for each year.

46. Stuart to the secretary of state, January 12 and January 5, 1949, *FRUS, 1949*, vol. 8: *The Far East: China*, pp. 933–935.

47. McConaughy to the secretary of state, October 21, 1949, *FRUS, 1949*, vol. 9: *The Far East, China*, p. 137.

48. Stuart to the secretary of state, 893.00B/5-1149, May 11, 1949; 893.00 B/5-1449, May 14, 1949; 711.93/6-849, June 8, 1949; 123 Stuart J. Leighton, June 30, 1949, in Kenneth W. Rea and John C. Brewer, eds., *The Forgotten Ambassador*, pp. 322–334.

49. According to Warren I. Cohen's interview with Huang Hua in 1986, Huang countered Stuart's report that Mao and Zhou initiated a possible meeting with Stuart. Huang claimed that the Communists did not reach out to the United States. Warren I. Cohen, "Conversations with Chinese Friends: Zhou Enlai's Associates Reflect on Chinese-American Relations in the 1940s and the Korean War," *Diplomatic History* 11, no. 3 (July 1987): 283–289; Michael M. Sheng, "Chinese Communist Policy toward the United States and the Myth of the 'Lost Chance' 1948–1950," *Modern Asian Studies* 28, no. 3 (July 1994): 475–502.

50. Kenneth S. Chern, "Politics of American China Policy, 1945: Roots of the Cold War in Asia," *Political Science Quarterly* 91, no. 4 (Winter 1976–1977): 631–647.

51. Lyman P. Van Slyke, introduction, in U.S. Department of State, *The China White Paper August 1949* (Stanford, Calif.: Stanford University Press, 1967), originally issued as *United States Relations with China with Special Reference to the Period 1944–1949*, published in August 1949.

52. Dean Acheson, letter of transmittal, in U.S. Department of State, *The China White Paper August 1949*.

53. Dorothy Borg and Waldo Heinrichs, eds., *Uncertain Years: Chinese-American Relations, 1947–1950* (New York: Columbia University Press, 1980); Nancy B. Tucker, *Patterns in the Dust: Chinese-American Relations and the Recognition Controversy, 1949–1950* (New York: Columbia University Press, 1983).

# SEVEN

# Facing East and West: Agents of Encounter

In addition to state-to-state diplomacy, a variety of cultural, religious, economic, and social forces also shaped American-Chinese relations through the flow of goods, peoples, and ideas—agents of encounter, both tangible and intangible. What did Chinese and Americans learn about each other from their interactions in the first half of the twentieth century? The following three broad observations will help understand the American-Chinese encounter.

First, American learning (values, ideals, and institutions, as well as innovations and manufacturing) both inspired and assisted many American-trained Chinese from varying backgrounds to embark on their future careers, in the belief that China should learn from the American model. Second, for many Americans—representing diverse sectors of American society and working in China as missionaries, educators, and journalists, for example—their Chinese experience not only gave them knowledge of the East but also raised their consciousness with respect to both countries. Third, this reservoir of Chinese-American ties at the personal level underlined the imbalance of power between the American and Chinese states.

## TRAINED IN THE UNITED STATES: V. K. WELLINGTON KOO
## (1887–1985)

The trend for Chinese nationals to study in the United States began in 1872 with Yung Wing (1828–1912), who escorted thirty young men to study military science, shipbuilding, and navigation in the United States under the auspices of the Qing government.[1] In 1895, China's military defeat by Japan—which had undergone a rapid modernization of technology and political institutions following the 1868 Meiji Restoration—convinced many Chinese of the superiority of Western civilization and the need to introduce the technological advances of the West on a large scale. Several government decrees encouraged students to study abroad and promised rapid promotion to those who returned and made contributions to national well-being.

In the United States, a series of landmark political decisions paved the way for a stream of young Chinese students who later became notable figures in their homeland. In May 1908, the U.S. Congress passed a resolution returning to China the bulk of the unexpended Boxer Indemnity Fund, totaling about US$12,000,000, to be used by the Qing government to sponsor Chinese students to study in America.[2] In 1911, Tsing Hua College was founded in Beijing as a preparatory institution for students intending to enter American universities and colleges. In May 1924, a resolution was passed in Congress, providing for the remission to China of the remainder of the Boxer Indemnity Fund to help develop educational and cultural projects.

Commenting on the hundreds of Chinese students in the United States, a remark made in 1909 by W. W. Yen (1876–1950), a graduate of the University of Virginia and a key diplomat and politician in Republican China, was to prove uncannily prophetic: "The influence of such young men, the future leaders of China, over their country's predilections and policies will be enormous."[3] One member of this elite power base in the making was Soong Mayling, a graduate of Wellesley College and well known as a China lobbyist in the United States. Her marriage to Chiang Kai-shek in 1927 secured him important American, Protestant connections and was featured in *Time* magazine and the weekly cinema newsreel, watched by millions, celebrating all things "made in the USA." Madame Chiang's brother, T. V. Soong (finance minister in the Nanjing government), was a Harvard and Columbia graduate.

The story of Wellington Koo—China's most celebrated diplomat of modern times—is no less revealing about the extent of American influence. In 1900, Koo entered St. John's University in Shanghai. He recollected that "the atmosphere both inside and outside the college was then filled with talk of reform"—constitutional and social reform as well as the establishment of modern schools founded largely on Western learning and technology.[4] In 1904 Koo traveled to the United States together with a group of students on government scholarships.

After a year's preparatory study at Cook Academy, in Montour Falls, New York, Koo matriculated in liberal arts at Columbia University. He received an MA in 1909 and a PhD in 1912 in political science and international law under John Bassett Moore (1860–1947), an eminent jurist specializing in international law. Responding to a call by Tang Shaoyi, premier of the new Chinese Republic, and with the encouragement of Moore, Koo left for China where he first worked as English secretary to President Yuan Shikai. Koo's diplomatic and interpersonal skills made him stand out among his peers, and his services were retained by successive governments. In 1915, just three years after launching his career, Koo was promoted to the position of Chinese minister to the United States.

Following World War I, Koo was a leading member of the Chinese delegation to the Paris Conference and the Washington Conference. In the aftermath of the Mukden Incident of 1931, as minister to France, Koo represented Nationalist China on the Lytton Commission of Inquiry and later at the League of Nations in Geneva, where he solicited support for China against Japan's invasion of Manchuria. In 1943, as Chinese ambassador to the Court of St. James's in London, Koo negotiated two important treaties with Britain and the United States dealing with the relinquishment of extraterritoriality. After retiring from his post as the Nationalist government's ambassador to Washington in 1956, he was elected an international judge at the Hague, a position he held until 1966.[5]

Koo's years in America convinced him of the value of international law as a medium for resolving international disputes and promoting world peace. The author of many authoritative books on international law and diplomacy including the eight-volume *Digest of International Law* (1906), Moore was Koo's sponsor and leading advisor, and taught him the fundamental skills and tactics of diplomacy.[6] According to Moore, diplomacy was essentially a kind of warfare waged in peacetime with different weapons. For him, a diplomat must study the situations of the contracting parties with great care, always urging reconciliation and compromise for the sake of reaching agreement. Koo incorporated Moore's ideas in his doctoral dissertation on Sino-foreign cooperation and compromise in relation to the free flow of commerce and China's desire to recover its jurisdictional rights. Koo underscored the injustice and inequality imposed on China as a sovereign nation and reciprocity as a leading principle in international law.[7] Koo (and other Chinese diplomats) challenged the legality of China's unequal treaties in international law particularly at the Paris Peace Conference and Washington Conference, as I have argued in other places.[8] Just before the Paris Peace Conference, Moore advised Koo (at that time China's minister to Washington) that, despite the divisions between the foreign-recognized Beijing government and the Canton Nationalist authorities, China should preserve the facade of unity. As it turned out, the Chinese did dispatch a nominally united delegation representing both governments to Paris.[9]

Unlike many anti-imperialist activists, Koo was committed to improving China's international position through international law and diplomatic negotiations. This approach, as detailed in the previous chapter, mirrored the burgeoning interest in international law and foreign relations as well as the promotion of the foreign service as a professional career among American academics and diplomats in the fifteen years before World War I. With backing from figures such as Archibald C. Coolidge, John B. Moore, Lewis Einstein, and Paul S. Reinsch (minister to China), great hopes were held for the role of international law in regulating international competition and power politics, thus making the world a more peaceful and predictable place.[10]

As a highly skilled professional diplomat, Wellington Koo showed what could be achieved when the respective cultural contributions of the United States and China were combined and harmonized. Commenting on Koo's trouncing of the Japanese delegation in Paris over the return of Shandong to China, Robert Lansing, secretary of state (1915–20), wrote,

> In a note on the meeting I recorded that "He [Koo] simply overwhelmed the Japanese with his argument." I believe that that opinion was common to all those who heard the two presentations [Japanese and Koo's]. In fact it made such an impression on the Japanese themselves, that one of the delegates called upon me the following day and attempted to offset the effect by declaring that the United States, since it had not promised to support Japan's contention, would be blamed if

Kiao-chow [Jiaozhou, part of Shandong] would be [sic] returned directly to China.[11]

## GROWING UP IN CHINA: PEARL S. BUCK (1892–1973)

Drawing on the experiences of the first forty years of her life, Pearl S.
Buck was the most popular and most translated American writer on China. Her career as a writer was full of irony and paradox. She was the first
woman to win the Pulitzer Prize in 1932 and the first American female
laureate to hold the Nobel Prize in literature, which she won in 1938 for
her realistic portrayal of Chinese peasants and rural life in novels including *The Good Earth*, *Sons*, and *A House Divided*. Despite these achievements, she languished in obscurity for decades. There were two main
reasons for the "lack of respect" she received. First, she focused on China
and women, both of which were considered "marginal" subjects in
American literary tradition. Second, she alienated both ends of the political spectrum: the absence of Christian sentiment in her novels and her
civil rights activities irritated the right, while her anti-Communist stance
exasperated the left. Throughout her life, Buck devoted herself to furthering the mutual understanding of East and West, yet her books, celebrated
in the West for her grasp of the "real" China, were disparaged by Chinese
of varying political and cultural complexions who criticized her treatment of Chinese people as superficial and offensive. The Guomindang
government refused to attend her Nobel Prize award ceremony, and the
People's Republic denied her visa application in 1972 following President
Nixon's historic visit to China. Only in the late 1990s did Pearl Buck
become "rehabilitated" and begin to attract renewed interest in the United States and China.[12]

A further irony was the stir that Buck generated in the Christian community. Born to Presbyterian missionary parents (Absalom and Carie
Sydenstricker), once married to a missionary agriculturist (John Lossing
Buck), and a missionary herself, she questioned the misrepresentation by
some missionaries of the Christian message in China. In the thick of the
anti-Christian movement and the Nationalist revolution of the 1920s, she
called for an intellectual and spiritual overhaul of the missionary enterprise. In articles in the *Chinese Recorder* in 1927 and *Harper's Monthly* in
1933, Buck openly criticized the narrowness and racial superiority of
many Christian missions. Uncomfortable as it was for many American

Christians, Buck raised doubts about the unquestioned assumptions of many missionaries and their supporters about China—the wretched dwellings, the naked children, the bound feet, and the placid souls awaiting the word of redemption from the West. "I have seen him [the missionary] so filled with arrogance in his own beliefs, so sure that all truth was with him and him only, that my heart has knelt with a humble one before the shrine of Buddha rather than before the God of that missionary, if that God could be true." [13]

To Buck, many missionaries failed to appreciate the simple—but very different—logic of life in China: "this foreign missionary has, it is true, too often seen only what he allowed himself to see." Her exemplary missionary was blind to "the sunshine pouring in, even into the hovel, the placid little daily round carried on there in great contentment and good humor, the merry laughter of glistening little brown persons rolling in the dust and acutely happy in their freedom, the pride of the mother in her small feet, and the joy in life of the smiling, philosophical father, idling in the sunshine of the threshold." [14] And the missionaries had failed even to follow Christ's teaching:

> We have approached these foreign countries not in the spirit in which Christ approached men. We have come too often in lordliness and consciousness of race superiority. We have glorified in our own minds the conditions in our countries. It is true that in our loneliness home looked very sweet and good. But that is no excuse for failing to see the grave faults in our own civilizations. . . . When we took upon ourselves that vow to a higher loyalty, why did we not see that Christ's loyalty was to humanity and make ours that also? [15]

Buck's scathing candidness about missions and missionaries was an expression of her spiritual ideals—principles that transcended race and nation and promoted "the highest trained intelligence, the keenest sympathies, the most delicate perceptions, the most profound moral and spiritual convictions." In sum, Buck was a product of the liberal rethinking of Christianity in China inside and outside the church in both the United States and China.

In the history of American Christianity in China, no single year was marked by greater irony than 1922, when the publication of *The Christian Occupation of China*—a work which symbolized the "peak of missionary self-confidence"—coincided with the outbreak of what became known as the Anti-Christian Movement, which lasted five years to 1927. [16] On February 26, 1922, in reaction to the announcement that the World Student Christian Federation's eleventh conference would be held in Beijing, a group of students from Shanghai founded the Anti-Christian Student Federation (ACSF). Imbued with the Bolshevik revolutionary worldview and its theory of class struggle, the ACSF manifesto—published in the Socialist Youth League's magazine *Xianqu* (*Vanguard*) on March 9— linked Christianity to the Western capitalist exploitation of China. Anti-religious sentiments were again dominant in the manifesto issued two days later by the Grand Anti-religion Federation, organized by Beijing's intelligentsia. These events ignited a war against Christianity in China.[17] During the period 1922–27, Chinese critics castigated Christianity as a foreign import and the vanguard of imperialism.

Chinese yearning for independence, as Thomas F. Millard—a long-time *China Coast* journalist and founder of *Millard's Weekly*—put it,

> is a logical outcome of progress and must have been expected. It follows closely in the wake of the similar movement in Japan and reflected in other Asiatic countries and beyond doubt is the manifestation of the development of nationalistic consciousness among Asiatics. . . . The existing "anti-foreign" troubles here have given definite proof that the body of Chinese Christians are in complete sympathy with the national aspirations of New China.[18]

Although there were large numbers of missionaries in the field and many professed Chinese Christians, some reports, echoing Pearl Buck, spoke of the "shallow hold" of Christianity on the Chinese mind, especially among intellectuals. "How has foreign influence and the teaching and the example of foreigners in China affected the political institutions and practices of the country?" one commentator asked skeptically. Others reflected soberly on the influence of the missions and Chinese Christianity amid the intellectual ferment and social turbulence of the times. The Reverend James M. Yard, a Methodist missionary in Shanghai, noted gravely, "We are seeing weakness that we were not aware of and we are being roused mentally and spiritually by the great upheaval."[19]

Adding to the anti-religious forces at work in China, the Restoring Educational Rights Movement of 1924 formed the second phase of the Anti-Christian Movement, aimed at Christian colleges and schools and incorporating stronger anti-imperialist and nationalist elements.[20] Despite this "most severe setback" for Christianity in China, some American newspaper commentators called for patience and persistence. Like Millard, others espoused the naturalization of Christianity in China: "China can well be left to interpret the Gospel in its own way. Maybe they can do a better job than we can."[21]

With its intellectual precedents in imperial Ming and Qing China, the Anti-Christian Movement of 1922–27 formulated its assault on Christianity not just in anti-religious polemic, but in anti-capitalist, anti-imperialist, and nationalistic terms.[22] For Chinese Christians, the movement confronted them with two vital questions: How should Christians address the relationship between the Christian faith and imperialism? And was there a biblical justification for the proactive involvement of Christians in nationalist endeavors and social reform? Riding the wave of self-examination both within and outside the Christian community across the Pacific, Pearl Buck addressed these questions by looking at the other side of the same coin.

## MAVERICK VOICES: EDGAR SNOW (1905–72) AND CHEN XUJING (CH'EN SU-CHING, 1903–67)

American views of China have very often reflected the divisions within American society itself: "There were competing images, with varying degrees of correspondence to reality, which were used as weapons in struggles among different segments of American society to gain hegemony over one another by defining their society's relationship to a dimly understood Other."[23] The perceptions of China nurtured by Pearl Buck were a far cry from the first account in English of Mao Zedong and other Communist leaders written by Edgar Snow, the plucky journalist who first ventured into the Chinese Communist Party's base in Yan'an in 1936. A very different perspective is provided by Chen Xujing, a fine scholar and educator with expertise in sociology, political science, cultural studies, and history. Chen had gained a PhD from the University of Illinois in 1928 and went on to champion the total Americanization and Westernization (*quanpan xihua* 全盘西化) of Chinese higher education and culture.

During the 1930s and 1940s, American media tycoon Henry R. Luce — a missionary child who grew up in China and a passionate promoter of America's leading role in world affairs — was an enthusiastic supporter of Chiang Kai-shek, whom he saw as a natural ally of America. Primarily through *Time* and *Life* magazines, Luce fostered an image of Chiang as the authentic popular leader of China, dedicated to bringing Christianity, democracy, and modernity to the nation.[24] In the cinema, the American wartime film *The Battle of China*, directed by Frank Capra and Anatole Litvak, also fueled the U.S. infatuation with Chiang Kai-shek, treating him in almost hagiographical terms.

However, this favorable image of Chiang did not go unchallenged. Many Chinese and some Americans living in China did little to conceal their discontent with the Nationalist leader. Even in the Luce media stable, the doings of Mao and the Chinese Communists were paraded before American policy makers and ordinary readers. More than forty rare photographs of Communist troops, taken by Edgar Snow, were published in the January and February 1937 issues of *Life*, along with a positive commentary:

> Their leaders were Mao Tse-tung [Mao Zedong] as Chairman and Chu Teh [Zhu De], as field commander. Able commanders flocked to them. These men, unlike most Chinese warlords, could not be bribed. It took Chiang nearly four years to dislodge them. In 1934 they slipped past his lines and headed for the Chinese Northwest, in a great 7,000-mile circle of flight. In the course of this "Heroic Trek," the Communist army of 100,000 avidly battled with Chiang's troops. But once they had reached the Northwest, the Chinese Communists were in a strategically perfect spot. They rapidly extended their influence over an area with a population of some 20,000,000 people.[25]

In the February 1937 issue of *Life*, the Chinese Communists were presented as a decisive force in Chinese politics, in the context of the 1936 Xi'an Incident and the second United Front between Chiang and Mao:

> On Jan. 18 [1937] Chang's [Zhang Xueliang] allies in Sian [Xi'an], scene of the kidnapping, "rebelled" against Generalissimo Chiang, invited the nearby Communist agents to come to Sian and propagandize their troops. On Jan. 19, they gave field command of all Sian troops to P'eng Teh-huai [Peng Dehuai], Communist commander . . . and gave the Communist armies $250,000 and sorely needed arms. A Communist spokesman for P'eng announced: "We are not anti-foreign nor anti-religious, only anti-Japanese. If Chiang Kai-shek will declare himself against the Japanese, we will obey him. We want all parties to be represented in a parliament or congress and want a democratic constitution. If our suggestion is complied with, we will drop Sovietism. Our armies have been fought for ten years in many provinces but we are not yet exterminated. Instead we are stronger than ever." This cock's crow by

no means meant that the Communists were willing to be absorbed in
Chiang's armies. It was in fact accompanied by demands for arms and
money gifts from Chiang.[26]

Born in Kansas City, Missouri, and a journalism graduate from the University of Missouri, Edgar Snow worked as a writer and journalist in China from 1928 to 1941. In 1936, he broke through the Nationalist government's blockade and spent four months (June–October) in the Communist-controlled zone in Northwest China. Snow gave a detailed historical account of the rise of the Chinese Communist movement in his newspaper reports and in his book, *Red Star over China*, first published in 1937.[27] Based on personal interviews, although criticized at home for being too credulous, *Red Star over China* is still the most gripping account of the early years of the Chinese Communist Party. In his book, Snow concluded presciently that the "movement for social revolution in China . . . would not only continue to mature; in one mutation or another it would eventually win, simply because . . . the basic conditions which had given it birth carried within themselves the dynamic necessity for its triumph."[28]

The Snow story had a bitter sequel back in the United States. In the early 1950s, tolerance of dissenting views and independent inquiry fell prey to the "Red Scare" and demagogic McCarthyism, inflicting deep and lasting wounds on all parties involved. Since Snow had been the first to report what the Chinese Communists had said and done, he, like many other American "China hands," became the target of allegations that he was "un-American" and "pro-Communist." Renewed interest in Snow in the 1980s on both sides of the Pacific once again mirrored the constantly changing nature of the relationship and the political and cultural contradictions inherent in it.

On the Chinese side, Chen Xujing, displaying a maverick spirit similar to Snow's, was the first to propose that thoroughgoing Westernization was the solution to China's problems. A native of Hainan and a former student in the United States and Germany, Chen was on the faculty of Nankai University in Tianjin for ten years before taking up a teaching post and later the presidency (1948–52) at Lingnan University in Canton.[29]

Together with the Warring States and Weijin periods, the early twentieth century has been categorized as the third major phase of cultural pluralization in Chinese history. These decades witnessed heated debates about the direction of Chinese educational reforms and their likely impact on the relationship between tradition and modernity, and between East and West. Guangdong educator Xu Chongqing (1888–1969, president of Yat-sen University in 1931–32 and 1940–41) advocated education as a means of increasing social productivity: "the correlation between education and society is equivalent to the relationship between education and production."[30]

In contrast with Chinese tradition, which separated manual labor from education, Xu's concept was centered on production as the core of the new educational system. Another educator from Guangdong, Lin Liru (1889–1977, president of Canton Normal College, 1922–27, and of Beijing Normal University, 1950–52) called for the development of normal schools based on two educational principles, popularization and modernization.[31] Pondering the future of education in China, a third educator, Chen Qingzhi, proposed a three-tier system: basic education, education for production, and advanced study. Chen's system was intended to orient both primary and secondary education toward practical labor and production for national needs. He believed that universities should be replaced by specialized technical higher institutions and that research institutions should be reserved for an elite group able to engage in scholarly work.[32] Socialist educator Jiang Qi rejected foreign educational models and instead advocated specialized programs at primary, secondary, and tertiary levels.[33]

Standing in the forefront of these debates on Chinese and Western culture in the 1920s and 1930s, Chen Xujing stated that his ultimate aim was to find a way out for Chinese culture. He wrote, "[T]o save China from its present threat of extinction, we have to be thoroughly Westernized. Wholesale Westernization, however, will involve a complete break with the cultural monopoly enjoyed by Chinese tradition in order to provide individuals with the opportunities they need to fulfill their potential."[34] As a part of this Westernization process, Chen suggested that Chinese education, as an integral component of the culture, must be thoroughly modernized to avoid the danger of a regressive return to traditional ways. "Since 1872, when the first batch of government-sponsored students was sent to the U.S., all so-called educational modernization movements have become mired in the quagmire of superficiality." Chen pointed to the pitfalls in China's previous experience with sending students overseas:

Since the Chinese authorities did not want students studying abroad to forget their own culture, they built comfortable quarters to accommodate them. Hence, except for going to classes and on special occasions, Chinese students on government bursaries read Chinese classics, spoke Chinese, and made Chinese friends—their life in America was much the same as in China. . . . As a consequence, these Chinese students missed the opportunity to observe the true spirit of education and life in the West.[35]

Having witnessed for himself the prosperity and advanced state of American and European societies, Chen Xujing expressed his confidence in Western capitalist civilization: China "must utilize American learning to become more like America." Despite his cultural radicalism, Chen's aim was to save China—to save it from itself.[36] His work also focused on fundamental issues in higher education, advocating the acquisition of knowledge for its own sake. After the establishment of the People's Republic, Chen gradually fell out of favor with the government and shifted his energies to academic research on various topics including Southeast Asian history. During the Cultural Revolution, he was branded as an "American-imperialist spy," and he died of a heart attack in 1967.

## FURTHER OBSERVATIONS

These character portraits have been chosen to illustrate how a diverse set of personalities—each with their own areas of expertise—and particular circumstances shaped the rich array of encounters between Americans and Chinese who had lived on each other's soil. Wellington Koo and Chen Xujing's American experience helped mold their convictions that in the fields of international law, education, and culture, Western practices should be utilized to the fullest extent in China's national interests. In the case of Pearl Buck and Edgar Snow, by contrast, the complex and subtle realities of China challenged superficial idealism and exclusive claims to truth exhibited by some Americans—the truth about life, about progress, about China, and about humanity itself. To Buck and Snow, the encounter with China stimulated soul-searching on issues confronting Americans from all walks of life such as race, nationalism, revolution, imperialism, justice, equality, and freedom.

In all these interactions, however, the balance of forces was never equal. In 1929, when the Nationalist Nanjing government had only just come to power, half of the sixty or so foreign advisors already working for the GMD regime were Americans. It would have been inconceivable for a comparable number of Chinese nationals to have been hired as advisors by any U.S. government.

This imbalance was also manifested in trade figures. Between 1868 and 1945, the total volume of China's international trade increased more than threefold, from US$193.9 million to $709.4 million.[37] Within the same period, the value of America's foreign trade grew over nineteen times, from US$748 million to $14,377 million (over $14 billion). In 1945, China's total international export and import trade was just over 2 percent of that of the United States. As a net creditor on international accounts, the United States held no more than 7 percent of foreign investments in China by 1930—constituting only about 1 percent of total U.S. overseas investments ($17.2 billion) at the time—far behind British and Japanese holdings ($1.2 billion and $1.1 billion, respectively) in China.[38] However, America's wartime alliance with China substantially changed the situation. Before World War I, trade between the United States and China accounted for around 10 percent of China's total trade with all countries; by the end of World War II in 1945, the ratio was about 60 percent—a clear indication that political relations were an important driver in the process whereby the United States overtook Britain and Japan in the Chinese market.[39]

As one of the earliest agents of encounter between the United States and China, Christianity sheds further light on the complexities of the bilateral relationship, especially in the emerging Cold War culture at the dawn of Communist domination in China.

First, the burgeoning diversity of Chinese Protestantism in the four decades from the 1910s to the 1940s was a phenomenon little known to the American public. Alongside the institutionalized denominational churches—the direct offspring of missionary efforts—independent and sectarian Chinese-led churches, with names like the True Jesus Church, the Jesus Family, and the "Little Flock," were flourishing. Theologically, the situation was equally diverse. In China as elsewhere, conservative fundamentalists and liberal modernists drew their own lines between the "social gospel" and individual salvation.[40] A dynamic pluralism, corresponding to the major currents in world Christianity, defined the landscape of Protestantism in China prior to 1949.

A particular irony is found in the fact that the post-1949 official Protestant church, which had developed from the Three-Self Patriotic Movement (TSPM, the three selves being "self-supporting," "self-governing," and "self-propagating"),[41] was not the creation of the Chinese Communist Party, but had grown out of the American missions and the theological, social, and political divisions among Chinese Christians.

Before the Communist defeat of Chiang Kai-shek, a group of educated Chinese Christian leaders who adopted a liberal theology and who supported a national independence and reformist approach had already spoken positively of socialist revolution and the Communist worldview.[42] Influential figures such as Y. T. Wu (Wu Yaozong, 1893–1979) and K. H. Ting (Ding Guangxun, 1915– ) advocated integrating Gospel values with Chinese circumstances and the revolutionary movement in the 1940s. In 1948, Wu identified the lack of understanding of the Chinese revolution as a "present-day tragedy" for Chinese Christianity:

> There are many blind people who think that the expression "class struggle" is just a deceitful slogan of one political party, they do not recognize that the existence of classes is a historical fact. They do not grieve over the existence of classes, nor think how to abolish them, but only resent those who do. . . . Capitalism can no longer meet the needs of our time; it only creates economic inequality and imperialism.[43]

Wu called on Christians to relate their faith to the reality of contemporary China and bow to the spirit of the Anti-Christian Movement of the 1920s: "Now over twenty years have passed, and as we look back we cannot but admit that the charges had a good deal of truth in them. If our thinking had remained the same as Western Christian thinking, we should indeed have become unconscious tools of imperialism and cultural aggression."[44]

Such denunciations of Christianity's association with imperialism and capitalism drew fire from within the Christian camp. In China, leading Catholics were at odds with some of their Protestant counterparts on the question of self-governance, self-support, and self-propagation. A Catholic pamphlet, entitled "Tianzhu jiao Zhongguo quanti zhujiao xuanyan" [The manifesto of all China's Catholic bishops], stated that the pope—rather than the head of state—held supreme authority over the Catholic faithful, and that no external agency could undermine the structure and solidarity of the Roman Catholic Church.[45]

In seeking to explain the rapid growth of Chinese Protestantism in the 1980s and early 1990s, Alan Hunter and Kim-kwong Chan argued that the TSPM and the China Christian Council (CCC) "essentially maintains a church tradition inherited from western missionaries. Urban-based, its congregations are relatively [well] educated, and its intellectual environment increasingly modern and rationalistic."[46]

Second, the "loss of China" by the United States not only intensified the climate of fear about the international situation and perceptions of the Chinese Communist Party as a ruthless tyranny, but also ironically fueled frustration and anger over America's record of racism and religious conflict around the world. This in turn motivated the Truman administration to make limited improvements on human rights and race relations in the United States. One writer commented in the *Chicago Defender*:

> The communists were able to do with China in a few years what America was unable to do in a century. . . . Race prejudice in America has been Russia's theme song among the other nations of the world. You understand, we call ourselves Christians. But the American's [*sic*] idea of Christianity carries a limited approach. If you are White, then you are Heaven-bound; but if you are colored there is no space allotted to you in the American concept of Christianity. . . . We are profuse with words but are short on deeds.[47]

## FURTHER READING

Chinese students in the United States are discussed in Qingjia Edward Wang, "Guests from the Open Door: The Reception of Chinese Students into the United States, 1900s–1920s," *Journal of American-East Asian Relations* 3, no. 1 (Spring 1994): 55–75; Stacey Bieler, *"Patriots" or "Traitors"? A History of American-Educated Chinese Students* (Armonk, N.Y.: M. E. Sharpe, 2004); and Weili Ye, *Seeking Modernity in China's Name: Chinese Students in the United States, 1900–1927* (Stanford, Calif.: Stanford University Press, 2001).

For further information on cultural, social, and economic relations between the United States and China, see James Reed, *The Missionary Mind and American East Asian Policy, 1911–1915* (Cambridge, Mass.: Council on East Asian Studies, Harvard University, 1983); James C. Thomson Jr., *While China Faced West: American Reformers in Nationalist China, 1928–37* (Cambridge, Mass.: Harvard University Press, 1969); Randall E.

Stross, *The Stubborn Earth: American Agriculturalists on Chinese Soil, 1898–1937* (Berkeley, Calif.: University of California Press, 1986); Charles W. Hayford, *To the People: James Yen and Village China* (New York: Columbia University Press, 1990); Yu-ming Shaw, *An American Missionary in China: John Leighton Stuart and Chinese-American Relations* (Cambridge, Mass.: Council on East Asian Studies, Harvard University, 1992); Robert Edwin Herzstein, *Henry R. Luce,* Time, *and the American Crusade in Asia* (Cambridge: Cambridge University Press, 2005); R. David Arkush and Leo E. Lee, eds., *Land without Ghosts: Chinese Impressions of America from the Mid-Nineteenth Century to the Present* (Berkeley, Calif.: University of California Press, 1989).

In the text, although I was unable to make room to further explicate economic relations between the United States and the Republic of China, I have found the works below enlightening. Yu-Kwei Cheng, *Foreign Trade and Industrial Development of China: A Historical and Integrated Analysis through 1948* (Washington, D.C.: University Press of Washington, D.C., 1956); Peter Schran, "Minor Significance of Commercial Relations between the United States and China, 1850–1931," and Mira Wilkins, "The Impacts of American Multinational Enterprise on American-Chinese Economic Relations, 1786–1949," in Ernest R. May and John K. Fairbank, eds., *America's China Trade in Historical Perspective: The Chinese and American Performance* (Cambridge, Mass.: Committee on American-East Asian Relations, Harvard University, 1986), pp. 237–292; Tomoko Shiroyama, *China during the Great Depression: Market, State, and the World Economy, 1929–1937* (Cambridge, Mass.: Harvard University Asia Center, 2008); Parks M. Coble Jr., *The Shanghai Capitalists and the Nationalist Government, 1927–1937* (Cambridge, Mass.: Harvard University Press, 1986; 1st ed. in 1980); Morris Bian, *The Making of the State Enterprise System in Modern China: The Dynamics of Institutional Change* (Cambridge, Mass.: Harvard University Press, 2005).

## NOTES

1. Yung Wing, born in Guangdong Province in South China, was brought to the United States by an American missionary, Samuel Robbins Brown, at the age of sixteen. Following his graduation from Yale University in 1854, Yung returned to China to promote study overseas. Yung Wing, *My Life in China and America* (New York: Henry Holt, 1909).

2. For the various self-interested American proposals to use the Boxer indemnity funds, see Richard H. Werking, "The Boxer Indemnity Remission and the Hunt Thesis," *Diplomatic History* 2, no. 1 (January 1978): 103–106; Michael H. Hunt, "The American Remission of the Boxer Indemnity: A Reappraisal," *Journal of Asian Studies* 31, no. 3 (May 1972): 539–559.

3. W. W. Yen, "China and the United States," *Chinese Students' Monthly* 5, no. 2 (December 1909): 59.

4. Wellington Koo, *The Wellington Koo Memoir*, microfilm reel 1, under "Reform Sentiment at St. John's University, Shanghai, 1900–1904."

5. Hui-lan Koo (Madame Wellington Koo), *Hui-lan Koo: An Autobiography* (New York: Dial Press, 1945) and *No Feast Lasts Forever* (New York: Quadrangle, 1975). Stephen G. Craft, *V. K. Wellington Koo and the Emergence of Modern China* (Lexington, Ky.: University Press of Kentucky, 2004); Jonathan Clements, *Wellington Koo: China, Makers of the Modern World* (London: Haus Publishing, 2008).

6. Moore's other important works include *The Principles of American Diplomacy* (New York: Harper & Brothers, 1918); *The Collected Papers of John Bassett Moore* (New Haven, Conn.: Yale University Press, 1944).

7. Wellington Koo, *The Status of Aliens in China* (New York: Columbia University, 1912), PhD dissertation, p. 355.

8. Dong Wang, *China's Unequal Treaties: Narrating National History* (Lanham, Md.: Rowman & Littlefield, 2005), chapter 2.

9. Wunsz King, *Cong bali hehui dao guolian* [从巴黎和会到国联 From the Paris Peace Conference to the League of Nations] (Taipei: Zhuanji wenxue chubanshe, 1967), p. 4.

10. Robert D. Schulzinger, *The Making of the Diplomatic Mind: The Training, Outlook, and Style of United States Foreign Service Officers, 1908–1931* (Middletown, Conn.: Wesleyan University Press, 1975).

11. Robert Lansing, *The Peace Negotiations: A Personal Narrative* (Boston, Mass.: Houghton Mifflin, 1921), p. 253.

12. James Thomson, "Why Doesn't Pearl Buck Get Respect?" *Philadelphia Inquirer* (July 24, 1992), A15; Peter J. Conn, *Pearl S. Buck: A Cultural Biography* (Cambridge: Cambridge University Press, 1996); Kang Liang, *Pearl S. Buck: A Cultural Bridge across the Pacific* (Westport, Conn.: Greenwood Press, 1997); Gao Xiongya, *Pearl S. Buck's Chinese Women Characters* (Cranbury, N.J.: Associated University Press, 2000); Hilary Spurling, *Pearl Buck in China: Journey to The Good Earth* (New York: Simon & Schuster, 2010).

13. Pearl S. Buck, "Is There a Case for Foreign Missions?" *Harper's Monthly* (January 1933): 143–155.

14. Pearl S. Buck, "Is There a Place for the Foreign Missionary?" *Chinese Recorder* 58 (February 1927): 100–107.

15. Pearl S. Buck, "Is There a Place for the Foreign Missionary?"

16. Bob Whyte, *Unfinished Encounter: China and Christianity* (Harrisburg, Pa.: Morehouse Publishing, 1988), p. 151. The section below is drawn from Dong Wang, "Portraying Chinese Christianity: The American Press and U.S.-China Relations since the 1920s," *Journal of American-East Asian Relations* 13 (November 2008): 81–119.

17. Yang Tianhong, *Jidujiao yu minguo zhishi fenzi* [基督教与民国知识分子 Christianity and the intelligentsia in the Republic of China] (Beijing: Renmin chubanshe, 2005). Jessie Gregory Lutz, *Chinese Politics and Christian Missions: The Anti-Christian Movements of 1920–28* (Notre Dame, Ind.: Cross Cultural Publications, Cross Roads Books, 1988).

18. Thomas F. Millard, "Chinese Christians among Disaffected," *New York Times,* September 8, 1925, p. 6.

19. "Preachers See Good in Chinese Upheaval," *New York Times,* July 5, 1925, p. 8.

20. Yang Tianhong, *Jidujiao yu minguo zhishi fenzi,* pp. 235–249.

21. "Christian Revival in China Reported: Dr. T. W. Mitchell, Missionary, Lays Renewed Interest to Communist Persecution," *New York Times,* March 24, 1930, p. 19.

22. "Chinese Christians See Gain in Turmoil," *New York Times,* February 13, 1927, p. 16.

23. Richard Madsen's review of *American Images of China, 1931–1949* by T. Christopher Jesperson in the *Journal of American History* 83, no. 4 (March 1997): 1463–1464.

24. T. Christopher Jesperson, *American Images of China 1931–1949* (Stanford, Calif.: Stanford University Press, 1996).

25. Edgar Snow, in *Life,* February 1, 1937.

26. *Life,* February 1, 1937.

27. S. Bernard Thomas, *Season of High Adventure: Edgar Snow in China* (Berkeley, Calif.: University of California Press, 1996); John Maxwell Hamilton, *Edgar Snow: A Biography* (Bloomington, Ind.: Indiana University Press, 1988).

28. Edgar Snow, *Red Star over China,* revised and enlarged ed. (New York: Grove, 1968; 1st ed. published in 1937 by Random House), p. 409.

29. The section on Chen Xujing is drawn from Dong Wang, "Circulating American Higher Education: The Case of Lingnan University (1888–1951)," *Journal of American-East Asian Relations* 9, nos. 3–4 (delayed Fall–Winter 2000 issue; the back issue appeared in 2006): 147–167.

30. Xu Chongqing (许崇清), *Xu Chongqing wenji* [许崇清文集 Collected works of Xu Chongqing], ed. Xu Xihui (Guangzhou: Guangdong jiaoyu chubanshe, 2004), p. 164.

31. Ou Chu (欧初), *Minguo shiqi de jiaoyu* [民国时期的教育 Education in Republican China] (Guangzhou: Guangdong renmin chubanshe, 1996), pp. 67–80.

32. Chen Qingzhi (陈青之), *Zhongguo jiaoyushi* [中国教育史 A history of education in China] (Shanghai: Shanghai shangwu yinshu guan, 1936), pp. 794–810.

33. Ruth Hayhoe, ed., *Education and Modernization: The Chinese Experience* (Oxford: Pergamon Press, 1992), pp. 58–59.

34. Chen Xujing (陈序经), *Zhongguo wenhua de chulu* [中国文化的出路 The future of Chinese culture] (Shanghai: Commercial Press, 1934).

35. Yang Shen (杨深), ed., *Zuochu Dongfang: Chen Xujing wenhua lunzhu jiyao* [走出东方:陈序经文化论著辑要 Going beyond the East: A collection of Chen Xujing's works on culture] (Beijing: Zhongguo guangbo dianshi chubanshe, 1995), pp. 204–213.

36. Chen Xujing, *Dongxi wenhua guan* [东西文化观 A personal view of the cultures of East and West], *Lingnan xuebao* [岭南学报 Lingnan journal], vol. 5, nos. 1–4 (July, August, and December 1936).

37. Wang Xi (汪熙) and Hu Hanjun (胡涵钧), "Zhongmei maoyi de lishi, xianzhuang he qianjing" [中美贸易的历史、现状和前景 Sino-American trade—past, present, and future prospects], in Gu Yunshen (顾云深), Shi Yuanhua (石源华), and Jin Guangyao (金光耀), eds., *Jianzhi wanglai: bainian Zhongmei jingji guanxi de huigu yu qianzhan* [鉴知往来: 百年来中美经济关系的回顾与前瞻 Looking back and forward: A century of Sino-American economic relations] (Shanghai: Fundan daxue chubanshe, 1999), pp. 11–21.

38. Bureau of the Census with the Cooperation of the Social Science Research Council, *Historical Statistics of the United States: Colonial Times to 1957* (Washington, D.C.: U.S. Government Printing Office, 1960), p. 565; Michael H. Hunt, "Americans in the China

Market: Economic Opportunities and Economic Nationalism, 1890s–1931," *Business History Review* 51, no. 3 (Autumn 1977): 277–307.

39. Yang Yuqing (杨雨青), "Kangri zhanzheng shiqi Zhongmei jingji guanxi yanjiu shuping" [抗日战争时期中美经济关系研究述评 A bibliographic assessment of the study of Sino-American economic relations during the Anti-Japanese War], *Lishi yanjiu*, no. 3 (2006): 167–175. For the political influence of Britain and the United States on the Beijing government finances (1912–28), see Roberta Allbert Dayer, *Bankers and Diplomats in China 1917–1925* (London: Frank Cass, 1981). Also see "Further Reading" at the end of this chapter.

40. China had become an important mission battlefield for conservative fundamentalist and liberal modernist Protestants. Fundamentalist missionaries stressed the unerring authority of the Bible and the supernatural dimension of the Gospel "in response to the modernists' advocacy of higher criticism and their humanistic re-interpretation of the scripture." Chinese fundamentalists also "insisted on the central place of preaching in mission work and the priority of evangelism over social service. Furthermore, fundamentalist missionaries rejected the liberal missionaries' conciliatory and cooperative approach to non-Christian religions, and firmly stood for the uniqueness and finality of Christ." Kevin Xiyi Yao, *The Fundamentalist Movement among Protestant Missionaries in China, 1920–1937* (Lanham, Md.: University Press of America, 2003), pp. 281–282. Alan Hunter and Kim-kwong Chan, *Protestantism in Contemporary China* (Cambridge: Cambridge University Press, 1993), pp. 119–135. Also see Lian Xi, *The Conversion of Missionaries: Liberalism in American Protestant Missions in China, 1907–1932* (University Park, Pa.: Pennsylvania State University Press, 1997).

41. The early shapers of the self-reliant indigenous church included Henry Venn (1796–1873), Rufus Anderson (1796–1880), and John Livingstone Nevius (1829–93). Nevius and his impact on Christianity in China are discussed in part 1 of this book.

42. Yihua Xu, "'Patriotic' Protestants: The Making of an Official Church," in Jason Kindopp and Carol Lee Hamrin, eds., *God and Caesar in China* (Washington, D.C.: Brookings Institution Press), pp. 107–121.

43. Y. T. Wu (Wu Yaozong), "The Present Day Tragedy of Christianity," in National Council of the Churches of Christ in the U.S.A., comp., *Documents of the Three-Self Movement: Source Materials for the Study of the Protestant Church in Communist China* (New York: National Council of the Churches of Christ in the USA, 1963), pp. 1–5. K. H. Ting (Ding Guangxun), *Christian Witness in China Today* (Kyoto: Doshisha University Press, 1985).

44. Y. T. Wu, "The Present Day Tragedy of Christianity."

45. This pamphlet bears an additional title, "Tianzhu jiao duiyu ziyang zichuan zizhi yundong de guandian; Tianzhu jiao Zhongguo quanti zhujiao xuanyan" [天主教对于自养、自传、自治运动的观点: 天主教中国全体主教宣言 Catholics' views on the movement for self-support, self-propagation, and self-governance: The manifesto of all China's Catholic bishops], date unknown, Rongzeng dang 32, document donated by Rong Mengyuan and held at the Institute of Modern History, the Chinese Academy of Social Sciences in Beijing. This was a key document (circulated in 1950–51 in my judgment) in the Catholic resistance against the Chinese government drive for an "Independent Catholic Church," led by Archbishop Antonio Riberi (1897–1967), Nuncio to China (1946–58), and Bishop Gaetano Mignani (1882–1973), vicar apostolic of Ji'an in Jiangxi. In a circular letter to all the bishops in China, Archbishop Riberi stated that the Catholic religion was "superpolitical, indivisible by national boundaries or political differences. . . . And the so-called Independent Catholic Church . . . is simply a

schismatic church and not the true and one Catholic Church." See "Catholics in China," *Time*, July 2, 1951, http://www.time.com/printout/0,8816,815075,00.html (accessed August 3, 2008), and "Pray for China," *Time*, September 17, 1951, http://www.time.com/magazine/article/0,9171,815470,00.html (accessed August 3, 2008).

46. Alan Hunter and Kim-kwong Chan, *Protestantism in Contemporary China*, p. 138.

47. A N [*sic*] Fields, "Billions of Dollars Can't Stem Onward March of Communism," *Chicago Defender*, February 18, 1950, p. 7.

# EIGHT

## Deterrence and Negotiation: American-Chinese Relations during the Cold War

This chapter sheds new light on the deep conflicts as well as the positive dynamics in Sino-American relations in the 1950s and 1960s. Some scholars refer to these years as the "great interregnum" because formal diplomatic relations were not reestablished until 1979. American support for the Guomindang (GMD) in the Chinese civil war and its military involvement in the Korean War, combined with Chinese advocacy of Third World revolutions, fed political and ideological conflict. At the same time—behind the scenes—both nations were feeling their way toward some kind of equilibrium. Key issues during this period include U.S. recognition of the People's Republic of China (PRC), China's representation in the United Nations, the Korean and Vietnam wars, and continuing geopolitical maneuverings—spanning the spectrum from hostility to negotiation—between the two countries.

Three points are worth noting. First, while American-Chinese relations were publicly contentious, following the armistice in the U.S.-Korean War, the leaders of both nations sought ways of easing the tensions between them behind closed doors. No fewer than 136 bilateral ambassadorial exchanges punctuated the decade and a half between August 1955 and February 1970. In 1973 the PRC and the United States established liaison offices in each other's capitals.[1] Despite the overt atmosphere of hostility, the two nations maintained channels of communication at various levels—official and unofficial, direct and indirect.[2]

Second, the Taiwan issue—the "One China" or the "Two Chinas" question[3]—was a stumbling block to good relations, resulting from America's long-standing commitment to Taiwan (formerly known as Formosa) and, opposing this stance, mainland China's consistent claim that the island territory was integral to its sovereignty as accorded by the Cairo Declaration of 1943.[4] Arising from international and domestic developments in the 1950s, the Taiwan question posed a formidable obstacle to the normalization and improvement of relations between the United States and China. In negotiations of the 1950s, the United States sought repudiation of force in the Taiwan Strait by both mainland China and Taiwan, while China insisted on negotiating directly with Chiang Kai-shek and approached Taiwan as an issue of sovereign rights, an internal rather than an international matter.

The third proposition is that the road leading to the rapprochement achieved in 1971 was a slow but ongoing process which transformed both sides. A wide variety of views on whether the United States should recognize the PRC had been expressed within government policy-making circles, as well as by intellectuals, businessmen, and ordinary Americans.[5] The Chinese by contrast showed a firmer consensus, adhering to their One China policy while asserting that the "Chinese people did not want to pick a fight with the United States and the Chinese government was willing to sit down and negotiate with the American government."[6] In the 1950s and 1960s, American pluralism and the Chinese capacity to make policy adjustments gradually created the foundations for the final diplomatic breakthrough. Thus the rapprochement that occurred during the Nixon presidency (1969–74)—driven as it was by a rebalancing of global geopolitics—did not happen just overnight.

## THE POST–WORLD WAR II SETTING

Sino-American relations turned sour after both countries decided to retreat within their respective Cold War camps. As America sought global dominance after World War II, new Communist China took a defensive but firm stance on resisting the hegemonic ambitions of the United States.[7] Communist China opted for membership in the Soviet-led Communist bloc. Anti-Americanism manifested itself in mainland Chinese efforts to deter America's isolation of China and unite the "mid-zone" countries—including Britain, France, Japan, and the newly independent Asian and African nations which retained a nonaligned position rather than simply acting as the "poodles" of Washington or Moscow.

Chinese Communist leaders were in no rush to procure American and "imperialist" recognition of the People's Republic. Instead, their priority was to rid China of American influence in order to both consolidate their new regime and boost the Chinese revolutionary spirit.[8] In 1949, the People's Liberation Army reached nearly 5.5 million, and military expenditure was accounting for almost 40 percent of the PRC government's budget. With an additional 3.5 million public servants to support, the government felt that it was bearing a special burden, the "burden of victory," while Taiwan, Tibet, and Hainan "were still awaiting liberation."[9] Zhou Enlai (1898–1976)—premier and foreign minister of the People's Republic for over a quarter of a century (1949–76)—was resolute in asserting that China must maintain political independence and economic self-sufficiency. "The American imperialists have imposed embargoes on us, which have caused great difficulties. We, however, must not succumb to American imperialism."[10]

On the other side of the Pacific, convinced that the "cold war is in fact a real war," the United States did not hesitate to assume the mantle of leadership as the "center of power in the free world."[11] In two National Security Council reports approved by President Harry Truman (presidency 1945–53) in November and December 1949 (NSC 48/2 and NSC 58/2), the U.S. government set out a strategic plan aimed—if not in so many words—at countering the Soviet influence in China and other countries.[12] A further report (NSC 68), approved by Truman in mid-April 1950, was vague on exactly how the United States was to stop the spread of Communism, although it was clear about the threat to the security of the United States posed by the Soviet Union which possessed "armed forces far in excess of those necessary to defend its national territory."[13] The report continued: "The issues that face us are momentous, involving the fulfillment or destruction not only of this Republic but of civilization itself."

## RECOGNITION AND REPRESENTATION OF THE PEOPLE'S REPUBLIC OF CHINA

Although both Congress and the American public were opposed to rec-ognizing the People's Republic of China, the Truman administration was not overtly intransigent. The American government's efforts to reach a consensus with its allies over the issue proved futile. Britain recognized Communist China in January 1950 because of its plans to retain Hong Kong as a colony, its considerable investments in China, and the pro-recognition views of its Asian Commonwealth partners. Nevertheless, the PRC did not establish full diplomatic relations with Britain until 1972, in response to British support in the face of an American call for the postponement of the debate on China's representation in the United Na-tions.[14] Countries that established diplomatic relations with China earlier than the United States (1979) included the Soviet Union, Bulgaria, Roma-nia, Hungary, the Democratic Republic of Korea, Czechoslovakia, Po-land, Mongolia, the Democratic Republic of Germany, and Albania (all in 1949); Vietnam, Sweden, Denmark, and Finland (1950); Norway (1954); France (1964); Canada and Italy (1970); the UK, Japan, Germany, Austra-lia, and New Zealand (1972); and Spain (1973).[15]

As part of its military, economic, and diplomatic efforts to secure the containment of Communism in Asia, the United States was determined to keep the PRC out of the United Nations where the Taiwanese Nation-alists held a seat as a founding member. But, again, the United States failed to rally its allies to the cause. In an attempt to reconcile America's differences with Britain, in April 1951 the secretary of state, Dean Ache-son, proposed a moratorium to postpone discussion of the representation question while the war in Korea continued. Britain proved unwilling to support this measure, particularly when Anthony Eden took over as prime minister. In October 1971, the UN General Assembly voted, by seventy-six to thirty-five, in favor of admitting the PRC and expelling Taiwan (the Republic of China). Not only did Britain vote for Communist China to be represented in the United Nations, but it also failed to sup-port an American-sponsored "important question" resolution designed to maintain Taiwan's membership in the international body.[16]

## THE KOREAN WAR

Characterized by Bruce Cumings as a conflict "mostly forgotten or un-known in the United States,"[17] the Korean War was the only direct military clash between the United States and the People's Republic of China. Over 33,000 Americans died during the Korean War, and Chinese casualties might have been close to 1 million.[18] From the outset, the Korean War was both a civil war and an international war, inextricably complicated by big-power politics.

Korea had been a Japanese colony from 1910 to 1945 and, during the Pacific War, became an integral part of Japan's imperial war machine. In the Cairo Declaration of December 1, 1943, the leaders of the Three Great Allies, President Roosevelt, Chiang Kai-shek, and British prime minister Winston Churchill — "mindful of the enslavement of the people of Korea" — agreed they were "determined that in due course Korea shall become free and independent."[19] But the reality was not so easy. In 1945, the foreign ministers of the United States, the Soviet Union, and Britain met in Moscow to form a Joint Commission, consisting of representatives of the U.S. command in southern Korea and the Soviet command in northern Korea, to draw up plans for the restoration of Korea as an independent state based on democratic principles. Soon, however, the United States and the Soviet Union were in a deadlock, unable to agree on how to set up a provisional democratic government that would meet the various demands of client parties and organizations in their own zones on either side of the 38th Parallel that divided the Korean Peninsula into two.[20]

Dismissing Soviet opposition, the United States referred the Korean problem to the United Nations to recommend elections for March 1948.[21] By June 1949, the Soviets and Americans had each withdrawn most of their troops and had named their preferred persons — Kim Il Sung, leader of the Democratic People's Republic of Korea in the north, and Syngman Rhee, head of the Republic of Korea in the south. Both sides pushed for military unification of the peninsula and sought endorsement from Russia and the United States to this end. By the end of 1949, Kim Il Sung had made forty-nine such requests to Stalin.[22] Pleas to his northern neighbor went unheeded. While agreeing to unification through military means in principle, China argued that a period of three to five years was needed for peaceful reconstruction.[23] And although Syngman Rhee threatened to march north, there is no evidence that the Americans were in collusion with him.[24]

Despite the lack of overt big-power support, on Sunday, June 25, 1950, North Korean troops crossed the 38th Parallel and launched an armed attack on the Republic of Korea. The U.S. government was quick to utilize the new interstate apparatus provided by the United Nations to respond to the crisis, although it had not been its practice to take joint action with other interested powers before the outbreak of the Pacific War in 1941. Dean G. Acheson (secretary of state under the Truman administration, 1949–53) requested the UN Security Council to convene without delay. On the same day, the Security Council passed a resolution condemning the North's attack as a breach of peace, and called for the immediate cessation of hostilities, the withdrawal of North Korean forces above the 38th Parallel, and the assistance of member states in executing the resolution. President Truman denounced North Korea's unprovoked aggression as constituting "threats to the peace of the world,"[25] and ordered U.S. air and sea forces to come to the aid of South Korean troops within two days, without seeking the approval of Congress. In July, the UN Security Council passed two further resolutions requesting the United States to designate the commander of the UN joint forces to be used to compel the North Koreans to withdraw behind the 38th Parallel.[26] Commanded by Pacific War veteran General Douglas MacArthur, the United Nations Forces comprised around 1.1 million troops from sixteen countries, the bulk of which were drawn from South Korea and the United States, which each contributed around half a million personnel.

In the first two months following their attack, North Korean troops took control of over 90 percent of South Korean territory and cornered the UN forces in the Pusan area in the southeast of the peninsula. In mid-September 1950, General MacArthur successfully carried out an amphibious landing at Inchon, which cut off the North Korean supply lines and turned the military situation decisively in favor of the South. Within two weeks, American troops had retaken South Korea, including the capital Seoul, and North Korean forces retreated to the 38th Parallel.

On the basis of a report by the National Security Council (NSC 81/1),[27] the U.S. government decided to change tack and invade North Korea—a move which, in hindsight, commentators have perceived as a fatal mistake.[28] At the end of September 1950, George Marshall, secretary of defense (1950–51), authorized MacArthur to cross the 38th Parallel and attack North Korean forces. The U.S. military response was intended to be restricted in its scope and was particularly sensitive to encroaching on Soviet and Chinese territory. Marshall's directive provided that under no circumstances should MacArthur's forces "cross the Manchurian or USSR borders of Korea and, as a matter of policy, no non-Korean ground forces will be used in the northeast provinces bordering the Soviet Union or in the area along the Manchurian border."[29] In separate messages, Marshall heaped praise on MacArthur for giving inspiration to the freedom-loving peoples of the world, and encouraged him to present the world with a grand military fait accompli. "We want you to feel unhampered tactically and strategically to proceed north of 38th parallel," Marshall instructed. "Announcement above referred to may precipitate embarrassment in UN where evident desire is not to be confronted with necessity of a vote on passage of 38th parallel, rather to find you have found it militarily necessary to do so."[30]

In early October, American troops crossed the border zone, making the decisive transition from defensive to offensive operations. The People's Republic had earlier indicated that it was open to diplomatic negotiations provided that the United States stopped at the 38th Parallel. In a conversation with the Indian ambassador to China, K. M. Panikkar, Zhou Enlai stated that "American forces are intent on crossing the 38th to expand the war. If American forces indeed do so, we cannot sit still; rather, we will have to intervene," and asked Panikkar to convey this message to the British and American governments.[31] Similar warnings from the Chinese had been received by the United States through various channels, but the American government did not take the poorly equipped Communists seriously and was determined to take over North Korea by force of arms. In Korea, MacArthur, who was inclined to make his own policy decisions, exacerbated the military and political situation. He disobeyed instructions by ordering American air forces to bomb the Chinese Manchurian border region.[32] In response, on October 8, Chairman Mao Zedong ordered the Chinese People's Volunteer Army to enter Korea under the command of Peng Dehuai.[33] On October 19—the same day that American forces occupied Pyongyang—250,000 Chinese troops crossed the Yalu River on the Chinese–Korean border undetected. One week later, the Chinese People's Volunteer Army clashed openly with American forces, a turn of events that shocked the United States.

Between October 1950 and June 1951, Chinese troops launched five counterattacks and pushed the Americans back south of the 38th Parallel. Chastened by these military reversals, most of Truman's national security team believed that the United States should avoid being drawn into a war in China and that America should cut its losses and withdraw from North Korea as soon as possible. "Our great objective . . . must be to hold an area, to terminate the fighting, to turn over some areas to the Republic of Korea, and to get out so that we can get ahead with building up our own strength, and building up the strength of Europe." Dean Acheson took the same line: "We don't want to beat China in Korea—we can't. We don't want to beat China any place—we can't. . . . It would bleed us dry."[34] In early December, the National Security Council agreed to negotiate a cease-fire with mainland China.[35] The nation's feelings were running in the same direction: a national poll revealed that 77 percent of Americans felt that the United States should not start an all-out war with the People's Republic of China. And half of the American people regarded that the United States had made a mistake in going into the war in Korea.[36]

In April 1951, Truman replaced the bellicose, insubordinate MacArthur, who openly challenged an American back-down, with the more compliant General Matthew B. Ridgway. MacArthur had wanted to extend the military conflict on the peninsula to China and give Asia a higher containment priority than Europe in the fight against Communism. On July 10, Sino-American peace negotiations began in Kaesong, Korea, and lasted over two years amid continued fighting. Both sides exploited the military situation with a view to giving them advantages at the armistice negotiation table. Protracted fighting along the 38th Parallel between the United States and China proved very costly and in many ways resembled the Western Front during World War I.[37] For forty-two days in October and November 1952, the U.S. 8th Army became bogged down during the Battle of Triangle Hill—or Operation Showdown— fought over an area of 1.4 square miles; total casualties on both sides exceeded 20,000. In November 1952, a new president, Dwight D. Eisenhower (presidency 1953–61), was elected, promising to bring the protracted war to a swift end. An armistice was concluded, and on July 27, 1953, arrangements for a four-kilometer demilitarized zone along the 38th Parallel, and for the exchange of prisoners of war, were finally agreed in the "truce village" of Panmunjom.

The Korean War had different consequences for the United States and mainland China in both domestic and international contexts. First, although failing to defeat the Chinese People's Volunteer Army in North Korea, the United States was able to make a successful withdrawal from the peninsula, establishing the demilitarized zone which has endured to this day. Despite its poor showing on the battlefield, the United States ended the Korean War with a firm hold on East Asia, a permanent armed force on the peninsula, and an increase in the defense budget from $13 billion to $54 billion.

Second, the war created a political atmosphere that made it difficult for any American politician to significantly improve the relationship with the PRC, characterized in the West as the aggressor, over the following two decades. In addition, the exigencies of American domestic politics required that the United States maintain at least some support for the Chiang Kai-shek government on Taiwan.

Third, the tenacious Chinese resistance to American military intervention in Korea was driven by a deep commitment to national self-defense and underpinned by Communist ideology,[38] thus offering a serious challenge to American pretensions to hegemony in the hemisphere. As part of the global Third World movement which emphasized decolonization, nationalism, and nonalignment, Communist China had boosted its domestic morale and international standing through the conflict, while at the same time forcing America to break its isolationist stance.

## TAIWAN

This section traces the convoluted disputes between America, mainland China, and the Nationalist Chinese in "Fortress Taiwan" over the status of the island. The three sides' position on the Taiwan question originated in the Korean War, when President Truman's use of naval power in the Taiwan Strait to create a buffer zone between the Communists and the Nationalists only served to stoke fears on the mainland of continued American aggression. Taiwan has provided a major source of acrimony in Sino-American relations since the 1950s.

A large island across the Taiwan Strait from China's Fujian Province, Taiwan is today recognized by fewer than thirty small countries as an independent nation, the Republic of China. It was a Japanese colony until 1945 when Japan was defeated in World War II. Taiwan has no seat in the

United Nations or other major international organizations. At the end of
1943, as we have seen, Roosevelt, Chiang Kai-shek, and Churchill met in
Cairo and agreed to return Taiwan to the Republic of China, led by Chi-
ang. In the Cairo Communiqué, the Allies agreed that "all the territories
Japan has stolen from the Chinese, such as Manchuria, Formosa, and the
Pescadores, shall be restored to the Republic of China."[39]

From the outset, Truman and his secretary of state Dean Acheson
insisted that Taiwan be part of China and that, with a civil war raging in
China between Nationalist and Communist forces, the United States
would avoid getting involved "militarily in any way on the Island of
Formosa." In January 1950, Truman declared that the United States "has
no predatory designs on Formosa, or on any other Chinese territory. . . .
The United States Government will not pursue a course which will lead
to involvement in the civil conflict in China. . . . Similarly, the United
States Government will not provide military aid or advice to Chinese
forces on Formosa."[40]

At the outbreak of war in Korea in June 1950, President Truman dispatched the 7th U.S. Fleet to the Taiwan Strait. The conventional interpretation of Truman's move—in response to North Korea's invasion of the
South—is that it was intended to shield Formosa from possible attack by
Communist China. As one scholar puts it, "Previously the United States
had kept the Nationalist Chinese remnant on Formosa at arm's length.
Now it would be embraced. One of Truman's first acts after North Korea's attack was ordering the Seventh Fleet to cover Formosa."[41] However, Truman made it clear that America's interest was in preserving the
status quo, not only on Taiwan but also on the mainland:

> Accordingly, I have ordered the Seventh Fleet to prevent any attack on
> Formosa. As a *corollary of this action* [my emphasis], I am calling upon
> the Chinese Government on Formosa to cease all air and sea operations
> against the mainland. The Seventh Fleet will see that this is done. The
> determination of the future status of Formosa must await the restora-
> tion of security in the Pacific, a peace settlement with Japan, or consid-
> eration by the United Nations.[42]

The British interpretation of Truman's statement, made in a note by the
minister of state for foreign affairs in 1955, preserved these nuances: "On
27th June, 1950, at the time of the invasion of South Korea, the President
of the United States (Mr. Truman) made a declaration which, among
other things, said that the 7th Fleet had been instructed to protect Formo-

sa but it had also been told to ensure that there were no attacks from Formosa on the mainland."[43]

However, mainland China did not seem interested in acknowledging the intent behind Truman's "double shield" put in place to neutralize the Taiwan region. In response to Truman's declaration, Zhou Enlai made a statement calling for a halt to "America's new aggression in the East":

> After instigating the Syngman Rhee puppet regime in South Korea to provoke the Korean civil war, American President Truman made a declaration on June 27. He declared that the American government has decided to use force to stop us from liberating Taiwan. The American 7th Fleet has already been ordered to move into the waters around Taiwan. . . . This is military aggression against Chinese territory, and an outright violation of the United Nations Charter. . . . There is no way of altering the fact that Taiwan belongs to China; this is not only an historical fact, but it has also been recognized in the Cairo Declaration, the Potsdam Declaration, and in the arrangements made following Japan's surrender.[44]

Zhou went on: "For us, the Korean question is not merely a question about Korea. The Taiwan issue is intimately related to it. American imperialism treats us as an enemy. It has extended its national defense line to the Taiwan Strait."[45]

Tensions increased another notch in February 1953 when, in retaliation for mainland China's refusal to accept the armistice proposals to end the Korean War, Eisenhower changed American policy on the "neutralization" of the Taiwan region. He declared that the "Seventh Fleet no longer be employed to shield Communist China."[46] Despite the undetermined legal status of Taiwan in American eyes—whether it was part of China or an independent nation state (a situation further complicated by the Nationalist Party's flight to the island in 1949)—the Nationalist government on Taiwan proved useful to American efforts to contain and isolate Communist China.[47] Chiang Kai-shek, outspoken about his desire to return to mainland China by force of arms, and his allies in Congress exerted considerable pressure on the Eisenhower administration to sign a mutual security defense treaty.[48]

In the fall of 1954 and again in 1958, two major crises arose over a handful of tiny islands (including Quemoy and Matsu) off China's Fujian coast—occupied by Nationalist forces, but within mainland Chinese territorial waters—when mainland China began shelling them. Although these offshore islands were of no military value in the eyes of most Americans, the Nationalists insisted on American protection, and many Americans, including Eisenhower, were convinced that Chiang's anti-Communist resolve would be fatally undermined if the United States abandoned the islands.[49] On December 2, 1954, Secretary of State John Foster Dulles (1953–59) signed a mutual security treaty with Taiwan—even though he was considering "neutralizing" the territory through the UN Security Council. In January 1955, Eisenhower stated that, for the United States and other free nations, Formosa and the neighboring Pescadores "in the island chain of the Western Pacific" constituted the "geographical backbone of their security structure in that ocean."[50] Two days later, Congress authorized the president to "employ the Armed Forces of the United States as he deems necessary for the specific purpose of securing and protecting Formosa and the Pescadores against armed attack."[51] However, the United States failed to gain the support of the British government for any military venture, Britain making it clear that these offshore islands formed part of the territory of mainland China.

The first Taiwan crisis was brought to an end in April 1955 when, at the Bandung Conference in Indonesia, Zhou Enlai expressed his willingness to enter into bilateral talks with the United States.[52] Meanwhile, the United States sent two representatives, Admiral Arthur Radford and Walter Robertson, to Taiwan, on a mission to persuade the Nationalists to evacuate the offshore islands, which would form the springboard for any invasion of the mainland. The Nationalist government remained unconvinced. In August 1955, the Sino-American ambassadorial talks began in Geneva. The Americans came to the negotiation table with the aim of securing the renunciation of force in the Formosa Strait, while the Chinese—sticking to their claim to Taiwan—were aiming to secure American withdrawal from the region. The notion of "Two Chinas" put forward by the American side—the coexistence of the Republic of China and the People's Republic of China—was rejected out of hand by the governments on both sides of the strait, each of which clung to the idea that Taiwan should be part of China—their own version of the "One China" concept.[53]

Chiang Kai-shek's first priority was to maneuver the Americans into making a further military and economic commitment toward the realization of his goal of retaking mainland China by armed force.[54] Nevertheless, in an exchange of notes signed on December 10, 1954, Chiang's government agreed that Taiwan would not invade mainland China, or draw the United States into a war, without prior agreement with America.[55]

In 1958, the Nationalists turned up the heat by sending planes over Beijing and other major mainland cities to drop propaganda leaflets attacking the Communist Party. By the summer of 1958, Nationalist forces in the disputed offshore islands of Quemoy and Matsu had reached 100,000—one-third of Taiwan's total ground forces. In response to this provocation, beginning on August 23, 1958, mainland China subjected Quemoy to heavy artillery bombardment for seven weeks. Although the United States had no wish to expand the conflict, the use of atomic weapons was seriously considered as a possible American response to mainland attacks on the disputed islands.[56] In terms of potential military action, the 1958 crisis was something of a "guessing game" for both the United States and mainland China.[57] Both sides were concerned to avoid direct military conflict and not to "engage in a level of military effort which is likely to provoke a general war."[58] In the end, the standoff petered out. For its part, the United States was at last able to get Chiang to renounce the use of force in his plans for returning to the mainland. Mainland China announced a pause in its artillery bombardment, and later stopped shelling on even-numbered days and might bomb Quemoy on odd-numbered days. Mao Zedong explained this deliberate tactic that had irritated the Americans:

> [O]n some occasions China deliberately makes a loud noise, as for example around Quemoy and Matsu. . . . Consider what could be accomplished by firing some blank shells within those Chinese territorial waters. Not so long ago the United States 7th Fleet in the Taiwan Strait was deemed insufficient to reply to the shell. The US also dispatched part of its 6th Fleet in this direction and brought over part of the Navy from San Francisco. Arrived here, they had found nothing to do, so it seemed that China could order the American forces to march here, to march there. . . . Of course when Navy men are warm and have full bellies they must be given something to do. But how was it that shooting off empty guns at home could be called aggression, while those who actually intervened with arms and bombs and burned people of other lands were not aggressors?[59]

The Taiwan question illustrated the complex array of forces at work in the region in the 1950s. While the United States drew itself into the conflict, albeit unwillingly, it found that it could not easily push Chiang Kai-shek or Mao Zedong around. At home, the political climate that viewed mainland China as a threat to American national security became entrenched as the United States strengthened its geopolitical hold on East Asia. On the other hand, between 1955 and 1970, a total of 136 meetings took place in Geneva and Warsaw between the United States and mainland China at the ambassadorial level, keeping the door open for communication.[60] At the same time, Chiang defied American efforts to reduce the Nationalists' military presence on the offshore islands.

## THE VIETNAM WAR AND SINO-AMERICAN RELATIONS IN THE 1960S

During the 1960s, American-Chinese relations were set against the backdrop of America's escalating war in Vietnam and, on China's side, domestic turbulence and an open split with the Soviet Union.[61] During this decade, the United States was absorbed in expanding its presence and promoting its values in Asia. The People's Republic of China was plunged into political and social turmoil, largely the result of the Great Leap Forward of 1958–59 and the Cultural Revolution (1966–69, more broadly 1966–76).[62] Strategically, each side viewed the other as the enemy, while privately hoping for a relaxation in the relationship.

In terms of Taiwan, the Lyndon B. Johnson administration (1963–69) continued the U.S. policy of discouraging Chiang from considering military or paramilitary operations against the mainland. Instead, the United States encouraged Taiwan to rely more on political and psychological efforts in seeking to undermine Communist control of mainland China.[63]

While recognition of the People's Republic of China was regarded by American policy makers as only a matter of time, politically it was seen as a poisoned chalice. President John F. Kennedy called for further cultural and economic contact with mainland China.[64] Dean Rusk—secretary of state (1961–69) in the Kennedy and Johnson administrations—and his subordinates Chester Bowles (the undersecretary of state), Adlai Stevenson (ambassador to the UN), and Lewis W. Douglas (former American ambassador to Britain) were all strong advocates of a relaxation in American policy toward mainland China. The Council on Foreign Relations, the Rockefeller Foundation, and the Ford Foundation took the same line.[65] The political price to be paid, however, would have been too high for immediate action, as the transcript of a guarded telephone conversation between President Johnson and Senator Richard Russell on January 15, 1964, suggests. Commenting on France's imminent recognition of mainland China, Russell said, "The time's going to come when we might well—can't talk about it now—the time's going to come when we're going to have to recognize them." Johnson replied, "Yeah, I think so—don't think there's any question about it."[66]

As with Taiwan, America's self-appointed role as the watchdog of the "free world" in Asia led it to become inexorably drawn into the developing conflict in Indochina. The collapse of the Japanese colonial empire in Southeast Asia following World War II had fatally undermined the efforts of its Dutch, French, and British predecessors. The United States found the process of "liquidating colonial regimes and replacing them by new and stable independent governments" a difficult one; French Indochina was the "toughest case." In 1950, the American government recognized the Bao Dai regime, the French puppet government based in Saigon in southern Vietnam, and gave France over $2 billion to help support it. Even with substantial American support, the French Indochinese states—Tonkin, Annam, Cochin China, Laos, and Cambodia—were unable to defeat the Democratic Republic of Vietnam, founded by militant Communist nationalists (the Vietcong) in September 1945 and led by Ho Chi Minh, a leading opponent of the French colonial presence. In 1954, Dien Bien Phu, a fortress city in northern Vietnam, fell to the Communists with assistance from mainland China—a fatal blow to France, leading to its retreat from Vietnam. The United States decided to move in to fill the vacuum, reasoning that if Southeast Asia "fell to Communist control, this would enormously add to the momentum and power of the expansionist Communist regimes in Communist China and North Vietnam and thus to the threat to the whole free-world position in the Pacific."[67]

At the Geneva Conference of 1954, where the Soviet Union, Britain, France, the United States, China, and the two Vietnamese governments participated, the bulk of Indochina was divided along the 17th Parallel pending elections to be held in 1956 which were intended to reunify Vietnam. However, the United States was unwilling to sign an agreement that "other parties—for very different reasons—were keen to conclude, but which, from the American point of view, might amount to enshrining French military defeat in a dishonorable document."[68] In the end, the United States signed a statement of intent not to violate the Geneva Accords. However, with American concurrence, South Vietnam refused to hold elections because the Communists were expected to win.

Following Bao Dai's retirement, the Eisenhower administration supported the unpopular Ngo Dinh Diem while at the same time insisting on political reform. The U.S. government staged the overthrow and killing of the noncompliant Diem in 1963, but this failed to solve the Vietnam problem. The Kennedy administration increased American military involvement in the country, including sending 16,000 advisors, but failed to turn the tide. Johnson cautiously committed U.S. air and ground forces to South Vietnam and bombed North Vietnam for the first time in August 1964. Congress then passed the Tonkin Gulf resolution, authorizing the president to use force in the region. By 1968, over half a million American forces had been dispatched to Vietnam. At the same time, Johnson was eager to negotiate with the Vietcong in Hanoi in order to avoid a wider conflict. In Henry Kissinger's view, "Johnson opted for halfway measures which staked America's international position without achieving goals."[69] The fall of Saigon in 1975 brought the Vietnam War to an end, with the North claiming victory.

The United States and mainland China publicly treated each other as strategic enemies, and they were very close to hostile contact in Indochina. The success of China's first nuclear test on October 16, 1964, failed to undermine Johnson's resolve: "The United States reaffirms its defense commitments in Asia. Even if Communist China should eventually develop an effective nuclear capability, that capability would have no effect upon the readiness of the United States to respond to requests from Asian nations for help in dealing with Communist Chinese aggression."[70] Beijing provided North Vietnam with moral support and supplied nearly all the arms and ammunition that reached anti-American forces in South Vietnam between 1962 and 1966. On the other hand, mainland China gave public assurances that China would not initiate a war with the United States in Vietnam unless the United States extended the war onto Chinese territory. "Fighting beyond one's borders was criminal. Why should the Chinese do that?" Mao Zedong commented.[71]

The deterioration of Sino-Soviet relations that began in 1956—when the Soviet 20th Party Congress was held—was one of the key external factors influencing mainland China to seek a more positive relationship with the United States. In 1972, Zhou Enlai told Richard Nixon,

> We came apart then because of ideology, and because it was unfair at
> that time to write off all of Stalin's achievements at one stroke. . . .
> Anyway we must recognize that he (Stalin) made contributions in the
> Second World War. Even our American friends recognize this. . . . It
> was utter nonsense for him [Khrushchev] to claim that it was not Stalin,
> but he, Khrushchev, who led the battle.[72]

Long in the brewing, the Sino-Soviet split partly lay in the paternalistic
attitude of the Soviet Union toward China—evident in such terms as
"teacher," "father," or "big brother," and in the defiant response of Mao
Zedong who loathed being characterized as a "student," "son," or "little
brother" by the Soviet bloc. Five elements mainly contributed to the collapse of the Sino-Soviet alliance by the end of the 1960s, despite their
efforts to confine and repair the rupture within the Communist camp.

First, mainland China was dissatisfied with the Soviet leader Nikita
Khrushchev who failed to support China's embryonic nuclear program,
denying China's requests for assistance in 1954–56. Disputes over Soviet
aid projects and bilateral trade also played a role. Second, Mao Zedong
refused to go along with the de-Stalinization program carried out by
Khrushchev after the death of Stalin. Mao viewed Stalin as a great Marxist leader although Stalin had made serious mistakes. To the Chinese
Communist Party, the Soviet Union's policy of revisionism and complete
denial of Stalin's achievements had derailed the world Communist revolution.

Third, the Soviet Union and mainland China diverged in their stance
toward the United States, Taiwan, Vietnam, Albania, India, and a number of other countries, and were unwilling to coordinate their policies
toward them. Fourth, although in 1964 Leonid Brezhnev ousted Khrushchev, Brezhnev's policies were the same as those of his former boss in the
eyes of the Chinese. Fifth, the two Communist powers engaged in a direct
military conflict over their long-disputed borders in 1969.[73]

While still in the throes of the Sino-Soviet breakup, mainland China
was gripped by a period of domestic anarchy and turmoil—the Great
Proletarian Cultural Revolution—leaving the United States and other
China watchers in a state of bewilderment.[74] At best, the Cultural Revolution can be described as a social convulsion. Beginning on May 16,
1966, Mao launched an intensive attack on the political establishment
aimed at waging a violent class struggle and completing the revolution
under socialism.[75] He called for the eradication of the "four olds"—old

customs, old habits, old culture, and old thinking. Bands of high school students—the Red Guards—were urged to take to the streets to take over government bodies, universities, and other organizations and not to hang back from carrying out personal assaults and other violent acts against those seen as class enemies. Lacking a cohesive economic and social vision, neither Mao nor his Communist followers had any real idea of where the nation should be heading.

At the end of the Cultural Revolution, the People's Republic of China—with only CNY 76 per capita income (less than US$10)—found itself twenty years behind Taiwan, Hong Kong, and South Korea, which, in terms of living standards, had all begun the 1950s on a par with mainland China.[76] In *Life*, Ma Sicong, China's foremost violinist and composer, told Americans about the violence and sheer madness at the height of the Cultural Revolution: "Someone dumped a bucket of paste over me and rammed a tall dunce cap labeled 'Cow Demon' on my head. . . . We were paraded. All the way people hit out at us and spit upon us. I recognized the distorted faces of my own students."[77]

## CONCLUSION

By the end of the 1960s both the United States and China had come to the realization that they needed to work together, within their own limits, ready to enter a new phase of their relationship.

The defining character of American-Chinese relations in the 1950s and 1960s was the American-led crusade against Communism which attempted to set the ground rules for the governance of China and other parts of the world. For the first decade, mainland China conducted its foreign relations within the coalition headed by the Soviet Union, seen by the United States as a threat to an American-led international order.

At home, the American public had adopted a mind-set that, in the main, perceived Communist China in negative terms. The "loss of China" was a scar seared into the national memory.[78] Americans found little solace in the "gain" of Japan from its postwar occupation of that country (1945–53), used as an anchor hold for containing Communism in Asia.

Holding two-thirds of the world's gold reserves and producing half of the world's goods, the United States emerged from World War II as the world's leading power. By 1957, American gross national product per capita was over US$2,500,[79] whereas mainland China could muster no more than US$10. Despite this imbalance in national wealth, the United States had recognized that there were limits to the projection of its power abroad. Differences among the United States and important allies such as Britain and France in dealing with the new Communist state helped mainland China find a place in the postwar world order.[80] On the other hand, the Sino-Soviet feud and a turbulent domestic situation prompted China to moderate its approach to America.[81]

Mainland China learned to play the game by exacerbating the differences between the United States and its allies. Through military and diplomatic channels, Mao's China countered the American world order and gradually projected itself as an important player in world affairs. The Geneva Conference of April 1954 and the 1955 Bandung Conference were major steps in this direction. At Geneva—through the good offices of Russian foreign minister Vyacheslav M. Molotov—Zhou Enlai, British foreign secretary Anthony Eden, and French prime minister Pierre Mendes discovered many shared viewpoints on Korea and Indochina. In Bandung, delegates from twenty-nine African and Asian states convened to form a neutral bloc outside the American-Soviet framework. Led by India's Jawaharlal Nehru, Egypt's Gamal Abdul Nasser, and Yugoslavia's Josip Broz Tito, this fledgling nonaligned movement was actively supported by mainland China through funding for economic development and championing of the Five Principles of equitable international relations.[82]

Scholars have increasingly recognized that American policy toward Mao's China in the 1960s was not a simple continuation of the antagonism that marked the preceding decade.[83] Although the political will necessary for reconciliation did not yet exist in the 1960s, the thawing of Sino-American relations that began in 1972 grew not only out of the rebalancing of the Washington-Moscow-Beijing strategic relationship, but was also the result of sustained efforts by a host of national and international players to secure a more productive approach to the bilateral relationship[84]—seeking and exploiting areas of agreement rather than fostering antagonisms.

The change in the atmosphere was abundantly evident in a declassified document signed by Dean Rusk, secretary of state (1961–69), on February 18, 1968:

> [I]t must be perfectly clear to anyone who has looked at this history of last 18 years that USG [the U.S. government] does not doubt existence

of Communist China. We fought against its soldiers in Korea. We have negotiated with its representatives in international conferences in Geneva twice. We have maintained regular bilateral contact with it on an Ambassadorial level for 14 years, first in Geneva and now in Warsaw. Territory controlled and administered by Peking is well known to Government of US and when matters arise which pertain to this area and involve interests of US or American citizens, obviously our approach is to Chinese Communist authorities. This is reality and it is fully acknowledged by this Government. . . . We are convinced that no war is inevitable. Seen in terms of national interests of our two countries, there [is] no fundamental reason why United States and Communist China should come into conflict and every reason for us both to exert every effort to avert such a disaster.[85]

## FURTHER READING

Further material on China's foreign relations and the United States can be found in Jerome Alan Cohen, ed., *The Dynamics of China's Foreign Relations* (Cambridge, Mass.: East Asian Research Center, Harvard University, 1973); Nancy Bernkopf Tucker, *Patterns in the Dust: Chinese-American Relations and the Recognition Controversy, 1949–1950* (New York: Columbia University Press, 1983) and *The China Threat: Memories, Myths, and Realities in the 1950s* (New York: Columbia University Press, 2012); Harry Harding and Yuan Ming, eds., *Sino-American Relations 1945–1955: A Joint Assessment of a Critical Decade* (Wilmington, Del.: Scholarly Research, 1989); John Garver, *The Sino-American Alliance: Nationalist China and American Cold War Strategy in Asia* (Armonk, N.Y.: M. E. Sharpe, 1997); Jian Chen, *Mao's China and the Cold War* (Chapel Hill, N.C.: University of North Carolina Press, 2001); Shu Guang Zhang, *Economic Cold War: America's Embargo against China and the Sino-Soviet Alliance, 1949–1963* (Stanford, Calif.: Stanford University Press, 2001); and Simei Qing, *Visions of Modernity, Identity, and U.S.-China Diplomacy, 1945–1960* (Cambridge, Mass.: Harvard University Press, 2007).

Additional studies of the Korean War and the Taiwan Strait crises include Philip West, ed., *Remembering the "Forgotten War:" The Korean War through Literature and Art* (Armonk, N.Y.: M. E. Sharpe, 2000); J. H. Kalicki, *The Pattern of Sino-American Crises: Political and Military Interactions in the 1950s*, reissue ed. (Cambridge: Cambridge University Press, 2010; 1st ed. 1975); Nancy Bernkopf Tucker, *Strait Talk: United States-Taiwan*

*Relations and the Crisis with China* (Cambridge, Mass.: Harvard University Press, 2011); and Shu Guang Zhang, *Deterrence and Strategic Culture: Chinese-American Confrontations, 1949–58* (Ithaca, N.Y.: Cornell University Press, 1992). In addition to the works on John S. Service and Edgar Snow cited in the notes to chapters 6 and 7, the McCarthyite purges are treated in Robert P. Newman, *Owen Lattimore and the "Loss" of China* (Berkeley, Calif.: University of California Press, 1992) and Gary May, *China Scapegoat: The Diplomatic Ordeal of John Carter Vincent* (Washington, D.C.: New Republic Books, 1979).

For American-Chinese relations in the 1960s, see Noam Kochavi, *A Conflict Perpetuated: China Policy during the Kennedy Years* (Westport, Conn.: Praeger, 2002), and Warren I. Cohen and Nancy B. Tucker, eds., *Lyndon Johnson Confronts the World: American Foreign Policy, 1963–1968* (Cambridge: Cambridge University Press, 1994). Leonard A. Kusnitz, *Public Opinion and Foreign Policy: America's China Policy, 1949–1979* (Westport, Conn.: Greenwood Press, 1984) is a useful book on public opinion of China in the United States. The role of Congress in Sino-American relations is discussed in Guangqiu Xu, *Congress and the U.S.-China Relationship, 1949–1979* (Akron, Ohio: Akron University Press, 2007).

## NOTES

1. Yafeng Xia, *Negotiating with the Enemy: U.S.-China Talks during the Cold War, 1949–1972* (Bloomington, Ind.: Indiana University Press, 2006). Wang Bingnan (王炳南), *Zhongmei huitan jiunian huigu* [中美会谈九年回顾 Recollections of nine years of Sino-American talks] (Beijing: Shijie zhishi chubanshe, 1985).

2. Evelyn Goh, "Competing Images and American Official Reconsiderations of China Policy, 1961–1968," *Journal of American-East Asian Relations* 10, nos. 1–2 (Spring–Summer 2001): 53–92.

3. The "One China" concept refers to international recognition of either the People's Republic of China (mainland China) or the Republic of China (Taiwan). "Two Chinas" refers to international recognition of both the People's Republic of China and the Republic of China.

4. For a legal approach to the Taiwan controversy, see Christopher J. Carolan, "The 'Republic of Taiwan': A Legal-Historical Justification for a Taiwanese Declaration of Independence," *New York University Law Review* 75 (May 2000): 429–468; Frank S. T. Hsiao and Lawrence R. Sullivan, "The Chinese Communist Party and the Status of Taiwan, 1928–1943," *Pacific Affairs* 52, no. 3 (Autumn 1979): 446–467.

5. Priscilla Roberts, "William L. Clayton and the Recognition of China, 1945–1966: More Speculations on the 'Lost Chances in China,'" *Journal of American-East Asian Relations* 7, nos. 1–2 (Spring–Summer 1998): 5–37.

6. Zhou Enlai's announcement on relaxing tensions in the Far East, especially with regard to Taiwan, was made at the Africa-Asia Bandung Conference on April 23, 1955, in Zhou Enlai, *Zhou Enlai xuanji* [周恩来文选 Selected works of Zhou Enlai] (Beijing: Renmin chubanshe, 1984), vol. 2, p. 476.

7. Christian F. Ostermann, ed., *Inside China's Cold War, Cold War International History Project Bulletin*, no. 16 (Fall 2007/Winter 2008); Yafeng Xia, "The Study of Cold War International History in China: A Review of the Last Twenty Years," *Journal of Cold War Studies* 10, no. 1 (Winter 2008): 81–115.

8. Mao Zedong, *Mao Zedong xuanji* [毛泽东选集 Selected works of Mao Zedong] (Beijing: Renmin chubanshe, 1966), vol. 4, p. 1373. Yang Kuisong (杨奎松), "Huade shijian yu xin Zhongguo dui Meiguo zhengce de queli" [华德事件与新中国对美国政策的确立 The Ward Incident and the formulation of new China's policy toward the U.S.], *Lishi yanjiu* 5 (1994): 104–118.

9. Zhonggong zhongyang wenxian yanjiushi (中共中央文献编辑委员会), ed., *Zhou Enlai xuanji* [周恩来选集 Selected works of Zhou Enlai] (Beijing: Renmin chubanshe, 1980), vol. 1, pp. 1–14. Zhonggong zhongyang wenxian yanjiushi, comp., *Zhou Enlai nianpu (1949–76)* [周恩来年谱 A Chronology of Zhou Enlai] (Beijing: Zhongyang wenxian chubanshe, 1997), vol. 1, pp. 12–13.

10. Zhonggong zhongyang wenxian yanjiushi, *Zhou Enlai xuanji*, vol. 2, p. 10.

11. "A Report to the National Security Council by the Executive Secretary (Lay)," NSC-68, April 14, 1950, in Department of State, *Foreign Relations of the United States [FRUS], 1950: National Security Affairs; Foreign Economic Policy*, ed. S. Everett Gleason and Fredrick Aandahl (Washington, D.C.: Government Printing Office, 1950), vol. 1, pp. 234–292.

12. NSC 58/2, "United States Policy toward the Soviet Satellite States in Eastern Europe," December 8, 1949, *FRUS, 1949*, vol. 5, pp. 42–54. NSC 48/2, "The Position of the United States with Respect to Asia," December 30, 1949, *FRUS, 1949*, vol. 7, p. 1219. John Lewis Gaddis, *Strategies of Containment: A Critical Appraisal of American National Security Policy during the Cold War*, revised and expanded ed. (Oxford: Oxford University Press, 2005), chapters 3–4.

13. "A Report to the National Security Council by the Executive Secretary (Lay)," NSC-68.

14. Wang Jianlang, "Xin Zhongguo chengli chunian Yingguo guanyu Zhongguo Lianheguo daibiaoquan wenti de zhengce yanbian" [新中国成立初年英国关于中国联合国代表权问题的政策演变 The Evolution of British policy on the Chinese representation question in the UN in the early years of new China], *Zhongguo shehui kexue* 3 (2000): 179–190; Warren I. Cohen, "Ambassador Philip D. Sprouse on the Question of Recognition of the People's Republic of China in 1949 and 1950 (Document)," *Diplomatic History* 2, no. 2 (Spring 1978): 213–217.

15. Dong Wang, "China's Trade Relations with the United States in Perspective," *Journal of Current Chinese Affairs* 39, no. 3 (November 2010): 165–210.

16. Victor S. Kaufman, "'Chirep': The Anglo-American Dispute over Chinese Representation in the United Nations, 1950–71," *English Historical Review* 115, no. 461 (April 2000): 354–377.

17. Bruce Cumings, *Dominion from Sea to Sea: Pacific Ascendancy and American Power* (New Haven, Conn.: Yale University Press, 2009), p. 340.

18. There is no agreement on the numbers of Chinese or American troops killed (figures for the latter have been put variously at 33,629, nearly 50,000, and 54,000). Roderick MacFarquhar, ed., *Sino-American Relations, 1949–71: Documented and Intro-*

duced by Roderick MacFarquhar (New York: Praeger, 1972), p. 82; Michael Hunt, *The American Ascendancy: How the United States Gained and Wielded Global Dominance* (Chapel Hill, N.C.: University of North Carolina Press, 2007), chapter 6.

19. Arthur M. Schlesinger Jr., ed., *The Dynamics of World Power: A Documentary History of United States Foreign Policy 1945–1973, vol. 4, The Far East,* ed. Russeli Buhite (New York: Chelsea House Publishers, 1973), p. 7.

20. Central Intelligence Group, "The Situation in Korea," Office of Reports and Estimates 5/1, January 3, 1947, President's Secretary's Files, Truman Papers, Truman Library.

21. "General Assembly Resolution on the Independence of Korea," November 17, 1947, in Arthur M. Schlesinger Jr., ed., *The Dynamics of World Power*, vol. 4, pp. 347–350.

22. Katheryn Weathersby, "New Findings on the Korean War," *Cold War International History Project Bulletin,* no. 3 (Fall 1993): 1, 14–18.

23. Kim Tong-kil (金东吉), "Zhongguo renmin jiefangjun Chaoxianshi guiguo wenti xintan" [中国人民解放军朝鲜师归国问题新探 A reexamination of the return to North Korea of the Korean divisions of the Chinese People's Liberation Army], in Wang Jianlang (王建朗) and Luan Jinghe (栾景河), eds., *Jindai Zhongguo, Dongya yu shijie* [近代中国、东亚与世界 Modern China, East Asia, and the world] (Beijing: Shehui kexue chubanshe, 2008), vol. 2, pp. 942–965.

24. Bruce Cumings, *The Korean War: A History* (New York: Modern Library, 2010), chapter 1; Edward Friedman and Mark Selden, eds., *America's Asia: Dissenting Essays on Asian-American Relations* (New York: Vintage, 1971).

25. "Statement by President on the Violation of the 38th Parallel in Korea on June 26, 1950," Public Papers of the Presidents: Harry S. Truman, 172, Truman Library, http://www.trumanlibrary.org/publicpapers/index.php?pid=799&st=&st1= (accessed April 8, 2011).

26. http://www.un.org/documents/sc/res/1950/scres50.htm (accessed May 8, 2011).

27. National Security Council Report 81, "United States Courses of Action with respect to Korea," September 1, 1950, the Korean War and Its Origins, 1945–1953, Documents, Truman Library, http://www.trumanlibrary.org/whistlestop/study_collections/korea/large/documents/pdfs/ki-17-1.pdf (accessed May 8, 2011).

28. William L. O'Neill, *American High: The Years of Confidence, 1945–1960* (New York: Free Press, 1989), chapter 5. Michael Hunt, *The American Ascendancy,* chapter 5.

29. George C. Marshall to Harry S. Truman, with Attached Directive to Commander of United Nations Forces in Korea, September 27, 1950, Truman Library, http://www.trumanlibrary.org/whistlestop/study_collections/korea/large/documents/pdfs/ki-18-3.pdf (accessed May 8, 2011).

30. Department of the Army Staff Message Center, Outgoing Classified Message, September 29, 1950, Truman Library, http://www.trumanlibrary.org/whistlestop/study_collections/korea/large/documents/pdfs/ki-22-19.pdf (accessed May 8, 2011).

31. "Meijun ru yueguo Sanba xian, women yaoguan" [美军如越过三八线,我们要管 If American forces cross the 38th Parallel, we will intervene], October 3, 1950, Zhonghua renmin gongheguo waijiaobu (中华人民共和国外交部) and Zhonggong zhongyang wenxian yanjiushi (中共中央文献研究室), compiled, *Zhou Enlai waijiao wenxuan* [周恩来外交文选 Selected works of Zhou Enlai on diplomacy] (Beijing: Zhongyang wenxian chubanshe, 2000), pp. 25–27.

32. Hong Xuezhi (洪学智), *Kangmei yuanchao zhanzheng huiyi* [抗美援朝战争回忆 Memoirs of the anti-American Korean War], 2nd ed. (Beijing: Jiefangjun wenyi chubanshe, 1991), chapter 2. Warren I. Cohen, "Conversations with Chinese Friends: Zhou

Enlai's Associates Reflect on Chinese-American Relations in the 1940s and the Korean War," *Diplomatic History* 11, no. 3 (July 1987): 283–289.

33. Nie Rongzhen (聂荣臻), *Nie Rongzhen huiyilu* [聂荣臻回忆录 Memoirs of Nie Rongzhen] (Beijing: Jiefangjun chubanshe, 2007), chapter 23. Peng Dehuai zhuan bianxie zu (彭德怀传编写组), *Peng Dehuai zhuan* [彭德怀传 The biography of Peng Dehuai] (Beijing: Dangdai Zhongguo chubanshe, 2006), chapters 20–22.

34. Minutes of the National Security Council Meeting with Harry S. Truman, November 28, 1950, Truman Library, http://www.trumanlibrary.org/whistlestop/study_collections/korea/large/documents/pdfs/ci-2-11.pdf (accessed May 9, 2011).

35. Minutes of National Security Council Meeting, December 11, 1950, and "United States Position Regarding a Cease-Fire in Korea," National Security Report no. 95, December 13, 1950, Truman Library, http://www.trumanlibrary.org/whistlestop/study_collections/korea/large/documents/pdfs/ci-4-9.pdf.

36. George H. Gallup, *The Gallup Poll: Public Opinion, 1935–1971, vol. 2, 1949–1958* (New York: Random House, 1972), p. 968.

37. Xu Yan (徐焰), *Diyi ci jiaoliang: Kangmei yuanchao zhanzheng de lishi huigu yu fansi* [第一次较量:抗美援朝战争的历史回顾与反思 The first showdown: Reflections on the anti-American Korean War] (Beijing: Zhongguo guangbo dianshi chubanshe, 1990); Junshi kexueyuan lishi yanjiubu (军事科学院历史研究部), *Zhongguo renmin zhiyuanjun kangmei yuanchao zhanshi* [中国人民志愿军抗美援朝战史 A history of the Chinese People's Voluntary Army in the anti-American Korean War] (Beijing: Junshi kexue chubanshe, 1988); Li Qingshan (李庆山), *Zhiyuanjun yuanchao jishi* [志愿军援朝纪实 A true account of the People's Voluntary Army in Korea] (Beijing: Zhonggong dangshi chubanshe, 2008).

38. On the influence of the Sino-Soviet alliance on China's role in the Korean War, see Chen Jian, *China's Road to the Korean War: The Making of the Sino-American Confrontation* (New York: Columbia University Press, 1994).

39. *FRUS, The Conference at Cairo and Tehran, 1943* (Washington, D.C.: Government Printing Office, 1943), pp. 448–449.

40. Harry S. Truman's news conference at the White House on January 5, 1950, Public Papers of the Presidents: Harry S. Truman, Truman Library, http://www.trumanlibrary.org/publicpapers/index.php?pid=574&st=news+conference&st1= (accessed August 25, 2012).

41. William L. O'Neill, *American High: The Years of Confidence, 1945–1960*, chapter 5. Another example is, "He [Truman] sent the Seventh Fleet to protect Taiwan from invasion and substantially increased military aid to fight Communist insurgencies in the Philippines and Indochina." Michael Schaller, *The United States and China: Into the Twenty-First Century*, 3rd ed. (Oxford: Oxford University Press, 2002), p. 128.

42. Statement by the president on the situation in Korea on June 27, 1950, Truman Library, Public Papers of the Presidents: Harry S. Truman, 173.

43. "The Formosa Strait: Note by the Minister of State for Foreign Affairs," September 24, 1958, C. (58) 192, CAB/129/94, the National Archives, UK.

44. "Guanyu meiguo wuzhuang qinlüe Zhongguo lingtu Taiwan de shengming" [关于美国武装侵略中国领土台湾的声明 A statement on the American military invasion of the Chinese territory of Taiwan], Zhonghua renmin gongheguo waijiaobu and Zhonggong zhongyang wenxian yanjiushi, comp., *Zhou Enlai waijiao wenxuan*, pp. 18–19.

45. "Kangmei yuanchao, baowei heping" [抗美援朝, 保卫和平 Resist America and assist Korea, preserve peace], October 24, 1950, in Zhonggong zhongyang wenxian yanjiushi, *Zhou Enlai xuanji*, vol. 2, pp. 50–54.

46. U.S. Department of State, *American Foreign Policy 1950–1955: Basic Documents* (Washington, D.C.: Government Printing Office, 1957–58), vol. 2, p. 2475. *FRUS, 1952–54*, vol. 14, p. 140.

47. John W. Garver, *Foreign Relations of the People's Republic of China* (Upper Saddle River, N.J.: Prentice Hall, 1993), pp. 50–51.

48. Nancy Bernkopf Tucker, *Taiwan, Hong Kong, and the United States, 1945–1992* (New York: Twayne Publishers, 1994), chapter 3.

49. "The Formosa Strait: Note by the Minister of State for Foreign Affairs," September 24, 1958, C. (58) 192, CAB/129/94, the National Archives, UK.

50. Arthur M. Schlesinger Jr., ed., *Dynamics of World Power*, vol. 4, pp. 210–213.

51. Arthur M. Schlesinger Jr., ed., *Dynamics of World Power*, vol. 4, pp. 213–214.

52. For two contrasting interpretations of the Taiwan crises, see Nancy Bernkopf Tucker, *Taiwan, Hong Kong, and the United States, 1945–1992*, chapter 3, and Tao Wenzhao, ed., *Zhongmei guanxishi (1949–1972)* (Shanghai: Shanghai renmin chubanshe, 1999), chapter 4.

53. Zhou Enlai (周恩来), "Jianjue fandui zhizao 'liangge Zhongguo' de yinmou" [坚决反对制造"两个中国"的阴谋 Fiercely opposing the "Two-China" conspiracy], January 5, 1955, in *Zhou Enlai waijiao wenxuan*, pp. 94–105.

54. Appu K. Soman, "'Who's Daddy' in the Taiwan Strait? The Offshore Islands Crisis of 1958," *Journal of American-East Asian Relations* 3, no. 4 (Winter 1994): 373–398.

55. U.S. Department of State, John P. Glennon, ed., *FRUS, 1952–54: China and Japan* (Washington, D.C.: Government Printing Office, 1952–54), vol. 14, part 1, pp. 870–880.

56. Memorandum of Conference with the President, August 14, 1958, Dwight D. Eisenhower (DDE) Papers as President, DDE Diaries, Box 35, the Dwight D. Eisenhower Presidential Library.

57. Zhou Enlai, "Taiwan haixia xingshi he women de zhengce" [台湾海峡形势和我们的政策 The Taiwan Strait situation and our policy], October 5, 1958, in *Zhou Enlai waijiao wenxuan*, vol. 2, pp. 262–267. Edgar Snow, "Interview with Mao Zedong," *New Republic* 52 (February 27, 1965): 17–23.

58. Comments by John Foster Dulles at a news conference, Arthur M. Schlesinger Jr., ed., *The Dynamics of World Power*, vol. 4, pp. 254–155.

59. Edgar Snow, "Interview with Mao Zedong."

60. Zhang Baijia (章百家) and Jia Qingguo (贾庆国), "Duikang zhong de fangxiangpan, huanchongqi he ceshiyi: Cong Zhongguo jiaodu kan Zhongmei dashiji huitan" [对抗中的方向盘、缓冲器和测试仪:从中国角度看中美大使级会谈 Sino-American ambassadorial talks seen from the Chinese perspective], *Dangdai Zhongguoshi yanjiu*, no. 1 (2000): 40–51; Steven M. Goldstein, "Dialogue of the Deaf? The Sino-American Ambassadorial-Level Talks, 1955–1970," in Robert S. Ross and Jiang Changbin, eds., *Re-examining the Cold War: U.S.-China Diplomacy, 1954–1973* (Cambridge, Mass.: Harvard University Asia Center, 2001), pp. 200–237.

61. Robert D. Schulzinger, "The Johnson Administration, China, and the Vietnam War"; Rosemary Foot, "Redefinitions: The Domestic Context of America's China Policy in the 1960s"; Li Jie, "Changes in China's Domestic Situation in the 1960s and Sino-American Relations," in Robert S. Ross and Jiang Changbin, eds., *Re-examining the Cold War*, pp. 238–320.

62. Victor S. Kaufman, "A Response to Chaos: The United States, the Great Leap Forward, and the Cultural Revolution, 1961–1968," *Journal of American-East Asian Relations* 7, nos. 1–2 (Spring–Summer 1998): 73–92. Roderick MacFarquhar and Michael Schoenhals, *Mao's Last Revolution* (Cambridge, Mass.: Harvard University Press, 2006).

63. *FRUS, 1964–1968*, vol. 30, *China*, ed. Harriet Dashiell Schwar (Washington, D.C.: Government Printing Office, 1998), pp. 86–94.

64. John F. Kennedy, "A Democrat Looks at Foreign Policy," *Foreign Affairs* 36, no. 1 (October 1957): 44–59.

65. Priscilla Roberts, "William L. Clayton and the Recognition of China, 1945–1966," June M. Grasso, *Truman's Two-China Policy* (Armonk, N.Y.: M. E. Sharpe, 1987).

66. Recordings and Transcripts, Recording of a Telephone Conversation between Johnson and Russell, January 15, 1964, Tape F64.06, PNO 1, Special Files, Lyndon B. Johnson Library.

67. Richard P. Stebbins, ed., *Documents on American Foreign Relations 1965* (New York: Harper & Row, 1966), pp. 120–134.

68. Paul Wingrove, introduction, "Russian Documents on the 1954 Geneva Conference," and Document no. 3, "From the Journal of Molotov: Secret Memorandum of Conversation at Dinner in Honor of Mendes-France, French Prime Minister and Foreign Minister," July 10, 1954, in *Cold War International History Project Bulletin*, no. 16 (Fall 2007/Winter 2008): 85–91.

69. Henry Kissinger, *Diplomacy* (New York: Simon & Schuster, 1994), chapter 26.

70. Statement by President Lyndon B. Johnson, in Arthur M. Schlesinger Jr., ed., *The Dynamics of World Power*, pp. 282–283.

71. Edgar Snow, "Interview with Mao Zedong." Zhou Enlai (周恩来), "Zhongguo jianjue zhichi Yuenan renmin de kangmei zhanzheng" [中国人民坚决支持越南人民的抗美战争 The Chinese people are resolved to support the Vietnamese people's anti-American war], April 2, 1965; "Guanyu Zhongguo dui Meiguo zhengce de sijuhua" [关于中国对美国政策的四句话 Four points regarding China's policy toward the U.S.], April 10, 1966, in *Zhou Enlai waijiao wenxuan*, pp. 436–444, 460–461.

72. Memorandum of Conversation between President Richard Nixon, Henry Kissinger, et al., and Prime Minister Zhou Enlai, Qiao Guanhua, et al., February 23, 1972, in Beijing, National Archives, Nixon Presidential Materials Project, White House Special Files, President's Office Files, box 87, Memorandum for the President Beginning February 20, 1972, http://www.gwu.edu/~nsarchiv/NSAEBB/NSAEBB106/NZ-2.pdf (accessed May 30, 2011).

73. Lorenz M. Lüthi, *The Sino-Soviet Split: Cold War in the Communist World* (Princeton, N.J.: Princeton University Press, 2008). Liu Xiao (刘晓), *Chushi Sulian banian* [出使苏联八年 Eight years as ambassador to the Soviet Union] (Beijing: Zhonggong dangshi ziliao chubanshe, 1986). Li Yueran (李越然), *Waijiao wutai shang de xin Zhongguo lingxiu* [外交舞台上的新中国领袖 New Chinese leaders on the diplomatic stage] (Beijing: Waiyu jiaoxue yu yanjiu, 1999). Yang Kuisong (杨奎松), *Zhonggong yu Mosike de guanxi (1920–1960)* [中共与莫斯科的关系 The Chinese Communist Party's relations with Moscow] (Hong Kong: Haixiao chuban shiye youxian gongsi, 1997), chapter 5 and conclusion. Niu Jun, "1962: The Eve of the Left Turn in China's Foreign Policy," Cold War International History Project, Woodrow Wilson International Center for Scholars, working paper no. 48, October 2005.

74. CIA report, January 19, 1967, Harriet Dashiell Schwar, ed., *FRUS, 1964–1968*, pp. 503–507.

75. Xi Xuan (席宣) and Jin Chunming (金春明), *"Wenhua dageming" jianshi* ["文化大革命"简史 A brief history of the "Cultural Revolution"], expanded ed. (Beijing: Zhonggong dangshi chubanshe, 2006).

76. Chen Yung-fa, *Zhongguo gongchan geming qishi nian*, vol. 2, chapter 9.

77. Ma Sitson, "In the Hands of the Red Guard Torture and Degradation," *Life* (June 2, 1967), p. 22.

78. Barbara W. Tuchman, "If Mao Had Come to Washington: An Essay in Alternatives," *Foreign Affairs* 51, no. 1 (October 1972): 44–64; James Claude Thomson et al., *Sentimental Imperialists: The American Experience in East Asia*, 2nd ed. (New York: Harper & Row, 1985), pp. 218–219.

79. U.S. Bureau of the Census, *Historical Statistics of the United States, Colonial Times to 1957* (Washington, D.C.: Government Printing Office, 1960), p. 139.

80. Dong Wang, review of Anthony Best, ed., *The International History of East Asia, 1900–1968: Trade, Ideology and the Quest for Order* (London: Routledge, 2010), geschichte.transnational (history.transnational, University of Leipzig, Germany), H-Soz-u-Kult (March 11, 2011), http://geschichte-transnational.clio-online.net/rezensionen/2011-1-182.

81. Tao Wenzhao (陶文钊), ed., *Zhongmei guanxishi (1949–1972)* [中美关系史 Sino-American relations] (Shanghai: Shanghai renmin chubanshe, 1999; reprinted ed. in 2004), chapter 7 by Niu Jun.

82. The Five Principles are mutual respect for each other's territorial integrity and sovereignty, mutual nonaggression, mutual noninterference in each other's internal affairs, equality and mutual benefit, and peaceful coexistence. Dong Wang, *China's Unequal Treaties: Narrating National History* (Lanham, Md.: Rowman & Littlefield, 2005), p. 127. Chen Jian and Shen Zhihua, "The Geneva Conference of 1954," and documents, *Cold War International History Project Bulletin*, no. 16 (Fall 2007/Winter 2008): 7–14.

83. Rosemary Foot, *The Practice of Power: US Relations with China since 1949* (Oxford: Clarendon Press, 1995); Evelyn Goh, *Constructing the U.S. Rapprochement with China, 1961–1974: From "Red Menace" to "Tacit Ally"* (Cambridge: Cambridge University Press, 2005).

84. A. M. Halpern, ed., *Policies toward China: Views from Six Continents* (New York: McGraw-Hill, 1965), pp. 490–494.

85. "Telegram from the Department of State to the Embassy in the Republic of China," February 13, 1968, *FRUS, 1964–1968*, vol. 30, *China*, ed. Harriet Dashiell Schwar, pp. 638–641.

*Part III*

# Rapprochement, the Default Superpower, and China Resurgent, 1970–Present

# NINE

## Renewing the Bilateral Relationship, 1970–1989

Strategic opportunities for détente were created by both the United States and China during the early 1970s. On the American side, President Richard Nixon (presidency 1969–74) was assisted by Henry Kissinger, his national security advisor (1969–75). China was led by Chairman Mao Zedong and Premier Zhou Enlai at the turn of the 1960s–70s. During this period, making meaningful contact was anything but a straightforward endeavor. While harsh words continued to be uttered in public forums throughout the 1960s, U.S.-Chinese relations were quietly improving, slowly building toward the diplomatic breakthrough that occurred in 1972.

The normalization of Sino-American relations was a gradual process, taking three American administrations and two generations of Chinese leaders under Mao Zedong and Deng Xiaoping (1904–97) to bring it to completion. Attempts at reconciliation had to contend with China's anti-American and anti-Russian revolutionary radicalism and America's anti-Communist ideology, directed chiefly at China.[1] On the other hand, the improvement in relations during the 1970s and 1980s also grew out of China's renewed, century-long search for a strong, unified nation and from America's conscious efforts to redefine its role in a changing, diversified world.

## NIXON'S "RACE IN ASIA" AND MAO'S "AMERICAN GAME"

Given the overt antagonism between the United States and the People's Republic of China (PRC), stretching over more than two decades, how are we to account for President Nixon's visit to China in 1972 and the warming of relations that followed? What lay behind the tactics adopted by both sides?

The leaders of both nations were prompted to cultivate a new kind of geopolitical strategy toward each other by a number of developments—the emergence of a new power structure in the world, and in East Asia in particular, and the changing domestic situation in both countries.[2] The need for a new orientation in bilateral affairs had been systematically discussed among policy makers and elites on both sides throughout the 1960s and early 1970s—a significant political and diplomatic factor that served to counterbalance the populist anti-Communist and anti-imperialist rhetoric of the times.

### Reorienting U.S. Foreign Policy

In 1967, to mark the fiftieth anniversary of the Russian Revolution, a group of reflective articles was published in the semiofficial magazine *Foreign Affairs* in the United States against the backdrop of a widened American military involvement in Vietnam, the changing nature of the "great contention" between the United States and the Soviet Union, and the demise of the Sino-Soviet alliance. For historian Arthur Schlesinger, "the once implacable struggle" between America and Russia had "lost its familiar clarity of outline."

> As the Cold War has begun to lose its purity of definition, as the moral absolutes of the fifties become the moralistic clichés of the sixties, some have begun to ask whether the appalling risks which humanity ran during the Cold War were, after all, necessary and inevitable; whether more restrained and rational policies might not have guided the energies of man from the perils of conflict into the potentialities of collaboration.[3]

Schlesinger's unspoken assumption was that the same considerations may well apply to America's relationship with its other great antagonist in the East. In China, in just a couple of years, Mao Zedong's Cultural Revolution had gutted the machinery of government, and China's foreign relations apparatus had ground to a halt. Senior statesmen such as Liu Shaoqi, president of the P. R. China (1959–68), and Deng Xiaoping were vilified and persecuted.[4] Despite the extreme violence witnessed during the Cultural Revolution, American commentator Robert Elegant concluded that after devoting the first two-thirds of the twentieth century to sweeping destruction, the Chinese people "appear ready to give themselves again to the great work of construction"[5]—the rebuilding of a political system as well as the reinstatement of moral values. "It would be excessively optimistic to declare definitely that China is now coming to the adjustment with the outside world . . . which she has sought by so many different roads for the past century and a half. It would be excessively cynical not to recognize that she is moving in that direction."[6]

For Richard Nixon in 1967, Vietnam was driving Americans to distraction. As he wrote in the same issue of *Foreign Affairs*, other nations must recognize that "the role of the United States as world policeman is likely to be limited in the future." As an anchor and partner in the Pacific community, the United States should avoid a heavy-handed paternalism and must disengage its combat forces from Southeast Asia.

> [America] must recognize that a highly sophisticated, highly advanced political system, which required many centuries to develop in the West, may not be best for other nations which have far different traditions and are still in an earlier stage of development. What matters is that these governments are consciously, deliberately and programmatically developing in the direction of greater liberty, greater abundance, broader choice and increased popular involvement in the processes of government.[7]

In Nixon's view, the United States needed to capitalize on the rapid economic development recorded by Japan—which had sustained an average growth rate of 9 percent per year since 1950—Hong Kong, Taiwan, Thailand, South Korea, Singapore, and Malaysia by encouraging these nations to play an independent economic and political role.[8] However, four giants would play key roles in Asia's future—India, Japan, China, and the United States. In his article, Nixon sketched out a set of measures—both long and short range—designed to meet the danger of China as Asia's "most immediate threat." In the short term, China must be persuaded that "its interests can be served only by accepting the basic rules of international civility." In the long term, it meant "pulling China back into the world community—but as a great and progressing nation, not as the epicenter of world revolution." "The struggle for influence in the

Third World is a three-way race among Moscow, Peking and the West. . . . In this race we cannot afford to wait for others to act, and then merely react. And the race in Asia is already under way."[9]

*Putting the Chinese "House" Back in Order*

For its part, the Chinese approach to managing Sino-American rapprochement was equally a tactical one. In his 1969 inaugural address, Nixon had lauded the ideals of peacemaking, negotiation, and the possibility of an open world, "in which no people, great or small, will live in angry isolation."[10] It seemed to have cut no ice in Beijing. Maintaining its posture of adamant opposition to the world's two superpowers (the United States and the Soviet Union), mainland China kept up the war of words, denouncing Nixon's speech as the shameful confession of a nation driven to the wall in Vietnam, and condemning the Soviet Union's softened stance toward the United States as "shameless claque."[11]

Despite this public polemic, however, two major considerations determined China's shifting assessment of the world situation in 1969–70.

The first involved the question of whether the United States was indeed China's most dangerous antagonist, from both the perspective of world revolution and China's national security. In the first half of 1969, the answer was still yes. The examples of Taiwan and the Korean and Vietnam wars all showed that America still posed a serious military threat to mainland China. In January 1966, Zhou Enlai stated that American imperialism was the main target of the united front of the international socialist movement, because the United States was spearheading military aggression and wanted to control the world on its own. Russia had been duped into supporting America's hegemonic ambitions. "[American] imperialism and [Soviet] revisionism are both reactionary ideologies in essence, but they vary in their origins and forms of development. The Soviet Union wants to cooperate with the U.S. Although they both desire to dominate the world, the Soviet Union is a *de facto* accomplice of America and they are in effect America's shock troops."[12]

Nevertheless, beginning in the latter half of 1969, and against the background of possibly over 4,000 Sino-Russian border skirmishes between 1964 and 1969, the Chinese leadership was inclining to the view that the Soviet Union was a more dangerous threat to China than the United States was. A Soviet military attack on China was even a distinct possibility.

The second determinant was the Chinese concern over the possibility of collusion between America and Russia, at a time when China was ill prepared to deal with a two-pronged attack from its two chief foes.[13] China's diplomacy was in transition at the turn of the 1960s–70s. The three chaotic years of the Cultural Revolution (1966–69) had left its foreign affairs apparatus in a virtual state of paralysis. During this time, Premier and Foreign Minister Zhou Enlai had barely managed to arrange a single state visit. The country had been unable to dispatch any diplomatic personnel since their mass recall in 1967. With the sole exception of Ambassador Huang Hua in Egypt, all other ambassadorial posts abroad were vacant.[14] China was on the back foot. At the 9th Congress of the Chinese Communist Party in April 1969, the political report—given by Lin Biao, Mao Zedong's newly designated successor—concluded that the American imperialists and the "Soviet social revisionist imperialists" were collaborating with each other in the oppression of national liberation movements and in pursuing wars of aggression against China, Communism, and the peoples of the world. In the second half of 1969, Chinese policy makers were engaged in a close study of the world situation while making efforts to put the nation's diplomatic apparatus back in action. Between July and September 1969, a group of four leading military figures and statesmen—Chen Yi, Ye Jianying, Xu Xiangqian, and Nie Rongzhen—concluded that the probability of the United States and the Soviet Union launching full-scale war against China was not very high, and that while the areas of conflict between China and Russia outnumbered those between the United States and China, they were fewer than those between the United States and the Soviet Union. At the top level of government, Mao and Zhou were slowly showing some signs of response to Nixon's signal for détente.[15]

Building on Nixon's initiative, America was eager to placate Chinese fears as to its intentions. In his face-to-face conversations with them in Beijing in February 1972, Henry Kissinger sought to reassure the Chinese leadership that America had no intentions of "ganging up" with Russia against China, despite appearances to the contrary: "We understand that part of the Soviet strategy is to create the impression that they and we are establishing a two-power directory over the world. And therefore they have started negotiations on a whole range of topics, some of very secondary importance, especially since my visit to Peking last July."[16]

Kissinger assured the Chinese that the United States would "do nothing that looks to us as if it could be collusion against you [China]." "Our policy is . . . to take your views very seriously."[17]

## THE NIXON/KISSINGER–MAO/ZHOU INITIATIVE

On taking office in 1969, Nixon began implementing his strategic foreign relations policies, albeit in a variety of understated and measured forms. In May 1969, he made the secret decision to "move generously to liberalize" American trade policy toward the Soviet Union and other Eastern European countries whenever there was sufficient improvement in America's overall relations with them. Then, in June, he took steps to remove the restraints imposed by the Foreign Assets Control regulations on foreign subsidiaries of U.S. firms relating to nonstrategic transactions with China. This move allowed Americans traveling or residing abroad to purchase Chinese goods in limited quantities for noncommercial import into the United States, and permitted general licenses for the export of food, agricultural equipment, chemical fertilizer, and pharmaceuticals. The ultimate goal of these measures was to facilitate the gradual development of balanced trade.[18]

Diplomatic approaches were made indirectly and cautiously. In August, on a visit to Pakistan, Nixon met with Mohammad Yahya Khan—the Pakistan president and a friend of China—and indicated that the United States would welcome an accommodation with mainland China. He asked if Yahya would convey an important, but not urgent, message to Zhou Enlai "at some natural and appropriate time" and "in a low-key factual way."[19] In response, Yahya conveyed to Nixon China's concerns that "China feels surrounded by hostile forces—India, the Soviet Union and the United States in Southeast Asia. China seeks no territory or war but will fight with no holds barred if war is thrust upon it."[20] Yahya passed on Nixon's reconciliatory message, which assured China that the United States had no interest in joining the Soviet Union to form an Asian collective security system against China. In September, Zhou Enlai and Vice Premier Li Xiannian met with a Romanian delegation in Beijing and learned through them that Nixon was interested in normalizing Sino-American relations. In mid-November and early December, Nixon and Kissinger informed the Chinese—again via Pakistan, and through the American ambassador to Poland—of their wish to establish secret contacts at the highest level. Zhou Enlai alerted Mao to Nixon and Kissinger's approach. In December, the Chinese ambassador to Poland invited his U.S. counterpart to visit the Chinese embassy in Warsaw. [21]

In January and February 1970, the 135th and 136th ambassadorial talks between the United States and China resumed in Warsaw after a two-year hiatus. The American invasion of Cambodia in March–June 1970 created a potential hitch, prompting fierce criticism from mainland China, which supported Cambodia's exiled Sihanouk government. However, China's new stance of openness to the world was not to be hindered, and diplomatic relations were established with Canada, Italy, and a handful of other countries. By the end of 1970, Mao and Zhou had signaled their willingness to talk with Nixon in person. [22]

Although Nixon understood that American public opinion was still opposed to any rapprochement with Communist China, his formulation of America's new role in a changed world—self-defined as the "Nixon Doctrine"—was explicitly spelled out to Congress on February 25, 1971: "Around the globe, East and West, the rigid bipolar world of the 1940s and 1950s has given way to the fluidity of a new era of multilateral diplomacy." [23] In American eyes, the problem of the People's Republic of China was twofold. In economic terms, China was lagging behind. With a population of 750 million—eight times greater than that of Japan—and possessing much greater resources, mainland China's GDP was only 40 percent of that of Japan.

Another "unresolved problem" was the continuing animosity between the United States and China in the geopolitical arena. Integrating China into the international system was an important challenge, and the United States understood that this process would have to begin with the opening of bilateral dialogue. The American Ping-Pong team visited the country in April, followed by Nixon's easing of trade and travel restrictions to China. Taken together, these initiatives created a welcome diversion from Vietnam. At the end of May, once again using President Yahya as an intermediary, Zhou Enlai signaled China's willingness to receive a visit from Henry Kissinger in Beijing, reaffirming that the main obstacle to improved Sino-American relations was the withdrawal of American forces from Taiwan and the Taiwan Strait. [24]

On July 9, 1971, Kissinger made a top-secret visit to Beijing followed by a further visit in October, laying the groundwork for Nixon. On July 15, Nixon publicly announced his forthcoming visit to Beijing as a "journey for peace"—labeled the "Beijing Primary" by the media in light of the forthcoming elections. In October 1971, United Nations General Assembly Resolution 2758 brought China onto the Security Council in place of the Republic of China in Taiwan. Following a quarter of a century of marginalization, chiefly promoted by the United States, mainland China had at last assumed its position as a leading political power on the international stage.[25]

The dynamic cooperation between the two sides—led by Nixon and Kissinger, and Mao and Zhou, respectively—during this short but crucial period can be summarized under four major heads. First, the United States and China had each taken energetic steps toward establishing mutual confidence while maintaining a veil of secrecy over their initiatives. Working behind the scenes, both sides succeeded in partially clearing the obstacles left over from two decades without contact.

Despite Nixon's previous public disclosure of his strategies toward mainland China, both short and long term, his presidential visit to China in the final week of February 1972 still stunned most observers. At the same time, the political fuel provided by past contacts, and mutual knowledge and interest—however minuscule—remained a flickering ember that had never died away completely. A report in *Life* magazine conveyed the sense of separation, distance, and awe felt by American observers and participants alike at the grand banquet given for Nixon by Zhou Enlai:

> Seated way off there at one of them [the tables] was right-wing columnist William Buckley, staring at the gigantic U.S. and China flags side by side on the backdrop. He seemed in mild shock to find himself there, just then, in such company. . . . Even farther in the distance was Nixon, trying his chopsticks on shark's fin in three shreds, up on the stage of this cavernous hall taking back everything he had said about the old adversary China for the last 20 years, loping from table to table, clinking, bowing slightly, toasting the prime minister while the central band of the People's Liberation Army played *America the Beautiful*.[26]

Second, the United States offered mainland China some tangible "stakes" in a future relationship. Kissinger and Nixon pressed the theme that the United States was not working with the Soviet Union against China. They were meticulous in keeping the Chinese informed of any American negotiations with Russia that concerned China. Detailed top-secret intelligence information on Russia's military deployments near its borders with China was shared with the Chinese leaders.[27] American assurances went further. In his conversations with Zhou Enlai, Nixon promised that "the U.S. would oppose any attempt by the Soviet Union to engage in an aggressive action against China. This we would do because we believe it is in our interest, and in the interest of preserving peace as well, world peace."[28]

The Shanghai Joint Communiqué, issued on February 28, 1972, was the outcome of the first American presidential visit to a country with which it had had no diplomatic relations. It can be seen as the initial cornerstone laid down in the rebuilding of postwar Sino-American relations. Both sides identified the common ground on which they could work. They recognized the potential significance of their bilateral relationship for regional and world peace and agreed that it should be firmly based on the principles of "respect for the sovereignty and territorial integrity of all states, non-aggression against other states, non-interference in the internal affairs of other states, equality and mutual benefit, and peaceful coexistence." Both sides agreed that trade, as well as people-to-people contacts and exchanges, were mutually beneficial and should be facilitated. They were also candid about their "long-standing serious disputes" over Taiwan and disagreement on other issues.[29] The talks were dominated by the Taiwan question. The Chinese side reaffirmed its firm position on "One China," a nation that included Taiwan:

> The Taiwan question is a crucial question obstructing the normalization of relations between China and the United States; the Government of the People's Republic of China is the sole legal government of China; Taiwan is a province of China which has long been returned to the motherland; the liberation of Taiwan is China's internal affair in which no other country has the right to interfere; and all U.S. forces and military installations must be withdrawn from Taiwan.[30]

The U.S. side expressed its willingness to compromise on the Taiwan issue, and the Chinese, while remaining firm on the issue, showed flexibility in refraining from setting definite deadlines for the withdrawal of American forces from the territory. The American delegation acknowledged that Chinese on both sides of the Taiwan Strait wanted one China and that Taiwan was a part of China. The U.S. government did not challenge this position, asserting that the Taiwan question should be settled by the Chinese themselves. America's "ultimate objective" was to withdraw all U.S. forces and military installations from the island. Addressing

Chinese concerns over Japan's expansion in the Pacific, Nixon stated that the United States "have not and will not support any Taiwan independence movement," and that the United States would "discourage Japan from moving into Taiwan as our [American] presence becomes less, and also discourage Japan from supporting a Taiwan independence movement."[31] In May 1973, Sino-American liaison offices were opened in both Beijing and Washington, headed by senior diplomats David Bruce and Huang Hua, respectively.

In many ways, the Nixon/Kissinger–Mao/Zhou initiative corresponded to the changing pulse of world affairs and set Sino-American relations in a new direction. However, as a result of political constraints at both the domestic and global levels, both sides lacked a realistic timetable for bringing the bilateral relationship onto a productive new plane.

## THE FORD ADMINISTRATION (1974–77) AND AMERICAN-CHINESE RELATIONS

Despite the 1972 breakthrough that shook the world, the development of U.S.-Chinese relations did not follow a straight course. Official diplomatic relations did not become a reality until January 1, 1979—this step had been pushed aside by American and Chinese domestic politics, the Taiwan issue, and other priorities between 1973 and 1977.

Both Nixon and Mao had other geopolitical objectives in mind. Alongside the rhetoric promoting a new, diverse, multipolar world, the Nixon administration remained unchanged in treating mainland China as a potential source of threat, a guiding principle of American military planning for Asia from August 1973:

> U.S. forces should be planned so that U.S. and Allied forces would be capable of conducting a combined conventional defense against a joint PRC/Communist ally attack in either Northeast or Southeast Asia as well as a non-PRC attack in the other Asian theater. . . . This does not preclude early use of tactical nuclear weapons in the event of a major PRC attack . . . improvements in Allied capabilities to enhance a joint U.S./Allied defense will be planned as a lower priority goal. . . . U.S. planning for the next five years should include Asian baseline deployments at essentially current levels in Korea, Japan/Okinawa, and the Philippines. . . . There will be no increases in forces or manpower on Taiwan without prior Presidential approval.[32]

The Mutual Defense Treaty of 1954 between the United States and Taiwan and the seeming relaxation of American-Russian tensions were also a barrier to improved relations with China. In June 1973, Zhou Enlai expressed his concerns to David Bruce over Russian leader Leonid Ilyich Brezhnev's forthcoming visit to the United States and the signing of two arms limitation agreements—the Basic Principles of Negotiations on Strategic Arms Limitation and the Agreement between the United States of America and the Union of Soviet Socialist Republics on the Prevention of Nuclear War.[33] In 1974, a rehabilitated Deng Xiaoping—substituting for Zhou Enlai who was being treated for liver cancer—told Kissinger in Beijing that diplomatic relations between the United States and Taiwan must be severed, and that the Mutual Defense Treaty between the United States and Taiwan must be rescinded. The Taiwan question should be solved by the Chinese themselves, in their own way.[34]

In 1973, the internal political struggles racking China served only to compound the obstacles to the normalization of Sino-American relations. On September 13, 1971, Lin Biao—Mao's constitutionally designated successor at the 9th Congress of the Chinese Communist Party in 1969—died in a mysterious plane crash after being accused of plotting against Mao. Lin's downfall strengthened the hand of Zhou and a group of senior military leaders—Marshals Chen Yi, Ye Jianying, Xu Xiangqian, and Nie Rongzhen—in foreign affairs, and aided the gradual rehabilitation of formerly influential cadres persecuted in the Cultural Revolution. The restoration of order, however, proved temporary. In June 1973 Mao expressed his displeasure with Zhou for allegedly taking his instructions less than seriously and for his overcautious approach to the question of American-Soviet collusion in Zhou's published report on the Nixon and Brezhnev summit.

At the same time, Mao was playing one political rival off against another. The Gang of Four—the ultra-leftist clique led by Mao's wife, Jiang Qing, along with Zhang Chunqiao, Yao Wenyuan, and Wang Hongwen—was promoted at the CCP's 10th Congress, where Wang was elected vice chairman of the Party, an important position next to Zhou and making him an obvious heir to Mao. In November–December 1973, Mao again expressed his dissatisfaction with Zhou for his handling of talks with Kissinger and for his carelessness in being duped by the Americans. His snubbing of Zhou ultimately led to Mao's decision to entrust Deng Xiaoping with the daily management of the Chinese government in early 1974, a move opposed by Jiang Qing. At the end of 1975, however, Deng was purged once again. The Gang of Four was riding high, and Mao's failing health and indecisiveness had some serious repercussions. Political instability in China had left Zhou and Deng in a vulnerable position when it came to moving U.S.-Chinese relations forward.[35] For example, there was little dialogue and communication between the Chinese leaders and David Bruce and his successor George Bush during their tenure at the Beijing Liaison Office. As Donald Anderson, a political officer stationed there from 1973 to 1975, recalled, "[I]t was a time when the power struggle in Beijing was very intense, so no one was going to stick their neck out."[36]

The situation was not helped by Mao's view of the United States and China as fundamentally incommensurable. In opposition to American and Soviet hegemonism, Mao Zedong put forward the "three world" division theory. In February 1974, in a meeting with Zambian president Kenneth Kaunda, Mao proposed that the United States and the Soviet Union constituted the "First World"; that Japan, Europe, Canada, and Australia belonged to the Second World; and that the Third World comprised Asia (except for Japan), all of Africa, and Latin America. In political and economic terms, China was thus lumped in with some of the world's poorest countries.[37]

Nevertheless, the obstacles faced by the relationship came from both sides. In August 1974, the Watergate crisis forced Nixon to resign from office, and he was succeeded by Gerald R. Ford. In his address to a joint session of Congress on August 12, 1974, Ford pledged to bring inflation under control as his first priority, but he also reaffirmed American commitment to the principles of the Shanghai Communiqué.[38] However, by 1975 U.S.-Chinese relations had backtracked. Both sides were wrangling over a series of incidents including the cancellation of the visit by a Chinese artists' delegation and America's support of the Dalai Lama and other exiled Tibetan leaders. On a visit to China in October 1975, Kissinger received the cold shoulder from Mao and Zhou, who were both very ill.

Although Ford's visit to China in December 1975 failed to move American-Chinese relations forward to any real degree, at least the relationship did not deteriorate. However, the finalization of normalized relations, which Deng Xiaoping had lobbied for, simply lost momentum. While the welcome and farewell toasts given by Deng and Ford affirmed the principles of the Shanghai Communiqué, both parties lacked the commitment to work together to make further progress. According to information released by the Chinese authorities, at the state banquet held for Ford, Deng warned of the threat to peace posed by global hegemonies and the rise of the Third World as an important international force that should not be ignored.[39]

The "quiet" years in U.S.-Chinese relations (1972–78) were the product of a variety of factors, both international and domestic—the Watergate scandal; political instability and opposition within mainland China; the deaths of the Chinese leaders, Mao Zedong and Zhou Enlai, in 1976; and the U.S.-Soviet détente, together with China's consequently weak bargaining position. All these events had a bearing on the shape and timing of the eventual normalization of relations.

## MOVING FORWARD: NORMALIZATION AND ITS CONSEQUENCES

The diplomatic relationship between China and the United States was not normalized until January 1, 1979—trailing behind around one hundred other countries that had already recognized the People's Republic of China. The factor that eventually made formal recognition of China a reality was America's change in stance toward the Soviet Union. In 1977–78 the Soviet invasion of Afghanistan, the appearance of Soviet combat troops in Cuba, and its other activities around the Mediterranean littoral and in Africa undermined U.S.-Soviet cooperation. The American government was concerned that the Soviets might be heading for superiority, rather than parity, in military terms. China was taking a tough stance against the expansion of Soviet influence, especially regarding the latter's ally Vietnam. Sino-Vietnamese relations worsened substantially as Vietnam continued to threaten Cambodia, a menace taken seriously by China.[40] Vietnam's invasion of Cambodia at the end of 1978 triggered a Chinese reaction, and war broke out on February 17, 1979. These geopolitical changes in Asia created a new opportunity for moving Sino-American relations forward, in combination with more favorable domestic political environments in both countries. However, this opportunity was undercut by multiple political clashes over Taiwan in particular—represented in the American political system by disagreements over the issue between the White House and Congress.[41]

In 1977, James Earl Carter Jr. (Jimmy Carter) took office as president (presidency 1977–80). Meanwhile, a rehabilitated Deng Xiaoping had returned to power once again. Sino-American relations took a fresh turn as China embarked on a new path in the quest for national wealth and international advantage. Aware of the need to put its economy on a stronger footing, China was now eager to seek diplomatic relations with the United States and to get American help in industrializing its backward economy. Efforts and adjustments on the part of both new Chinese and American governments led slowly to the establishment of full diplomatic relations.

The normalization negotiations were driven by a mutual mistrust of the Soviet Union and a desire to resolve the Taiwan question. Particularly for the latter reason, they were conducted in secret. James Lilley (American ambassador to China, 1989–91) wrote of Carter's national security advisor that "[Zbigniew] Brzezinski's proprietary handling of the matter shut out virtually all government agencies."[42] One major reason for the administration's caution was Taiwan and its longtime friends in Congress. A small group of Carter's staff were given—albeit highly restricted—access to records of the many hours of conversation between Kissinger and Zhou and Mao, which they studied to ascertain the best way of handling the negotiations. Carter did not want Congress to "know too far in advance" what direction the talks might take.[43] The Chinese compromised on the issue of American arms sales to Taiwan, leaving it for future negotiation.[44] However, the United States agreed to break its diplomatic relations with Taiwan on short notice.

On December 15, 1978, Carter made a public announcement that the United States would henceforth recognize "One China"—the People's Republic of China—as the sole legal government of China, and that it would withdraw its embassy and military forces from Taiwan, effective January 1, 1979. In response, Congress challenged the president's prerogatives and weighed in on the side of Taiwan, passing the Taiwan Relations Act in April 1979.[45] Among other measures, the act committed the United States to the security of Taiwan, without specifying under what circumstances, and to providing Taiwan with "arms of a defensive character." There was still one further obstacle to reckon with. In 1980, during his presidential campaign, Ronald Reagan (presidency 1981–89) vowed to reestablish diplomatic relations with "the Republic of China," meaning Taiwan. The Chinese were inflamed with resentment over this apparent double-dealing.[46] Tensions grew over America's continuing arms sales to Taiwan, always a source of conflict between the two nations.

The conflict over Taiwan aside, the breakthrough in relations aroused feelings of euphoria and elicited expressions of mutual admiration in China and the United States. On January 28, 1979, Vice Premier Deng Xiaoping, the de facto leader of China, began a weeklong visit to the United States—the first official visit by a top Chinese Communist leader since 1949. There was a "fierce scramble" for invitations to the state dinner held on January 29. "People will kill for a ticket to the state dinner," declared one businessman. "If we invited everyone who claims an undeniable right to come, we'd have to hold the damn thing in the Capital Center [the 19,000-seat Washington sports arena]," sighed one senior White House official.[47] Vocal in condemning Soviet hegemonism and commending a Sino-American alliance against the Soviet Union, Deng appealed to America and Western Europe for assistance in modernizing China, including its backward military.

In the end, both China and the United States compromised on normalization. The Carter administration acknowledged the Chinese position that there was only one China and that Taiwan was part of China. And Deng Xiaoping acceded to the American request that China seek a peaceful resolution of the Taiwan issue. Moving away from its previous confrontational stance, mainland China expressed a willingness to negotiate peacefully with Taiwan over the question of unification, and agreed that "the Taiwan authorities as a local government" would maintain their own armed forces and system of governance, "but it must be within the context of one China."[48] Deng also agreed that the United States would give Taiwan a year's notice of these changes and that the defense treaty between the United States and Taiwan would remain in place through 1979. Among other factors driven by geopolitics and domestic reform, one important motive driving Deng's willingness to compromise on Taiwan was the need "to clear the American flank before addressing the issue of Vietnamese imperialism and the occupation of Cambodia."[49]

## ADJUSTMENT AND REORIENTATION IN THE 1980S

The 1980s witnessed strategic adjustments and adaptations in both America's China policy and China's America policy. The Reagan and Deng leaderships proved sufficiently flexible to accommodate ideology to practical reality and to change policy direction as their respective ideologies evolved. Both leaders should be credited for their success in maintaining relative stability in the relationship during the first decade of formal diplomatic relations.

After taking office, Ronald Reagan—a staunch conservative Republican carrying a good deal of ideological baggage on the China question—was gradually convinced by his secretary of state, the forceful Alexander M. Haig Jr., to retreat from his "Two Chinas" or "One China, Two Governments" rhetoric that could have seriously undermined America's China policy.[50] American arms sales to Taiwan continued to be controversial: the Chinese wanted them stopped, but the Americans saw their continuation as vital to helping defend Taiwan. Intense negotiations took place in Beijing. The two sides failed to reach a satisfactory agreement, and the third joint communiqué issued in August 1982 reflected a compromise on the issue. In the communiqué, China permitted the United States to sell weapons to Taiwan (the only country allowed to do so), and the United States agreed to the gradual diminution of arms sales to Taiwan; they would be kept at the existing level until a final solution was agreed.[51]

In 1982, China began a process of systematically reorienting and consolidating its approach to the outside world, distancing the United States, and relaxing tensions with the Soviet Union.[52] This shift in policy was introduced with the clear understanding that the core task of China's foreign policy was to create a peaceful international environment for economic development. Making China an affluent country was the first national priority. "Everything depends on whether we can get our own affairs in order," Deng Xiaoping explained.[53] Independence, nonalignment, and multilateralism became consistent objectives of Chinese foreign policy. In September 1982, Hu Yaobang—Deng's handpicked successor and general secretary of the Chinese Communist Party—declared at the 12th CCP Congress that China would pursue an independent course in relation to the two superpowers, the United States and the Soviet Union, on the basis of its own national interests. Hu also expressed China's willingness to normalize relations with the Soviet Union as long as the Soviets took concrete measures to remove the threat posed by their military activities to China's security. This position was reaffirmed at the fifth meeting of the 5th National People's Congress in December 1982.[54] Three years after the death of the Soviet leader Leonid Brezhnev in 1982,

Mikhail Gorbachev came to power ushering in dramatic economic and social reforms. As part of the Soviet Union's own reorientation process, the withdrawal of Soviet troops from Afghanistan and a substantial reduction in military deployments along the Soviet–Chinese borders helped promote a rapprochement in Sino-Soviet relations in 1985–86.[55]

From both the American and Chinese perspectives, the five years following the signing of their 1982 communiqué was a relatively stable, even a "golden" period.[56] As James Lilley commented, "For the first time in a long while, the State Department and the White House were in agreement on China policy."[57] Frequent high-level visits to both capitals—by President Reagan, President Li Xiannian, and Vice President George H. W. Bush, among others—helped maintain a progressive trend in the bilateral relationship.

## CONCLUSION

During the 1970s and 1980s, the United States and mainland China slowly found positive ways of working with each other. This process itself suggests that Cold War studies, especially in relation to China, ought to be moved beyond the 1950s and 1960s—where they have been conventionally stalled—and deep into the 1970s and 1980s.[58]

Both the American and Chinese leaderships and their political elites were broadly in favor of a reasonably amicable bilateral relationship. At the turn of the 1960s–70s, mainland China was quietly embarking on rectifying the wrongs of the Cultural Revolution, putting its own house back in order, and rebuilding a strong nation-state while working to shape an international environment in which China could flourish. Premier Zhou Enlai, who nevertheless deferred to Mao's authority, even discussed the "excesses" of the Cultural Revolution with Henry Kissinger. Zhou said that "he was hesitant to discuss mistakes but that the Chairman [Mao], with his greater inner strength, was free in admitting past errors."[59] In the Chinese view, it was the open, dynamic character of the relationship—driven less by ideology than by national interest—that had set in motion the historic, complex process of normalization.[60]

The progressive American approach was perhaps best exemplified by A. Doak Barnett, an influential, visionary scholar who was well known for working behind the scenes in Congress and the executive branch to improve relations between China and the United States. In 1970, Barnett asserted that the "China threat" had been exaggerated for twenty years and that America needed to take a more relaxed approach to the issue. A "new configuration of power" was emerging in East Asia, marking a fundamental shift from the bipolar pattern of the 1950s to a quadrilateral structure made up of Russia, America, China, and Japan. The demise of the Sino-Soviet alliance and their occasional border clashes had served to intensify Russia's competition with the Chinese as well as the Americans throughout East Asia and the Third World. As a result of these developments, the United States should "adjust its policies toward China" and "continue to probe"—to Moscow's discomfort—the possibilities for lessening tensions and expanding contacts with China. The United States should not "align with Moscow in any general policy of hostile pressure against Peking and should avoid both the act and appearance of any anti-Chinese 'collusion.'"[61] According to Barnett, the normalization of Sino-American relations and the removal of restrictions on nonstrategic trade with China was the right course, one that should not be inhibited by the "kinds of restrictions from Congressional and public opinion that existed some years ago."[62]

What had threatened to derail relations at times was that in the 1980s both sides had problems accommodating to each other's systems of government and political culture. The Chinese government found it irritating that often American presidents made promises—on the Taiwan issue, for instance—which Congress then failed to carry out. The struggle over the control of foreign policy between the American executive and legislative branches was embedded in the Constitution. The American political system did not always provide tidy results with regard to China, as well as other countries; it depended on the open exchange of views in debate and on bargaining and compromise.[63] In the United States, where "Anti-Communism has conditioned our foreign and military policy for too long,"[64] the "return" of China—following two decades of estrangement—was approached in a sentimental manner or with inflated expectations. These cultural and political assumptions were to be tested in the Tiananmen crisis of 1989 and the end of the Cold War.

## FURTHER READING

In addition to the works cited in the notes, valuable studies of U.S.-Chinese relations during the 1970s–80s include Harry Harding, *A Fragile*

*Relationship: The United States and China since 1972* (Washington, D.C.: Brookings Institution, 1992); Henry Kissinger, *On China* (New York: Penguin, 2011); Robert S. Ross, *Negotiating Cooperation: The United States and China, 1969–1989* (Stanford, Calif.: Stanford University Press, 1997); James H. Mann, *About Face: A History of America's Curious Relationship with China, from Nixon to Clinton* (New York: Knopf, 1998); Margaret MacMillan, *Nixon and Mao: The Week That Changed the World* (New York: Random House, 2007); Patrick Tyler, *A Great Wall: Six Presidents and China, an Investigative History* (New York: PublicAffairs, 1999).

Useful primary source material can be found in Scott Kennedy, *China Cross Talk: The American Debate over China Policy since Normalization: A Reader* (Lanham, Md.: Rowman & Littlefield, 2003); William Burr, ed., *The Kissinger Transcripts: The Top Secret Talks with Beijing and Moscow* (New York: New Press, 1998); Nicholas Platt, *China Boys: How U.S. Relations with the PRC Began and Grew. A Personal Memoir* (Round Top, N.Y.: Vellum, 2010); Cyrus Vance, *Hard Choice: Critical Years in America's Foreign Policy* (New York: Simon & Schuster, 1983); and Jeffrey A. Engel, ed., *The China Diary of George H. W. Bush: The Making of a Global President* (Princeton, N. J.: Princeton University Press, 2008).

Supplementary studies in Chinese include Wei Shiyan (魏史言), *Nikesong fanghua* [尼克松访华 Nixon's visit to China], vol. 3 of *Xin Zhongguo waijiao fengyun* [新中国外交风云 New China's diplomatic experience] (Beijing: Shijie zhishi chubanshe, 1994); and Li Tiecheng (李铁城) and Qian Wenrong (钱文荣), eds., *Lianheguo kuangjia xia de Zhongmei guanxi* [联合国框架下的中美关系 U.S.-Chinese relations within the framework of the United Nations] (Beijing: Renmin chubanshe, 2006).

## NOTES

1. Both the American and Chinese leaders understood that their own national domestic politics and public opinion needed to be accommodated in their foreign policy rhetoric, a tactic summarized as "firing empty guns," or "empty words," by Mao and Zhou. Memorandum of conversation between Nixon and Zhou Enlai in Beijing, February 22, 1972, National Archives, Nixon Presidential Materials Project, White House Special Files, President's Office Files, box 87, Memorandum for the President Beginning February 20, 1972, http://www.gwu.edu/~nsarchiv/NSAEBB/NSAEBB106/NZ-1.pdf (accessed May 30, 2011); also see William Burr's introduction at http://www.gwu.edu/~nsarchiv/NSAEBB/NSAEBB106/index2.htm (accessed May 30, 2011). Henry A. Kissinger's memo to Richard Nixon, November 11, 1972 [*sic*, 1971], "My October China Visit: Discussions of the Issues," National Archives, RG59, State

Department Top Secret Subject-Numeric Files, 1970–1973, POL 7 Kissinger, http://www.gwu.edu/~nsarchiv/NSAEBB/NSAEBB70/doc20.pdf (accessed July 6, 2012).

2. Harry Schwartz, "The Moscow-Peking-Washington Triangle," *Annals of the American Academy of Political and Social Science*, vol. 414, USA-USSR: Agenda for Communication (July 1974): 41–50. Lorenz M. Lüthi, *The Sino-Soviet Split: Cold War in the Communist World* (Princeton, N.J.: Princeton University Press, 2008).

3. Arthur Schlesinger, "Origins of the Cold War," *Foreign Affairs* 46, no. 1 (October 1967): 22–52.

4. David Shambaugh, ed., *Deng Xiaoping: Portrait of a Chinese Statesman* (Oxford: Clarendon Press, 1995); Ezra F. Vogel, *Deng Xiaoping and the Transformation of China* (Cambridge, Mass.: Belknap Press, 2011). Melvin Gurtov, "The Foreign Ministry and Foreign Affairs in China's 'Cultural Revolution,'" memorandum, RM-5934-PR, March 1969, RAND.

5. Robert S. Elegant, "China's New Phase," *Foreign Affairs* 46, no. 1 (October 1967): 137–150.

6. Arthur Schlesinger, "Origins of the Cold War."

7. Richard M. Nixon, "Asia after Viet Nam," *Foreign Affairs* 46, no. 1 (October 1967): 111–125.

8. Richard M. Nixon, "Asia after Viet Nam"; Donald W. White, *The American Century: The Rise and Decline of the United States as a World Power* (New Haven, Conn.: Yale University Press, 1996), p. 419.

9. Richard M. Nixon, "Asia after Viet Nam."

10. John T. Woolley and Gerhard Peters, American Presidency Project, http://www.presidency.ucsb.edu/ws/?pid=1941 (accessed May 27, 2011).

11. Editorial, "Zoutou wulu de zigongzhuang" [走投无路的自供状 A personal confession made in an impasse], *Renmin ribao*, January 28, 1969.

12. Zhou Enlai's speech at the fourth diplomatic personnel meeting at the Chinese Ministry of Foreign Affairs, January 1966, in Wang Yongqin (王永钦), "1966–1976 nian Zhong Mei Su guanxi jishi" [1966–76年的中美苏关系纪事 A chronicle of China-U.S.-USSR relations, 1966–76], part 1, *Dangdai Zhongguoshi yanjiu*, no. 4 (1997): 112–126.

13. Niu Jun (牛军), "1969 nian Zhongsu bianjie chongtu yu Zhongguo waijiao zhanlue de tiaozheng" [1969年中苏边界冲突与中国外交战略的调整 The Sino-Soviet border conflict in 1969 and the adjustment of China's diplomatic strategy], *Dangdai Zhongguo yanjiu* 1 (1999): 66–77. Winston Lord's memorandum for Henry A. Kissinger on Kissinger's conversations on July 9, 1971, in Beijing with Zhou Enlai, July 29, 1971. National Archives, Nixon Presidential Materials Project, NSC files, box 1033, China HAK Memcons, July 1971, http://www.gwu.edu/~nsarchiv/NSAEBB/NSAEBB145/09.pdf (accessed May 29, 2011); also see William Bur's introduction at http://www.gwu.edu/~nsarchiv/NSAEBB/NSAEBB145/index.htm (accessed May 29, 2011).

14. Jin Chongji (金冲及), ed., *Zhou Enlai zhuan* [周恩来传 A biography of Zhou Enlai] (Beijing: Zhonggong zhongyang wenxian yanjiushi, 1998), vol. 4, chapter 71.

15. Zhonggong zhongyang wenxian yanjiushi, comp., *Zhou Enlai nianpu (1949–1976)* [周恩来年谱 A chronology of Zhou Enlai] (Beijing: Zhongyan wenxian chubanshe, 1997), vol. 3, pp. 274–342. Xiong Xianghui (熊向晖, 1919–2005, assistant to Zhou Enlai during the Kissinger and Nixon visits to China), *Lishi de zhujiao: Huiyi Mao Zedong, Zhou Enlai ji si laoshuai* [历史的注脚:回忆毛泽东、周恩来及四老帅 Footnotes of history: Reflections on Mao Zedong, Zhou Enlai, and the four marshals] (Beijing: Zhongyang dangxiao chubanshe, 1995), pp. 173–204.

16. Memorandum of conversation between Henry Kissinger, John Holdridge, Winston Lord, Jonathan Howe, Ye Jianying, Qiao Guanhua, Zhang Wenjin, etc., on February 23, 1972, in Beijing, p. 14. National Archives, Nixon Presidential Materials Projects, NSC files, HAK office files, box 92, Dr. Kissinger's meetings in the PRC during the presidential visit February 1972, http://www.gwu.edu/~nsarchiv/NSAEBB/NSAEBB145/10.pdf (accessed May 29, 2011).

17. Memorandum of conversation between Henry Kissinger, John Holdridge, Winston Lord, Jonathan Howe, Ye Jianying, Qiao Guanhua, Zhang Wenjin, etc., on February 23, 1972, in Beijing, p. 14.

18. East-West Trade, Relaxation of Economic Controls againt China, National Security Memorandum 15 and 17, May 28 and June 26, 1969, Nixon Library, http://nixon.archives.gov/virtuallibrary/documents/nsdm/nsdm_015.pdf and http://nixon.archives.gov/virtuallibrary/documents/nsdm/nsdm_017.pdf (both accessed May 27, 2011).

19. Memorandum of conversation participated in by Agha Hilaly, Pakistan ambassador to the United States, and Harold H. Saunders, National Security Council staff, on August 28, 1969. Nixon Presidential Materials Project, National Security Files, box 1032, cookies II, http://www.gwu.edu/~nsarchiv/NSAEBB/NSAEBB145/02.pdf (accessed May 29, 2011).

20. Memorandum of conversation participated in by Agha Hilaly, Pakistan ambassador to the United States, and Harold H. Saunders, National Security Council staff, on August 28, 1969.

21. Wang Yongqin, "1966–1976 nian Zhong Mei Su guanxi jishi," part 1, *Dangdai Zhongguoshi yanjiu*, 4 (1997): 112–126.

22. Wang Yongqin, "1966–1976 nian Zhong Mei Su guanxi jishi," part 2, *Dangdai Zhongguoshi yanjiu*, 5 (1997): 110–127.

23. John T. Woolley and Gerhard Peters, American Presidency Project, http://www.presidency.ucsb.edu/ws/print.php?pid=3324 (accessed June 4, 2011). Nixon and Kissinger telephone conversation (Telecon), April 14, 1971, Henry A. Kissinger Telephone Conversation Transcripts (Telecons), Nixon Presidential Materials Project, National Archives II, College Park, Md., box 29, http://www.gwu.edu/~nsarchiv/NSAEBB/NSAEBB145/05.pdf (accessed May 29, 2011).

24. Message from Zhou Enlai to Nixon on May 29, 1971, National Archives, Nixon Presidential Materials Project, NSC files, box 1031, Exchanges Leading up to HAK Trip to China, December 1969–July 1971 (1), http://www.gwu.edu/~nsarchiv/NSAEBB/NSAEBB145/06.pdf (accessed May 29, 2011).

25. For an eyewitness account of many key events between the 1930s and 1970s, see Xiong Xianghui (P. R. China's first chief representative to the UN), *Wode qingbao yu waijiao shengya* [我的情报与外交生涯 My careers in espionage and diplomacy], expanded ed. (Beijing: Zhonggong dangshi chubanshe, 2006; 1st ed. 1999).

26. Hugh Sidey, "A President Wrapped in an Enigma," *Life* 72, no. 8 (March 3, 1972), p. 12.

27. Memorandum of conversation between Henry Kissinger, John Holdridge, Winston Lord, Jonathan Howe, Ye Jianying, Qiao Guanhua, Zhang Wenjin, etc., on February 23, 1972, in Beijing. Kissinger's memo of his meeting with Huang Zhen, the Chinese Ambassador to France, in Paris to Nixon on August 16, 1971, National Security Archive, RG59, Records of the Policy Planning Staff, Director's Files (Winston Lord), 1969–1977, box 330, China Exchanges July–October 20, 1971, http://www.gwu.edu/~nsarchiv/NSAEBB/NSAEBB70/doc2.pdf (accessed July 6, 2012).

28. Memorandum of Conversation between Nixon and Zhou Enlai in Beijing, February 23, 1972, National Archives, Nixon Presidential Materials Project, White House Special Files, President's Office Files, box 87, Memorandum for the President Beginning February 20, 1972, http://www.gwu.edu/~nsarchiv/NSAEBB/NSAEBB106/NZ-2.pdf (accessed May 30, 2011).

29. http://usinfo.state.gov/eap/Archive_Index/joint_communique_1972.html (accessed March 25, 2007). *Hongqi* no. 3 (1972): 5–7 published the Chinese version of 1972 Joint Communiqué in its entirety without any editorial.

30. http://usinfo.state.gov/eap/Archive_Index/joint_communique_1972.html (accessed March 25, 2007).

31. Memorandum of conversation between Nixon and Zhou Enlai in Beijing, February 22, 1972. This point was repeated by both Nixon and Zhou in their February 24 meeting; see Memorandum of Conversation, National Archives, Nixon Presidential Materials Project, White House Special Files, President's Office Files, box 87, Memorandum for the President Beginning February 20, 1972, http://www.gwu.edu/~nsarchiv/NSAEBB/NSAEBB106/NZ-3.pdf (accessed May 30, 2011).

32. U.S. Strategy and Forces for Asia, National Security Memorandum 230, August 9, 1973, Nixon Library, http://nixon.archives.gov/virtuallibrary/documents/nsdm/nsdm_230.pdf (accessed May 27, 2011).

33. Li Jie, "China's Domestic Politics and the Normalization of Sino-U.S. Relations, 1969–1979," in William C. Kirby, Robert S. Ross, and Gong Li, eds., *Normalization of U.S.-China Relations: An International History* (Cambridge, Mass.: Harvard University Asia Center, 2005), pp. 56–89.

34. Huang Hua (黄华), *Qinli yu jianwen: Huang Hua huiyi lu* [亲历与见闻: 黄华回忆录 Witnessing and experiencing at first hand: The memoirs of Huang Hua] (Beijing: Shijie zhishi chubanshe, 2007).

35. Gong Li (宫力), *Kuayue honggou: 1969–1979 nian Zhongmei guanxi de yanbian* [跨越鸿沟: 1969–1979 年中美关系的演变 Overcoming the chasm: The evolution of U.S.-China relations, 1969–79] (Zhengzhou: Henan renmin chubanshe, 1992).

36. Nancy Bernkopf Tucker, ed., *China Confidential: American Diplomats and Sino-American Relations, 1945–1996* (New York: Columbia University Press, 2001), chapter 5.

37. Wang Yongqin, "1966–1976 nian Zhong Mei Su guanxi jishi," part 4, *Dangdai Zhongguoshi yanjiu* 1 (1998): 103–118. Chen Mingxian (陈明显), ed., *Zhonghua renmin gongheguo zhengzhi zhidushi* [中华人民共和国政治制度史 A history of the political system of the People's Republic of China] (Tianjin: Nankai daxue chubanshe, 1998), chapter 8.

38. John T. Woolley and Gerhard Peters, American Presidency Project, http://www.presidency.ucsb.edu/ws/print.php?pid=4694 (accessed May 27, 2011).

39. *Renmin ribao*, December 2 and 5, 1975. In the three meetings between Deng and Ford held on December 1–5, 1975, Deng underscored the common ground between China and the United States, emphasizing that both nations were opposed to the hegemonic activities of other countries and interest groups. He stressed that the leaders of both nations should therefore stay in close contact and exchange ideas despite their different positions on international issues. See Zhongyang wenxian yanjiushi (中央文献研究室), ed., *Deng Xiaoping nianpu: 1975–1997* [邓小平年谱 A chronology of Deng Xiaoping] (Beijing: Zhonggong zhongyang wenxian chubanshe, 2004), vol. 1, pp. 134–135.

40. Memorandum of conversation between Deng Xiaoping and Zbigniew Brzezinski, May 25, 1978, Declassified Documents Reference System (Farmington Hills, Mich.: Gale, 2011), document no. CK3100155890.

41. Deng Xiaoping's interview with Earl W. Foell, *Christian Science Monitor*, December 3, 1980, B1. Robert S. Ross, "International Bargaining and Domestic Politics: U.S.-China Relations since 1972," *World Politics* 38, no. 2 (January 1986): 255–287; Gong Li (宫力), *Deng Xiaoping yu Meiguo* [邓小平与美国 Deng Xiaoping and the United States] (Beijing: Zhonggong dangshi chubanshe, 2004).

42. James Lilley with Jeffrey Lilley, *China Hands: Nine Decades of Adventure, Espionage, and Diplomacy in Asia* (New York: PublicAffairs, 2004), p. 210.

43. Nancy Bernkopf Tucker, ed., *China Confidential*, p. 325.

44. Wang Taiping (王泰平), *Zhonghua renmin gongheguo waijiaoshi* [中华人民共和国外交史 A diplomatic history of the People's Republic of China] (Beijing: Shijie zhishi chubanshe, 1999), vol. 3, p. 380.

45. United States Code, Title 22: Foreign Relations and Intercourse, Chapter 48: Taiwan Relations, http://uscode.house.gov/download/pls/22C48.txt (accessed June 24, 2011).

46. Huang Hua (黄华), "Zhongmei 'Bayiqi gongbao' douzheng shimo" [中美《八一七公报》斗争始末 The struggle over the Sino-American Communiqué of August 17], *Lishi kuandai* (September 2010): 93–97.

47. Cover story, "Teng's Great Leap Outward," *Time*, February 5, 1979, p. 26.

48. Hedley Donavan's interview with Deng Xiaoping, *Time*, February 5, 1979, p. 35. Michael D. Swaine, "Chinese Decision-Making Regarding Taiwan, 1979–2000," in David M. Lampton, ed., *The Making of Chinese Foreign and Security Policy in the Era of Reform* (Stanford, Calif.: Stanford University Press, 2001), pp. 289–336.

49. Nancy Bernkopf Tucker, ed., *China Confidential*, pp. 342–347.

50. Deng Xiaoping (邓小平), January 4, 1981, *Deng Xiaoping wenxuan* [邓小平文选 Selected works of Deng Xiaoping], 2nd ed. (Beijing: Renmin chubanshe, 1994, 1st ed. 1983), vol. 2, pp. 375–378.

51. http://usinfo.state.gov/eap/Archive_Index/joint_communique_1982.html (accessed March 27, 2007). Huang Hua, "Zhongmei 'Baiyiqi gongbao' douzheng shimo." Nancy Bernkopf Tucker, ed., *China Confidential*, pp. 359–370. Author unknown, "Risky Balancing Act," *Los Angeles Times*, January 22, 1981, C10.

52. Zhang Baijia (章百家), "Zhongyu shidai, chaoyue shidai: Zhou Enlai yu Zhongguo waijiao" [忠于时代,超越时代:周恩来与中国外交 Loyal to his time, and transcending his time: Zhou Enlai and Chinese diplomacy], *Zhonggong dangshi yanjiu*, no. 4 (2008): 52–60. Tao Wenzhao (陶文钊), ed., *Zhongmei guanxishi (1949–1972)* [中美关系史 A history of Sino-American relations (1949–1972)] (Shanghai: Shanghai renmin chubanshe, 2004), vol. 2, chapter 8.

53. Deng Xiaoping, August 21, 1982, *Deng Xiaoping wenxuan*, pp. 415–417. Deng Xiaoping, January 16, 1980, *Deng Xiaoping wenxuan*, pp. 239–273.

54. *Renmin ribao*, September 5 and 8, and December 6, 1982.

55. U.S. Department of State, compiled, *American Foreign Policy: Current Documents, 1986* (Washington, D.C.: Government Printing Office, 1987).

56. Tao Wenzhao, *Zhongmei guanxishi (1972–2000)* (Shanghai: Shanghai renmin chubanshe, 2004), vol. 3, chapter 5, p. 168. Ni Shixiong (倪世雄), *Jiejiao yiyan zhong, xiangqi qianli zhi: Yige Zhongguo xuezhe yanli de Zhongmei jianjiao sanshi nian* [结交一言重,相期千里至: 一个中国学者眼里的中美建交30年 Keeping one's word regardless of the obsta-

cles: The 30th anniversary of the U.S. and China diplomatic relations seen through the eyes of a Chinese scholar] (Shanghai: Fudan chubanshe, 2009), chapter 1.

57. James Lilley with Jeffrey Lilley, *China Hands*, p. 250.

58. David Shambaugh, "Studies of China's Foreign and Security Policies in the United States," in Robert Ash, David Shambaugh, and Seiichiro Takagi, eds., *China Watching: Perspectives from Europe, Japan and the United States* (London: Routledge, 2007), pp. 213–240.

59. Kissinger's memo to Nixon, "Your Encounter with the Chinese," February 5, 1972, National Archives, Nixon Presidential Materials Project, HAK Office files, box 13, China, http://www.gwu.edu/~nsarchiv/NSAEBB/NSAEBB70/doc27.pdf (accessed May 30, 2011).

60. Qian Qichen (钱其琛), "Qingshan zhe buzhu, bijing dongliu qu: Jinian Zhong-mei Shanghai gongbao fabiao sanshi zhounian" [青山遮不住,毕竟东流去:纪念中美上海公报发表三十周年 High mountains cannot hold the river back from flowing east: Commemorating the 30th anniversary of the announcement of the Sino-American Communiqué], *Qiushi zazhi* [求是杂志 Seeking the truth magazine] 4 (2002): 4–9. Zhang Baijia (章百家), "Cong 'Yibiandao' dao 'Quanfangwei': Dui wushi nian lai Zhongguo waijiao geju yanjin de sikao" [从"一边倒"到"全方位":对50年来中国外交格局演进的思考 From "Leaning to One Side" to "Multidirectional": Thoughts on the evolution of China's diplomatic framework over the last 50 years] *Zhonggong dangshi yanjiu* 1 (2000): 21–37.

61. A. Doak Barnett, "The New Multipolar Balance in East Asia: Implications for United States Policy," *Annals of the American Academy of Political and Social Science* 390 (July 1970): 73–86.

62. A. Doak Barnett, "The New Multipolar Balance in East Asia."

63. Stephen E. Ambrose, "The Presidency and Foreign Policy," *Foreign Affairs* 70, no. 5 (Winter 1991): 120–137. The Commission on the Bicentennial of the United States Constitution, *The Constitution of the United States with Index and the Declaration of Independence*, 18th ed. (Washington, D.C.: Government Printing Office, 1992).

64. Barbara W. Tuchman, *Notes from China* (New York: Collier Books, 1972), pp. 73–74.

# TEN

## The China Market and the Allure of the United States

Official and unofficial exchanges—in a wide spectrum of areas other than politics—helped rebuild relations between the United States and China. The late 1970s and 1980s witnessed China's historic domestic reforms, a new openness to the West, and increasing stature on the international stage. This was a time of hope and optimism. But meanwhile, both sides were struggling with issues arising from differences in their respective political, economic, and social systems, as well as their national values—issues that often led to conflict in a variety of international contexts.

### THE FIRST DECADE, 1971–80: FRAMEWORK BUILDING

*A Social and Economic Note*[1]

The year 1972 marked the end of a long freeze in contacts between the United States and the People's Republic of China. During the preceding twenty-two years of hostility (1949–71), only 1,500 Americans had traveled to mainland China.[2] By the end of 1987, however, 300,000 American citizens had visited China, and over 30,000 Chinese students and visiting scholars were living in the United States.[3]

China's "return" to the United States after a long hiatus created a sense of disorientation and generated fragmented impressions of the "new" China among "old" China hands. "China again—and one wonders where to begin, how to thread the memory from past to present,"

247

wrote Theodore White, a journalist who had visited Yan'an (the center of the Chinese Communist revolution) in 1944 on the first official American mission to the Chinese Communists, and who again found himself in China during President Nixon's visit in 1972.[4] White found Mao Zedong's ubiquitous presence "difficult to adjust to":

> There is no easy way of describing it—this is no classic tyranny or dictatorship but a presence that overpowers and smothers. From it there is no escape, no crevice, for private thought. . . . He [Mao] is there: his picture hanging ten feet high at every airport. On every street, above factory, apartment block, government hall, in red and white by day, in flaring light by night, the same five characters: "Mao Chu Hsi Wan Sui" (Long Live Mao Tse-tung).[5]

The acclaimed author Barbara W. Tuchman made a six-week trip to China in July–August 1972, one of the first generation of American visitors since the diplomatic thaw. Tuchman was able to observe the "new" China in both a positive and negative light: "In a country where misery and want were the foundation of the social structure, famine was periodic, death from starvation common, disease pervasive, thievery normal, and graft and corruption taken for granted, the elimination of these conditions in Communist China is so striking that negative aspects of the new rule fade in relative importance."[6] Yet, similar to Theodore White, Tuchman found what she described as the country's "mental monotone" troubling: "All thought, all ideas past, present, and future, not to mention the historic record, are twisted, manipulated, rolled out, and flattened into one, expressed in half a dozen slogans dinned incessantly and insistently into the heads of the public."[7]

In the realm of the economy, China was almost totally insulated from the outside world in 1971 when Nixon announced his upcoming visit to China. As a *New York Times* reporter wrote, "The news of President Nixon's coming trip to Communist China, sensational as it is politically, produced virtually no effect on the stock market."[8] China was a "puzzle" to be pieced together, as a major fiscal initiative would soon illustrate. On August 15, 1971, in an attempt to redress inflation and unemployment, the Nixon administration devalued the U.S. dollar by 8 percent by imposing a system of wage and price controls and fixing the exchange rates for American currency. As a result, "one country after another began to float its currency against the dollar."[9] A few days later, James Reston filed this report from Shanghai:

The "dollar crisis" was no crisis in China. Even here in this commercial capital of the People's Republic there was no public evidence that anybody was paying the slightest attention to Washington's "new economic policy." . . . Two days after President Nixon devalued the old greenback and sent a hiccup through all the banks and stock exchanges of Europe, I cashed $500 worth of American travelers checks at the old exchange rate in Peking. No problem. No questions asked. And even a day later, the banks here in Shanghai were still paying out on cabled dollars from New York as if nothing had happened.[10]

However, this economic insulation was not to last. The decade 1971–80 witnessed rapid institutional growth and the lifting of some of the barriers to the flow of goods, technology, and people. Already in 1971–72, China's international trade and its trade with the United States were increasing by levels of 20 percent per year. In March 1971, the State Department eased restrictions on U.S. citizens visiting China, and the following month American table tennis players toured the country in what became known as "ping-pong diplomacy." On April 14, the Nixon administration announced five measures aimed at removing restrictions on commerce and travel between the United States and China. Under this initiative, the United States would expedite visas for visitors from the People's Republic. In the other direction, U.S. currency controls were to be relaxed, allowing American citizens to remit money to Chinese citizens or organizations without prior Treasury approval.

There was also limited liberalization of commercial activity. Restrictions were to be lifted "on American oil companies providing fuel to ships or aircraft proceeding to and from China except on Chinese-owned or Chinese-chartered carriers bound to or from North Vietnam, North Korea, or Cuba."[11] The *New York Times* reported, "A list of 'non-strategic' goods will be drafted and U.S. companies will be allowed to export these items directly to mainland China without prior government permission. Selected direct imports from there will be authorized in the future. . . . American carriers will be allowed to haul Chinese cargo between non-Chinese ports."[12] Then on June 10, following these carefully calibrated measures, Nixon officially ended the trade embargo, sweeping aside the legal barriers which had hindered significant economic interaction between the United States and China since 1950.

While taking note of the geopolitical sea change, the American media remained wary about the prospects for bilateral trade. Some newspapers characterized the China market as illusory, given that the gross national product of a nation with five times its population constituted only about 7 percent of that of the United States. A headline in the *Wall Street Journal* could hardly have been more explicit: "Illusory Market: Trade with China, Long a Dream of Americans, Remains Only a Mirage; Peking Policy Limits Imports; China's Potential Exports Unlikely to Spur Demand; Want to Buy Any Pig Bristle?" Its author made no attempt to conceal his sarcasm: "Since the U.S. embargo on China trade was lifted last June, trade has totaled about $5 million; all of this has been through third parties because the Chinese still refuse to deal directly with American firms. From this tiny level, trade has nowhere to go but up."[13]

A more temperate journalistic assessment expressed a widely held view: "In straight economic terms, it is difficult to see United States trade with Communist China amounting to a great deal for years to come."[14] An editorial in the *New York Times* commented,

> In the short run, there are fairly narrow constraints on how much trade can take place bilaterally between China and the United States. Chinese economic capacities are extremely limited—per capita income is about $120 a year. Total Chinese exports are only about one-tenth those of Japan. . . . There are many goods China would like to import from the United States, such as locomotives, industrial chemicals, fertilizers, construction equipment, steel mills, machine tools, wheat—which this country can produce in abundance. But China's ability to pay is tightly bound by her narrow export list. . . . Since June [1971] when trade with China was opened, total American imports from that country have amounted to a mere $5 million.[15]

Many Americans believed that China would be unable to "finance any great increase of imports until it can begin to earn enough foreign exchange by increasing its own exports."[16] Hence, the growth of Sino-American economic relations would likely depend on U.S. "willingness to extend export credits or other forms of aid to China."[17]

In February 1972, Nixon decided to upgrade China from Country Group Z of the Commodity Control List to Country Group Y, and to eliminate the Foreign Assets Control requirement that subsidiaries of American firms in CoCom (the Coordinating Committee for Multilateral Export Controls) countries had to obtain a Treasury license, in addition to a host country license, for the export of strategic goods to the P. R. China, and to rescind the requirement that subsidiaries of American firms abroad obtain prior Treasury licensing for the export of foreign technology to mainland China.[18] In 1973 Nixon decided that the United States should approve the export of eight state-of-the-art inertial navigational systems (INS) to be included on four Boeing 707 aircraft, in addition to the INS required for three Anglo-French Concorde aircraft sold to mainland China.[19]

With full diplomatic relations established, the United States and Chinese governments set out to clear the remaining legislative and administrative hurdles and move trade relations forward. On May 11, 1979, Michael Blumenthal, the U.S. secretary of the treasury, and Zhang Jinfu, the Chinese finance minister, reached a settlement on the US$280 million worth of claims and assets resulting from the reciprocal confiscation of assets and property that had followed the outbreak of the Korean War in 1950.[20] The next twelve months saw a wide range of developments encouraging the full normalization of trade relations including a bilateral trade agreement; the opening of the first American law firm (Coudert Brothers of New York City) in mainland China since 1950; U.S. assistance with Chinese hydroelectric power development, consumer goods manufacturing, and petroleum production and transportation; export-import bank credits; approval for expanded arms sales to China; and a Chinese commitment to exporting scarce strategic materials.

Most importantly, on January 24, 1980, Congress passed a trade agreement conferring most-favored-nation (MFN) status on China. This measure exempted Chinese exports to the United States from the high tariff rates stipulated by the Smoot-Hawley Act of June 1930. Enacted at the start of the Great Depression, this piece of legislation epitomized American protectionism and was subsequently used to distinguish friends from foes among its trading partners.

Despite this move, China's MFN trade status (which was not granted permanently) created new legal and political impediments to Sino-American trade relations which were not removed until 2001. Under U.S. law, the normalizing of trade relationships placed the People's Republic of China within the purview of the Jackson-Vanik Amendment contained in Title IV of the 1974 Trade Act. Regarded as the most important human rights legislation ever passed by the U.S. Congress, the Jackson-Vanik Amendment links trade benefits with the human rights policies of Communist (or former Communist) countries and was originally directed at Russian restrictions on Jewish emigration to the United States. Not only does it deny preferential trade relations to offending nations, but "such a country shall not participate in any program of the Government of the United States which extends credits or credit guarantees or investment guarantees, directly or indirectly."[21] The U.S. president has the authority to waive the application of the Jackson-Vanik Amendment to a particular country, and Congress must review his semiannual reports on that country's continued compliance in upholding rights to freedom of emigration.[22] Therefore, the Jackson-Vanik Amendment provided the legal grounds for the annual congressional renewal of China's most-favored-nation status until 2001 when China joined the World Trade Organization (WTO), whose rules prohibit members from imposing such trade restrictions on other members.

Tables 10.1 and 10.2, compiled from U.S. and Chinese sources respectively, present trade data for the first decade of renewed commercial activity between the two countries. They show continued growth, but at quite low levels, with a hiccup from 1975 to 1977, with respect to U.S. exports to China. Although, with the exception of 1979 and 1980, the two sets of figures rarely agree with each other, their differences were marginal compared with the considerable divergence that began in the mid-1980s (see figures 10.1 and 10.2). Especially noteworthy is the fact that, during this period, America's trade with China never amounted to more than 1 percent of total U.S. world trade—a situation very like U.S. trade relations with China in the eighteenth and nineteenth centuries. Overall, during this period the United States sold more than it bought from China. By the end of the decade, however, the total business conducted between the two nations was doubling each year, from US$1.1 billion in 1978 (U.S. figures; Chinese statistics recorded $991.7 million), to $2.3 billion in 1979 (Chinese figures: $2.4 billion), to $4.8 billion in 1980.

Following Mao Zedong's death in 1976, Deng Xiaoping made his way back into power, removing Mao's designated successor, Hua Guofeng, and waging a peaceful revolution—comprising the "Four Modernizations" of agriculture, industry, science and technology, and the military—that began with the 11th Plenary Session of the 13th CCP Congress held in December 1978.[23] The extraordinary reforms that followed have made China the second-largest economy in the world in 2011.

In foreign trade, raw materials such as iron and steel (rather than technology and industrial equipment) formed the bulk of China's imports. In 1977 China spent 22 percent of its foreign exchange on iron and steel, followed by foodstuffs (17 percent), chemicals (12 percent), trans-

Table 10.1.  U.S.-Chinese Trade, 1971–80 (U.S. figures, in millions of current U.S. dollars)

| Year | U.S. Imports from PRC | U.S. Exports to PRC | Total Bilateral Trade | U.S. Trade Balance | Percent of Total U.S. Trade | Percent of Total PRC Trade |
|------|------|------|------|------|------|------|
| 1971 | 4.7 | 0.0 | 4.7 | −4.7 | 0.0 | — |
| 1972 | 32.2 | 60.2 | 92.4 | 28 | 0.1 | — |
| 1973 | 63.5 | 689.1 | 752.6 | 625.6 | 0.5 | — |
| 1974 | 114.4 | 806.9 | 921.2 | 692.5 | 0.4 | — |
| 1975 | 157.9 | 303.6 | 461.6 | 145.7 | 0.2 | — |
| 1976 | 201.5 | 134.4 | 335.9 | −67.1 | 0.1 | — |
| 1977 | 200.7 | 171.3 | 372.1 | −29.4 | 0.1 | 2.5 |
| 1978 | 324.0 | 820.7 | 1,144.6 | 496.7 | 0.3 | 5.4 |
| 1979 | 592.3 | 1,724.0 | 2,316.3 | 1,131.7 | 0.6 | 7.9 |
| 1980 | 1,058.3 | 3,754.4 | 4,812.7 | 2,696.1 | 1.0 | 12.7 |

*Source:* Harry Harding, *A Fragile Relationship: The United States and China since 1972* (Washington, D.C.: Brookings Institution, 1992), p. 364.

port equipment (9 percent), and textile fibers (7 percent).[24] U.S. exports reflected this: in 1978 the United States sold China cereals, raw textile fibers and waste, machinery, fertilizers, and vegetable oils and fats, while the chief items exported by China were feathers, cotton fabrics, basketwork, fireworks, pig bristles, and mats and matting screens.[25] It needs to be said that this situation also reflected continued American restrictions on exports of technology and equipment.

These historic trade developments, as well as the lure of the China market, generated considerable enthusiasm in the United States:

> Within weeks of diplomatic recognition, seminars and conferences on trade with China proliferated throughout the country (U.S.), playing to packed houses of several hundred business executives at a time. U.S. Department of Commerce officials reported an average 350 calls a day and a flood of inquiries in the mail. Teng Hsiao-p'ing's [Deng Xiaoping's] pointed interest in automobiles, petroleum equipment, and aircraft manufacturing plants gave an additional impetus to the snowballing interest in Chinese markets.[26]

**Table 10.2. U.S.-Chinese Trade, 1971–80 (Chinese figures, in millions of current U.S. dollars)**

| Year | PRC Exports to U.S. | PRC Imports from U.S. | Total Bilateral Trade | China Trade Balance |
|------|------|------|------|------|
| 1971 | — | — | — | |
| 1972 | 9.6 | 3.3 | 12.9 | 6.3 |
| 1973 | 39.72 | 220.66 | 260.38 | −180.94 |
| 1974 | 102.86 | 372.85 | 475.71 | −269.99 |
| 1975 | 128.88 | 341.83 | 470.71 | −212.95 |
| 1976 | 156.04 | 160.64 | 316.68 | −4.6 |
| 1977 | 179.63 | 114.62 | 294.25 | 65.01 |
| 1978 | 270.6 | 721.1 | 991.7 | −450.5 |
| 1979 | 595.01 | 1,856.59 | 2,451.6 | −1,261.58 |
| 1980 | 981.06 | 3,830.21 | 4,811.27 | −2,849.15 |

*Source:* Tao Wenzhao (陶文钊), ed., *Zhongmei guanxishi (1972–2000)* [中美关系史 The history of Sino-American relations (1949–1972)] (Shanghai: Shanghai renmin chubanshe, 2004), vol. 3, p. 339. Some minor adjustments have been made to the figures published here, and I have added the China trade balance column.

*Religion and Culture: On Chinese Terms* [27]

In the religious sphere, the forced termination of American missions in China in 1949–51 had left scars on both sides. In the early 1950s, in both the United States and China, fear of the other country's baleful influence was palpable. Christianity became a vehicle for pro-Communists and anti-Communists alike to take a stance on either "Red China" or "free China."

In May 1950, a document known as *The Christian Manifesto* was released by the Chinese government. It stated that the Christian church must unite behind the leadership of the new Communist government and disavow the ecclesiastical and financial influence of foreign imperialism. According to the *New York Times*, this call for the reform of Chinese Christianity—characterized as "the Chinese Communist church-state declaration" by American Protestants—"closely followed a pattern set by Communists in other satellite territories." [28] The press also highlighted the cooperation of Protestant leaders such as Y. T. Wu with the new Chinese government. [29]

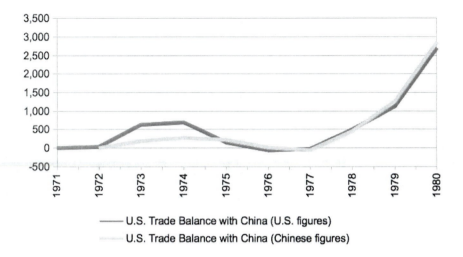

Figure 10.1. U.S. Trade Balance with China, 1971–80 (in millions of current U.S. dollars)

Today, the official Protestant establishment in the People's Republic of China consists of two partly overlapping organizations, the Three-Self Patriotic Movement Committee (TSPM, established in 1954) and the China Christian Council (CCC, founded in 1980), commonly known as the "two committees." Although both serve as arms of the state, the TSPM is "more overtly political," [30] while the CCC functions in a more pastoral capacity and deals with foreign relations. Other manifestations of Protestantism in China include house churches, sectarian groups, and groups of uncertain descent. [31] To ordinary Americans, the Three-Self Patriotic Movement was at the Communist regime's beck and call. The American print media rarely mentioned that the official Chinese church was the direct child of the American missions (as we saw in chapter 7).

In June 1950, the Korean War sparked a barrage of news stories that attested to the mutual fear and hatred between China and the United States. China's entry into the war in October was accompanied by a stepping up of the anti-American campaign in China and by a vigorous drive to eradicate American influence among Chinese. At the same time, the Committee to Defend America by Aiding Anti-Communist China issued an appeal to President Harry Truman and Secretary of State Dean Acheson, "urging the United States government to 'remain firm' in not recognizing the Communist regime in China." [32] It was signed by two hundred American clergy, missionaries, and laymen—many of whom had spent

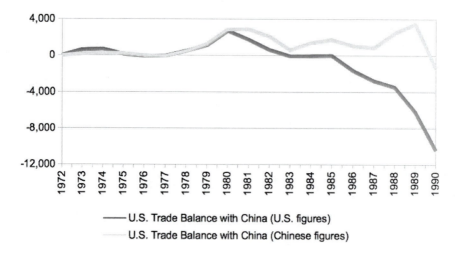

— U.S. Trade Balance with China (U.S. figures)
— U.S. Trade Balance with China (Chinese figures)

**Figure 10.2. U.S. Trade Balance with China, 1972–90 (in millions of current U.S. dollars)**

time in East Asia. The statement asserted that U.S. recognition of the People's Republic would be a "moral compromise" and a "political mistake," and would endorse the CCP's authority in what the *New York Times* described as "occupied China."

Pro-Communist missionaries—albeit few and far between—found themselves at odds with mainline Christians and other Americans who looked on the CCP as "Reds," and on Chinese Christians as a persecuted minority. In late 1950, the American Baptist Foreign Mission Society summoned home missionary Dryden L. Phelps—who had been stationed in China since 1921—for hailing the restructuring of Christianity in China as the "most profoundly religious experience I have ever been through. . . . God is working alongside of these Communists."[33] Similarly, the Anglican cleric Hewlett Johnson, dean of Canterbury Cathedral, came under attack for siding with China over the use of germ warfare by the United States in Korea.[34]

The estrangement between the United States and China was aptly summed up by historian John K. Fairbank: "Since 1950 Washington has officially sent more men to the moon than it has to China, even though China is closer, more populous, and the trip less costly and dangerous."[35] However, attempts to renew direct contact with China were discouraged in Protestant circles.[36]

In 1971, President Nixon's announcement of his forthcoming visit to Beijing awoke memories of a bygone missionary era in China, but most importantly it provided a ray of sunshine. American Protestants reacted to the thaw in Sino-American relations with a variety of responses, venting long-smoldering emotions. One fundamentalist group called for a thousand three-man missionary teams to evangelize every city in China: "Let us be ready to be first with the message of Christ as this great nation opens its doors to the outside world again."[37] But this approach set off alarm bells among some evangelicals who were aware of the linkage between Christianity and imperialism in China. "There will never be a foreign-dominated church in China again, and this is good."[38]

Not all Americans lambasted the Chinese Communist Party over the state of the church in China. In many quarters, Nixon's state visit to China spurred self-examination over the mistakes made in the pre-1952 missionary era. A *New York Times* piece speculated that official hostility to religion "reflected a traditional Marxist disdain for Christianity, but it also had its roots deep in Chinese nationalism. In moving to reorder the church in China, the Communists were appealing to a widespread sentiment among the people, who had come to link Christianity with Western imperialism."[39] In recognition of common social goals such as the eradication of public prostitution and poverty, other Christian leaders called for a coming to terms with Maoism and Chinese Communism. Some observers even called for dialogue between Christianity and Marxism in China.[40]

In reaction to Nixon's historic announcement, some American evangelical civil rights activists again linked the opening of "Red China" with the race issue in the United States. In 1971, Hosea L. Williams, who had served as Martin Luther King Jr.'s chief field general and held the record for civil rights arrests (eighty-one), visited China for four weeks. In a sermon, Williams proclaimed,

> I went to China as a Christian, and I have returned as a better Christian. Recognizing the religious hypocrisy of America, it makes me wonder whether or not God has decided to entrust the moral regeneration of man into the hands of the non-believer because the believers have become so corrupt, so sinful and so evil.[41]

## THE SECOND DECADE, 1980–89: IMPROVEMENTS AND OBSTACLES

*Trade*

Throughout the 1980s, the normalization of political relations and China's nascent economic reforms paved the way for an acceleration in the transfer of goods, values, ideas, personnel, and technology. These interactions were mutually beneficial, although from the U.S. point of view, the China trade was still small beer. Nevertheless, by 1984 the United States had become China's third-largest trading partner, trailing only Japan and Hong Kong, then still a British colony. As America's fourteenth-largest trading partner, on the other hand, China accounted for a paltry 1.7 percent of total American foreign trade in 1988 and 2.2 percent in 1990.[42] While these developments represented a strengthening of the web of mutual relations, they also planted the seeds of new issues and conflicts that went on to arouse fierce debate in the 1990s. For example, the two nations differed on the extent of China's exports and the trade imbalance, and the battle over statistical discrepancies in this area is an ongoing one.

The 1980s witnessed the initial phase of what would turn out to be a massive and continuing process of economic reform in China. In the late 1970s, the Deng leadership was concerned that China's chief economic unit since the 1950s—communal farming—could no longer produce sufficient grain to feed over 1 billion Chinese and was moreover undermining the potential for new agricultural technology. In place of the collective farming system, the "household responsibility" system was introduced: every village household was given a piece of land previously held by a commune to manage for itself. This radical change in land use practices motivated peasants to work hard and seek new avenues of profitability in small rural businesses.

State-owned heavy industry was also a target of the reforms. Mao Zedong's planned economy had failed to provide the Chinese people and the state sector with sufficient services and consumer goods such as bus, railway, and taxi transport; hotels and catering outlets; repair shops; convenience stores; and construction materials. These long-neglected areas were opened up to both state and private investment as China became increasingly geared toward a market economy. Foreign investment was also courted. By 1987 several special economic zones had been established in coastal areas of Guangdong and Fujian—sites where foreign firms could set up industries or establish joint enterprises with Chinese firms and operate with a degree of economic freedom. This initiative provided China with much-needed foreign capital, technology, expertise, and ideas.

This "Second Revolution,"[43] led by Deng Xiaoping, Zhao Ziyang, and Hu Yaobang, brought prosperity to more Chinese than at any time since the founding of the People's Republic in 1949. The introduction of private farming, along with a huge bump in prices for agricultural products, spearheaded the steady advance of the Four Modernizations. The household contract system led to a surge in grain output in the period 1978–84, strengthening China's ability to feed 22 percent of the world's population on only 7 percent of its arable land. The new policies encouraged the proliferation of village and township enterprises, which set the stage for further market-led reforms. In the industrial sector, the central government gradually loosened its control over state-owned enterprises (20 percent of which recorded losses in 1986), while permitting dynamic rural industries and joint-stock companies to diversify their industrial production as well as expand market outlets. As competition increased, profitability criteria began to extend to state-run industries. Managers were given greater freedom in hiring and firing.[44]

The restructuring of the domestic economy coincided with China's opening up to the outside world. Here, the position of Hong Kong as an entrepôt linking East with West was crucial. The first step in connecting China to global trade involved harnessing Hong Kong's trading power in world markets by encouraging Hong Kong firms to sign export-processing contracts with businesses in the newly established special economic zones in Guangdong and Fujian provinces. Direct international trade grew apace as well. By the mid-1980s the number of companies engaged in the direct export and import trade had increased dramatically, and the central government relaxed controls over local agencies and prioritized revenue creation. The government also offered tax incentives to both domestic and foreign investors, which virtually turned China's entire littoral into a lucrative export-processing zone. These dual trade reforms resulted in annual growth of around 10 percent in China's gross national product from 1983 to 1987 and a 15.8 percent annual expansion in international trade.[45] China's foreign trade almost tripled from US$20.6 billion in 1978 to US$60.2 billion in 1985. The acceleration in China's international trade was reflected in its trade with the United States—but here the growth was sevenfold, from about US$1 billion to over US$7 billion during the same period.

One noteworthy change facilitating U.S.-Chinese economic relations was the steady liberalizing of controls over American exports of advanced technology. In 1980, such exports to China were reassigned from category Y (the Warsaw Treaty countries) to category P (new trading partners with the United States), and then to category V (American allies) in May 1983 under the Reagan administration (1981–89). A three-tiered system of export licenses further streamlined the licensing process, placing 75 percent of export license applications in a "green zone" under the sole control of the Department of Commerce.

In the 1980s, the commodities traded between the two countries were complementary rather than competitive. In contrast to the heavy emphasis on iron and steel in the 1970s, Chinese imports from the United States diversified to include grain ($699 million in 1988), chemicals and industrial raw materials ($596 million), fertilizer ($379 million), instruments and communications and transportation equipment ($905 million), wood products, and chemical fibers. In the second half of the decade, finished manufactures and technologically advanced products began to enter the China market. Among American imports from China, textiles and clothing accounted for more than 40 percent of the total value of Chinese exports to the United States. After Hong Kong and Macau, the United States was the largest investor in China, with about $3 billion in assets by 1985.

Following the Chinese economic reforms of the 1980s, U.S. companies manufacturing consumer goods were increasingly drawn to China. American companies entered the country by forming joint ventures with a Chinese company or government agency. Early participants included H. J. Heinz, R. J. Reynolds Tobacco, Coca-Cola, American Express, American Motors, AMF Inc., General Foods, Beatrice, Gillette, Pepsi-Cola, Eastman Kodak, AT&T, Nabisco, and Bell South. By 1985, four Coke bottling plants were operating in Beijing, Guangzhou, Xiamen, and Zhuhai, and by 2000, Coca-Cola had invested US$1.2 billion in twenty-three plants, accounting for 70 percent of China's domestic soft drink market. In spring 1985, the Great Wall Sheraton Hotel in Beijing became the first internationally managed corporation in China to accept American Express.[46]

*The Road to Conflict: The Problem of Re-traded Goods*

While bilateral trade advanced at a breakneck pace, the two nations differed on the extent of trade and the trade imbalance, a situation which fueled the wrangling over statistics that broke out and continues to this day. The most striking discrepancies in the American and Chinese trade statistics, as illustrated in figure 10.2 and tables 10.3 and 10.4, centered on disagreement over the extent of China's exports. In 1984, for example, the *Los Angeles Times* reported that bilateral trade had reached a record US$6.1 billion, 50.6 percent higher than in 1983. The Chinese claim of a deficit in this figure was disputed by American data, with U.S. officials "insisting that two-way trade balanced at 3 billion for each side, whereas China claimed a 1.5 billion trade deficit. Washington concluded that the numbers were concocted by the Chinese in order to extract concessions from the United States in talks on textiles and other trade negotiations."[47] And while official U.S. estimates of Chinese exports varied to some degree, the figures were relatively consistent on American exports to China.[48] U.S. statistics show that 1986 was a turning point, with a US$1.67 billion trade deficit against the United States which not only made the previous year's US$9.9 million deficit look paltry, but also kicked off a deep twenty-year trade deficit with the People's Republic. In stark contrast, the Chinese figures for 1986 show a more than US$1 billion deficit against the PRC—one point on the long curve of a trade deficit stretching from 1973 through 1992. (See figures 10.3 and 12.1.)

While these statistical differences were to lead to escalating frictions in the future, in the 1980s both sides recognized the rapid growth in their commercial relationship since the establishment of diplomatic relations in 1979—producing an annual average growth rate of 44 percent.[49] The controversy over the bilateral trade imbalance calls for an analysis of a complex array of local, regional, and international factors. The disagreements over the size and causes of the deficit originated in a number of areas: the two sides' different accounting approaches to re-exports to and from China via Hong Kong, U.S. policy constraints on exports to China, the role of foreign firms in China, the multinational trade in commercial services, and global outsourcing and capital flows in the increasingly interdependent East Asian and world economy. Here, we will focus on one of these disputed areas—whether American exports and imports channeled through Hong Kong should legitimately be considered part of U.S.-China trade.

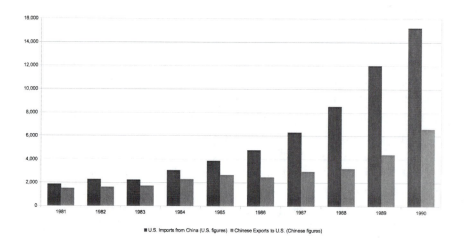

**Figure 10.3. Chinese Exports to the United States, 1981–90 (in millions of current U.S. dollars)**

Hong Kong's intermediary role in connecting China with the world was vital to the national economy. In the mid-1980s, over 30 percent of China's foreign exchange passed through Hong Kong. The United States was the largest foreign investor in Hong Kong with 54 percent of the total, followed by Japan (21 percent) and the United Kingdom (7 percent).[50] In 1984 the United States was the leading export market for Hong Kong with about US$7.8 billion worth of exports, and was the colony's second-largest re-export market, handling trade worth approximately US$1.5 billion. In 1984, China provided 25 percent of Hong Kong's imports (and 45 percent of its food imports), overtaking Japan as the territory's leading supplier. In the same year, American exports channeled through Hong Kong to China amounted to US$375.9 million, while China in turn exported over US$1,125 million worth of goods through Hong Kong to the United States.[51] The Chinese insisted that these Hong Kong re-exports account for 50 percent of China's total exports to the United States that year (almost one-third in the U.S. statistics).

According to Chinese trade figures, 60 percent of Chinese exports to the United States were initially consigned to buyers in Hong Kong who resold them to a third party, who then shipped them to the United States. On top of this, a further 20 percent of Chinese exports to the United States were re-exported via a third country. Although the Chinese accepted that such goods had originated in China, they argued that the 40 to 100 per-

Table 10.3. U.S.-Chinese Trade, 1981–90 (U.S. figures, in millions of current U.S. dollars)

| Year | U.S. Imports from PRC | U.S. Exports to PRC | Total Bilateral Trade | U.S. Trade Balance | Percent of Total U.S. Trade | Percent of Total PRC Trade |
|------|------|------|------|------|------|------|
| 1981 | 1,865.3 | 3,602.7 | 5,468.0 | 1,737.4 | 1.1 | 12.7 |
| 1982 | 2,283.7 | 2,912.1 | 5,195.8 | 628.4 | 1.1 | 12.7 |
| 1983 | 2,244.1 | 2,176.1 | 4,420.2 | −68.0 | 0.9 | 10.2 |
| 1984 | 3,064.8 | 3,004.0 | 6,068.8 | −60.8 | 1.1 | 11.8 |
| 1985 | 3,861.7 | 3,851.7 | 7,713.4 | −9.9 | 1.4 | 10.0 |
| 1986 | 4,770.9 | 3,105.4 | 7,876.3 | −1,665.5 | 1.3 | 10.5 |
| 1987 | 6,293.5 | 3,488.4 | 9,781.8 | −2,805.1 | 1.4 | 11.8 |
| 1988 | 8,512.2 | 5,022.9 | 13,535.1 | −3,489.3 | 1.7 | 13.2 |
| 1989 | 11,988.5 | 5,807.4 | 17,795.9 | −6,181.1 | 2.1 | 16.1 |
| 1990 | 15,223.9 | 4,807.3 | 20,031.2 | −10,416.6 | 2.2 | 17.6 |

*Source:* Harry Harding, *A Fragile Relationship*, p. 364.

cent appreciation accrued through re-export markups should not be computed as China's direct imports to the United States. They argued, for example, that the added value of re-exports to the United States in 1992 and 1993, amounting to US$5.23 billion and US$6.3 billion respectively, should be deducted from Chinese export figures for those years.

Although U.S. trade statistics did not record goods traded to China via Hong Kong, they did trace the countries of origin of all imports, including re-exported goods. Similarly, prior to 1993 the Chinese authorities did not keep an account of the final destinations of goods exported through Hong Kong—figures which might have compromised the value and volume of Chinese exports to the American market. The differences in accounting practices suggest that "the discrepancies between official trade figures may be brought down by as much as three-quarters when adjustments are made."[52]

## Clashes of Opinion: Religion, Tibet, and Human Rights

Developments in the 1980s contributed to positive news reporting about Christianity in China and China's religious tolerance. American media portrayals of Chinese Christianity fostered a sense of hope and desire for reconciliation, although concerns over religious rights, imprisoned Christians, and the running sore of Tibet tended to converge. Meas-

**Table 10.4. Sino-American Trade, 1981–90 (Chinese figures, in millions of current U.S. dollars)**

| Year | PRC Exports to U.S. | PRC Imports from U.S. | Total Bilateral Trade | China Trade Balance |
|------|-----|-----|-----|-----|
| 1981 | 1,505.79 | 4,382.53 | 5,888.32 | −2,876.74 |
| 1982 | 1,619.25 | 3,716.75 | 5,336.00 | −2,097.50 |
| 1983 | 1,720.17 | 2,321.67 | 4,041.84 | −601.50 |
| 1984 | 2,299.71 | 3,663.38 | 5,963.09 | −1,363.67 |
| 1985 | 2,651.60 | 4,373.36 | 7,024.96 | −1,721.76 |
| 1986 | 2,466.43 | 3,527.09 | 5,993.25 | −1,060.66 |
| 1987 | 2,962.66 | 3,809.36 | 6,772.02 | −846.70 |
| 1988 | 3,209.96 | 5,651.93 | 8,261.89 | −2,441.97 |
| 1989 | 4,410.00 | 7,860.00 | 12,270.00 | −3,450.00 |
| 1990 | 6,580.00 | 5,190.00 | 11,770.00 | 1,390.00 |

*Source:* Based on Tao, *Zhongmei guanxi shi,* vol. 3, pp. 339–340. Figures adjusted by the present author.

ured criticism of the Communist handling of indigenous Christianity in the 1980s was followed by the sharp debate over religious freedom in the U.S. printed press in the 1990s, to be discussed in a later chapter.

During the 1980s, many Americans applauded the revival of religious practices in China and the opening and restoration of mosques, churches, and temples, all the fruits of China's new political liberalism.[53] Encouraged by the changes taking place in China, on his Asian trip in March 1981, Pope John Paul II expressed a desire to repair the broken ties between the Vatican and independent Chinese Catholics. The pope urged China "to forget the past and to emphasize the patriotism of Chinese Catholics."[54] The loosening of state control over religion in China, which accompanied the country's drive for modernization and national unification, was noted by the media. "Religious life in China is at the moment a matter of mutual accommodation," observed one report in the *New York Times.*[55] As part of this public relations campaign, the China Christian Council hosted visits by foreign Christians, creating a generally positive impression in the outside world. Three American clergy—Rabbi Arthur Schneier of Park East Synagogue in New York City, the Reverend Herbert Anderson of the Brick Presbyterian Church in New York, and the Reverend Donald R. Campion of the U.S. Jesuit Conference—were members of a delegation that visited China in 1983. They found that "there has been a substantial growth of religious freedom in China in the past two years."[56] During his visit to China, the archbishop of Canterbury, Robert Runcie—the first Western church leader officially received by the Chinese government—gained a similar impression: "Recent legislation seems to have eased the pressure Christians suffered in China during the Cultural Revolution."[57] American evangelist Billy Graham was cautiously optimistic after his own visit in April 1988. Encouraged by the "limited" measure of religious freedom and the fact that "thousands of churches have reopened in recent years," Graham said that "Christians in China could be salt and light in Chinese society and could be a great moral and spiritual force for good in the nation where God has placed them."[58]

Despite this generally positive response from church leaders in the West, questions such as the Chinese government's policies toward unregistered churches and, in particular, religious freedom in Tibet were sometimes given hostile coverage in the press. One American journalist noted, "Chinese rulers have taken a double-edged approach in their effort to find a place for religion in the post-Mao society, on the one hand reopening churches and printing and distributing Bibles, while insisting that churches be registered with the government and creating the China Christian Council to oversee the churches."[59] Pro-independence demonstrations and disturbances in Tibet received considerable attention in the press throughout the 1980s.[60] However, criticism of China's handling of Tibet—which alternated between the use of "jackboot tactics and embarrassed concessions"[61] —did not go unchallenged. One *New York Times* reader reacted negatively to news coverage of Tibet:

> I've read and heard much about how Tibetans are oppressed and have no religious freedom. I won't comment on the ancient three-to-four-foot drum made from human skin that hangs in the Potala, the Dalai Lama's palace. But there are monks everywhere and praying Tibetans everywhere you look. It's also known that in some places the monks themselves torched their temples in past episodes of defiance. The remaining palaces and residences, of which there are plenty, have not been maintained by these religious zealots, who now eagerly accept money to restore and expand them from the same government they vilify.[62]

Another reader responded strongly to media condemnation of China's restrictions on foreign travel to Tibet, which were put in place as a result of riots that broke out there in 1987 and 1988:

> In the United States, minorities are coerced to adopt English in schools. You speak of human rights violations in China, yet isn't the forced depletion of ethnic identity a blatant permanent violation of human rights? . . . The Chinese government has sealed up Tibet from foreign journalists because many tend to only report one side of the story. I am free to go to Tibet because I make no attempt to brainwash the Tibetans into thinking their ethnic and religious rights have been violated. If you want to report on these topics, look in your own backyard.[63]

## CHALLENGES AND IMPLICATIONS

As we have seen, initially Sino-American rapprochement was based primarily on geopolitical considerations but with no immediate impact on their respective economies. In the closing years of the 1980s, economic factors had assumed a weight. At the beginning of the Bush administration in 1989, American direct investment in China stood at US$284 million, and an estimated 100,000 American jobs were dependent on exports to China (not including "service" exports). China had also begun to play a role in the U.S. Treasury notes and bond market.

Three developments were noteworthy: First, in the 1980s, the growing involvement of Congress and political lobby groups in making China policy reduced the power of the executive branch and its ability to engage in the kind of clandestine diplomacy that had led to the thawing of relations during the Nixon and Carter years. The annual renewal of China's most-favored-nation (MFN) status was a continuing irritant for the Chinese right up until China's accession to the WTO in 2001. By law, members of Congress were at liberty to raise any concerns about China, especially human rights issues, and the president was obliged to respond. The heated debate over China made an annual spectacle on Capitol Hill, particularly after 1989, as Congress, the president, the Chinese, and other interest groups wrangled over the issues. The result was that economic relations became embroiled in foreign policy, ideology, and domestic politics. Looking back in 2005, James McGregor, former China bureau chief of the *Wall Street Journal* and corporate executive, offered his rule of thumb on the relationship between trade and politics: "[T]echnology companies doing business in China require significant investments in proactive government relations in Washington. The mission isn't only to make friends, but to educate officials."[64] Otherwise, such firms "could find their business short-circuited by political storms."[65] This lesson was as important then as now.

Second, the problems experienced by both sides were largely a natural consequence of the rapid advances in communication between two vastly different societies. For example, in 1979, the first Chinese joint venture law came into force, representing a step forward in opening China to foreign investment. In the following three years, a long list of new organizations and regulations was created, intended to attract and channel foreign funds. However, in the first half of the 1980s, the much anticipated "floodgate" failed to eventuate as far as investment from the United States was concerned.

Chinese concerns were similar. From their perspective, potential problems were caused by the mutual lack of experience and inadequate understanding of each country's laws, accounting systems, markets, pricing policies, management systems, fund-raising methods, and the financial situations of the enterprises concerned.[66]

Rapid commercial growth sometimes resulted in a major backlash. As more and more Chinese textile products entered the American market, China provoked the ire of the American textile industry and its powerful political supporters, triggering surging protectionism in the United States. In reaction to its escalating global trade deficit and increasing pressure from the manufacturing sector in the 1980s, the U.S. Congress moved to create legal barriers to Chinese textile imports. Under the Multifiber Agreement and the Agreement on Textiles and Clothing (ATC) that governed the international trade in textiles and apparel from 1974 through 2004, developed countries could unilaterally impose quotas on the quantity and categories of textile imports from developing countries to prevent disruption of existing markets. During the seven years from the signing of the first Sino-American agreement on textiles in 1980 to the third accord in 1987, the categories of Chinese textiles restricted by quotas grew from eight to eighty-seven, and over 85 percent of Chinese exports were put under the quota system. From 1987 through 1991, the period covered by the third agreement, the permitted annual growth rate for Chinese textile exports was 3 percent, dropping from 19 percent in previous years.

The third major development in the late 1980s was surging American anxiety over the trade deficit with China—just one aspect (but an important one) of the growing international debt accrued by the United States, rising from $26 billion in the late 1970s to $126 billion in 1988. The China trade imbalance, like that with Japan and Taiwan, fed American domestic demands for counterprotectionist measures as well as calls for the further opening up of the Chinese market and increasing the transparency of trade rules.[67]

It would be fanciful to subscribe to the notion that both sides were critical to each other's economies and polity at the time. The example of Taiwan provides a useful reality check. With a population of a little over 22 million, Taiwan has a land area of only 35,960 square kilometers, slightly larger than Belgium. Nevertheless, with US$82 billion in foreign exchange reserves—the largest in the world in 1992—and a per capita income of US$10,000 a year, in the 1980s Taiwan ranked sixth among America's trade partners, while the United States was Taiwan's top foreign trader.[68]

As the 1980s came to an end, the China market and the allure of the United States gave people hope. Nevertheless, a decade of sustained improvement in Sino-American relations suffered serious setbacks sparked by the Tiananmen crisis of 1989.


## FURTHER READING

Richard Madsen's *China and the American Dream: A Moral Inquiry* (Berkeley, Calif.: University of California Press, 1995) examines the American reaction to the 1989 Tiananmen event in terms of the "liberal myth" of China developed over many years. The evolving images of "China" and the "United States" as viewed by Americans and Chinese respectively are an important topic for which there is unfortunately no room in the present text. Useful works on the subject include the following[69]: Richard Baum, *China Watcher: Confessions of a Peking Tom* (Seattle, Wash.: University of Washington Press, 2010); Jing Li, *China's America: The Chinese View the United States, 1900–2000* (New York: State University of New York Press, 2011); Sigrid Schmalzer, "Speaking about China, Learning from China: Amateur China Experts in 1970s America," *Journal of American-East Asian Relations* 16 (2009): 313–352; Hongshan Li and Zhaohui Hong, eds., *Image, Perception, and the Making of U.S.-China Relations* (Lanham,

Md.: University Press of America, 1998); David L. Shambaugh, *Beautiful Imperialist: China Perceives America, 1972–1990* (Princeton, N.J.: Princeton University Press, 1991); Steven W. Mosher, *China Misperceived: American Illusions and Chinese Reality* (New York: Basic Books, 1990); Paul M. Evans, *John Fairbank and the American Understanding of Modern China* (New York: Basil Blackwell, 1988); John King Fairbank, *Chinabound: A Fifty-Year Memoir* (New York: Harper & Row, 1982); and Paul Hollander, *Political Pilgrims: Travels of Western Intellectuals to the Soviet Union, China, and Cuba 1928–1978* (Oxford: Oxford University Press, 1981).

For the movement of ideas and people between the United States and China, see Cheng Li, *Bridging Minds across the Pacific: U.S.-China Educational Exchanges, 1978–2003* (Lanham, Md.: Lexington Books, 2005); Howard Gardner, *To Open Minds: Chinese Clues to the Dilemma of Contemporary American Education* (New York: Basic Books, 1989); Rosemary Mahoney, *The Early Arrival of Dreams: A Year in China* (New York: Fawcett Columbine, 1990); Mark Salzman, *Iron and Silk* (New York: Random House, 1986); and Vera Schwarcz, *Long Road Home: A China Journal* (New Haven, Conn.: Yale University Press, 1984).

## NOTES

1. Some of the material below is drawn from Dong Wang, "China's Trade Relations with the United States in Perspective," *Journal of Current Chinese Affairs* 39, no. 3 (October 2010): 165–210.

2. Qian Qichen (钱其琛), "Qingshan zhe buzhu, bijing dongliu qu: Jinian Zhongmei Shanghai gongbao fabiao sanshi zhounian" [青山遮不住, 毕竟东流去: 纪念中美上海公报发表三十周年 High mountains cannot hold the river back from flowing east: Commemorating the thirtieth anniversary of the announcement of the Sino-American Communiqué], *Qiushi zazhi* [求是杂志 Seeking the truth magazine] 4 (2002): 4–9.

3. Liu Liandi (刘连第) and Wang Dawei (汪大为), eds., *Zhongmei guanxi de guiji: Jianjiao yilai dashi zonglan* [中美关系的轨迹: 建交以来大事纵览 The trajectory of U.S.-China relations: An overview of major events since the establishment of diplomatic relations] (Beijing: Shishi chubanshe, 1995), p. 262.

4. Theodore H. White, "An Old China Hand in the New China," *Life*, March 17, 1972, p. 47.

5. Theodore H. White, "An Old China Hand in the New China," p. 50B.

6. Barbara W. Tuchman, *Notes from China* (New York: Collier Books, 1972), p. 3.

7. Barbara W. Tuchman, *Notes from China*, p. 3.

8. Leonard S. Silk, "Nixon, China and Wall St.: Why Has News of Nixon's Trip Had No Effect on the Market?" *New York Times*, July 21, 1971, pp. 45, 48.

9. Gary M. Walton and Hugh Rockoff, *History of the American Economy*, 8th ed. (Fort Worth, Tex.: Dayton Press, 1998), p. 650.

10. James Reston, "China and the Dollar," *New York Times*, August 20, 1971, p. 33.

11. Roderick MacFarquhar, ed., *Sino-American Relations, 1949–71* (New York: Praeger, 1972), p. 254.

12. Robert Keatley, "Melting the Ice: U.S. Announces Five More Steps to Spur Commerce with Red China," *New York Times*, April 1, 1971, p. 2.

13. William R. Galeota, "Illusory Market: Trade with China, Long a Dream of Americans, Remains Only a Mirage," *Wall Street Journal*, February 29, 1972, p. 1.

14. "End of an Embargo," *New York Times*, June 11, 1971, p. 34. Authors unknown unless otherwise specified.

15. "The China Trade," *New York Times*, February 16, 1972, p. 38.

16. Brendan Jones, "China Trade: Wary Hope," *New York Times*, April 18, 1971, F1.

17. "The China Trade," *New York Times*, February 16, 1972, p. 38.

18. Relaxation of Restrictions on Trade with the People' s Republic of China, National Security Decision Memorandum 155, February 17, 1972, Nixon Library, http://nixon.archives.gov/virtuallibrary/documents/nsdm/nsdm_155.pdf (accessed May 27, 2011).

19. Sale of Inertial Navigation Systems to the People's Republic of China, National Security Decision Memorandum 204, February 6, 1973, Nixon Library, http://nixon.archives.gov/virtuallibrary/documents/nsdm/nsdm_204.pdf (accessed May 27, 2011).

20. Richard T. Devane, "The United States and China: Claims and Assets," *Asian Survey* 18, no. 12 (December 1978): 1267–69; Joseph A. Martellaro, "Some Aspects of Sino-American Economic Relations: Post-1950," *China Report* 18 (July–August 1982): 19–33.

21. http://frwebgate.access.gpo.gov/cgi-bin/getdoc.cgi?dbname=browse_usc&docid=Cite:+19USC2432 (accessed November 23, 2007).

22. http://www.whitehouse.gov/news/releases/2001/11/20011113-16.html (accessed November 23, 2007).

23. Flemming Christiansen and Shirin M. Rai, *Chinese Politics and Society: An Introduction* (London: Prentice Hall, 1996), part 3. Flemming Christiansen, "Food Security, Urbanization and Social Stability in China," *Journal of Agrarian Change* 9, no. 4 (October 2009): 548–575.

24. Bohdan O. Szuprowicz, "China Fever: Scrambling for Shares in a $600 Million Buying Spree," *Management Review* 68, no. 5 (May 1979): 8–16.

25. Paul A. Varg, "Sino-American Relations Past and Present," *Diplomatic History* 4, no. 2 (April 1980): 101–112.

26. Bohdan O. Szuprowicz, "China Fever."

27. The material in this section is drawn from Dong Wang, "Portraying Chinese Christianity: The American Press and U.S.-China Relations since the 1920s," *Journal of American-East Asian Relations* 13 (November 2008): 81–119.

28. "Peiping Launches Christian Reform," *New York Times*, September 25, 1950, p. 6.

29. Henry R. Lieberman, "Peiping Executes 2 Chinese Priests," *New York Times*, October 21, 1950, p. 4.

30. Jacqueline E. Wenger, "Official vs. Underground Protestant Churches in China: Challenges for Reconciliation and Social Influence," *Review of Religious Research* 46, no. 2 (2004): 169–182.

31. For a comprehensive seventy-four-page report on the divisions in Chinese Protestantism, see Jonathan Walton (Long Term Strategy Group), "Contemporary Chinese Protestantism and Ongoing Developments in Church-State Relations," January 2007, manuscript (courtesy of Daniel Bays).

32. "Clergy Urge U.S. Bar to Communist China," *New York Times*, October 2, 1950, p. 5.

33. "Red Letter Causes Missionary Recall," *New York Times*, December 20, 1950, p. 7. Dan L. Thrapp, "Spread of Christianity in China Halted by Reds," *Los Angeles Times*, December 1, 1951.

34. "'Red Dean' Draws British Fire by Statement Backing Peiping Charges on Germ Warfare," *New York Times*, July 9, 1952, p. 3.

35. John K. Fairbank, "The Time Is Ripe for China to Shift Outward Again," *New York Times*, April 18, 1971, E1.

36. George Dugan, "Churchman Cool to Visiting China," *New York Times*, January 18, 1957, p. 7.

37. Edward B. Fiske, "China: Still Some Life in the Church," *New York Times*, December 5, 1971.

38. Edward B. Fiske, "China: Still Some Life in the Church."

39. "Protestants in Peking: A Church Survives," *New York Times*, October 14, 1972, p. 5.

40. John B. Sheerin, "The Nixon Visit and Religion in China," *Catholic World* 213, no. 1278 (September 1971): 259–260.

41. "Talks of Red China Trip," *Chicago Defender*, December 28, 1971, p. 8.

42. Jia Shi, "Future Prospects for Broadening US-China Economic and Trade Cooperation," trans. Thomas Apple, *Columbia Journal of World Business* 20, no. 4 (Winter 1985): 57–58. Harry Harding, *A Fragile Relationship: Reform after Mao* (Washington, D.C.: Brookings Institution, 1987), pp. 145–154.

43. Harry Harding, *China's Second Revolution: Reform after Mao* (Washington, D.C.: Brookings Institution, 1987). Yu Guangyuan, ed., *China's Socialist Modernization* (Beijing: Foreign Languages Press, 1984).

44. Barry Naughton, *The Chinese Economy: Transitions and Growth* (Cambridge, Mass.: MIT Press, 2007), chapters 4 and 16.

45. Harry Harding, *A Fragile Relationship*, pp. 145–154.

46. Joseph O. Eatlack Jr. and Roberta Lucker, "Is China Moving from Marx to Mastercard?" *Journal of Consumer Marketing* 3, no. 3 (Summer 1986): 5–21.

47. "U.S.-China Trade Hit a Record $6.1 Billion in 1984," *Los Angeles Times*, January 23, 1985, OC-C2.

48. The figures adopted by David Lampton differ from those quoted above from Harry Harding. According to Lampton, e.g., Chinese exports to the United States from 1981 to 1990 were valued at US$2,062 million, $2,502, $2,477, $3,381, $4,224, $5,241, $6,910, $9,261, $12,901, and $16,296 million respectively. David Lampton, *Same Bed, Different Dreams: Managing U.S.-China Relations, 1989–2000* (Berkeley, Calif.: University of California Press, 2001), p. 382.

49. Jia Shi, "Future Prospects for Broadening US-China Economic and Trade Cooperation."

50. K. C. Mun and T. S. Chan, "The Role of Hong Kong in United States-China Trade," *Columbia Journal of World Business* 21, no. 1 (Spring 1986): 67–73.

51. K. C. Mun and T. S. Chan, "The Role of Hong Kong in United States-China Trade."

52. Sarah Y. Tong, "The US-China Trade Imbalance: How Big Is It Really?" *China: An International Journal* 3, no. 1 (March 2005): 131–154.

53. Victoria Graham, "More Attending Beijing Mosque," *Los Angeles Times*, December 2, 1979, H10. Michael Parks, "China Gives Official Blessing to Resurgence of Is-

lam," *Los Angeles Times*, May 27, 1981. Christopher S. Wren, "Islam, after Persecutions, Rebounds in China," *New York Times*, June 15, 1983, A1. John Tagliabue, "China's Catholics Restore a Church in Peking," *New York Times*, December 18, 1985, A6.

54. Charles Austin, "China's Catholics: A Nation unto Itself Moves to Meet the Vatican," *New York Times* , March 29, 1981, E7; E. J. Dionne Jr., "Pope Lauds China's Effort to Modernize," *New York Times*, July 25, 1985, A3.

55. Christopher S. Wren, "Religion and China Make Accommodations," *New York Times*, December 20, 1981, E18.

56. "American Clergymen Note Growth of Religious Freedom in China," Associated Press, July 9, 1983, AM cycle, international news section.

57. "Archbishop Says China Improving Religious Tolerance," *Asian Week* (San Francisco) 5, no. 20 (January 13, 1984): 23. Edward A. Gargan, "It's Good News from China for Billy Graham," *New York Times*, April 17, 1988, p. 4.

58. "Billy Graham Sees Better Future for China's Christians," Associated Press, April 29, 1988, PM cycle, international news section.

59. David E. Anderson, "Religion in America; Degree of Religious Freedom in China Still at Issue," United Press International, February 17, 1984, BC cycle. William McGurn, "Forbidden Tibet Looks Outward," *Wall Street Journal*, April 14, 1988, p. 1.

60. Charlene L. Fu, "Young Monks Says [sic] Tibet Must Be Free," Associated Press, October 13, 1987, PM cycle.

61. "A Captive Tibet," *Globe and Mail*, April 11, 1988. David Holley, "Tension Erupts during Lhasa's Great Prayer Festival in Tibet, It's Butter Sculpture and Bitter Words," *Los Angeles Times*, March 6, 1988, p. 5.

62. Letter to editor, Michele Hoffman, *New York Times*, August 9, 1988.

63. Teh-han P. Chow, "'Chinese Gulag' in Tibet," *Los Angeles Times*, March 4, 1988, p. 10.

64. James McGregor, *One Billion Customers: Lessons from the Front Lines of Doing Business in China* (New York: Free Press, 2005), p. 186.

65. James McGregor, *One Billion Customers*, p. 188.

66. Rudy Ruggles Jr., "The Environment for American Business Ventures in the People's Republic of China," *Columbia Journal of World Business* 18, no. 4 (1983): 67–73.

67. Julia Chang Bloch, "Commercial Diplomacy," in Ezra F. Vogel, ed., *Living with China: U.S./China Relations in the Twenty-First Century* (New York: Norton, 1997), pp. 185–216.

68. Nancy Bernkopf Tucker, *Taiwan, Hong Kong, and the United States, 1945–1992* (New York: Twayne Publishers, 1994), p. 168.

69. I am indebted to Charles Hayford for most of these references.

# ELEVEN

## Clashes and Cooperation

Three sets of dynamics gave rise to the unsettled relationship between the United States and China between 1990 and 2012. First, the two powers had weathered a number of major crises, demonstrating their mutual interest in sustaining stability and peace despite changes in leadership in both countries and in the ongoing diffusion of global power. Second, since the end of the Cold War, the United States—the default superpower—has often had the upper hand in the relationship, while China—the rising power—has been challenged to limit America's regional and international reach. Third, following the demise of the Soviet Union, U.S. policy makers convinced themselves that there was only one remaining threat: China. Political irritants continued to disrupt relations between the two countries—although during the period 2002–12 the relationship became somewhat less turbulent. But tensions ramped up again by the end of 2011 with President Barack Obama's announcement of an increased American security commitment to the Asia-Pacific.

The 1990–2012 period spans four presidencies involving Republicans and Democrats with very different styles of governance—Presidents George H. W. Bush (1989–93), William Jefferson Clinton (1993–2001), George W. Bush (2001–9), and Barack Obama (2009– )—and two generations of Chinese leaders—President Jiang Zemin and Premier Zhu Rongji (1989–2002), and Hu Jintao and Wen Jiabao (2002–12). By the end of the two decades, well-wishers on both sides were hoping that the United States and China had developed the capacity to lift their relationship onto a new level. Unlocking the enormous potential of the relationship to promote peace and work for the common good of humanity is the only alternative to escalating levels of conflict and their unthinkable consequences.

## THE TIANANMEN CRISIS: A WATERSHED

The fall of the Berlin Wall in 1989 presaged the rapid collapse of Communist regimes in Eastern and Central Europe and the dissolution of the Soviet Union, marking the end of the Cold War only two years later. As the common threat of the Soviet Union dissipated, China and the United States drifted into an uneasy relationship in which their growing economic, social, and cultural ties often stood in marked contrast to the "roller-coaster" effect felt in the political domain.

The gravest challenge to the bilateral relationship since the rapprochement of 1972 originated in the Tiananmen student protests in Beijing in May–June 1989. This turned out to be a global event that put China under an unprecedented—and unfavorable—media spotlight. One American study reveals the extent of the coverage on television alone:

> [T]he evening news shows of the three major networks (ABC, CBS and NBC) totaled five hundred seventy-seven China stories in the first six months of 1989, by comparison with forty-four stories in all of 1988. There were three hundred ninety-seven stories in these shows in the month between May 14 and June 14, 1989, by comparison with three hundred forty-four stories in the ten years (1972–81) before China was opened to American television coverage.[1]

The Tiananmen Incident was long in the brewing. It had strong links with the democracy movement, symbolized by the "Democracy Wall" in Beijing, where a spontaneous popular movement resulted in the pasting up of political posters in the winter of 1978.[2] Drawing inspiration from a Chinese intellectual tradition of dissent and affecting China's major cities, this loosely defined movement expressed a variety of opinions on Mao Zedong, the Cultural Revolution, and other controversial issues in the form of commentaries, literary publications, and group actions. Although prominent activists such as Wei Jingsheng were strong supporters of Western liberalism, others were critical of American-style democracy. While this latter group espoused socialism, they insisted that it "must be steeped in popular democracy, a scientific socialism infused with the boundless vigor of life."[3] Notwithstanding the diversity exhibited by these activist groups, the newly consolidated Chinese leadership was irritated by their outspokenness which went beyond the bounds of criticism and free speech sanctioned by the Communist Party. Beginning in 1979, the government imprisoned a number of activists and outlawed unofficial publications, wall posters, and dissident organizations. Between 1985 and 1987 the suppressed democracy movement reemerged, but now with the support of a new group—militant university students—who were dissatisfied with corruption, inflation, the abuse of state power, the lag between economic and political reform, and the growing gap between rich and poor. These student demonstrations, however, defied the boundaries of the limited political participation and sanctioned dissent permissible in China. [4]

The massive demonstrations in Tiananmen Square in the heart of Beijing, less than a mile away from offices and residences of the top Chinese leadership, were triggered by the death on April 15, 1989, of former party general secretary Hu Yaobang—who had resigned in January 1987, allegedly because of his sympathy for dissident student rallies. Initially the government was reticent about the mass protests, but on April 26 the authorities denounced them as "disturbances" organized by a "handful" of subversive individuals. [5] Nevertheless, the Chinese government failed to move quickly to quell the unrest, "allowing the students, in effect, to get out of control and pose a direct challenge to their authority." [6]

Hundreds of thousands of students, workers, and other citizens camped out in the square for over a month. At the time, U.S. diplomatic and intelligence analyses offered warnings about the potential for political and social disorder posed by the demonstrations and the setback to reform efforts in China:

> Events of the last several months have cast doubt on China's ability to weather the social strains that accompany reform and modernization in a backward, Communist country. . . . Growing social disorder has slowed China's reform program by discrediting reform policies and providing ammunition to conservative critics of reform. . . . Further, the party [the Chinese Communist Party, CCP] no longer commands the moral authority it once did. In our judgment, the Cultural Revolution has left a legacy of bitterness and disillusionment with the party and Communist ideology that reformers have not been able to overcome. [7]

In mid-May, the Soviet leader Mikhail Gorbachev visited Beijing, seeking rapprochement with China. Student demonstrators disrupted the welcome ceremony, chanting Gorbachev's name as the symbol of the political changes they wanted for their own nation. Disagreements became apparent in the CCP leadership on how to handle the protests; the five members of the Politburo Standing Committee were locked in an impasse over whether to resort to force in Beijing. It has been claimed that while Zhao Ziyang, general secretary of the CCP (1987–89), and Hu Qili objected to the imposition of martial law, Li Peng and Yao Yilin supported it, and Qiao Shi abstained from voting. The final decision was made by a group of elder party statesmen led by Deng Xiaoping who decided to call on the People's Liberation Army to restore order. [8]

On May 20, Premier Li Peng declared martial law in Beijing in the hope that these measures would be sufficient to clear the square and resolve the standoff peacefully. However, many demonstrators continued to occupy the site. The options available to the government were diminishing. The leadership spent a "considerable amount of time and energy on convincing the military to agree to—or on negotiating the political price of its involvement in—the final use of force" against civilians. Deng allegedly signed the final order to send troops into the square. [9] On the night of June 3 and in the early morning of June 4, the People's Liberation Army (PLA) forced their way into Beijing and stormed the square, inflaming the ire of American observers and other protest sympathizers around the world. At home, many people feared that China might disintegrate into a number of states controlled by warlords—a situation similar to the first Republic of China (1912–28), the Chinese historical nightmare. In a similar vein, the State Department reported at one point that China was experiencing a "descent into chaos" as various military units engaged in clashes with each other and the army appeared to be running out of control. [10]

Confronted with this situation, the new Bush administration had to perform a subtle balancing act. President Bush had to balance his reactions to the Tiananmen Incident—finding a response that effectively condemned and punished the actions of the Chinese leadership, but one that did not undermine the realpolitik behind the relationship. In the words of a memo from one presidential advisor, it was important to "prevent Sino-Soviet normalization from jeopardizing its [China's] relationship with US which retains vital importance as counterbalance to USSR, key element for stability in East Asia, source of technology/investments." [11] On top of these considerations, there was a real concern that China was about to collapse into chaos. At a news conference held on June 5, 1989, President Bush called for a measured response: "This is not the time for an emotional response, but for a reasoned, careful action that takes into account both our long-term interests and recognition of a complex internal situation in China." [12] In reaction to the violent crackdown in China, he ordered suspension of all government-to-government sales and commercial exports of weapons, as well as suspension of bilateral visits between military leaders; he urged a sympathetic review of requests by Chinese students in the United States to extend their stay; and he offered humanitarian and medical assistance through the Red Cross to those injured during the army's assault on the square. In addition, he ordered a review of other aspects of the bilateral relationship.

Meanwhile, to keep the lines of communication open, Bush secretly dispatched his top aide, National Security Advisor Brent Scowcroft (1989–93), to visit China in June and again in December 1989 for discussions with Deng Xiaoping and other Chinese leaders. The president's moderate reaction prompted a hard-line response from Congress. Displeased with the limited sanctions imposed, both parties in Congress passed two pieces of legislation. The first was the Chinese Student Protection Act of 1992, sponsored by Democratic congresswoman Nancy Pelosi, which granted permanent residency to mainland Chinese students who had arrived in the United States on or before April 11, 1990. The second measure prompted by the Tiananmen Square Incident were the sanctions, including arms sales, that were signed into law in February 1990 by George H. W. Bush, following several months of bitter negotiations with Congress. In their final form, they included waiver provisions authorizing the president to end sanctions if China's progress on human rights warranted such a change, or if it was in the United States' national interest to do so. [13]

The Chinese Communist Party was steered through the Tiananmen crisis and the power transition that followed by Deng Xiaoping. The third generation of leadership represented by Jiang Zemin (1989–2002) and Zhu Rongji took the helm under Deng's tutelage. In the wake of the crisis, Deng made a series of statements which served as guidelines for Chinese foreign affairs officials in handling the sanctions imposed by the United States and six other countries. In December 1989, Deng met with Bush's secret envoy, Brent Scowcroft. "Your visit at this time is an important sign," Deng told him. "Despite the disputes between the United States and China, and despite problems and disagreements of all kinds, relations between the United States and China will have to improve ultimately. This is necessary for world peace and stability. . . . It is also our common desire." Deng offered Scowcroft assurances of goodwill:

> China will not threaten the United States, and the United States should not treat China as an enemy. We have never done anything to harm the United States. . . . The United States and China should avoid a fight. I do not mean a military confrontation; rather, I am referring to verbal and rhetorical conflict. I advise you not to encourage such things. We have said many times that China cannot emulate the American political system. Americans themselves must determine whether the American system is good or not, and we do not interfere. . . . For two countries to get along, they should respect each other, and do their best to accommodate the other party so as to resolve their disputes. . . . Appropriate, acceptable solutions can be found if both sides make certain compromises.[14]

It is important to understand the background to Deng's remarks. For Deng, there were two major international issues—peace and development—that were yet to be resolved. He believed that China should stand firm in its opposition to hegemonism and power politics and seek to maintain world peace through the formation of a new international political and economic order. It was in China's interests to maintain good relations with all countries, and strengthen contacts with both the Soviet Union and the United States without becoming involved in ideological debates.[15] In a meeting in 1990 with Pierre Trudeau, the former Canadian prime minister, Deng asserted that the seven countries that had imposed sanctions on China in response to the Tiananmen event had no right to do so, and that China had the capability to resist any sanctions. "Responsible foreign politicians understand that China cannot slide into chaos. A focus on human rights and people's rights cannot help with this issue."[16]

The Tiananmen crisis proved to be a setback for all sides involved. Innocent lives were lost, and China's progress toward the rule of law and political liberalism was pushed back. Chinese activists were persecuted, and a number of the leading figures sought sanctuary abroad. The Bush administration was under mounting pressure to punish China more than it had, revealing the significant differences between the executive and legislative branches on the issue. For its part, the Chinese government continued to roll out its economic development program in the face of its tattered reputation and an unfavorable international environment. The

Tiananmen Incident of 1989 has had major repercussions, for policy making and mutual perceptions in particular, right up to the present.

## MOVING ALONG THE BUMPY ROAD, 1990–2001

As a result of the Tiananmen crisis, American-Chinese relations were severely strained over the issues of human rights, Taiwan, and numerous other areas, while leaders in both countries attempted to improve the relationship and work toward a constructive strategic partnership. The annual renewal of most-favored-nation (MFN) status for China quickly became a vehicle for American debate over human rights, tougher economic sanctions, and revocation of China's MFN position. For its part China was on the defensive, constantly reiterating its position on key principles such as the superiority of national sovereignty over human rights, equality, independence, and democratization in international affairs. While there were numerous crises and rhetorical flash points, under Presidents George H. W. Bush (1989–93) and Bill Clinton (1993–2001) and President Jiang Zemin (1989–2002) and Premier Zhu Rongji, the United States and China avoided direct military confrontation.

Following the Tiananmen Incident, China continued with its forward-looking and growth-oriented policy, essential to the very survival of the People's Republic of China.[17] While it continued "opening up" to the outside world, it refused to acquiesce in the imposition of foreign sanctions and the demonization of China. This approach involved tactical flexibility combined with a firm stand over the defense of national interests such as China's claims on Taiwan and Tibet, the furthering of the "China Way"—socialism with Chinese characteristics—and the fostering of a favorable regional and global environment for the nation's economic development.[18] Jiang was firm with Richard Nixon on the Tiananmen question: "Dampening down this year's political disturbance is our own country's business. I do not know why it has caused such a stir in the United States. . . . The ideological differences between us have contributed to the different viewpoints on this incident."[19] In a speech to CCP cadres, Jiang admonished them to remain vigilant and to be ready to fight because "hostile Western forces want to 'Westernize' and 'divide' us, to impose their ideas of 'democracy' and 'freedom' on us."[20]

Following the broad lines laid down by Deng Xiaoping, Jiang Zemin emphasized two new themes. The first urged respect for the political system and development path chosen by individual nation-states. Without national sovereignty, there was no way of talking about human rights.[21] A second element shaping China's dealings with the outside world during 1990–2001 was a new understanding of security. Jiang asserted that institutions based on coercion could not lead to peace; the use of force was unable to resolve disputes or conflicts. Taking shape in the 1990s, China's new notions of security involved the fostering of mutual trust, mutual benefits, equality, and cooperation through dialogue and negotiation.[22]

Despite fears that bilateral relations would continue to deteriorate, anxiety gave way to new hopes when China averted the political chaos that many commentators predicted. Following a two-year setback period (1989–91), China's transition to a market-oriented economy rolled on, a trend symbolized by Deng Xiaoping's "Southern Tour" of Shenzhen and other special economic zones in South China in early 1992. Deng's strong endorsement provided the momentum for a new phase of economic reform. This second phase, led by Jiang Zemin and Zhu Rongji, rested on regulatory and administrative restructuring of the banking, taxation, and corporate governance systems, as well as further exposure to world markets through China's membership in the World Trade Organization (WTO). This strong commitment to reform yielded some significant outcomes, both positive and negative—price stability replaced rising inflation; the number of state-owned enterprises (SOEs) dwindled while private firms increased, hiring twice as many workers as the SOEs by the end of 2004; and increased market competition sharpened pressure on employers and employees alike, contributing to massive layoffs and social inequity.

In addition to the Tiananmen crisis, five major crises affected bilateral relations at the geopolitical level: the American decoupling of human rights issues from trade with China in 1994 and the general use of economic issues as a political tool in the post–Cold War era; the 1995–96 military standoff in the Taiwan Strait; the American bombing of the Chinese embassy in Belgrade in 1999; the midair collision between a U.S. spy plane and a Chinese jet fighter in spring 2001; and China's accession to the World Trade Organization in December 2001 (to be discussed in the next chapter).

*Human Rights*

The delinking of human rights issues from the annual extension of China's most-favored-nation trading status took place in spring 1994. Less than two weeks after his inauguration in January 1993, with Tiananmen and his campaign-trail attacks on President Bush's "soft" stance on China now behind him, President Bill Clinton appointed Winston Lord, former American ambassador to China, to head the Senior Steering Group (SSG) charged with advising him on China's MFN status. On May 28, 1993, Clinton bypassed Congress and issued Executive Order 128590, linking the renewal of China's MFN status to seven conditions tied to human rights issues—free emigration, cessation of exports manufactured by prison labor, observing the UN Declaration of Human Rights, preserving Tibetan indigenous religion and culture, access to prisons for international human rights organizations, the permitting of international radio and TV broadcasts, and the release of prisoners held on political and religious grounds. Clinton's intervention represented a sharp departure from George H. W. Bush's position that political democratization would occur as China's economic status improved. Nonetheless, a year later, on May 26, 1994, the Clinton administration reversed this stance and decoupled human rights issues from the MFN. This new approach had the support of the American business community, which argued that "[t]he only way to undermine the regime is to infiltrate it." Trade with China came to be seen as a "moral crusade," and business executives asserted that "missionaries and businessmen will work together to change China, unless Congress interferes." [23]

This striking policy turnaround had three major implications. First, Clinton's rapid reversal of his 1993 executive order raised questions about the way in which moral issues such as human rights violations should be addressed in American politics and foreign policy. Second, the China question became a "political football" in the United States. The intense debate over China policy during both terms of the Clinton presidency (1993–2001) involved a wide spectrum of interest groups. On the one hand, the debate highlighted the checks and balances operating in the presidential prerogative over foreign affairs and Congress's role in handling trade issues under the U.S. constitution. On the other hand, it showed the extent to which bilateral relations had expanded since 1972, explaining the "return" of China to American politics.

Third, this vacillating linkage of human rights to economic interests set the tone for the roller-coaster ride that was to mark political relations in the years to come. Since 1995, the United States had sought a resolution condemning Beijing's human rights practices from the UN Human Rights Commission in Geneva, but had been defeated, with virtually no support forthcoming from other countries. On the other hand, as critics and observers pointed out, in China political dissidents received little sympathy and were viewed as "stupid" idealists by the majority of Chinese.[24]

## The Taiwan Crisis

In the assessment of J. Stapleton Roy, American ambassador to China (1991–95), for nearly six decades Taiwan had constituted a major obstacle to improved relations; it "has bedeviled U.S. foreign policy in East Asia, complicated the U.S. relationship with the People's Republic of China, and generated domestic passions of unusual intensity."[25] From America's viewpoint, the rise of native Taiwanese nationalism was such that Taiwan's leaders were no longer predictable or trustworthy and that the Taiwan issue compromised American national interests and threatened to suck the United States into armed conflict in the Taiwan Strait.[26] Also, in the mid-1990s the Taiwan crisis, like the human rights question, exposed the divergence between the White House and Congress on the right way to handle China. To generations of Chinese leaders, Taiwan has been the "most important and sensitive issue" in bilateral relations.[27] They have viewed the U.S. Congress as the source of unnecessary trouble between China and the United States. Congress has been variously described as the "instigator," the "backstage boss," and the "behind-the-scenes patron" of the American approach to the Taiwan issue.[28] The Chinese were bitterly opposed to the ideas expressed by Taiwanese politicians such as Lee Teng-hui, who argued that Taiwan needed to expand its national footprint and solidify its identity as a democratic, economically developed, independent sovereign state on the world stage.[29]

The military tensions between Taiwan and mainland China in 1995–96 originated in the shifting dynamics of politics in Taiwan during the 1980s, which overturned the status quo on the island. As a result of political liberalization introduced by the ruling Nationalist Party (Guomindang, GMD), the long-suppressed Taiwanese independence movement and associated organizations formed the Democratic Progressive Party in 1986, and had grown powerful enough to challenge the Nationalist Party's political dominance. In 1988, Lee Teng-hui—a native Taiwanese Hakka—rose to power as the leader of the GMD and president of Taiwan (1988–2000), following the death of Chiang Ching-kuo, the son of Chiang Kai-shek.

Lee managed Taiwan's relations with both China and the United States through the ambivalent use of both sticks and carrots. First, under Lee's presidency, economic, political, and cultural contacts with the mainland had substantially increased. Lee abandoned the Nationalist Party's long-standing attachment to "One China" ruled by the GMD— not the Chinese Communist Party. In contrast to his predecessors, Lee accepted the reality of the Communist regime in mainland China and lifted some of the remaining travel restrictions across the Taiwan Strait. Between 1990 and 1995, Lee conducted secret talks with the mainland authorities. In 1992 and again in 1998, Koo Chen-fu, chairman of Taiwan's Straits Exchange Foundation, and Wang Daohan, chairman of the mainland-based Association for Relations across the Taiwan Strait, met in Singapore, where they launched the Wang-Koo summit that symbolized the effort being made by both sides toward peaceful relations.

Second, and in partial contradiction to his first position, Lee attempted to establish the popular sovereignty of the government of Taiwan—the Republic of China—as an equal entity within a divided "China" where the People's Republic of China formed the other equal part. In 1996, the first direct election for president in Taiwanese history was held. In order to gain votes from native Taiwanese electors against the increasing popularity of the pro-independence Democratic Progressive Party, Lee risked antagonizing mainland China by moving closer to a formal declaration of independence.[30] However, the Chinese government refused to consider the prospect of "Two Chinas" in any form; variations such as "One China, One Taiwan" or "one state, two governments" were also rejected as possible options.[31]

Third, Lee attempted to reverse Taiwan's marginal status and raise its formal profile on the world stage. Following the Tiananmen Incident, high-level private visits increased in frequency between the United States and Taiwan. Taiwan was also campaigning for representation in the United Nations. Since 1979, the U.S. government had been committed to the decisions incorporated in three communiqués with mainland China and so could not receive visits from Taiwanese leaders in their official capacity. In 1995, Lee pressed the United States for a work visa so he could give a reunion speech at his alma mater, Cornell University. With the second-strongest lobby in Congress (after Israel), Taiwan pressured Capitol Hill to grant Lee a visa; his case received overwhelming support in a Congress impressed by Taiwan's progress on democracy and human rights. In June, Lee made a personal visit to Cornell. The Clinton administration found itself in an awkward position but was assured by Taiwan's representative in Washington that Lee's Cornell speech would be nonpolitical. However, in his speech, Lee severely embarrassed the United States by referring to Taiwan as "the Republic of China on Taiwan" at least fifteen times. In retaliation, China withdrew its ambassador from Washington and refused to accept the credentials of the new American ambassador to China.

Tensions continued to mount. In July 1995 China began military exercises in the Strait region, firing six targeted missiles into the waters north of Taiwan, followed by live firing exercises and missile tests in the Eastern Sea in August and October. However, these intimidating displays of force failed to stem the rising influence of pro-independence groups in Taiwan. Then in March 1996, prior to elections in Taiwan, Chinese military exercises resumed—this time with artillery fire bracketing the island to home in on chosen targets. On March 8, four missiles landed inside the target area west of Kaohsiung—the second-largest city in southwest Taiwan, facing the Taiwan Strait—and east of Keelung, a port city on the northeast tip of the island. These exercises shook the island in every sense: support for independence declined and Taiwan's stock market fell sharply. The open independence candidate, Peng Ming-min, failed in his bid for the presidency, with only around 21 percent of the vote.

The military situation in the Taiwan Strait escalated, drawing in the U.S. Navy. While holding discussions with high-level Chinese officials, the Clinton administration dispatched two aircraft carriers, the USS *Independence* and the *Nimitz*, together with their accompanying battle escorts, to the one-hundred-mile zone east of the Strait. The Chinese responded by deploying nuclear submarines, the American warships retired one hundred miles away, China ended the exercise "ahead of schedule,"[32] and the United States withdrew its fighting forces. The crisis was over. In Taiwan, the Nationalist Party candidate Lee Teng-hui won the elections held at the end of March—the least worst choice for China compared with the other parties, especially Peng Ming-min, the Progressive Democratic Party candidate, who had campaigned against trade with China and the "One China" policy.

To all three parties involved, the crisis of 1995–96 had shown that the threat of direct military confrontation was dangerously real. Nevertheless, there was still room for compromise. The United States had no core interests that would lead it to seek conflict with China—it certainly did not want to be dragged into war with mainland China by Taiwan. For its part, Taiwan had been doing what it had done since the days of Chiang Kai-shek—playing the "America card" to achieve its strategic goals. While China was willing to negotiate with Taiwan, it was intransigent on the question of the island being integral to its territory, a principle that put the legitimacy of the CCP at stake. Further complicating the issue, Taiwan had grown more dependent on the China market for export, investment, and tourism opportunities.[33]

### The Embassy Bombing of 1999 and the Midair Collision of 2001

In 1997 and 1998, bilateral relations were settling into a relatively stable pattern. President Clinton and President Jiang Zemin expressed their joint commitment to building the relationship "from a long-term perspective on the basis of the principles of the three China-U.S. joint communiqués."[34] Jiang's visit to the United States in October 1997—the first by a Chinese leader in twelve years—and Clinton's trip to China in June 1998 were characterized by the Chinese government as a "milestone," a "solid step" toward building a constructive strategic partnership for the twenty-first century, and by U.S. secretary of state Madeleine Albright as a "dramatic step forward" in encouraging China to "define its own interests in ways that are compatible" with American aspirations in the region.[35] Their joint statement provided a framework for a constructive strategic partnership, to be achieved not just through high-level dialogue and official consultations, but also through "increasing cooperation" in a host of areas—clean energy projects; technology transfers; the promotion of biodiversity, trade, and peaceful uses of nuclear energy; managing climate change and desertification; combating international organized crime, narcotics trafficking, people smuggling, counterfeiting, and money laundering; consultation on military (especially maritime) safety to avoid accidents, misunderstandings, and miscalculations; humanitarian assistance and disaster relief; new applications of science and technology; the use of space for earth science research and other practical applications; and educational and cultural exchanges.[36]

However, things were not all smooth sailing. The optimistic tone of progress and engagement embodied by the joint communiqué was undercut by bitter wrangling over a host of intertwined issues including human rights, political prisoners, religious freedom, China's one-child policy, repression of the Falun Gong (an anti-government religious cult), the Cox Committee report on alleged technology leaks to China, and the allegations of spying brought against former Los Alamos scientist Wen Ho Lee. Also there was the bombing of the Chinese embassy in Belgrade in May 1999.

In March 1999, the United States and its NATO allies decided to bomb the Federal Republic of Yugoslavia to force its president, Slobodan Milosevic, to stop the "ethnic cleansing" of Albanians by Serb forces in the country's Kosovo Province. China and Russia did not support the NATO intervention. On May 7, American B-2 bombers dropped four precision-guided 2,000-pound munitions on the Chinese embassy in Belgrade, causing severe damage to the building, killing three Chinese journalists, and injuring more than twenty staff. In China, students as well as ordinary citizens were outraged, rejecting Washington's explanation that the bombing was a mistake resulting from the use of outdated maps. During May 8–11, massive anti-American demonstrations erupted in major cities—including Beijing, Shanghai, Canton, Shenyang, and Chengdu—until the Chinese government intervened and called for order. Between May 8 and 14, the American ambassador to China James Sasser (1995–99), CIA director George Tenet, Secretary of Defense William Cohen, Madeleine Albright, and President Clinton all contacted the Chinese authorities to express their regrets and apologies. The Chinese remained furious over what they perceived as the casual, insincere, and inadequate American response to the incident. However, on May 11, the Chinese media began reporting the earlier American condolences and apologies. On July 30, the United States announced that it would pay out $4.5 million in compensation to the families of the Chinese killed and injured. In December, Washington agreed to pay a further $28 million for damage to property, while Beijing agreed to pay out $2.87 million to the American embassy and U.S. consulates in China for damage caused by protest actions.

However, less than six months later, relations hit a low point once again. Beginning in 2000, the American air force stepped up its reconnaissance activities off the coast of China, with planes flying four to five times a week within international airspace but only fifty miles from the Chinese mainland. The People's Liberation Army responded by intercepting U.S. reconnaissance flights. This was not the first time that the two sides had been at loggerheads over this issue. On April 1, 2001, an American navy EP-3E Aries II airplane on a routine surveillance mission collided with an intercepting Chinese F-8 fighter jet which was tailgating it over the South China Sea. The midair collision killed the Chinese pilot; the damaged U.S. spy plane made an emergency landing on Hainan Island in China, and its twenty-four crew were detained in China for eleven days. China demanded an apology and held the United States responsible for the incident for several reasons. First, the American plane had veered suddenly into the Chinese jet and had landed on Chinese soil without permission. Second, the United States had violated the UN Convention on the Law of the Sea (UNCLOS), to which China, but not the United States, was a signatory. Articles 55–75 of UNCLOS provide for the sovereign rights and jurisdiction of a coastal state party over its exclusive economic zone, particularly its rights to maintain peace, security, and good order in the waters of the zone (extending two hundred miles from the Chinese coastline). According to Article 301, the American military intrusion posed a threat to the national security of China.[37] Third, the U.S. aircraft had violated the 1944 Chicago Convention on International Civil Aviation signed by both the United States and China. Article 3 stipulates that "no military airplanes shall land on the territory of a contracting party without authorization."[38] Finally, in Chinese eyes the incident had been inevitable in the light of the frequency of U.S. reconnaissance flights and the fact that they flew too close to the Chinese coast.

For Chinese observers, the roots of the incident were to be sought in American post–Cold War hegemonism. America's initial reaction in words and actions did little to placate China's sense of outrage. On April 2, President George W. Bush stated, "Our priorities are the prompt and safe return of the crew, and the return of the aircraft without further damaging or tampering. . . . Failure of the Chinese government to react promptly to our request is inconsistent with standard diplomatic practice, and with the expressed desire of both our countries for better relations."[39] The Pentagon ordered three American navy destroyers to monitor the situation in the South China Sea, a step which did nothing to mitigate the developing crisis.[40] However, this hard-line stance was soon to change. Eleven days later, on April 12, Joseph W. Prueher, American ambassador to China (1999–2001), sent a letter to Tang Jiaxuan, the Chinese minister of foreign affairs (1998–2003), stating that President George W. Bush and Secretary of State Colin L. Powell were "very sorry" for the loss of the Chinese pilot, Wang Wei, and that "the entering of China's airspace and the landing did not have verbal clearance." In response, the twenty-four detained crewmen were released to the United States. Following the release of the crew, the Pentagon rejected the claim that the EP-3 had veered into the Chinese fighter—it had been flying straight and level until struck by the Chinese aircraft. It asserted that military reconnaissance flights beyond the borders of a state's sovereign territory had been going on for decades and were nothing out of the ordinary. They were permissible under international law, and emergency landings were necessary when an aircraft was in distress.[41] After months of negotiations, on July 3, the MP-3 plane was dismantled and returned to the United States. However, the Chinese declined to take up the modest American offer of compensation for the emergency landing.

## DEVELOPMENTS DURING 2001–12: AN UPWARD SPIRAL

The geopolitical relationship between the United States and China in the first decade of the twenty-first century incorporated three major elements. First, American involvement with China represented the kind of Protestant idealism that sought to change the world as well as to get China to conform to the American way. For its part, the Chinese Communist Party had improved its capacity for governance by significantly raising living standards for China's 1.34 billion people. Facing the common threat posed by terrorism, the global financial meltdown, and sovereign debt that on average had exceeded 100 percent of GDP among industrialized countries, both nations worked together through high-level contacts, strategic dialogue, and institutionalized exchanges at bilateral, regional, and global levels.

Second, threatening the above positive outlook, a spirit of wariness and anxiety developed on both sides—as evidenced in their strategic and military preparations and, in the United States, in the polemics of the "China threat." In China, this attitude was mirrored in the discourse of the new American imperialism. While the United States kept up the pressure on China for democratic change, the China model appealed to some observers as an alternative to the economic, moral, and "democratic" decline shown in the "sunset club," as they called the developed world.[42] Taken together, these factors fueled the growth of an updated version of Cold War and nationalistic thinking as well as tactics on both sides. However, while the China question remained a live political issue in the United States, it was not as inflammatory as it had been in the 1990s.

Third, both countries sought to prepare for a faltering in bilateral relations by nurturing good relationships with and diverting resources to other countries, and by revitalizing existing regional and global security architecture or by developing new structures. Against this background, the United States and China continued their efforts to maintain a stable relationship, albeit one constrained by constant but manageable irritants. While this approach succeeded in maintaining the peace, it failed to tap the full potential of a real geo-partnership.

The terrorist attacks in the United States on September 11, 2001, and the response that followed redefined the relationship between the United States and the world's 1.4 billion Muslims.[43] These events also had consequences for U.S.-Chinese relations, resulting in some significant shifts in American attitudes toward China. Prior to the 9/11 attacks, a series of statements by President George W. Bush (2001–9) and others were widely interpreted as targeting China as a major strategic rival, rather than a strategic partner—a public stance different from that taken by the Clinton administration.[44] The 2001 *Quadrennial Defense Review Report*—largely prepared before September 11 but released on September 30—implicitly identified China as a potential "military competitor" in the Asia-Pacific and a future challenger to American interests in the region:

> Although the United States will not face a peer competitor in the near future, the potential exists for regional powers to develop sufficient capabilities to threaten stability in regions critical to U.S. interests. . . . The possibility exists that a military competitor with a formidable resource base will emerge in the region. The East Asian littoral—from the Bay of Bengal to the Sea of Japan—represents a particularly challenging area.[45]

In the aftermath of the 9/11 attacks, however, President Bush quickly sought to reassure China: "Our ties are mature, respectful and important to both our nations and to the world."[46] Within a year, the American and Chinese heads of state had met three times, a phenomenon unprecedented in their relationship. Between October 2001 and February 2002, Bush made two visits to China to meet with President Jiang Zemin in the wake of a string of crises. These two summits were followed by a third between Bush and Jiang in October 2002 at Bush's Prairie Chapel Ranch in Crawford, Texas.[47] Both leaders agreed to ease tensions and move toward a constructive relationship of collaboration, particularly on the nuclear issue that had newly surfaced on the Korean Peninsula. Consultations took place on mechanisms to combat terrorism, including the formation of a counterterrorism coalition; the Six-Party Talks on North Korea and a nuclear-free Korean Peninsula; curbing the spread of weapons of mass destruction in Iraq; food and energy security; climate change; and world health.

Despite these signs of progress and collaboration, the "National Security Strategy of the United States of America"—released in September 2002—sent mixed messages about the complex bilateral relationship. First and foremost, it made clear that America "seeks a constructive relationship with China," and welcomed "the emergence of a strong, peaceful, and prosperous China." Second, the report placed Sino-American trade relations within the new post-9/11 strategic coalition framework. However, in the list of U.S. friends and allies in the "war against terror," China ranked not only after Canada, the European countries, Japan, and Australia, but also after Russia and India. Ominously, the report warned that "[i]n pursuing advanced military capabilities that can threaten its neighbors in the Asia-Pacific region, China is following an outdated path that, in the end, will hamper its own pursuit of national greatness."[48] Not surprisingly, the Chinese found the report disturbing: "Although in recent years Beijing has refrained from identifying Washington as an adversary or criticizing its 'hegemonism,' . . . many Chinese still view the United States as a major threat to their nation's security and domestic stability."[49]

From 2003, P. R. China's fourth-generation leadership—President Hu Jintao and Premier Wen Jiabao—built on the gains achieved in earlier phases of market reform to deliver economic benefits to a larger slice of the population, particularly those living in rural areas. Rectifying the imbalance between economic development and social progress and coordinating development between the cities and the countryside were issues that remained high on China's domestic agenda. Externally, maintaining a low-profile, independent, and nonaggressive foreign policy and encouraging a favorable international and regional environment were at the core of the Chinese approach to dealing with U.S. pressure, or the "America threat." In a speech celebrating the 110th anniversary of Mao Zedong's birthday, Hu Jintao explained that, in the spirit of mutual respect, China sought common ground with the United States while seeking to set aside their differences. He stated that China "advocates the democratization of international relations and the diversification of development models, opposes the various forms of hegemonism and power politics, opposes terrorism in all its forms, and seeks to advance the establishment of an international political and economic new order that is fair and reasonable."[50]

The notion of China's peaceful rise and harmonious coexistence with other countries was promoted by the Hu–Wen administration in the face of the American-inspired rhetoric of the China threat and the China challenge. Senior Chinese leaders used national and international forums to express their views on democracy and China's peaceful character. In December 2003 Wen Jiabao visited the United States, the first visit by a Chinese head of state since the transition of power at the 16th Congress of the Chinese Communist Party. Before beginning his trip, he explained in an interview with the *Washington Post* that political reform "has to be done in an orderly fashion and in a well-organized manner." According to Wen, four items were at the top of the democratization agenda for the Chinese government:

> First of all, we should develop democracy to safeguard people's democratic rights and to respect and protect their human rights. Secondly, we should improve on the legal system through better legislation, better administration according to law, and greater judicial reform. Thirdly, we should run the country according to law, making our socialist democracy more institutionalized, standardized and proceduralized, and in this way we can make sure that it will not change because of changes in the leadership and changes in the views and focus of attention of leaders. Fourth, we must strengthen supervision, and we should make sure that the government is placed under the supervision of the people. We have to develop democracy and strengthen supervision. Only in this way can we make sure the government will not relent in its efforts, and this would help avoid a situation whereby the government would be a failure.[51]

In an article in *Foreign Affairs*, Zheng Bijian, a leading Party theorist who had participated in the drafting of the core reports of all CCP central committee meetings after 1982, explained China's grand strategy for its "peaceful rise":

> China will not follow the path of Germany leading up to World War I or those of Germany and Japan leading up to World War II, when these countries violently plundered resources and pursued hegemony. Neither will China follow the path of the great powers vying for global domination during the Cold War. Instead, China will transcend ideological differences to strive for peace, development, and cooperation with all countries of the world.[52]

The relatively steady development in American-Chinese relations continued throughout 2003–2011, particularly on the questions of Northeast Asian security and Taiwan. At the urging of the United States, China has gradually shifted its role in Northeast Asia from a cautious onlooker during the first nuclear crisis in 1993 and 1994, then to a host for multilateral negotiations, and finally to that of mediator. It has worked with the United States, the Democratic People's Republic of Korea (North Korea), the Republic of Korea (South Korea), Japan, and Russia to denuclearize the Korean Peninsula. Since the discovery by American intelligence in 2002 of North Korea's intention to develop nuclear weapons, China had shared its opposition to this possibility with the United States. The result was the Six-Party Talks between North Korea, the United States, China, South Korea, Japan, and Russia, four rounds of which were held between August 2003 and July 2005. In these discussions, China was caught in a deadlock between the American insistence on a complete cessation of all nuclear-related activity in North Korea (as a quid pro quo for favors granted to North Korea) and North Korea's demands for advanced economic aid and security guarantees. In contrast to America, China was opposed to sanctions, as it did not want to see the collapse of North Korea.

In November 2005, North Korea walked away from the fifth round of the Six-Party Talks until their resumption in December 2006 and February 2007. The sixth round of talks took place in March 2007 but was discontinued in April 2009 following North Korea's launch of a satellite, a second nuclear test, and further missile tests, and the resulting condemnation of these acts by the United States and the UN Security Council.[53] While China was given credit for being instrumental in bringing Washington and Pyongyang to the negotiating table—resulting in two joint statements by the six parties in September 2005 and February 2007—the issues raised by North Korea's nuclear program were far from being resolved. They were compounded by the sinking of the South Korean navy vessel *Cheonan* in disputed waters in March 2010, skirmishes between the two Koreas on Yeonpyeong Island the following November, and the death of North Korean leader Kim Jung Il in December 2011.[54]

On the Taiwan question, developments during the first decade of the twenty-first century showed that the United States was capable of accommodating China's core interests. Although veiled in his "pro-Taiwan" campaign rhetoric, President George W. Bush sought to address China's concerns over the issue. In 2000, Chen Shui-bian, the Democratic Progressive Party candidate, won the presidential election in Taiwan. A staunch native Taiwanese nationalist, Chen had publicly promoted the independence of Taiwan as a totally separate sovereign entity from the People's Republic of China—an open challenge to the accepted formula of "One China and Taiwan as part of China," a principle fiercely upheld by mainland China since its founding in 1949. To China, such a declaration of independence would be a formula for war.[55]

In 2002 and 2003, to help his reelection chances, Chen announced plans to hold a referendum on the sovereignty issue and draft a new constitution that would make Taiwan completely independent. However, American support for these proposals was not forthcoming. In December 2003, in the presence of Wen Jiabao, President George W. Bush publicly chastised Chen for provoking China over the issue. During a visit to China in April 2004, Vice President Richard (Dick) Cheney reaffirmed America's opposition to Taiwan independence and continued adherence to the One China "principle." His use of the term "principle"— rather than the expected "policy"—did not go unnoticed in China. Following his reelection, and ignoring the signals emanating from the White House, Chen asserted that he now had the "mandate" to make Taiwan independent. In response, James Kelley, American assistant secretary of state for East Asia, stated that it would be a misunderstanding to assume that the United States would protect Taiwan under any circumstances. In May 2005, Taiwan's political opposition leaders Lien Zhan and James Song, defeated by Chen in the presidential election of 2004, were invited to visit mainland China as part of a united front strategy. In a telephone conversation, Bush reassured Hu Jintao that the American government would not change its position on One China.[56] In the 2008 presidential election, the people of Taiwan gave the Nationalist Party candidate, Ma

Ying-jeou, decisive support against Chen Shui-bian, who was later sentenced and served a jail term for corruption.

Up until 2011, Presidents Hu and Ma's nonconfrontational approach toward each other had helped stabilize the situation. The existing network of economic and cultural links across the Strait culminated in the signing of the Economic Cooperation Framework Agreement in 2010 and continues to foster a positive and prosperous relationship between Taiwan and China. Nevertheless, continuing American arms sales to Taiwan elicited regular protests from the mainland and have frequently triggered suspension of military-to-military contacts with the United States.

Following the setback of the midair collision incident of 2001, military contacts between the United States and China were sporadic, and were closely linked with geopolitical variables such as American arms sales to Taiwan, Tibet, and the Dalai Lama. In 2004, Chairman of the U.S. Joint Chiefs of Staff Richard Myers visited China, followed by a visit to the United States by Liang Guanglie, chief of the General Staff of the People's Liberation Army. In 2005, a visit to China by American secretary of defense Donald Rumsfeld resumed exchanges between the two countries at the defense minister level after a five-year hiatus. Rumsfeld's visit was followed by meetings between Robert Gates, Bush's new secretary of defense, and Cao Gangchuan, the Chinese minister of national defense, and President Hu Jintao in Beijing in 2007. Both sides agreed to establish a hotline between their defense ministers, to foster regular military dialogue and exchanges at all levels, to share military archives in connection with locating American military personnel listed as missing during the Korean War, and to conduct joint exercises and training for humanitarian projects. In July 2011, Mike Mullen, chairman of the U.S. Joint Chiefs of Staff, made a trip to China, where he held talks with his Chinese counterpart, General Chen Bingde, chief of the General Staff of the Chinese People's Liberation Army.

However, friction over defense issues broke out from time to time. In 2007, China announced an 18 percent budget increase for defense spending to more than $45 billion, a figure described by Vice President Dick Cheney as "not consistent" with China's stated goal of a "peaceful rise" on the world stage. While some experts considered that Beijing had wildly understated its defense spending, others pointed out that the U.S. defense budget of $481 billion still dwarfed that of China. They emphasized that, in 2008, the United States led the world in terms of military activity by a huge margin, accounting for 41.5 percent of the military expenditures of all countries, followed by China and Russia at 5.8 percent and 4 percent respectively.[57] Although there is no institutionalized mechanism in place, a healthy, stable, and reliable military-to-military relationship between the United States and China has been reaffirmed as an important element of the developing ties between the two countries.[58]

Over the last two decades, the United States and China had struggled to define the nature of their relationship, and to identify potential partners, rivals, and enemies. China, now the world's second-largest economy, was the largest holder of U.S. debt at $1.7 trillion in 2011, giving it considerable influence over the American economy. China is also the United States' second-largest trading partner. Senior leaders were committed to frequent meetings and the regular exchange of visits. In 2009 alone, Presidents Obama and Hu met four times. In July 2009, two high-level forums—the Strategic Dialogue and the Strategic Economic Dialogue, launched in 2005 and 2006 respectively—merged into one, the Strategic and Economic Dialogue.

Despite these increasingly comprehensive links, both countries have grown increasingly wary of each other. There was a continuing war of words especially over Tibet, Taiwan, human rights, and the status of the Spratly Islands.[59] Are Chinese and American security interests really incompatible? Can the two countries break out of the fluctuating, polarized cycle into which the relationship has been locked for so long? In the United States, a wide range of observers—alarmists, pragmatists, and optimists—have offered their opinions in books. They include Richard Bernstein and Ross Munro's *The Coming Conflict with China*, Michel Oksenberg and Elizabeth Economy's *Shaping U.S.-China Relations: A Long-Term Strategy*, and Fareed Zakaria's *The Post-American World*.[60] In 2010, David Shambaugh argued that American strategy toward China needed to be reset. The United States should learn from China and regard China as a genuine working partner; Congress needs to reeducate itself about China and stop its ill-informed hectoring; both militaries need to pursue real cooperation; America should immediately institute a moratorium on arms sales to Taiwan in exchange for the withdrawal of Chinese missiles and fighters deployed across the Taiwan Strait; and the American media should report fairly on the complex realities of China.[61]

On the Chinese side, defiant, alarmist publications have gained enormous popularity in reaction to the frequent bilateral crises and the con-

tinuing "China threat" polemic in the United States. Two significant examples are the multiauthored *Zhongguo keyi shuobu* [China can still say
no], which sold 3 million copies on its publication in 1996, and the revised edition, *Zhongguo bugaoxing* [China is unhappy], published thirteen
years later.[62] Fang Ning's best-selling studies argue that the bilateral relationship follows the pattern of American deterrence and repression, regardless of the level of subservience adopted by China.[63] Other commentators have argued that the new American imperialism has five components—military dominance, political power, cultural imperialism, the imposition of democratic ideology, and preemptive military action.[64] As of
2011, Song Hongbin's *Huobi zhanzheng* [The currency war] sold over 2
million copies since its first appearance in 2007. Another popular writer,
Dai Xu, argued that the United States has "encircled" China through
strategic military bases, deployment of anti-missile systems, joint military
exercises, and alliances with China's neighbors.[65]

More moderate, but still critical, voices have also emerged. Yan Xuetong of Tsinghua University commented in 2007 that cooperation between the United States and China "is based on their frictions and conflicts, just like 35 years ago. . . . What they are trying to do is to seek
common interests from frictions and conflicts." This conflict is "structu-
ral" in character and has made it impossible for the two countries to
become real strategic partners because the United States "does not want
to see China rise to become the most powerful country in the world."[66]
China should demand that the United States follow its own counsel when
it called on China to become a "responsible stake-holder." Chinese are
becoming increasingly critical of the Chinese government's America policy; the time has come for the "teacher-student relationship," whereby
Beijing takes its lead from Washington, to be transformed into a mature
peer-to-peer relationship.[67]

According to another Chinese scholar, Yuan Peng, the continuing friction in bilateral relations is the consequence of two main factors. First, the
relative shift in the balance of national power between the two countries
over the past two decades—coincident with the transformation of the
international system under powerful globalizing trends—has created a
false impression of the comprehensive strategic rivalry between the United States and China. Second, complex changes in the geopolitical environment, together with the domestic political and social situation in both
nations, have affected their strategic judgment. Americans have adopted

a defensive attitude in the aftermath of the 9/11 attacks, the costly and unpopular Iraq War, and the 2008 financial tsunami. As a result, the conventional public rhetoric used by the Chinese leadership has been interpreted as aggressive and assertive. On the Chinese side, China's successful hosting of the 2008 Olympics and the 2010 Shanghai Expo has boosted its domestic morale and international influence. China's diplomatic and military sectors have gained more confidence and have taken a firmer stand on defending national core interests. Under these changing circumstances, Chinese tolerance of American criticism has visibly loosened. Chinese feel that "it is time to square off with the U.S."[68]

To a great extent, the China-bashing and the America-bashing did not help many Americans alleviate their anxieties about the decline of the United States, or help many Chinese get over their deep-seated sense of injustice in global affairs. In sociological theory, when a group finds itself in conflict with an external group, it produces an increase in internal solidarity which in turn strengthens their leaders and makes them more authoritative.[69]

## CONCLUSION

Compared with the ten years from 1990 to 2000, during the first decade of the twenty-first century the overall capacity of the bilateral relationship expanded at all levels, most notably in communications and crisis management. Although both countries have benefited when they have pooled their power and resources, it will take considerable time and effort to cultivate a relationship that brings peace and hope to the Asia-Pacific and other parts of the world.

Since the 1980s, China has shifted its world outlook from linking the progress of humanity with the decline and eventual demise of capitalism to connecting the development and prosperity of China with a stable and peaceful international environment. And China has given the United States due credit for helping steer this transformation in outlook.

The two countries have quarreled, often bitterly, but for the most part they have managed their uneasy relationship in a rational manner. Restraint has been evident on both sides. Andrew Scobell argues that the use of the Chinese military under the Communists has not been reckless or belligerent. He points out that a civil–military consensus has developed in China, based on rational, strategic thinking.[70] On the American side, David Lampton writes that "US presidents as different from one another as Richard Nixon and Jimmy Carter, and Bill Clinton and George H. W. Bush and George W. Bush, not to mention Ronald Reagan and Gerald Ford, have all ended up pursuing a broadly consistent China policy, even though they came to office with quite divergent inclinations and domestic contexts."[71]

## FURTHER READING

David M. Lampton's *Same Bed, Different Dreams: Managing U.S.-China Relations, 1989–2000* (Berkeley, Calif.: University of California Press, 2001) and his edited *The Making of Chinese Foreign and Security Policy in the Era of Reform, 1978–2000* (Stanford, Calif.: Stanford University Press, 2001) are excellent works on the period from the 1980s to 2000. Other recommended books include Robert Suettinger, *Beyond Tiananmen: The Politics of U.S.-China Relations* (Washington, D.C.: Brookings Institution, 2003); Jean A. Garrison, *Making China Policy: From Nixon to G. W. Bush* (Boulder, Colo.: Lynne Rienner Publishers, 2005); Christopher Marsh and June Teufel Dreyer, eds., *U.S.-China Relations in the Twenty-First Century: Policies, Prospects, and Possibilities* (Lanham, Md.: Lexington Books, 2003); Suisheng Zhao, ed., *China and the United States: Cooperation and Competition in Northeast Asia* (New York: Palgrave Macmillan, 2008); and Gerald Curtis, Ryosei Kokubun, and Wang Jisi, eds., *Getting the Triangle Straight: Managing China-Japan-US Relations* (Tokyo: Japan Center for International Exchange, 2010).

The Great Wall and the Empty Fortress by Andrew Nathan and Robert S. Ross (New York: Norton, 1997) is a comprehensive survey of the security issues surrounding China's post–Cold War foreign relations and an effective antidote to the "China threat" discourse prevalent in the United States. For additional readings on China-Taiwan-U.S. relations, see Alan M. Wachman, *Why Taiwan? Geostrategic Rationales for China's Territorial Integrity* (Stanford, Calif.: Stanford University Press, 2007); Jonathan Manthorpe, *Forbidden Nation: A History of Taiwan* (New York: Palgrave Macmillan, 2002); Edward Friedman, ed., *China's Rise, Taiwan's Dilemmas and International Peace* (London: Routledge, 2006); and John F. Copper, *Taiwan: Nation-State or Province?* 5th ed. (Boulder, Colo.: Westview Press, 2009).

The following publications in Chinese give a range of Chinese views about America: Qian Qichen (钱其琛), *Waijiao shiji* [外交十记 Ten diplomatic episodes] (Beijing: Shijie zhishi chubanshe, 2003); Su Ge (苏格), *Meiguo duihua zhengce yu Taiwan wenti* [美国对华政策与台湾问题 America's China policy and the Taiwan question] (Beijing: Shijie zhishi chubanshe, 1998); and Sun Zhe (孙哲), *Meiguo xue: Zhongguo dui Meiguo zhengzhi waijiao yanjiu, 1979–2006* [美国学: 中国对美国政治外交研究 American studies: Chinese writings on American politics and foreign relations] (Shanghai: Shanghai renmin chubanshe, 2008).

## NOTES

1. Michael Berlin, Ross Terrill, and Akira Iriye, "Tiananmen Two Years Later—How Did the Media Perform? A Study of American Media Coverage of the Beijing Spring of 1989," draft, for the Joan Shorenstein Barone Center on the Press, Politics and Public Policy, John F. Kennedy School of Government, Harvard University, August 20, 1991, p. 13.

2. Flemming Christiansen and Shirin Rai, *Chinese Politics and Society* (London: Prentice Hall, 1996), pp. 142–148.

3. 0538 (Xu Wenli's alias), "Zaitan Meiguo shi 'minzhu de leyuan ma'?" [再谈美国是"民主的乐园吗"? More on whether the U.S. is a "democratic paradise"?] *Siwu luntan* [四五论坛 April 5th forum], no. 9 (May 1979): 15–19.

4. Han Minzhu, ed., *Cries for Democracy: Writings and Speeches from the 1989 Chinese Democracy Movement* (Princeton, N.J.: Princeton University Press, 1990). Documents 1–6, cables from the American Embassy in Beijing to Department of State and IPAC daily intelligence summary, November 21, 1985–January 17, 1987. The U.S. "Tiananmen Papers," http://www.gwu.edu/~nsarchiv/NSAEBB/NSAEBB16/documents/index.html#d2 (accessed May 29, 2011). CIA, "China: Potential for Political Crisis," summary, February 9, 1989, http://www2.gwu.edu/~nsarchiv/NSAEBB/NSAEBB47/index2.html (accessed May 29, 2011).

5. Editorial, "Bixu qizhi xianmingde fandui dongluan" [必须旗帜鲜明地反对动乱 We must take a clear stand and oppose the disturbances], *Renmin ribao*, April 26, 1989, p. 1. For an analysis of three competing narratives about the Tiananmen Incident from the viewpoint of protesters, the Chinese government, and the Bush administration, see Randolph Kluver, "Rhetorical Trajectories of Tiananmen Square," *Diplomatic History* 34, no. 1 (January 2010): 71–94.

6. Nancy Bernkopf Tucker, ed., *China Confidential: American Diplomats and Sino-American Relations, 1945–1996* (New York: Columbia University Press, 2001), p. 443. Flemming Christiansen, "The 1989 Student Demonstrations and the Limits of the Chinese Political Bargaining Machine: An Essay," *China Information* 4, no. 1 (Summer 1989): 17–27.

7. Document 9, CIA intelligence assessment, "Perspectives on Growing Social Tension in China," May 1989, http://www2.gwu.edu/~nsarchiv/NSAEBB/NSAEBB47/index2.html (accessed May 29, 2011).

8. Andrew J. Nathan and Perry Link, *The Tiananmen Papers* (New York: PublicAffairs, 2001).

9. CIA research paper, "The Road to the Tiananmen Crackdown: An Analytic Chronology of Chinese Leadership Decision Making," September 1989, http://www2.gwu.edu/~nsarchiv/NSAEBB/NSAEBB47/index2.html (accessed May 29, 2011).

10. Document 19, "Secretary of State's Morning Summary for June 6, 1989, China: Descent into Chaos," http://www2.gwu.edu/~nsarchiv/NSAEBB/NSAEBB47/index2.html (accessed May 29, 2011).

11. Memo from James A. Baker III to the President, "Your China Visit," February 25–27, 1989, http://www2.gwu.edu/~nsarchiv/NSAEBB/NSAEBB47/index2.html (accessed May 29, 2011).

12. The President's News Conference, June 5, 1989, John T. Woolley and Gerhard Peters, American Presidency Project, http://www.presidency.ucsb.edu/ws/?pid=17103 (accessed July 21, 2011).

13. Section 902 of the Foreign Relations Authorization Act, Fiscal Years 1990 and 1991 (P.L. 101-246; 22 U.S.C. 2151 note). Dianne E. Rennack, "China: Economic Sanctions," Congressional Research Service, Library of Congress, May 18, 2005.

14. Deng Xiaoping (邓小平), "Zhongmei guanxi zhonggui yao hao qilai caixing" [中美关系终归要好起来才行 U.S.-Chinese relations will have to ultimately improve], December 10, 1989, *Deng Xiaoping wenxuan* [邓小平文选 Selected works of Deng Xiaoping], reprint (Beijing: Renmin chubanshe, 2008; 1st ed. 1993), vol. 3, pp. 350–351.

15. Deng Xiaoping, "Guoji xingshi he jingji wenti" [国际形势与经济问题 The international situation and economic questions], March 3, 1990, *Deng Xiaoping wenxuan*, vol. 3, pp. 353–356.

16. Deng Xiaoping, "Zhongguo yongyuan bu yunxu bieguo ganshe neizheng" [中国永远不允许别国干涉内政 China would never allow other countries to interfere in its internal affairs], July 11, 1990, *Deng Xiaoping wenxuan*, vol. 3, pp. 359–361.

17. Jiang Zemin's conversation with the American president's special envoy, Brent Scowcroft, national security advisor, "Fazhan Zhongmei guanxi yao xiangqian kan" [发展中美关系要向前看 The development of U.S.-Chinese relations needs to be forward-looking], in *Jiang Zemin wenxuan* [江泽民文选 Selected works of Jiang Zemin] (Beijing: Renmin chubanshe, 2006), vol. 1, pp. 84–86.

18. Jiang Zemin, "Guoji xingshi he junshi zhanlüe fangzhen" [国际形势和军事战略方针 The international situation and military strategic guidelines], January 13, 1993, in *Jiang Zemin wenxuan*, vol. 1, pp. 278–294.

19. Jiang Zemin's conversation with former president Richard Nixon in Beijing on October 31, 1989, "Zhongguo renmin lilai shi jiang minzu qijie de" [中国人民历来是讲民族气节 的 The Chinese people have always been concerned about national dignity], *Jiang Zemin wenxuan*, vol. 1, pp. 70–73.

20. Jiang Zemin, "Lingdao ganbu yiding yao jiang zhengzhi" [领导干部一定要讲政治 Leaders must deal with politics], September 27, 1995, in Zhonggong zhongyang xuanchuanbu, ed., *Mao Zedong, Deng Xiaoping, Jiang Zemin lun sixiang zhengzhi gongzuo* [毛泽东邓小平江泽民论思想政治工作 Mao Zedong, Deng Xiaoping, and Jiang Zemin on political work] (Beijing: Xuexi chubanshe, 2000), pp. 234–236.

21. Jiang Zemin's speech at the UN head of the state summit on September 12, 2000, http://www.investchina.org.cn/chinese/2000/Sep/5068.htm (accessed July 15, 2011).

22. http://big5.xinhuanet.com/gate/big5/news.xinhuanet.com/zhengfu/2002-08/06/content_512599.htm (accessed July 15, 2011). Jiang Zemin, "Dui Yatai jingji hezuo de yuanze jianyi" [对亚太经济合作的原则建议 Suggested principles for economic collabo-

ration in the Asia-Pacific], November 15, 1994, in *Jiang Zemin wenxuan*, vol. 1, pp. 413–417.

23. Joseph Kahn, "Executives Make Trade with China a Moral Issue," *New York Times*, February 13, 2000, http://www.nytimes.com/2000/02/13/us/executives-make-trade-with-china-a-moral-issue.html?pagewanted=print&src=pm (accessed December 14, 2011).

24. Erik Eckholm, "In China, So Many Liberties, So Little Freedom," *New York Times*, January 3, 1999, Section 4, p. 1.

25. J. Stapleton Roy's praise of Nancy Bernkopf Tucker, ed., *Strait Talk: United States-Taiwan Relations and the Crisis with China* (Cambridge, Mass.: Harvard University Press, 2009).

26. Nancy Bernkopf Tucker, *China Confidential*, p. 473.

27. Interview with Wen Jiabao by Leonard Downie Jr., executive editor of the *Washington Post*, on November 21, 2003, http://www.washingtonpost.com/ac2/wp-dyn/A6641-2003Nov22?language=printer (accessed July 16, 2011).

28. Sun Zhe (孙哲), *Meiguo Guohui yu Zhongmei guanxi: Anli yu fenxi* [美国国会与中美关系: 案例与分析 The American Congress and U.S.-Chinese relations: Case studies and analysis] (Beijing: Shishi chubanshe, 2004). Li Qingsi (李庆四), *Meiguo Guohui yu Meiguo duihua zhengce* [美国国会与美国对华政策 The American Congress and American China policy] (Beijing: Dangdai shijie chubanshe, 2002).

29. Lee Teng-hui, "Always in My Heart," speech at Cornell University in June 1995, http://www.news.cornell.edu/campus/Lee/Lee_Speech.html (accessed July 22, 2011).

30. Richard Bush, "Lee Teng-hui and 'Separatism,'" in Nancy Bernkopf Tucker, ed., *Dangerous Strait: The U.S.-Taiwan-China Crisis* (New York: Columbia University Press, 2005), pp. 70–92.

31. Jiang Zemin, "Wei cujin zuguo tongyi daye de wancheng er jixu fendou" [为促进祖国统一大业的完成而继续奋斗 Continue to strive to accomplish the great cause of the unification of the motherland], January 13, 1995, *Jiang Zemin wenxuan*, vol. 1, pp. 418–424.

32. Xiong Zhiyong (熊志勇), *Bainian Zhongmei guanxi* [百年中美关系 A century of Sino-U.S. relations] (Beijing: Shijie zhishi chubanshe, 2006), p. 363.

33. Christopher M. Dent, "Taiwan and the New Regional Political Economy of East Asia," *China Quarterly*, no. 182 (June 2005): 385–406. For a different view of the economic integration between Taiwan and China, see T. J. Cheng, "China-Taiwan Economic Linkage: Between Insulation and Superconductivity," in Nancy Bernkopf Tucker, ed., *Dangerous Strait*, pp. 93–130.

34. "China-US Joint Statement," October 29, 1997, http://www.china-embassy.org/eng/zmgx/zysj/jzxfm/t36249.htm (accessed July 24, 2011).

35. Editorial, *Renmin ribao*, November 3, 1997, June 18, 1998. Liu Liandi (刘连第), ed., *Zhongmei guanxi de guiji: 1993–2000 nian dashi zonglan* [中美关系的轨迹: 1993年–2000年大事纵览 The contours of U.S.-Chinese relations: An overview of major events from 1993 to 2000] (Beijing: Shishi chubanshe, 2001), pp. 186–189. Madeleine Albright, "U.S. Commitment to Security and Prosperity in Asia," June 27, 1998, *U.S. Department of State Dispatch* (August 1998): 1–9.

36. "China-US Joint Statement," October 29, 1997.

37. United Nations Convention on the Law of the Sea, December 10, 1982, 1833 UNTS 397, 21 ILM 1261 (1982).

38. The Convention on International Civil Aviation, December 7, 1944, 61 Stat. 1180, 15 UNTS 295.

39. "Statement by the President on American Plane and Crew in China," April 2, 2011, http://georgewbush-whitehouse.archives.gov/news/releases/2001/04/20010402-2.html (accessed July 25, 2011).

40. Michael D. Swaine and Zhang Tuosheng, with Danielle F. S. Cohen, eds., *Managing Sino-American Crisis: Case Studies and Analysis* (Washington, D.C.: Carnegie Endowment for International Peace, 2007).

41. "Secretary Rumsfeld Briefs on EP-3 Collision," April 13, 2001, http://www.defense.gov/transcripts/transcript.aspx?transcriptid=1066 (accessed July 25, 2011).

42. Stephen Sackur's interview with Angel Gurria, secretary-general of the Organisation for Economic Co-operation and Development (OECD) on BBC *HARDtalk*, July 6, 2011. Howard W. French, "Letter from Shanghai: Behind the U.S. Decline of Influence in China," *International Herald Tribune*, Asia Pacific, March 22, 2006, http://www.iht.com/articles/2006/o3/22/news/letter.php (accessed March 22, 2006).

43. Peter Warren Singer, "America, Islam, and the 9-11 War," *Current History: A Journal of Contemporary Trends* 105, no. 695 (December 2006): pp. 415–422.

44. Wu Xinbo, "The Promise and Limitations of a Sino-U.S. Partnership," *Washington Quarterly* 27, no. 4 (Autumn 2004): 115–126. Tony Karon, "Bush China Policy Defaults to Engagement," *Time*, July 31, 2001, http://www.time.com/time/columnist/karon/article/0,9565,169585,00.html (accessed January 7, 2008). Jing-dong Yuan, "Bush's Hawks Circle over Policy," Op-Ed, *South China Morning Post*, July 24, 2002, Section: News, p. 14, http://cns.miis.edu/pubs/other/bushhawk.htm (accessed January 7, 2008).

45. "2001 Quadrennial Defense Review Report," http://www.defenselink.mil/pubs/pdfs/qdr2001.pdf (accessed January 8, 2008).

46. Office of the Press Secretary, White House, "President Bush Meets with Chinese President Jiang Zemin," February 21, 2002, http://www.whitehouse.gov/news/releases/2002/02/20020221-7.html (accessed January 8, 2008).

47. Remarks by Presidents Bush and Jiang at the press conference, October 25, 2002, http://georgewbush-whitehouse.archives.gov/news/releases/2002/10/20021025.html (accessed July 17, 2011). Mike Allen and Karen DeYoung, "Bush Seeks China's Aid to Oppose N. Korea," *Washington Post*, October 26, 2002, http://www.washingtonpost.com/wp-dyn/content/article/2009/11/10/AR2009111009772_pf.html (accessed July 16, 2011). Editorial, "Xin shiji xin xingshi xin xingdong: Relie zhuhe Jiang Zemin zhuxi chufang yuanman chenggong" [新世纪, 新形势, 新行动:热烈祝贺江泽民主席出访圆满成功 New century, new situation, and new actions: Warmly celebrate the success of President Jiang Zemin's visit], *Renmin ribao*, October 30, 2002.

48. "The National Security Strategy of the United States of America," September 2002, pp. 25–28, http://www.whitehouse.gov/nsc/nss.pdf (accessed January 8, 2008).

49. Wang Jisi, "China's Search for Stability with America," *Foreign Affairs* 84, no. 5 (September/October 2005): 39–48.

50. Hu Jintao's speech on the 110th anniversary of Mao Zedong's birthday, http://news.xinhuanet.com/newscenter/2003-12/26/content_1250092.htm (accessed July 16, 2011).

51. Interview with Wen Jiabao by Leonard Downie Jr., executive editor of the *Washington Post*, on November 21, 2003.

52. Zheng Bijian, "China's 'Peaceful Rise' to Great-Power Status," *Foreign Affairs* 84, no. 5 (September/October 2005): 18–24.

53. Zhongguo guoji wenti yanjiu suo (中国国际问题研究所), *Guoji xingshi he Zhongguo waijiao lanpishu (2009/2010)* [国际形势和中国外交蓝皮书 The bluebook of the international situation and China's foreign affairs positions (2009/2010)] (Beijing: Shijie zhishi chubanshe, 2010), chapter 7. Jae Ho Chung, "China's Ascendancy and the Korean Peninsula: From Interest Reevaluation to Strategic Realignment?" in David Shambaugh, ed., *Power Shift: China and Asia's New Dynamics* (Berkeley, Calif.: University of California Press, 2005), pp. 151–169.

54. "Joint Statement of the Fourth Round of the Six-Party Talks," Beijing, September 19, 2005, http://www.state.gov/p/eap/regional/c15455.htm. "Initial Actions for the Implementation of the Joint Statement," February 13, 2007, Beijing, http://www.fmprc.gov.cn/eng/zxxx/t297463.htm. Jayshree Bajoria and Carin Zissis, "The Six-Party Talks on North Korea's Nuclear Program," http://www.cfr.org/proliferation/six-party-talks-north-koreas-nuclear-program/p13593 (all three files accessed July 17, 2011).

55. Richard C. Bush, *Untying the Knot: Making Peace in the Taiwan Strait* (Washington, D.C.: Brookings Institution, 2005). Nancy Bernkopf Tucker, ed., *Dangerous Strait: The U.S.-Taiwan-China Crisis* (New York: Columbia University Press, 2005).

56. *Renmin ribao*, overseas ed., May 6, 2005.

57. James B. Rule, "The Military State of America and the Democratic Left. George Packer Responds. Michael Walzer Responds. James B. Rule Replies," *Dissent* 57, no. 1 (Winter 2010): 81–90.

58. "Future of China-U.S. Military Ties Requires Mutual Respect, Trust," July 13, 2011, http://www.china-embassy.org/eng/gdxw/t839334.htm (accessed July 18, 2011).

59. For a summary of the views of liberal optimists, liberal pessimists, and liberal constructivists in relation to those of realist optimists, realist pessimists, and realist constructivists in the United States, see Aaron L. Friedberg, "The Future of U.S.-China Relations: Is Conflict Inevitable?" *International Security* 30, no. 2 (Fall 2005): 7–45. Aaron L. Friedberg, "Are We Ready for China?" *Commentary* (October 2007): 39–43, and *A Contest for Supremacy: China, America, and the Struggle for Mastery in Asia* (New York: Norton, 2011).

60. Richard Bernstein and Ross H. Munro, *The Coming Conflict with China* (New York: Vintage, 1998; 1st ed. by Knopf in 1997); Michel Oksenberg and Elizabeth Economy, *Shaping U.S.-China Relations: A Long-Term Strategy* (New York: Council on Foreign Relations, 1997); Fareed Zakaria, *The Post-American World* (New York: Norton, 2009; 1st ed. 2008).

61. David Shambaugh, "A New China Requires a New US Strategy," *Current History* 109, no. 728 (September 2010): 219–226.

62. Song Qiang (宋强) and Zhang Cangcang (张藏藏), et al., *Zhongguo keyi shuobu: Lengzhan houshidai de zhengzhi yu qinggan jueze* [中国可以说不: 冷战后时代的政治与情感抉择 China can say no: Politics and sentiment in the post–Cold War era] (Beijing: Zhonghua gongshang lianhe chubanshe, 1996). Song Xiaojun (宋晓军) and Wang Xiaodong (王小东), et al., *Zhongguo bugaoxing: da shidai, da mubiao ji women de neiyou waihuan* [中国不高兴:大时代、大目标及我们的内忧外患 China is unhappy: Broad picture, grand strategy, domestic concerns and external threats] (Nanjing: Jiangsu renmin chubanshe, 2009).

63. Fang Ning (房宁), *Chengzhang de Zhongguo: Dangdai Zhongguo qingnian de guojia minzu yishi yanjiu* [成长的中国:当代中国青年的国家民族意识研究 Growing China: A study of national consciousness among contemporary Chinese youth] (Beijing: Remin chubanshe, 2002). Fang Ning, *Xin Diguo zhuyi shidai yu Zhongguo zhanlüe* [新帝国主义

时代与中国战略 The age of new imperialism and China's counterstrategy] (Beijing: Beijing chubanshe, 2003).

64. Song Hongbin (宋鸿兵), *Huobi zhanzheng* [货币战争 The currency war] (Beijing: Zhongxin chubanshe, 2007). Lang Xianping of the Chinese University of Hong Kong has advised Chinese government agencies and private enterprise alike that, in the "new imperialist" era, China must strive to become a rule maker in the international competition game. Lang Xianping (郎咸平), *Lang Xianping shuo: Xin Diguo zhuyi zai Zhongguo* [郎咸平说:新帝国主义在中国 Lang Xianping on new imperialism in China], 8th printing (Beijing: Dongfang chubanshe, 2011; 1st ed. in January 2010); its sequel appeared four months afterward in May 2010, *Lang Xianping shuo: Xin Diguo zhuyi zai Zhongguo 2* [郎咸平说:新帝国主义在中国2 Lang Xianping on new imperialism in China 2] (Beijing: Dongfang chubanshe, 2010).

65. Dai Xu (戴旭), *C xing baowei: Neiyou waihuan xia de Zhongguo tuwei* [C形包围: 内忧外患下的中国突围 The C-shaped encirclement: China's way out of its domestic problems and the foreign threat] (Shanghai: Wenhui chubanshe, 2010).

66. Yan Wei, "Relations in Transition," interview with Yan Xuetong, director of the Institute of International Studies of Tsinghua University, *Beijing Review* (February 22, 2007), p. 16.

67. Yan Wei, "Relations in Transition."

68. Yuan Peng (袁鹏), "Zhongmei guanxi zhuanyuan, Meiguo ying xianxing" [中美关系转圜, 美国应先行 To improve U.S.-Chinese relations, the United States ought to make the first move], *Huanqiu shibao* [环球时报], no. 2243, August 23, 2010.

69. Georg Simmel, *Georg Simmel on Individuality and Social Forms* (Chicago, Ill.: University of Chicago Press, 1972).

70. Andrew Scobell, *China's Use of Military Force: Beyond the Great Wall and the Long March* (Cambridge: Cambridge University Press, 2003).

71. David M. Lampton, "The China Fantasy, Fantasy," *China Quarterly* 191 (September 2007): 745–749.

# TWELVE

# China's Catch-Up: A Game-Changer for America?

Since the late 1970s, a major mismatch has emerged from the American-Chinese encounter—the gap between their fluctuating political and military relations, on the one hand, and their expanded ties in the areas of trade, society, religion, and culture, on the other. Would economic convergence—China's endeavor to catch up with developed countries like the United States—and increasing social and cultural interchange ultimately overcome the barriers to bring both countries closer in terms of security concerns?[1]

## OVERALL TRADE PERFORMANCE

This section charts the broad contours of American-Chinese trade relations in the 1990s and 2000s in an interlocking Asian and world economy.

During the last two decades, Sino-American economic relations, to some observers, formed the most important bilateral economic and financial relationship in the world.[2] In 2010, China became the world's second-largest economy. Nevertheless, early 2011 data showed that the U.S. economy (with a GDP of US$14,624 billion) was still well over twice the size of China's ($5,745 billion), and the U.S. GDP per capita (US$47,132) was eleven times that of China ($4,283).[3]

In terms of overall trade performance, as of December 2010 the United States was China's largest export market, whereas China was America's third-largest export market (buyer of U.S. goods and services), according to American statistics.[4] And the United States was the fourth-largest supplier of imports to China in the Chinese figures.[5]

Trade data from the period presented in tables 12.1 and 12.2 reveal four significant trends. First, and most generally, economic factors have played an important role in both countries, appropriate to the level of bilateral trade and investment. At the beginning of the 1990s, the total volume of bilateral trade was less than 3 percent of total U.S. trade; it would grow to over 14 percent by 2010 and 13.6 percent in 2011. Since 1980, China's trade with the United States has varied between 10 and 18 percent of its total international trade volume. Clearly, both countries have benefited from expanded commercial links.

Second, there has been a tremendous increase in the level of trade between the two countries since 1971 (when it stood at a mere US$4.7 million),[6] but the statistics from both countries often show substantial disagreement (figure 12.1). In China's list, the United States was its largest trade partner, and the total trade volume between the two countries was US$385.3 billion in 2010 and $446.7 billion in 2011.[7] But according to U.S. statistics, the trade volume between the two countries had risen to US$458.8 billion in 2010 and $503.2 billion in 2011 (of which $273.1 billion and $295.5 billion was a trade deficit respectively run by America). China overtook Mexico as America's second-largest trading partner in 2005, and has retained that position since, with Canada as the largest U.S. trade partner.[8]

Third, since joining the WTO in 2001, China's international export and import trade has increased more rapidly than its trade with the United States. In other words, China's fastest trade growth lay in the rest of the world (Europe, Africa, the Middle East, South America, and Asia), but not in North America, as shown in figure 12.2. In part, this trend reflects China's outward-oriented growth path noted above.[9] It also underscores China's avoidance of dependence on the U.S. market by diversifying its partnerships as a hedge against future uncertainty.

Fourth, according to the American figures, from 1995 to 2011 the United States ran a trade deficit with China, snowballing from US$33.8 billion in 1995 to US$295.4 billion in 2011—a close to ninefold increase over fifteen years. However, the American statistics also reveal a degree of instability in the economic relationship. For instance, between a 10.9 percent growth in exports to China in 1998 and a 24.4 percent increase in 2000, U.S. exports fell by 8 percent in 1999; and sandwiched between a

22.3 percent increase in U.S. imports from China in 2000 and 22.4 percent in 2002, a figure of only 2.2 percent was recorded in 2001.

## CHINA'S ENTRY INTO THE WTO

During the last two decades, in both countries, domestic politics as well as security considerations figured large in influencing such economic matters as sanctions, most-favored-nation status, and negotiations over China's application for membership in the World Trade Organization (WTO). Alongside these larger issues, trade relations continued on a relatively steady course despite the vagaries of politics.

As we saw in the preceding chapter, the imposition of sanctions on China as a result of the 1989 Tiananmen Incident, and the linking and delinking of China's most-favored-nation status with its human rights record during the Clinton administration in the early 1990s illustrate how economic issues have provided the United States with a lever to obtain concessions from China in the political sphere. The cover story of the October 1990 issue of *The Atlantic* reflected the dampened enthusiasm for trade in the immediate aftermath of the Tiananmen storm: "American business in China in the eighties fell victim to the naïve optimism with which it contemplated the vast 'China market.'" To these critics, the Chi-

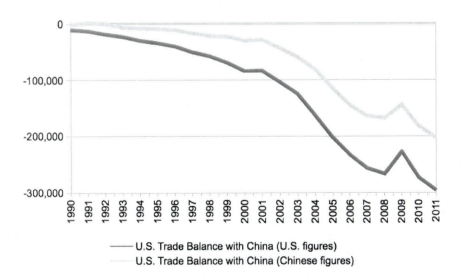

Figure 12.1.  **U.S. Trade Balance with China, 1990–2011 (in millions of current U.S. dollars)**

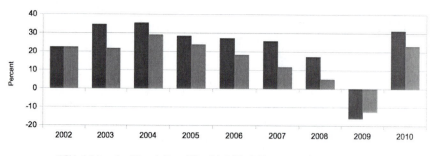

**Figure 12.2. Comparison of the Growth in China's Exports to the World and to the United States, 2002–10 (percent annual growth)**

na market was a chimera: "U.S.-China bilateral trade totaled $18 billion in 1989, scarcely half of U.S. trade with Taiwan, and today direct U.S. investment in China amounts to less than half of one percent of direct U.S. investment worldwide. And these days Eastern Europe would seem to provide business with far more fertile ground."[10]

The atmosphere could not have been more different a short decade later. Together with the Chinese government, the United States was the prime mover in China's accession to the WTO on December 11, 2001. Although the WTO came into being on January 1, 1995, its predecessor, the General Agreement on Tariffs and Trade (GATT), dates back to 1948. China was one of the original signatories of the GATT. In 1971, the GATT revoked Taiwan's membership in line with the UN's recognition of the People's Republic of China as the only legitimate government of China, and invited China to join the organization. In the opinion of Long Yong-tu, chief Chinese WTO negotiator, readmission should have been a relatively straightforward process at the time. However, China regarded the GATT through ideological lenses as "a rich countries' club," mainly comprised of developed nations, and decided not to join in the early 1970s. In 1986, China formally applied to rejoin the GATT; the Chinese leadership, now committed to the process of reform and "opening up," were afraid that being outside the organization might inflict enormous financial losses (e.g., in the textile industry) on China.

Originally set up to regulate international trade in commodities, over the years the role of the GATT has evolved through several rounds of negotiations aimed at settling trade disputes. The last and largest of these was the Uruguay Round from 1986 to 1994, which led to the birth of the

**Table 12.1. U.S.-Chinese Trade, 1991–2011 (U.S. figures, in billions of current U.S. dollars)**

| Year | U.S. Imports from PRC/World* | U.S. Exports to PRC/World | Total U.S.-China/U.S.-World Trade | U.S.-China/U.S.-World Trade Balance | Percent of Total U.S. Trade |
|------|------|------|------|------|------|
| 1991 | 19.0/488.2 | 6.3/421.9 | 25.6/910.1 | −12.7/−66.3 | 2.8 |
| 1992 | 25.7/532.7 | 7.4/448.2 | 33.1/980.9 | −18.3/84.5 | 3.4 |
| 1993 | 31.5/580.7 | 8.8/465.1 | 40.3/1,045.8 | −22.8/−115.6 | 3.9 |
| 1994 | 38.8/663.3 | 9.3/512.6 | 48.1/1,175.9 | −29.5/−150.6 | 4.1 |
| 1995 | 45.6/743.5 | 11.8/584.7 | 57.4/1,328.2 | −33.8/−158.8 | 4.3 |
| 1996 | 51.5/795.3 | 12.0/625.1 | 63.5/1,420.4 | −39.5/−170.2 | 4.5 |
| 1997 | 62.6/869.7 | 12.8/689.2 | 75.4/1,558.9 | −49.8/−180.5 | 4.8 |
| 1998 | 71.2/911.9 | 14.3/682.1 | 85.8/1,594.0 | −56.9/−229.8 | 5.4 |
| 1999 | 81.8/1,024.6 | 13.1/695.8 | 94.9/1,719.6 | −68.7/−328.8 | 5.5 |
| 2000 | 100.0/1,218.0 | 16.3/781.9 | 116.3/1,999.9 | −83.7/−436.1 | 5.8 |
| 2001 | 102.3/1,141.0 | 19.2/729.1 | 121.5/1,870.1 | −83.0/−411.9 | 6.5 |
| 2002 | 125.2/1,161.4 | 22.1/693.1 | 147.3/1,854.5 | −103.1/−468.3 | 7.9 |
| 2003 | 152.4/1,257.1 | 28.4/724.8 | 180.8/1,981.9 | −124.0/−532.4 | 9.1 |
| 2004 | 196.7/1,469.7 | 34.7/818.8 | 231.4/2,288.5 | −162.0/−650.9 | 10.1 |
| 2005 | 243.5/1,673.5 | 41.8/906.0 | 285.3/2,579.5 | −201.6/−767.5 | 11.1 |
| 2006 | 287.8/1,854.0 | 55.2/1,037.0 | 343/2,891.0 | −232.5/−817.3 | 11.9 |
| 2007 | 321.5/1,957.0 | 65.2/1,148.2 | 386.7/3,105.2 | −256.3/−808.7 | 12.5 |
| 2008 | 337.8/2,103.6 | 71.5/1,287.4 | 409.2/3,391.0 | −266.3/−816.2 | 12.1 |
| 2009 | 296.4/1,558.1 | 69.6/1,056.9 | 366.0/2,615.0 | −226.8/−501.3 | 14 |
| 2010 | 364.9/1,913.2 | 91.9/1,278.3 | 458.8/3,191.5 | −273.1/−634.9 | 14.4 |
| 2011 | 399.3/2,207.8 | 103.9/1,480.4 | 503.2/3,688.3 | −295.4/−727.4 | 13.6 |

*Source:* 1995–2011 figures are drawn from the U.S.-China Business Council's website, http://www.uschina.org/statistics/tradetable.html (accessed December 20, 2007; April 17, 2010; July 29, 2011; and July 19, 2012). 1991–1994 U.S.-China trade data are based on U.S. Census Bureau, Trade in Goods (Imports, Exports, and Trade Balance) with China, http://www.census.gov/foreign-trade/balance/c5700.html (accessed December 27, 2007).

*American world trade figures are based on data from U.S. Census Bureau, Foreign Trade Statistics, http://www.census.gov/foreign-trade/balance/c0004.html (accessed December 25, 2007; April 26, 2010; and July 29, 2011). These figures have been rounded and totaled by the present author.

WTO. Reflecting changes in world trade, the WTO extended its purview to trade in services and intellectual property.[11] Legally, WTO agreements and other instruments constitute binding rules intended to help exporters and importers trade as efficiently as possible. Beginning in 2001 the WTO

**Table 12.2.  U.S.-Chinese Trade, 1991–2011 (Chinese figures, in billions of current U.S. dollars)**

| Year | PRC Exports to U.S./World | PRC Imports from U.S./World | Total China-U.S./China-World Trade | China Trade Balance with U.S./World | Percent of Total PRC Trade |
|------|--------------------------|----------------------------|-------------------------------------|--------------------------------------|----------------------------|
| 1991 | 6.2/71.9                 | 8.0/63.8                   | 14.2/135.7                          | −1.8/8.1                             | 10.5                       |
| 1992 | 8.6/84.9                 | 8.9/80.6                   | 17.5/165.5                          | −0.3/4.4                             | 10.6                       |
| 1993 | 17.0/91.7                | 10.7/104.0                 | 27.7/195.7                          | 6.28/−12.2                           | 14.2                       |
| 1994 | 21.5/121.0               | 14.0/115.6                 | 35.4/236.6                          | 7.5/5.4                              | 15.0                       |
| 1995 | 24.7/148.8               | 16.1/132.1                 | 40.8/280.9                          | 8.6/16.7                             | 14.5                       |
| 1996 | 26.7/151.1               | 16.2/138.8                 | 42.9/289.9                          | 10.5/12.3                            | 14.8                       |
| 1997 | 32.7/182.7               | 16.3/142.4                 | 49.0/325.2                          | 16.4/40.4                            | 15.1                       |
| 1998 | 38.0/183.7               | 17.0/140.2                 | 55.0/323.9                          | 21.0/43.5                            | 17.0                       |
| 1999 | 41.9/194.9               | 19.5/165.7                 | 61.4/360.6                          | 22.4/29.2                            | 17.0                       |
| 2000 | 52.1/249.2               | 22.4/225.1                 | 74.5/474.3                          | 29.7/24.1                            | 15.7                       |
| 2001 | 54.3/266.2               | 26.2/243.6                 | 80.5/509.8                          | 28.1/22.6                            | 15.8                       |
| 2002 | 69.9/325.6               | 27.2/295.2                 | 97.2/620.8                          | 42.7/30.4                            | 15.7                       |
| 2003 | 92.5/438.2               | 33.9/412.8                 | 126.3/851.0                         | 58.6/25.4                            | 14.8                       |
| 2004 | 125.0/593.3              | 44.7/561.2                 | 169.6/1,154.6                       | 80.3/32.1                            | 14.7                       |
| 2005 | 162.9/762.0              | 48.6/660.0                 | 211.5/1,422.0                       | 114.3/102.0                          | 14.8                       |
| 2006 | 203.4/969.0              | 59.2/791.5                 | 262.7/1,760.4                       | 144.2/177.5                          | 14.9                       |
| 2007 | 232.7/1,218.0            | 69.4/955.8                 | 302.1/2,173.8                       | 163.3/262.2                          | 13.9                       |
| 2008 | 248.4/1,428.6            | 81.1/1,133.1               | 329.5/2,561.7                       | 167.3/295.5                          | 12.9                       |
| 2009 | 220.8/1,201.7            | 77.4/1,005.6               | 298.2/2,207.3                       | 143.4/196.1                          | 13.5                       |
| 2010 | 283.3/1,577.9            | 102.0/1,394.8              | 385.3/2,972.8                       | 181.3/183.1                          | 13.0                       |
| 2011 | 324.5/1,898.6            | 122.2/1,743.5              | 446.7/3,642.0                       | 202.3/155.1                          | 12.3                       |

*Sources:* Statistics for 1991–2000 are drawn from Tao, *Zhongmei guanxi shi*, pp. 339–340, with adjustments by the present author. For statistics on China's trade with the United States for 2001–6 and with the world for 1978–2006, respectively, see Zhongguo guojia tongjiju (National Bureau of Statistics of China), *Zhongguo tongji nianjian* [China Statistical Yearbook] (Beijing: China Statistics Press, 2001–7). Figures for 2007–11 are taken from *Caijing* [Finance], http://www.sina.com.cn, January 15, 2008; the Ministry of Commerce of the People's Republic of China, http://zhs.mofcom.gov.cn/aarticle/Nocategory/200801/20080 105333370.html, http://zhs.mofcom.gov.cn/aarticle/Nocategory/200901/20090106003675.html, http://zhs.mofcom.gov.cn/aarticle/Nocategory/201001/20100106747574.html, http://zhs.mof com.gov.cn/aarticle/aa/201105/20110507536961.html, and the US-China Business Council, http://www.uschina.org/statistics/tradetable.html. All the above websites were accessed on April 27, 2010, and July 29, 2011. http://english.mofcom.gov.cn/aarticle/statistic/Brief Statistics/201201/20120107927531.html (accessed July 19, 2012).

hosted a new round of trade negotiations, the Doha Development Round, which collapsed in July 2006, and again in 2007 and 2008.

It took fifteen years of negotiations (1986–2001) for China to become the 143rd member of the WTO. The first six years were spent debating whether China was indeed developing a market economy—the Chinese negotiating team explained little more beyond asserting that China was developing a system combining market forces with a planned economy. Progress was made in 1992 when, during his "Southern Tour" of the nation's special economic zones, Deng Xiaoping announced that China under socialism could adopt the market economy structure. [12]

Compared with the talks held with thirty or so other countries, China's negotiations with the United States were arduously protracted. The Chinese, who felt that the American negotiators were domineering, dug their heels in. The WTO talks were suspended in 1989 in the wake of the Tiananmen Incident and were not resumed for over two years when senior Chinese leaders became personally involved in the process, aware that membership in the WTO would function as an important tool to break through Western sanctions and deterrence. [13] The Sino-American negotiators considered trade issues relating to over 4,000 classes of merchandise, in addition to access to the Chinese banking, insurance, and telecommunication industries. While China was eager to be part of the WTO, it wanted to join it as a developing country and insisted that the balance between obligations and rights be respected, especially by developed member states. "The developed countries, as the initiators and the biggest beneficiaries of globalization and liberalization, ought to shoulder even more international responsibilities and obligations and create conditions for the developing countries to actively participate in the process of globalization and liberalization and fully integrate into the world economy." [14]

By the time Premier Zhu Rongji visited the United States in April 1999, China was offering serious concessions in the areas of agricultural tariffs, market access, and service industries. The proffered terms were well received by the U.S. WTO negotiators and the American business community. Nevertheless, anticipating opposition from Congress and from labor and human rights groups, at the last minute President Clinton veered away from an agreement with China during Premier Zhu's visit. Realizing his political misjudgment, Clinton quickly did another about-face and contacted Zhu, who was still in the United States, urging that the Chinese team stay on for further talks. Zhu responded that they could discuss the WTO again in Beijing. [15]

The embassy bombing incident in May 1999 pushed U.S.-Chinese relations into a corner. At the time, anti-American sentiment was running high in China. Terms such as "unequal treaties," "national heroes," and "traitors" were being bandied about and were applied to the WTO talks and the Chinese negotiators. A report in Hong Kong's *Wen Wei Po* newspaper asserted that membership would simply open China up to exploitation by foreign business interests once again:

> [I]f China cannot "join the WTO" as a developing country, and if there is no balance on the rights and obligations of joining, that means China's national interests will be compromised. If an "unequal treaty" is signed against China's will, China can do little to expand its export market, but rather must open all its markets to foreign businessmen. Such a treaty is senseless for China; it only means an unbearable bitter pill. [16]

Despite such misgivings, the leaders of both countries saw the potential of WTO membership for improving their relationship. President Jiang Zemin and the Politburo made the political decision to push trade negotiations with the United States, and Zhu Rongji himself participated directly in the final round. Representatives of both countries, led by Charlene Barshefsky and Shi Guangsheng, met at 4:30 a.m. on November 15, 1999, and an agreement was signed the same day. The biggest hurdle to China's WTO membership was cleared, and negotiations with other countries were completed over the following two years. On December 11, 2001, China officially became a member of the WTO.

Joining the WTO turned out to be a win-win situation for China, the United States, and the world. It prompted China to implement a new round of economic reforms aimed at increased prosperity, liberalization of trade, and integration into the global community. The financial sector was liberalized by allowing foreign banks to compete on the domestic market. China's WTO commitments included lower tariffs and nondiscriminatory trading rights for both domestic and foreign private firms. The average tariff rate was reduced from 43 percent in 1992 to 17 percent in 1999 and to under 10 percent by 2004. China also lowered average agricultural tariffs to 15 percent. Many imports are now exempt from tariffs, and in fact many goods enter the country duty free. As a result, in

2006 actual tariffs levied relative to the value of imports were a mere 2 percent.[17]

Membership in the WTO has contributed to major growth in international trade and investment, matched by the widening scope and increasing sophistication of commercial operations both in China and overseas. In the space of thirty years, China has emerged from relative insignificance to become, in 2005, the world's third-largest trading nation after the United States and Germany. In 1978, the total value of China's trade was US$20 billion, and it stood at thirtieth among world trading nations—in 2005 this figure had rocketed to $1.4 trillion.

During the ten years since China's admission, the volume of Chinese-American trade increased from US$80.5 billion to $385.3 billion on the Chinese books, or from $121.5 billion to $458.8 billion according to the U.S. figures. To look at this from another angle, American exports to China increased by 81 percent in the three years after China joined the WTO, compared with 34 percent in the three previous years. Similarly, American imports from China rose by 92 percent in the three years following China's WTO entry; they had risen by just 46 percent—exactly half this figure—in the three previous years.

As the business environment improved, American entrepreneurs spared no time in exploring new opportunities. The draw of the China market has been felt across the board by the American business sector. In 2004, Wal-Mart was America's largest corporation, with revenues making up 2 percent of the nation's GDP. Of Wal-Mart's 6,000 suppliers, 80 percent were in China.[18] In 2011, the American-based company Starwood Hotels & Resorts built one hotel in China every two weeks, and China represented 30 percent of its worldwide growth.

Elite sports also proved to be a promising area. The popularity of Chinese center Yao Ming of the Houston Rockets boosted the NBA's China business. In an interview in Guangzhou, NBA commissioner David Stern—the architect of the league's push into the international market—stated that "the China market is our most important and largest market outside the United States."[19]

Another development involves the Chinese automobile sector, which many feared would collapse when foreign competitors swarmed in following China's successful WTO bid. To meet WTO requirements, China reduced its tariff on car imports from 200 percent to 25 percent and scrapped the import quota on automobiles in 2005. Despite price cuts on imported cars, auto sales soared at home, and China began to tap export markets. Some 43,000 Chinese-made vehicles were exported in 2003, an increase of 96 percent over 2002, and auto exports surged to 173,000 units in 2005.[20] In July 2007, Chery Automobile Co. Ltd, the largest Chinese auto exporter, and the Chrysler Group, the third-largest car manufacturer in the United States, signed a cooperation agreement in Beijing.

Frictions remain in spite of the enhanced economic cooperation over the last ten years. Trade imbalances, intellectual property rights, industrial policy, and investment environment are America's main concerns. China on the other hand expects fair business and investment opportunities on the American and world markets.[21]

## SOCIAL AND ECONOMIC "CONVERGENCE" WITH A NATIONAL AND INTERNATIONAL STAMP

Both countries have attached great political importance to trade relations. From the Chinese government's standpoint, bilateral trade has been important for modernization, although China's economic strategies are often driven more by political than economic considerations. For its part, the U.S. government has regularly subjected economic activity involving China to security and moral constraints. The restrengthening of the U.S. military presence in the Asia-Pacific was a strategic decision. It was made public in November 2011 by President Obama and has been seen as a muscular approach to China by some of America's allies including Australia, Japan, and India. This "new" turn of American security and economic policy toward Asia also promises increased business opportunities in the region.

As happened in the United States following World War II, the expansion of legislative and executive control over foreign trade and the economy has occurred at all levels of government in China. The parallels can be taken further. To a large extent, the American public looks to the government to provide it with increasing levels of security—protection from unemployment and job-related risks, racial or sex discrimination, environmental pollution, and so on.[22] In the last few years, similar trends have found expression in the "security development" (*anquan fazhan* 安全 发展) policy implemented by the Chinese state. As more and more new laws and regulations are put in place, the demands of WTO obligations have increased the scope and capabilities of the state's governance role.[23]

In both countries, some economic issues can no longer circumvent political scrutiny because they are often not purely commercial or legal in character. Some observers would disagree with this assessment, attributing the absence of intellectual property rights in China, for instance, to persisting infrastructural problems; these critics cite facts such as that, in July 2011, China had only as many patent firms as the city of Chicago.[24]

Five interrelated shifting vectors of national and international character have molded the development of Sino-American economic relations from 1990 to 2011.

First and most important are the profound changes wrought in both the American and Chinese economies and their impact on foreign trade, a factor that helps explain the U.S. trade deficit with China. Until the 1970s in the United States, the gap between government spending and taxes, and the gap between imports and exports, were small. In the 1970s and 1980s, however, the U.S. federal budget deficit soared, savings regularly exceeded investment, and the foreign trade balance moved deeply into the red. Borrowing to service the growing national debt became the order of the day. At the time, some Chinese economists speculated that "the large share of the national economy financed by debt and the large share of the government budget allocated to interest payments will eventually bankrupt the U.S. economic system."[25] American economists, however, still dispute whether reducing the budget would have positive effects on investment, economic growth, and the foreign trade deficit. Two senior economists asserted that "it is by no means clear that the foreign trade deficit owes its existence to the budget deficit."[26] Rather, they attributed it to higher levels of imports from Canada, Mexico, Asia, Latin America, Eastern Europe, and other U.S. trading partners. Nevertheless, policy makers in the 1970s and 1980s were concerned about both the deficit in the federal budget and the trade deficit.

It is against this background that America's trade imbalance with China has sparked debate. As one Chinese economist puts it, the U.S. trade deficit with China in 2005 and 2006 was "the largest deficit it has ever recorded with a single economy in history."[27] Critics of China attribute the deficit to a raft of factors, most of which are related to job losses in the U.S. manufacturing sector and obstacles to U.S. exports to China. These include the low cost of Chinese goods and services, arbitrary devaluation of the currency (renminbi, CNY), market-access barriers, poor handling of intellectual property rights, and a low level of government transparency.[28]

China's accession to the WTO has not only liberalized its foreign trade and investment regime but also "institutionalized the process of China's domestic reform externally through the force of WTO obligations."[29] The WTO commitment, for instance, has prodded the Chinese government into easing limits on foreign ownership of domestic financial institutions and loosening restrictions on foreign investment in certain areas. In April 2007 four branches of foreign-funded banks—HSBC Bank (China) Co. Ltd., Standard Chartered Bank (China) Ltd., the Bank of East Asia (China) Ltd., and Citibank (China) Co. Ltd—were duly incorporated and began trading in renminbi retail business. To enhance the protection of intellectual property, China has also mandated the installation of licensed operating software on all computers manufactured in China prior to sale—although implementing these rules throughout the country remains a challenge.

Some economists downplay the significance of the bilateral trade gap: "Given today's globalized manufacturing network, in which most products are made in a multistage process distributed across several countries, the bilateral trade balance has lost much of its economic meaning."[30] One Chinese commentator takes this argument to an extreme:

> The bilateral trade balance is a hot issue in official discussions and news media. However, to economists it is a non-issue. A country's total trade deficit reflects the excess of its national spending over its domestic savings, and bilateral trade balances reflect international comparative advantages and consumer preference. They are topics in different areas of economics. Mixing them is a common mistake. . . . We have to ask ourselves whether it is total trade balance or bilateral trade balance that we care about. More basically, for an international-currency country such as the U.S., one needs to ask why we should care about either at all.[31]

The second major factor impacting U.S.-Chinese economic relations is the shifting role of East Asia in the world economy. Despite its rapid increase in trade, over the decade 1997–2006 China's share of the U.S. global trade deficit remained static in percentage terms, increasing from 27 percent to 28 percent.[32] During the same period, however, the share of the American global trade deficit held by all East Asian countries declined from 70 percent to 45 percent, while the U.S. trade imbalance with the rest of the world increased from 30 percent to 55 percent.

The sharp fall in trade surpluses with the United States experienced by other East Asian nations was explained by the change of destination in Asian manufacturing and direct investment from the United States to China. In 2004, funds from Hong Kong, Japan, South Korea, Singapore, and Taiwan accounted for nearly 60 percent of foreign direct investment in China. According to Swiss investment bank UBS AG and the US-China Business Council, although more than 50 percent of PRC exports by value were products of foreign companies operating in China, most of these firms are based in Hong Kong, Taiwan, and Korea.

Consider toys, footwear, and laptop computers: in the 1960s–70s, Hong Kong was the center of world toy manufacturing—until the entire industry moved to the mainland shortly after China reopened its doors to the outside world. The same phenomenon transformed the shoe industry in the 1980s when Taiwanese manufacturers relocated to the mainland. Laptop production followed suit twenty years later.[33] For many years, Taiwanese companies had accounted for 80 percent of global laptop assembly. But, beginning in 2001, within five years they had transferred all production lines to China to take advantage of the mainland market. By 2006, 80 percent of the world's laptops were being assembled in China.

The integration of the stronger East Asian economies is primarily a business-driven phenomenon, combining China's low-cost manufactures and efficient export arrangements with capital from its regional partners. During the first few years of the twenty-first century, Asian investors have opened 20,000 manufacturing facilities a year in China, amounting to a wholesale shift in their operations.

This dynamic regional interpenetration extends to other commercial sectors such as pop culture. Aside from the success of Japanese manga and animation in Hong Kong, Taiwan, China, South Korea, Thailand, and Singapore, South Korea's vibrant cultural industry has also been creating waves in East Asian markets, as a story from 2006 in the *Wall Street Journal* (Europe) illustrates:

> Tokyo. Thin and gorgeous in a slinky black dress, Mikimoto pearls and a low-slung diamond Tiffany pendant, 26-year-old Kazumi Yoshimura already had looks, cash and accessories. There is only one more thing this single Japanese woman says she needs to find eternal bliss—a Korean man. . . . She may just have to take a number and get in line. In

recent years, the wild success of male celebrities from South Korea—
sensitive men but *totally* ripped—has redefined what Asian women
want, from Bangkok to Beijing, from Taipei to Tokyo. . . . Today, South
Korea's trend-setting screen stars and singers dictate everything from
what hair gels people use in Vietnam to what jeans are bought in China. . . . Though the Korean Wave hit Japan relatively late, washing
ashore only within the past 24 to 36 months, the country has quickly
become the largest market for Korean stars. . . . Almost all the major
Korean male stars have opened lucrative "official stores" in Tokyo. In
the three-story boutique of Ryu Siwon, a baby-face[d] Korean actor-
crooner who sings in phonetic Japanese for the local market, the top
floor boasts a recreation of his living room, complete with a life-size,
high-tech plastic model of Mr. Ryu lounging casually on a white leath-
er sofa. It has become a meeting place of sorts for his Japanese fans,
where a gaggle of women sat and stared longingly at his statue on a
recent afternoon.[34]

The third major factor influencing the direction of bilateral business relations is China's openness to and dependence on international trade. The
extent of this shift can be gauged by three separate measures. First, the
growth rate of China's imports has kept pace with exports since 1998. In
the eight years following China's entry into the WTO (2002–10), U.S.
exports to China increased by 416 percent (see table 12.1). Not only was
China the largest importer of high value-added semiconductors, micro-
processors, and airplanes in the world, but it was also an important export market for both raw materials and manufactures for a number of
countries/regions including Singapore, Malaysia, Taiwan, and Brazil. A
report by Oxford Economics and the Signal Group in January 2006 concluded that "China was one of the principal locomotives of global economic growth" over the previous decade.[35] Second, average import tariffs were lowered from over 50 percent in 1982 to under 10 percent in
2005—a low figure compared with 2004 tariff levels in India (29.1 percent), Mexico (18 percent), and Brazil (12.4 percent). This marked reduction in trade barriers is part of China's ongoing economic reform process
aimed at making its market more accessible to foreign imports. Third, the
surging ratio of imports to GDP in China, from 5 percent in 1978 to 30
percent in 2005, is roughly twice the ratio in the United States (17 percent)
and more than three times that in Japan (10 percent). It is also higher than
other large developing countries such as Argentina, Brazil, and India.[36]

America's advantage in commercial services is the fourth factor affecting bilateral trade, which is by no means restricted to the exchange of commodities. Commercial services include a large variety of trade-related activities such as data processing, banking, accounting, insurance and education, legal counsel, management consulting, royalties and license fees, telecommunications, and transportation and travel. As the world's largest importer and exporter of commercial services since the 1970s, the United States ran a total surplus of $64 billion in 2003. In comparison, China has been a net importer of commercial services, especially since joining the WTO in 2001. With China's trade deficit in commercial services reaching US$9 billion in 2003, for example, the United States has a golden opportunity in this lucrative sector.[37] Both countries also have mutual obligations to curb violations of intellectual property rights, in particular in the software and culture industries.

Fifth, in reaction to the post-2008 financial downturn, as well as the sovereign debt and Euro crises, advocates of a new world economic order have called for a rebalancing of global demand, a question which will arguably become a major, politically charged issue in U.S.-Chinese economic relations in the years to come.[38] There will no doubt be controversy over the definition of "imbalances" and the measures needed to address them. To some, this means that the United States will need to significantly reduce its deficit, save more, and spend less, whereas emerging markets and economies with large surpluses—such as China—should spend more and reduce exports. On the other hand, pro-China critics argue that the characterization of China as a "currency manipulator" is unfounded, and that rebalancing the global economy will be achieved through fine-tuning the decision-making structures of the IMF, the World Bank, and other international organizations, adjustments that would allow emerging economies to play a greater role in monitoring American economic policies.[39] These disagreements, however, merely serve to underscore the perception that the economic relationship between the United States and China will "play a large part in determining the future of humanity."[40]

As Greece, Ireland, Spain, and Italy are beleaguered by national indebtedness, the sovereign debt and Euro troubles have dragged on around the world. Developing countries including the BRIC states (Brazil, Russia, India, and China) called on the national leaders of the European Union member states, Japan, and the United States to carry out urgent reforms—measures similar to those introduced by the Chinese, for example, to restructure their own political and financial system in the 1990s.

## "PROSELYTIZING" AMERICA AND "CULTURAL CHINA"

Shifting the focus to religion, society, and culture, this section investigates U.S.-Chinese relations from another angle. It sheds further light on a "crucial global relationship" that is warm in some aspects but lukewarm and even icy in others. A composite of ideological and cultural forces have, since the 1990s, been absorbed into a sharpened moral crusade which pitted American politics and values against those of China. This represented a major shift away from America's "softness" on human rights abuses in China during the previous decade; in the 1980s, while courting China for strategic reasons, the U.S. government did not hesitate to condemn political repression in the Soviet Union and South Africa. In the 2000s, China's response to hardened American criticism has been the promotion of "Cultural China"—a loose phrase for the concerted official efforts at spreading Chinese civilization and influence overseas, although it also reflects China's renewed confidence in the efficacy of the Chinese way in the contemporary world.

### *"Proselytizing" America: Human Rights, Religion, and Politics*

Support for human rights—in close association with religious freedom and independence for Tibet in the case of China—has remained an important component of American foreign policy.[41] More than just policy questions, they have proven to be controversial, emotional, and sentimental issues for Chinese and American officials and ordinary citizens alike. While the renewed controversy over China in the United States in the 1990s was triggered by the Tiananmen crisis of 1989, it continued to play a role in defining the political and cultural predicaments of the bilateral relationship.

An amalgam of highly contentious issues—trade, advanced technology exports, human rights, religion, Tibet, and China's one-child policy—lay in the eye of the storm when President Bill Clinton visited China in late June 1998. Although condemnation of China in the United States in the post-Tiananmen 1990s did not necessarily translate into coordinated action, these issues provided the American executive branch, Congress, Christian lobbyists, human rights advocates, and business corporations—bodies linked by a murky enmeshment of interests—plenty of political ammunition.[42]

In 1996, American Christian groups, including the National Association of Evangelicals—allegedly numbering more than 10 million Christians in forty-seven denominations—launched a mass movement that framed persecution of Christians as a global concern. The movement aimed at moralizing American foreign policy, urging the U.S. federal government to respond to anti-Christian actions in countries such as China, North Korea, Vietnam, Cuba, Sudan, Pakistan, Saudi Arabia, Iran, Egypt, and Algeria.[43] In response to this pressure, in November 1996 President Clinton appointed a twenty-member advisory committee on religious freedom abroad to the secretary of state. In July 1997, the U.S. State Department released its first comprehensive report on the global persecution of Christians, directing sharp criticisms at China in particular.

As religious and human rights activists in the United States honed their rhetoric against the Chinese government, they garnered support for legislation such as the International Religious Freedom Act (the Nickles-Lieberman bill) of 1998.[44] This act reflected the growing efforts by evangelical Christians at shaping politics, foreign policy, and public life in America since the Reagan years (1981–89). The new "China bashers" of the 1990s were well on the way to linking the persecution of Christianity with the "free Tibet" movement, demanding that the U.S. government take a tough stance on the Chinese state.

Congressional opponents called Clinton's intended visit a "tragedy" and a "disaster." Over 150 lawmakers urged him not to go.[45] China's control over religion was "totally unacceptable and ought to be condemned," exclaimed Chris Smith, a Republican representative from New Jersey.[46] "Can religion and communism peacefully coexist?" asked one online news report, highlighting the fissure between officially approved churches and underground worshipers.[47]

Nevertheless, Americans were far from unanimous in their criticisms of China. A 1997 piece in the *Christian Science Monitor* downplayed the issue: "Most Christians who monitor the situation in China closely say they have not detected any special crackdown of late. Comparisons with the 1966 to 1969 Cultural Revolution, when all religion was banned and churches closed or turned into warehouses, are considered absurd."[48]

The business sector—China's chief advocates in the United States—including many Fortune 500 companies, frowned on turning the campaign against China into a political football. According to Jeffrey Goldberg, the American business community discerned "distinctly political, and not humanitarian, motivations behind the evangelical right's interest in China."[49] When asked about his attitude to human rights violations in China, Philip M. Condit, chairman and CEO of the Boeing Company, responded with caution: "They are the same ones that I have about human rights violations in the United States. . . . I happened to be in China during the Rodney King beating. Now, there is a whole bunch of background that goes along with that. But watching that on CNN in China, their perspective was, 'What was that about?'"[50]

Unlike the situation in the 1970s, in the 1990s any lingering memories of the historical anti-Christian movements in China were pushed aside, replaced in the United States by a strong, indeed triumphalist, sense of moral superiority—an attitude that corresponded to the booming American economy in the Clinton era.

In February 2002 and November 2005, President George W. Bush made two trips to China. He openly criticized the Chinese government for controlling the practice and promotion of Christianity, indicating the kind of American idealism that sought to change the world as well as get China to conform to the American way.

Perceived as one of the most pro-evangelical presidents in recent American history, George W. Bush expanded the federal government's involvement with religion. China's progress in the areas of religion and social freedom was outrun by American expectations.

In contrast to his predecessor, President Bush was more than willing to use strong rhetoric against the Chinese government. Bush prefaced his talks with Chinese President Jiang Zemin by stating that he hoped that "as a president of a great nation, Jiang would understand the important role of religion in an individual's life."[51] By contrast, before his 1998 China trip, Clinton had argued for a conciliatory understanding of China's "historical nightmares" to avoid criticizing China too harshly. Clinton's attitude to the Chinese president was almost playful; the *New York Times* reported that he had spent "'a lot of time' coaching Mr. Jiang [Zemin] during his trip to Washington last year on how to handle their joint news conference. . . . Mr. Clinton said he had told Mr. Jiang, 'You've got to learn how to smile when they hit you right between the eyes.' I said, 'That's the way we do it over here.'" [52]

During his 2005 visit, while Bush affirmed that the Gangwashi Church, one of the officially authorized churches in Beijing, was "a real church," he explicitly called for more religious freedom. [53] By contrast, on his visit, Clinton had joined in worship at the Chongwenmen Church in Beijing, another official church. In public, Clinton's comments about the state of Protestantism in China were guarded: "I believe our faith calls upon us to seek unity with people across the world of different races and backgrounds and creeds." [54]

Compared with his two immediate predecessors, President Obama's visit to China in mid-November 2009 was low key and less fractious, leaving both Chinese dissidents and American China activists disappointed. [55] Obama steered clear of public meetings with political activists and lawyers while in Beijing, despite numerous requests that he promote the United States as the protector of universal values on the trip. His skirting of sensitive issues of human rights led some reporters to joke that Obama's trip "had driven the homeless from Beijing and brought more censorship to China." [56] The American press commented that, in many ways, Obama had assumed the role of "profligate spender coming to pay his respects to his banker." [57]

Repeated American criticism has encouraged the Chinese state to develop a legal framework to increase its control over its domestic religious affairs. Through the Regulations on Religious Affairs passed in 2005, to give one example, the state strengthened its management of religious bodies across all sectors of society. [58] Flourishing religious activity has given the Chinese government the ammunition needed to justify the imposition of strict parameters managed by state agencies. To defend their actions, Chinese officials have employed the same language of human rights and the rule of law as their critics. In response to a question by a senior American journalist about political reform, Premier Wen Jiabao brought up the issue of freedom of religion without prompting: "[F]reedom of religious beliefs is actually written into China's constitution. . . . Since the beginning of reform and opening up, one religious site has been either newly built or restored every three days." [59]

*"Cultural China" (wenhua Zhongguo 文化中国) and Its Predicaments*

Since the beginning of the new millennium, the notion of "Cultural China" has gained currency both inside and outside the nation as the "third pillar" of Chinese diplomacy, next to economic and political diplomacy.[60] Guided by the government, Cultural China is both internally and externally driven. Domestically, it is integral to the national program for cultural rejuvenation. In his keynote report to the 17th National Congress of the Central Committee of the Communist Party of China, President and General Secretary Hu Jintao outlined the party's goals for cultural and international development: "The great rejuvenation of the Chinese nation will definitely be accompanied by the thriving of Chinese culture."[61] On the international front, the Cultural China ideology took shape as China became frustrated with the misalignment between its self-image as a peace-loving, harmonious nation and its image in the United States and other countries as authoritarian, militaristic, and obstructive. For the Chinese government, public diplomacy became a favored route for promoting China to the catbird seat in the court of international opinion.[62]

Among many of the projects associated with it, two important aspects of Cultural China include the preservation of Chinese heritage and the establishment of branches of the Confucius Institute throughout the world.[63] Over the last thirty years, China's flourishing cultural industry has added a substantial number of locations to UNESCO's World Heritage sites. Following its admission to the World Heritage Convention in 1985, in 2010 China ranked third in the total number of World Heritage properties (forty sites), hard on the heels of Italy (forty-four) and Spain (forty-two), among 187 state members. China is also proud of its significant role in the drafting of the Convention for the Safeguarding of Intangible Cultural Heritage adopted in 2003 and the Convention on the Protection and Promotion of the Diversity of Cultural Expressions in 2005.

The Confucius Institute, a nonprofit government organization headquartered in Beijing, represents another strategic investment in the cultural industry both inside and outside of China. Within just six years of the opening of the first institute in Maryland in 2004, seventy Confucius Institutes have been planted in the United States, taking the grand total to 322 in ninety-one countries and regions in five continents. The institute teaches Chinese language and culture, administers the Chinese Proficiency Test overseas, and hosts international visits and cultural events.[64]

This is also a convenient place to mention an important intercultural phenomenon, the Chinese-American educational exchange programs that since 1978 have facilitated a high volume of people-to-people contact. In 2009, China regained its place as the largest supplier—outstripping India—of students (nearly 130,000 that year) who have gone to the United States for study purposes. In 2010, U.S. educational institutions admitted over 150,000 mainland Chinese students. In the same year, China ranked as the fifth-largest destination for American students (over 13,000) wanting to study abroad. Between 2001 and 2010, over 800,000 Chinese students traveled to the United States to study, with over half a million in the last five years of the decade.[65] What does this human capital investment bring to American-Chinese relations? The asymmetrical flow of personnel itself mirrors the imbalance of power in the relationship, even after taking into account the population ratio between the two nations (1.3 billion versus 0.3 billion). Despite the wide-ranging and complex issues involved, during the last ten years both countries have been growing progressively more open to each other in particular areas.[66]

Have these varied cultural and educational encounters helped improve American views of China? The findings of a recent study about the impact of the 2008 Beijing Olympics on American attitudes toward China are revealing. An academic survey conducted in the United States in August 2008, the month the Olympics took place, indicated that Americans viewed China more negatively than before. China's successful hosting of and competition in the games appeared to have heightened American anxieties about a resurgent China—in addition to other factors such as the scandals involving underage Chinese gymnasts and lip-synching by a child singing star at the opening ceremony.[67]

Finally, the incongruities inherent in U.S.-Chinese relations are no better illustrated than by the fate of the Bible in contemporary China, where the Christian scriptures have become the object of commercial mass production. Since its founding in 1986, the Amity Printing Press in Nanjing has printed over 50 million copies of the Bible in seventy-five languages and exported Bibles to more than sixty countries, leading the *Los Angeles Times* to assert that "a booming Bible industry is on its way to turning the world's biggest atheist nation into the world's largest producer of the Good Book."[68]

## FURTHER READING

Based on oral interviews, Sang Ye's *China Candid: The People on the People's Republic*, ed. Geremie R. Barmé with Miriam Lang (Berkeley, Calif.: University of California Press, 2006) is packed with witty commentary by ordinary Chinese from a wide range of backgrounds about contemporary China and its opening up to the United States and the wider world. This book forms a sharp contrast with Perry Link's *Evening Chats in Beijing: Probing China's Predicament* (New York: Norton, 1992), which presents, through the pen of an American academic, the responses of some Chinese intellectuals to the dilemmas inherent in Chinese history, society, and Deng Xiaoping's reforms at the time of the 1989 Tiananmen crisis.

For China's engagement with America and other countries over the last twenty years, see Robert S. Ross, Øystein Tunsjø, and Zhang Tuosheng, eds., *US-China-EU Relations: Managing the New World Order* (London: Routledge, 2010); Elizabeth Economy and Michel Oksenberg, eds., *China Joins the World: Progress and Prospects* (New York: Council on Foreign Relations Press, 1999); David Zweig, *Internationalizing China: Domestic Interest and Global Linkages* (Ithaca, N.Y.: Cornell University Press, 2002). They are usefully read together with Michael H. Hunt, *Ideology and U.S. Foreign Policy* (New Haven, Conn.: Yale University Press, 1987); William R. Keylor, *A World of Nations: The International Order since 1945* (Oxford: Oxford University Press, 2003); Joseph S. Nye Jr., *The Paradox of American Power: Why the World's Only Superpower Can't Go It Alone* (New York: Oxford University Press, 2002); and David M. Lampton, *The Three Faces of Chinese Power: Might, Money, and Minds* (Berkeley, Calif.: University of California Press, 2008).

## NOTES

1. Economic convergence is a component of the neoclassical concept about economic growth known as the Robert Solow-Trevor Swan model. The model holds that, in the long run, poor countries will eventually catch up or converge with rich nations in production output and per capita income, and that each economy has its own growth ceiling to its GDP, dependent on variables such as the level of technological innovation, the rate of savings, labor levels and depreciation, and the adequacy of state management. Robert M. Solow, "A Contribution to the Theory of Economic Growth," *Quarterly Journal of Economics* 70, no. 1 (February 1956): 65–94; Trevor W. Swan, "Economic Growth and Capital Accumulation," *Economic Record* 32, no. 63 (November 1956): 334–361.

2. Zhongguo guoji wenti yanjiusuo (中国国际问题研究所), *Guoji xingshi he Zhong-guo waijiao lanpishu (2009/2010)* [国际形势和中国外交蓝皮书 The bluebook of the international situation and China's foreign affairs] (Beijing: Shijie zhishi chubanshe, 2010), chapter 18.

3. The US-China Business Council, April 2011, "China and the US Economy: Advancing a Winning Trade Agenda, a Guide for the 112th Congress," p. 12, https://www.uschina.org/info/trade-agenda/uscbc-trade-agenda-report.pdf (accessed July 29, 2011).

4. The US-China Business Council, April 2011, "China and the US Economy," p. 5.

5. The People's Republic of China General Administration of Customs, *China's Customs Statistics*, US-China Business Council, http://www.uschina.org/statistics/tradetable.html (accessed July 29, 2011).

6. This estimate is based on figures in Harry Harding's *A Fragile Relationship: The United States and China* (Washington, D.C.: Brookings Institution, 1992), p. 99, where the 1971 figure is set at US$4.7 million, and Tao Wenzhao's *Zhongmei guanxishi* [中美关系史 A history of Sino-American relations] (Shanghai: Shanghai renmin chubanshe, 2004), vol. 3, 1972–2000, p. 339, where the figure is set at zero.

7. "US-China Trade Statistics and China's World Trade Statistics," US-China Business Council, http://www.uschina.org/statisticss/tradetable.html (accessed July 29, 2011, and July 18, 2012).

8. U.S. Census Bureau, Foreign Trade Statistics, http://www.census.gov/foreign-trade/top/index.html #top_partners (accessed December 2, 2007, and July 29, 2011).

9. Raphael Kaplinsky and Dirk Messner, "Introduction: The Impact of Asian Drivers on the Developing World," *World Development* 36, no. 2 (February 2008): 197–209.

10. Lynn Chu, "The Chimera of the China Market," *The Atlantic* 266, no. 4 (October 1990): 56–64.

11. http://wto.org/english/thewto_e/whatis_e/tif_e/fact1_e.htm (accessed April 23, 2007).

12. Zhang Shengqiu (张盛秋), "Long Yongtu yu jiaru Shimao zuzhi" [龙永图与加入世贸组织 Long Yongtu and the WTO accession], in Zhang Shengen (张神根) and Duanmu qinghua (端木清华), comps., *Gaige kaifang sanshi nian zhongda juece shimo, 1978–2008* [改革开放三十年重大决策始末 A comprehensive study of important policy-making over 30 years of reform] (Chengdu: Sichuan renmin chubanshe, 2008), pp. 317–322.

13. Long Yongtu, "'Rushi' tanpan shi zheyang wanchengde" ["入世"谈判是这样完成的 How the WTO talks were completed], in Wang Gang (王刚), Lu Lin (鲁林), and Jin Baochen (金宝辰), eds., *Zhongguo Gongchandang lishi koushu shilu, 1978–2000* [中国共产党历史口述实录 An oral history of the Chinese Communist Party, 1978-2000] (Jinan: Jinan chubanshe, 2002), pp. 436–450.

14. Chinese UN envoy Huang Xueqi's speech at the UN second committee, November 13, 1999, *Summary of World Broadcasts*, November 15, 1999, FE/3692 G/1and G/2.

15. Long Yongtu, "'Rushi' tanpan shi zheyang wanchengde."

16. Author unknown, "Selected Documents on the China-US Agreement on the WTO," *China Report* 36, no. 2 (2000): 293–321.

17. Nicholas R. Lardy, "The Only Way Is Up," *Beijing Review* 50, no. 16 (April 19, 2007): 18–19.

18. Fareed Zakaria, "China's Century," *Newsweek*, May 9, 2005, pp. 28–29.

19. Associated Press, "Stein's Foreign Policy Tilts toward China," *Korean Herald*, August 8, 2006, p. 15.

20. Yunyun Liu, "Growing Pains or Growing Gains," *Beijing Review*, December 21, 2006, 32–34.

21. See the *People's Daily*'s interview on February 15, 2012, with Gao Hucheng, China international trade representative and vice commerce minister, http://english .mofcom.gov.cn/aarticle/newsrelease/significantnews/201202/20120207966357.html (accessed July 19, 2012).

22. Price Rishback, Robert Higgs, Gary D. Libecap, et al., *Government and the American Economy: A New History* (Chicago, Ill.: University of Chicago Press, 2007), chapter 17.

23. Chen Jiagui (陈佳贵) and Li Yang (李扬), eds., *2011 Nian Zhongguo jingji xingshi fenxi yu yuce* [2011年中国经济形势分析与预测 The Chinese economy: An analysis and forecast for 2011] (Beijing: Shehui kexue wenxian chubanshe, 2010).

24. CCTV-9 International (English channel), *Dialogue* (Europe July 11, 2011).

25. Teh-wei Hu, "Teaching about the American Economy in the People's Republic of China," *Journal of Economic Education* 19, no. 1 (Winter 1988): 87–96.

26. Gary M. Walton and Hugh Rockoff, *History of the American Economy*, 8th ed. (Fort Worth, Tex.: Dayton Press, 1998), pp. 733–735.

27. Pingfan Hong, "China's Economic Prospects and Sino-US Economic Relations," *China & World Economy* 14, no. 2 (2006): 45–55.

28. Han Yugui (韩玉贵), *Lengzhan hou de Zhongmei guanxi* [冷战后的中美关系 Sino-American relations in the post–Cold War era] (Beijing: Shehui kexue wenxian chuban-she, 2007). Yang Guohua (杨国华), *Zhongmei zhishi chanquan wenti gaiguan* [中美知识产权问题概观 A brief examination of the U.S.-Chinese intellectual property question] (Beijing: Zhishi chanquan chubanshe, 2008). Ling Jintao (凌金涛), *Zhishi chanquan yu Zhongmei guanxi, 1989–1996* [知识产权与中美关系 Intellectual property rights and Sino-American relations] (Shanghai: Shanghai renmin chubanshe, 2007). John Frisbie, "China's Implementation of Its World Trade Organization Commitments: An Assessment by the US-China Business Council," Testimony for the Trade Policy Staff Committee on October 2, 2009, (Washington, D.C.: US-China Business Council, 2009).

29. Julia Ya Qin, "Trade, Investment and Beyond: The Impact of WTO Accession on China's Legal System," *China Quarterly*, special issue, no. 191 (September 2007): 720–744.

30. Pingfan Hong, "China's Economic Prospects and Sino-US Economic Relations."

31. Hang-Sheng Cheng, "Comments on Xianquan Xu's Chapter," in Shuxun Chen and Charles Wolf Jr., ed., *China, the United States, and the Global Economy* (Santa Monica, Calif.: RAND, 2001), p. 253.

32. "US-China Trade in Context," http://www.uschina.org/public/documents/2007/ 05/uscbc-us-china-trade-in-context-2007.pdf (accessed October 22, 2007).

33. Tse-Kang Leng, "State and Business in the Era of Globalization: The Case of Cross-Strait Linkages in the Computer Industry," *China Journal*, no. 53 (January 2005): 63–79.

34. Anthony Faiola, "All around Asia, Love-Struck Women Want Men with a Little Bit of Seoul," *Wall Street Journal* (Europe), September 1–3 (Friday–Sunday), 2006.

35. "The China Effect: Assessing the Impact on the US Economy of Trade and Investment with China," *China Business Forum*, January 2006, p. 3, http:// www.chinabusinessforum.org/pdf/the-china-effect.pdf (accessed April 15, 2007).

36. Fred C. Bergsten, Bates Gill, Nicholas R. Lardy, and Derek Mitchell, *China: The Balance Sheet; What the World Needs to Know about the Emerging Superpower* (New York: PublicAffairs, 2006), pp. 81–84.

37. Sarah Y. Tong, "The US-China Trade Imbalance: How Big Is It Really?" *China: An International Journal* 3, no. 1 (March 2005): 131–154.

38. Secretary of the Treasury Timothy F. Geithner, "Written Testimony before the Senate Foreign Relations Committee," November 17, 2009, http://www.ustreas.gov/press/releases/tg410.htm (accessed July 1, 2010).

39. Xiaojing Zhang, "Rebalancing the Global Economy," in Foresight, ed., *Global Power Revisited: The United States in a Changing World Order* (Berlin: Foresight, 2009), pp. 15–17.

40. John King Fairbank, *The United States and China*, 4th enlarged ed. (Cambridge, Mass.: Harvard University Press, 1976), foreword by Edwin O. Reischauer.

41. WikiLeaks, December 21, 2009, cable, Reference ID: 09BEIJING3416, released on December 9, 2010. Michael Wines, "Leaked Cables Offer Glimpses into Relations of U.S. and China," *New York Times*, September 4, 2011, http://www.nytimes.com/2011/09/05/world/asia/05china.html (accessed November 4, 2011).

42. Donald D. A. Schaefer, "U.S. Foreign Policies of Presidents Bush and Clinton: The Influence of China's Most Favored Nation Status upon Human Rights Issues," *Social Science Journal* 35, no. 3 (July 1998): 407–415. David Skidmore and William Gates, "After Tiananmen: The Struggle over U.S. Policy toward China in the Bush Administration," *Presidential Studies Quarterly*, 27, no. 3 (Summer 1997): 514–526.

43. Peter Steinfels, "Evangelicals Lobby for Oppressed Christians," and "Evangelicals Ask Government to Fight Persecution of Christians," *New York Times*, January 23 and September 15, 1996. Jeffrey Goldberg, "Washington Discovers Christian Persecution," *New York Times*, December 21, 1997.

44. Carol Lee Hamrin, "Advancing Religious Freedom in a Global China: Conclusions," in Jason Kindopp and Carol Lee Hamrin, eds., *God and Caesar in China: Policy Implications of Church-State Tensions* (Washington, D.C.: Brookings Institution Press, 2004), pp. 165–185. Xu Yihua, "Meiguo '1998 nian guoji zongjiao ziyoufa'" [美国"1998年国际宗教自由法" The U.S. International Religious Freedom Act of 1998], in Xu Yihua, ed., *Zongjiao yu Meiguo shehui* [宗教与美国社会 Religion and American society] (Beijing: Shishi chubanshe, 2004), vol. 2, pp. 515–546.

45. Ann Scott Tyson, "Clinton vs. Nixon: Changed US Views on Trip to China," *Christian Science Monitor*, June 24, 1998, p. 3.

46. Erik Eckholm, "Wary Flock: A Special Report; China's Churches: Glad, and Bitter, Tidings," *New York Times*, June 17, 1998, A1.

47. Rebecca Mackinnon, "Chinese Christians a Small but Growing Minority," http://www.cnn.com/WORLD/asiapcf/9806/27/china.christians (accessed April 2, 2008).

48. Todd Crowell, "China's Crusade against Christians: No Change," *Christian Science Monitor*, October 31, 1997, p. 6, 1c.

49. Jeffrey Goldberg, "Washington Discovers Christian Persecution."

50. Jeffrey Goldberg, "Washington Discovers Christian Persecution."

51. Todd Hertz, "Bush: 'I'm One of Them,'" *Christianity Today*, February 2002, http://www.ctlibrary.com/ct/2002/februaryweb-only/2-25-31.0.html (accessed February 4, 2007).

52. Elaine Sciolino, "Clinton Argues for 'Flexibility' over Sanctions," *New York Times* , April 28, 1998, A1.

53. "President Attends Church Service at Gangwashi Church in Beijing, China," November 20, 2005, http://www.whitehouse.gov/news/releases/2005/11/print/20051120-5.html (accessed February 4, 2007).

54. Erick Eckholm, "Clinton in China: Christians; Protestants, Delighted, Feel Clinton's Visit Moves the Cause Onward," *New York Times*, June 29, 1998, A8.

55. Elizabeth Lynch, "The Obama Visit to China: What the U.S. Press Missed," *Huffington Post*, November 23, 2009, http://www.huffingtonpost.com/elizabeth-lynch/the-obama-visit-to-china_b_367459.html (accessed July 31, 2011).

56. Michael Wines and Sharon LaFraniere, "During Visit, Obama Skirts Chinese Political Sensitivities," *New York Times*, November 18, 2009, http://www.nytimes.com/2009/11/18/world/asia/18prexy.html?pagewanted=print (accessed July 29, 2011).

57. Helene Cooper, Michael Wines, and David E. Sanger, "China's Role as Lender Alters Obama's Visit," *New York Times*, November 15, 2009, http://www.nytimes.com/2009/11/15/world/asia/15china.html (accessed July 31, 2011).

58. For the full text of the regulations in Chinese and English, see http://www.china.com.cn/chinese/PI-c/732332.htm and http://www.amityfoundation.org/cms/user/3/docs/decree_426.pdf (both files accessed August 7, 2011).

59. Interview with Wen Jiabao by Leonard Downie Jr., executive editor of the *Washington Post* on November 21, 2003, http://www.washingtonpost.com/ac2/wp-dyn/A6641-2003Nov22?language=printer (accessed July 16, 2011).

60. Cai Wu (蔡武), *Gaige kaifang sanshi nian Zhongguo wenhua de fazhan* [改革开放三十年中国文化的发展 China's cultural development over thirty years of reform and opening up] (Beijing: Waiwen chubanshe, 2009), pp. 37–68.

61. Beijing Review, "Charting Roadmap for China: Special Report, 17th CPC Congress," *Beijing Review* 50, no 43 (October 11, 2007).

62. Lü Hong (吕鸿) and Zheng Hong (郑红), "Jixinge duihua Zhao Qizheng: Zui zhengui de bushi gaolou dasha, ershi gonggong waijiao" [基辛格对话赵启正:最珍贵的不是高楼大厦,而是公共外交 A dialogue between Henry Kissinger and Zhao Qizheng: The most valued assets are not skyscrapers but public diplomacy], March 22, 2011, Renminwang, http://world.people.com.cn/GB/14203342.html# (accessed January 27, 2012).

63. Dong Wang, "Internationalizing Heritage: UNESCO and China's Longmen Grottoes," *China Information* 24, no. 2 (July 2010): 123–147; Dong Wang, "Restructuring Governance in Contemporary Urban China: Perspectives on State and Society," *Journal of Contemporary China* 20, no. 72 (November 2011): 723–733.

64. http://www.hanban.org (accessed January 26, 2012).

65. Data gathered from the Institute of International Education, Open Doors Data, http://www.iie.org/en/Research-and-Publications/Open-Doors (accessed January 26, 2012).

66. The issues and problems around educational exchanges are further discussed in David Zweig, Chen Changgui, and Stanley Rosen, "Globalization and Transnational Human Capital: Overseas and Returnee Scholars to China," *China Quarterly* 179, (September 2004): 735–757; Tricia Coverdale-Jones and Paul Rastall, eds., *Internationalizing the University: The Chinese Context* (New York: Palgrave, 2009).

67. Peter Hays Gries, H. Michael Crowson, and Todd Sandel, "The Olympic Effect on American Attitudes towards China: Beyond Personality, Ideology, and Media Exposure," *Journal of Contemporary China* 19, no. 64 (2010): 213–231.

68. Ching-Ching Ni, "Bibles Are Big Business in China," *Los Angeles Times*, June 21, 2008, http://www.latimes.com/news/nationworld/world/la-fg-bible22-2008jun22,0,2725020.story (accessed June 22, 2008).

# Epilogue

My account of American-Chinese relations begins with private commerce in 1784—relatively minuscule in terms of global geopolitics and the world economy—and concludes with the conviction that political cooperation between the world's two economic powerhouses is in the interests of the United States, China, and indeed the world in the twenty-first century. What lessons and legacies can their shared past offer to help improve their contemporary relationship?

Over the last 230 years, the United States has rapidly developed from thirteen former British colonies into a strong, self-conscious nation-state, and then into an empire that has a privileged position in international political, financial, and military institutions. China, on the other hand, has transformed itself from a decaying empire into a staunch defender of its national sovereignty—although it has had only a limited part to play in the postwar construction of the international order.

China's historic "catch-up" over the last thirty years has boosted its cultural confidence and sense of place in the world, following two centuries of dynastic decline and constant revolutions. But China has yet to earn respect for a political system that has been openly disdained by Americans and others.[1] The Chinese people are yet to make skeptics believe that they are a peaceful nation with no military designs on other countries. Many Americans will take some comfort in the likelihood that the socioeconomic gap between the United States and China will remain in place for the foreseeable future.[2] In 1980, when China's economic reconstruction had only just begun, the U.S. population stood at 235 million and its gross domestic product (GDP) per capita was over US$25,000 (in 2005 dollars). China's population at the time was over 900 million and its GDP per capita was about $220. Thirty years later, although the economic gulf has been significantly reduced, the American GDP per capita (with 0.3 billion people) is more than ten times that of China (1.3 billion people), and the American economy is nearly 2.5 times larger than China's (2011 figures).

At the beginning of the new millennium, the bilateral relationship is a major security concern for each side. Many critics have pointed out that the United States needs an external enemy to stay focused, and that it has a near-pathological need to maintain "absolute security at all costs."[3] But strategic rivalry and military confrontation, in today's entangled and diverse world, are not only too costly but also bring no benefits to either the countries involved or humanity as a whole.

Drawing on his personal experience as an architect of American-Chinese relations and a scholar of international diplomacy, Henry Kissinger spoke in 2011 of the necessity of avoiding a military solution to the Sino-U.S. conflict in the twenty-first century. He described this as the "great challenge of our time":

> The foreign policy of Moscow followed an imperialist tradition. The expansion of its power was always to some extent linked to asserting military might. By contrast, China has historically asserted its influence through some sort of cultural imperialism. China's influence on its neighbors did not depend on the threat of invasion. Containing China's power, therefore, does not primarily mean military containment. It means creating foreign policy frameworks. It is a totally different type of containment. . . . America continues to believe in its exceptional status, its exceptionalism—basically like China does. Two different kinds of exceptionalism stand face to face in the form of the U.S.A. and China. American exceptionalism is missionary. The Chinese exceptionalism is culturally influential, but does not seek to convert people.[4]

In an atmosphere of complex fluidity in the Asia-Pacific and across the Pacific in summer 2012 when I was finishing the last few lines of this book in Northern Europe, it may sound naive to suggest that the United States and China need to work together on friendly terms to secure a better future for all. But progress, patience, and, most importantly, peace are the proven historical cure for the various ills engendered by their interactions.

## FURTHER READING[5]

John King Fairbank—doyen of American China scholars—reshaped the study of U.S.-Chinese relations through his emphasis on educating Americans about China. His single-authored volume *The United States and China* offers a corrective to studies such as those by Tyler Dennett and

Alfred Whitney Griswold, which focus on American high diplomacy in East Asia. But this new emphasis has created its own set of predicaments. Its title notwithstanding, Fairbank's work devotes half of its 632 pages to Chinese history, politics, and society before turning to the American approaches to China. His book also omitted discussion of Chinese experiences of and perspectives on the relationship. See:

> Tyler Dennett, *Americans in East Asia: A Critical Study of United States Policy in the Far East in the Nineteenth Century*, reprint (New York: Barnes & Noble, 1963; 1st ed. in 1922 by Macmillan).
>
> Alfred Whitney Griswold, *The Far Eastern Policy of the United States* (New Haven, Conn.: Yale University Press, 1966; 1st ed. in 1938 by Harcourt, Brace).
>
> John K. Fairbank, *The United States and China*, 4th ed. (Cambridge, Mass.: Harvard University Press, 1983; 1st ed. in 1948).

There are several other useful general studies of the subject. Primarily grounded in English-language sources, Michael Schaller's survey is succinct, but focuses on American-Chinese relations during the 1930s–60s. While Warren I. Cohen places American policy toward China in a broad international setting, his main concern is "the response of American statesmen who sought to devise an East Asian policy consistent with the ideals and interests of their people" (preface to the 1st ed.). Understandably, Cohen's paradigm of "American-response-to-China" does not pretend to cover the Chinese side of the relationship. Robert Sutter's book represents a contemporary social sciences approach, with most of the volume devoted to analyzing the fluctuations in issues of security, the economy, the environment, Taiwan, and human rights since 1989. Sutter concludes that while a rapid improvement in the relationship is unrealistic, a drastic reversal is equally unlikely. Henry Kissinger in his *On China* examines the bilateral relationship in an evolving world. See:

> Michael Schaller, *The United States and China: Into the Twenty-First Century*, 3rd ed. (Oxford: Oxford University Press, 2002; 1st ed. in 1979).
>
> Warren I. Cohen, *America's Response to China: A History of Sino-American Relations*, 5th ed. (New York: Columbia University Press, 2010; 1st ed. in 1971).
>
> Robert Sutter, *U.S.-Chinese Relations: Perilous Past, Pragmatic Present* (Lanham, Md.: Rowman & Littlefield, 2010).

Henry Kissinger, *On China* (New York: Penguin, 2011).

Complementary to the few general works in English discussed above, a comparable list of texts in Chinese would start with Tao Wenzhao (陶文钊), *Zhongmei guanxi shi* [中美关系史 A history of Sino-American relations] (Shanghai: Shanghai renmin chubanshe, 2004, vol. 1, 1911–49; vol. 2, 1949–72; vol. 3, 1972–2000). Drawing on original research, this three-volume study highlights Chinese viewpoints on important issues, particularly the political and geo-economic aspects of the bilateral relationship. Two single-volume works that I have consulted are Xiang Liling's (项立岭) *Zhongmei guanxi shi quanbian* [中美关系史全编 A comprehensive history of U.S.-China relations] (Shanghai: Huadong shifan daxue, 2002) and Xiong Zhiyong's (熊志勇) *Bainian Zhongmei guanxi* [百年中美关系 A century of Sino-U.S. relations] (Beijing: Shijie zhishi chubanshe, 2006).

In addition to the works by Fairbank and Cohen cited above, annotated bibliographical guides can also be found in Charles W. Hayford, ed., *Draft Bibliography of American-East Asian Relations*, a special volume of the *Journal of American-East Asian Relations* 8, nos. 1–4 (1999, published in 2002); Warren I. Cohen, ed., *Pacific Passage: The Study of East Asian Relations on the Eve of the Twenty-First Century* (New York: Columbia University Press, 1996) and *New Frontiers in American-East Asian Relations: Essays Presented to Dorothy Borg* (New York: Columbia University Press, 1983); Akira Iriye's *Across the Pacific: An Inner History of American–East Asian Relations*, revised ed. (Chicago, Ill.: Imprint Publications, 1992; 1st ed. 1967), pp. 395–408; and Ernest R. May and James C. Thomson Jr., eds., *American-East Asian Relations: A Survey* (Cambridge, Mass.: Harvard University Press, 1972). An extensive bibliography of studies in Chinese, English, and Japanese is published in *150 nian Zhongmei guanxishi lunzhu mulu (1823–1990)*, ed. Wang Xi (汪熙) and Tajiri Tōru (田尻利), (150年中美关系史论著目录 A bibliography of works on the history of Sino-American relations over the last 150 years) (Shanghai: Fudan daxue chubanshe, 2005), p. 603.

On the American history side, the two-volume *American Foreign Relations: A History*, 7th ed. (Florence, Ky.: Wadsworth Publishing, 2009) by Thomas Paterson et al., provides a point of entry. For further references on the historiography of American foreign relations, see Michael H. Hunt's *The American Ascendancy: How the United States Gained and Wielded Global Dominance* (Chapel Hill, N.C.: University of North Carolina Press, 2007), pp. 357–385; and Robert L. Beisner and Kurt W. Hanson, eds.,

*American Foreign Relations since 1600: A Guide to the Literature,* 2nd ed. (Santa Barbara, Calif.: ABC-CLIO, 2003), 2 vols. Michael J. Hogan and Thomas G. Paterson's *Explaining the History of American Foreign Relations,* 2nd ed. (Cambridge: Cambridge University Press, 2004) surveys research trends and analytical approaches to U.S. foreign affairs.

## NOTES

1. Ramon H. Myers, Michel C. Oksenberg, and David Shambaugh, eds., *Making China Policy: Lessons from the Bush and Clinton Administrations* (Lanham, Md.: Rowman & Littlefield, 2001).

2. See Fareed Zakaria's buoyant analysis of America's future power in his *The Post-American World* (New York: Norton, 2009; 1st ed. 2008).

3. Walter A. McDougall, *Promised Land, Crusader State: The American Encounter with the World since 1776* (Boston, Mass.: Houghton Mifflin, 1998). David C. Unger, *The Emergency State: America's Pursuit of Absolute Security at All Costs* (New York: Penguin, 2012).

4. Henry Kissinger's interview with Matthias Nass, "Der Anfang einer neuen Zeit" [The beginning of a new age], *Die Zeit,* no. 22 (May 26, 2011), p. 23.

5. In formulating my ideas and analysis, I have also benefited from the following works: Ulrich Beck, *The Risk Society: Towards a New Modernity* (Newbury Park, Calif.: Sage, 1992); Ulrich Beck, *Cosmopolitan Vision* (Cambridge: Polity Press, 2007); Craig Calhoun, *Nations Matter: Culture, History, and the Cosmopolitan Dream* (London: Routledge, 2007); Kenneth N. Waltz, *Theories of International Politics* (New York: McGraw-Hill, 1979); Robert O. Keohane and Joseph S. Nye, *Power and Interdependence,* 4th ed. (Boston, Mass.: Longman, 2011); Scott Burchill et al., *Theories of International Relations* (Basingstoke: Palgrave Macmillan, 2005); Robert Powell, *In the Shadow of Power: States and Strategies in International Politics* (Princeton, N.J.: Princeton University Press, 1999); Michael P. Sullivan, *Theories of International Relations: Transition and Persistence* (New York: Palgrave, 2001); and Immanuel Wallerstein, *Geopolitics and Geoculture: Essays on the Changing World-System* (New York: Columbia University Press, 1991).

# Bibliography

Abramowitz, Morton, and Stephen Bosworth. "America Confronts the Asian Century." *Current History* 105, no. 690 (2006): 147–152.

Aldridge, Alfred Owen. *The Dragon and the Eagle: The Presence of China in the American Enlightenment.* Detroit, Mich.: Wayne State University Press, 1993.

Alford, William P. *To Steal a Book Is an Elegant Offense: Intellectual Property Law in Chinese Civilization.* Stanford, Calif.: Stanford University Press, 1997.

Ambrose, Stephen E. "The Presidency and Foreign Policy." *Foreign Affairs* 70, no. 5 (Winter 1991): 120–137.

Asada, Sadao. "Japan's Special Interests and the Washington Conference, 1921–1922." *American Historical Review* 67, no. 1 (October 1961): 62–70.

Atkins, Martyn. *Informal Empire in Crisis: British Diplomacy and the Chinese Customs Succession, 1927–1929.* Ithaca, N.Y.: Cornell University Press, 1995.

Atwell, Pamela. *British Mandarins and Chinese Reformers: The British Administration of Weihaiwei (1898–1930) and the Territory's Return to Chinese Rule.* Oxford: Oxford University Press, 1985.

Auerbach, Sascha. *Race, Law, and "the Chinese Puzzle" in Imperial Britain.* New York: Palgrave Macmillan, 2009.

Bailey, Thomas A. *A Diplomatic History of the American People.* 10th ed. Englewood Cliffs, N.J.: Prentice Hall, 1980.

Barnett, A. Doak. *The Making of Foreign Policy in China: Structure and Process.* Boulder, Colo.: Westview Press, 1985.

———. "The New Multipolar Balance in East Asia: Implications for United States Policy." *Annals of the American Academy of Political and Social Science*, no. 390 (July 1970): 73–86.

Barnett, Susan Wilson, and John King Fairbank, eds. *Christianity in China: Early Protestant Missionary Writings.* Cambridge, Mass.: Harvard University Press, 1985.

Barrett, David D. *Dixie Mission: The United States Army Observer Group in Yenan, 1944.* Berkeley, Calif.: Center for Chinese Studies, University of California, 1979.

Barrett, David P., and Lawrence N. Shyu, eds. *Chinese Collaboration with Japan, 1932–1945: The Limits of Accommodation.* Stanford, Calif.: Stanford University Press, 2001.

Bates, M. Searle. "The Theology of American Missionaries in China, 1900–1950." In *The Missionary Enterprise in China and America*, edited by John King Fairbank. Cambridge, Mass.: Harvard University Press, 1974.

Baum, Richard. *China Watcher: Confessions of a Peking Tom.* Seattle, Wash.: University of Washington Press, 2010.

Bays, Daniel H. *A New History of Christianity in China.* Malden, Mass.: Wiley-Blackwell, 2012.

Beck, Ulrich. *Cosmopolitan Vision.* Cambridge: Polity Press, 2007.

———. *The Risk Society: Towards a New Modernity.* Newbury Park, Calif.: Sage, 1992.

Beeching, Jack. *The Chinese Opium Wars*. San Diego, Calif.: Harvest/HBJ Book, 1975.

Beisner, Robert L., and Kurt W. Hanson, eds. *American Foreign Relations since 1600: A Guide to the Literature*. 2nd ed. 2 vols. Santa Barbara, Calif.: ABC-CLIO, 2003.

Benton, Gregor. *Chinese Migrants and Internationalism: Forgotten Histories, 1917–1945*. New York: Routledge, 2007.

Berger, Peter L., and Samuel P. Huntington. *Many Globalizations: Cultural Diversity in the Contemporary World*. Oxford: Oxford University Press, 2002.

Bergsten, C. Fred, Bates Gill, Nicholas R. Lardy, and Derek Mitchell. *China: The Balance Sheet; What the World Needs to Know Now About the Emerging Superpower*. New York: PublicAffairs, 2006.

Bernstein, Richard, and Ross H. Munro. *The Coming Conflict with China*. New York: Vintage, 1998. 1st ed. in 1997 by Knopf.

Best, Antony, ed. *The International History of East Asia, 1900–1968: Trade, Ideology and the Quest for Order*. London: Routledge, 2010.

Bian, Morris. *The Making of the State Enterprise System in Modern China: The Dynamics of Institutional Change*. Cambridge, Mass.: Harvard University Press, 2005.

Bickers, Robert, and R. G. Tiedemann, eds. *The Boxers, China, and the World*. Lanham, Md.: Rowman & Littlefield, 2007.

Bliss, Edward, Jr. *Beyond the Stone Arches: An American Missionary Doctor in China, 1892–1932*. New York: Wiley, 2001.

Boardman, Eugene P. "Christian Influence Upon the Ideology of the Taiping Rebellion." *Far Eastern Quarterly* 10, no. 2 (February 1951): 115–124.

Borg, Dorothy. *American Policy and the Chinese Revolution, 1925–1928*. New York: Macmillan, 1947.

———. *The United States and the Far Eastern Crisis of 1933–1938: From the Manchurian Incident through the Initial Stage of the Undeclared Sino-Japanese War*. Cambridge, Mass.: Harvard University Press, 1964.

Borg, Dorothy, and Waldo Heinrichs, eds. *Uncertain Years: Chinese-American Relations, 1947–1950*. New York: Columbia University Press, 1980.

Brinkley, Alan. *The Unfinished Nation: A Brief, Interactive History of the American People*. New York: McGraw-Hill, 2005.

Brook, Timothy. *Collaboration: Japanese Agents and Local Elites in Wartime China*. Cambridge, Mass.: Harvard University Press, 2005.

Brook, Timothy, and Bob Tadashi Wakabayashi, eds. *Opium Regimes: China, Britain, and Japan, 1839–1952*. Berkeley, Calif.: University of California Press, 2000.

Buck, Pearl S. "Is There a Place for the Foreign Missionary?" *Chinese Recorder* 58 (February 1927): 100–107.

Burchill, Scott, et al. *Theories of International Relations*. Basingstoke: Palgrave Macmillan, 2005.

Burr, William, ed. *The Kissinger Transcripts: The Top Secret Talks with Beijing and Moscow*. New York: New Press, 1998.

Bush, Richard C. *Untying the Knot: Making Peace in the Taiwan Strait*. Washington, D.C.: Brookings Institution, 2005.

Butterfield, Fox. "A Missionary View of the Chinese Communists (1936–1939)." In *American Missionaries in China: Papers from Harvard Seminars*, edited by Kwang-Ching Liu, 249–301. Cambridge, Mass.: Harvard University Press, 1966.

Calavita, Kitty. "The Paradoxes of Race, Class, Identity, and 'Passing': Enforcing the Chinese Exclusion Acts, 1882–1910." *Law and Social Inquiry* 25, no. 1 (Winter 2000): 1–40.

Calhoun, Charles W., ed. *The Gilded Age: Essays on the Origins of Modern America.* Wilmington, Del.: Scholarly Resources, 1996.

Carpenter, Francis Ross. *The Old China Trade: Americans in Canton, 1784–1843.* New York: Coward, McCann & Geoghegan, 1976.

Chan, Sucheng. *This Bittersweet Soil: The Chinese in California Agriculture, 1860–1910.* Berkeley, Calif.: University of California Press, 1987.

———, ed. *Entry Denied: Exclusion and the Chinese Community in America, 1882–1943.* Philadelphia, Pa.: Temple University Press, 1991.

Chan, Sucheng, and Madeline Yuan-yin Hsu, eds. *Chinese Americans and the Politics of Race and Culture.* Philadelphia, Pa.: Temple University Press, 2008.

Cheek, Timothy, ed. *A Critical Introduction to Mao.* Cambridge: Cambridge University Press, 2010.

———. *Mao Zedong and China's Revolutions: A Brief History with Documents.* Boston, Mass.: Bedford, 2002.

Ch'en, Kuo-Tung. *The Insolvency of the Chinese Hong Merchants, 1760–1843.* Taipei: Institute of Economics, Academia Sinica, 1990.

Chen, Hansheng (陈翰笙), ed. *Huagong chuguo shiliao huibian* [华工出国史料汇编 A comprehensive collection of historical sources on overseas Chinese laborers]. Beijing: Zhonghua shuju, 1980–1985, 10 vols.

Chen, Helen. "Chinese Immigration into the United States: An Analysis of Changes in Immigration Policies." PhD dissertation, Brandeis University, 1980.

Chen, Jiagui (陈佳贵), and Li Yang (李扬), eds. *2011 nian Zhongguo jingji xingshi fenxi yu yuce* [2011年中国经济形势分析与预测 The Chinese economy: An analysis and forecast for 2011]. Beijing: Shehui kexue wenxian chubanshe, 2010.

Chen, Jian. *China's Road to the Korean War: The Making of the Sino-American Confrontation.* New York: Columbia University Press, 1994.

———. *Mao's China and the Cold War.* Chapel Hill, N.C.: University of North Carolina Press, 2001.

———. "The Ward Case and the Emergence of Sino-American Confrontation, 1948–1950." *Australian Journal of Chinese Affairs,* no. 30 (July 1993): 149–170.

Chen, Yung-fa (陈永发). *Zhongguo Gongchan Geming qishi nian* [中国共产革命七十年 The seventy years of the Chinese Communist Revolution]. Revised ed. Taipei: Lianjing, 2001.

Cheng, Hang-Sheng. "Comments on Xianquan Xu's Chapter." In *China, the United States, and the Global Economy,* edited by Shuxun Chen and Charles Wolf Jr., p. 253. Santa Monica, Calif.: RAND, 2001.

Cheong, Weng Eang. *The Hong Merchants of Canton: Chinese Merchants in Sino-Western Trade.* Richmond, Surrey: Curzon, 1997.

Chern, Kenneth S. "Politics of American China Policy, 1945: Roots of the Cold War in Asia." *Political Science Quarterly* 91, no. 4 (Winter 1976–1977): 631–647.

China Continuation Committee. *The Christian Occupation of China: A General Survey of the Numerical Strength and Geographical Distribution of the Christian Forces in China.* Shanghai: China Continuation Committee, 1922.

Chow, Tse-tsung. *The May Fourth Movement: Intellectual Revolution in Modern China.* Cambridge, Mass.: Harvard University Press, 1960.

Christensen, Thomas J. "A 'Lost Chance' for What? Rethinking the Origins of U.S.-PRC Confrontation." *Journal of American-East Asian Relations* 4, no. 3 (Fall 1995): 249–278.

Christiansen, Flemming. "The 1989 Student Demonstrations and the Limits of the Chinese Political Bargaining Machine: An Essay." *China Information* 4, no. 1 (Summer 1989): 17–27.

Christiansen, Flemming, and Shirin M. Rai. *Chinese Politics and Society: An Introduction.* London: Prentice Hall, 1996.

Clarke, Prescott, and J. S. Gregory, comps. *Western Reports on the Taiping: A Selection of Documents.* Honolulu, Hawaii: University Press of Hawaii, 1982.

Coble, Parks M., Jr. *Facing Japan: Chinese Politics and Japanese Imperialism, 1931–1937.* Cambridge, Mass.: Harvard University Press, 1991.

———. *The Shanghai Capitalists and the Nationalist Government, 1927–1937.* 2nd ed., 1st ed. in 1980. Cambridge, Mass.: Harvard University Press, 1986.

Cohen, Jerome Alan, ed. *The Dynamics of China's Foreign Relations.* Cambridge, Mass.: East Asian Research Center, Harvard University, 1973.

Cohen, Paul A. "The Anti-Christian Tradition in China," *Journal of Asian Studies* 20, no. 2 (February 1961): 169–180.

———. *China and Christianity: The Missionary Movement and the Growth of Chinese Antiforeignism, 1860–1870.* Cambridge, Mass.: Harvard University Press, 1963.

———. *China Unbound: Evolving Perspectives on the Chinese Past.* New York: Routledge-Curzon, 2003.

———. *History in Three Keys: The Boxers as Event, Experience, and Myth.* New York: Columbia University Press, 1997.

Cohen, Warren I. "Ambassador Philip D. Sprouse on the Question of Recognition of the People's Republic of China in 1949 and 1950 (Document)." *Diplomatic History* 2, no. 2 (Spring 1978): 213–217.

———. *America's Response to China: A History of Sino-American Relations.* 5th ed., 1st ed. in 1971. New York: Columbia University Press, 2010.

———, ed. *The Cambridge History of American Foreign Relations: America in the Age of Soviet Power.* Vol. 4. Cambridge: Cambridge University Press, 1993.

———. "Conversations with Chinese Friends: Zhou Enlai's Associates Reflect on Chinese-American Relations in the 1940s and the Korean War." *Diplomatic History* 11, no. 3 (July 1987): 283–289.

———, ed. *New Frontiers in American-East Asian Relations: Essays Presented to Dorothy Borg.* New York: Columbia University, 1983.

———. *Pacific Passage: The Study of American-East Asian Relations on the Eve of the Twenty-First Century.* New York: Columbia University Press, 1996.

Cohen, Warren I., and Nancy B. Tucker, eds. *Lyndon Johnson Confronts the World: American Foreign Policy, 1963–1968.* Cambridge: Cambridge University Press, 1994.

Conn, Peter J. *Pearl S. Buck: A Cultural Biography.* Cambridge: Cambridge University Press, 1996.

Coolidge, Mary Robert. *Chinese Immigration.* New York: Henry Holt, 1909.

Cooney, Kevin. *Japan's Foreign Policy since 1945.* Armonk, N.Y.: M. E. Sharpe, 2007.

Copper, John F. *Taiwan: Nation-State or Province?* 5th ed. Boulder, Colo.: Westview Press, 2009.

Craft, Stephen G. *V. K. Wellington Koo and the Emergence of Modern China.* Lexington, Ky.: University Press of Kentucky, 2004.

Crouch, Archie R., et al., ed. *Christianity in China: A Scholar's Guide to Resources in the Libraries and Archives of the United States.* Armonk, N.Y.: M. E. Sharpe, 1989.

Cumings, Bruce. *Dominion from Sea to Sea: Pacific Ascendancy and American Power.* New Haven, Conn.: Yale University Press, 2009.

————. *The Korean War: A History*. New York: Modern Library, 2010.

Curtis, Gerald, Ryosei Kokubun, and Wang Jisi, eds. *Getting the Triangle Straight: Managing China-Japan-US Relations*. Tokyo: Japan Center for International Exchange, 2010.

Dai, Xu (戴旭). *C xing baowei: Neiyou waihuan xia d e Zhongguo tuwei* [C形包围: 内忧外患下的中国突围 The C-Shaped encirclement: China's way out of its domestic problems and the foreign threat]. Shanghai: Wenhui chubanshe, 2010.

Davids, Jules, ed. *American Diplomatic and Public Papers: The United States and China*. Wilmington, Del.: Scholarly Resources, 1973.

Davies, John Paton, Jr. *China Hand: An Autobiography*. Philadelphia, Pa.: University of Pennsylvania Press, 2012.

Davis, Donald E., and Eugene P. Trani. *The First Cold War: The Legacy of Woodrow Wilson in U.S.-Soviet Relations*. Columbia, Mo.: University of Missouri Press, 2002.

Dayer, Roberta Allbert. *Bankers and Diplomats in China 1917–1925*. London: Frank Cass, 1981.

Deng, Yong, and Fei-ling Wang, eds. *In the Eyes of the Dragon: China Views the World*. Lanham, Md.: Rowman & Littlefield, 1999.

Dennett, Tyler. *Americans in East Asia: A Critical Study of United States Policy in the Far East in the Nineteenth Century*. New York: Barnes & Noble, 1963. 1st ed. in 1922 by Macmillan.

Dent, Christopher M. "Taiwan and the New Regional Political Economy of East Asia." *China Quarterly* 182 (June 2005): 385–406.

Dingman, Rodger. *Power in the Pacific: The Origins of Naval Arms Control*. Chicago, Ill.: University of Chicago Press, 1976.

Downs, Jacques M. "American Merchants and the China Opium Trade, 1800–1840." *Business History Review* 42 (Winter 1968): 418–422.

————. *The Golden Ghetto: The American Commercial Community at Canton and the Shaping of American China Policy, 1784–1844*. Bethlehem, Pa.: Lehigh University Press, 1997.

Duara, Prasenjit. *Sovereignty and Authenticity: Manchukuo and the East Asian Modern*. Lanham, Md.: Rowman & Littlefield, 2003.

Dudden, Arthur Power. *The American Pacific: From the Old China Trade to the Present*. New York: Oxford University Press, 1992.

Dulles, Foster Rhea. *The Old China Trade*. Cambridge, Mass.: Riverside Press, 1930.

Economy, Elizabeth, and Michel Oksenberg, eds. *China Joins the World: Progress and Prospects*. New York: Council on Foreign Relations Press, 1999.

Egerton, George W. "Britain and the 'Great Betrayal': Anglo-American Relations and the Struggle for United States Ratification of the Treaty of Versailles, 1919–1920." *Historical Journal* 21, no. 4 (December 1978): 885–911.

Elegant, Robert S. "China's New Phase." *Foreign Affairs* 46, no. 1 (October 1967): 137–150.

Eng, Robert Y. *Economic Imperialism in China: Silk Production and Exports, 1861–1932*. Berkeley, Calif.: University of California Press, 1986.

Engel, Jeffrey A., ed. *The China Diary of George H. W. Bush: The Making of a Global President*. Princeton, N.J.: Princeton University Press, 2008.

Eperjesi, John. "The American Asiatic Association and the Imperialist Imaginary of the American Public." *Boundary 2*, vol. 28, no. 1 (Spring 2001): 195–219.

Esherick, Joseph W. *Lost Chance in China: The World War II Dispatches of John S. Service*. New York: Random House, 1974.

————. *The Origins of the Boxer Uprising*. Berkeley, Calif.: University of California Press, 1987.

————. "Ten Theses on the Chinese Revolution." *Modern China* 21, no. 1 (January 1995): 44–76.

Esherick, Joseph W., Hasan Kayali, and Eric Van Young, eds. *Empire to Nation: Historical Perspectives on the Making of the Modern World*. Lanham, Md.: Rowman & Littlefield, 2006.

Etō, Shinkichi. "China's International Relations 1911–1931." In *The Cambridge History of China*, edited by John King Fairbank and Albert Feuerwerker, 74–115. Cambridge: Cambridge University Press, 1986.

Evans, Paul M. *John Fairbank and the American Understanding of Modern China*. New York: Blackwell, 1988.

Ewell, Judith. *Venezuela and the United States: From Monroe's Hemisphere to Petroleum's Empire*. Athens, Ga.: University of Georgia Press, 1996.

Fairbank, John K. "'American China Policy' to 1898: A Misconception." *Pacific Historical Review* 39, no. 4 (November 1970): 409–420.

————. *Chinabound: A Fifty-Year Memoir*. New York: Harper & Row, 1982.

————. *Trade and Diplomacy on the China Coast: The Opening of the Treaty Ports, 1842–1854*. 2nd ed. Stanford, Calif.: Stanford University Press, 1969. 1st ed. in 1953 by Harvard University Press.

————. *The United States and China*. 4th and enlarged ed. Cambridge, Mass.: Harvard University Press, 1983. 1st ed. in 1948.

Fang, Ning (房宁). *Chengzhang de Zhongguo: Dangdai Zhongguo qingnian de guojia minzu yishi yanjiu* [成长的中国:当代中国青年的国家民族意识研究 Growing China: A study of national consciousness among contemporary Chinese youth]. Beijing: Renmin chubanshe, 2002.

————. *Xin Diguo zhuyi shidai yu Zhongguo zhanlüe* [新帝国主义时代与中国战略 The age of new imperialism and China's counter-strategy]. Beijing: Beijing chubanshe, 2003.

Fewsmith, Joseph. *China since Tiananmen: From Deng Xiaoping to Hu Jintao*. 2nd ed. Cambridge: Cambridge University Press, 2008. 1st ed. in 2001.

Fic, Victor M. *The Collapse of American Policy in Russia and Siberia, 1918*. New York: Columbia University Press, 1995.

Fine, Gary Alan, and Bin Xu. "Honest Brokers: The Politics of Expertise in the 'Who Lost China?' Debate." *Social Problems* 58, no. 4 (2011): 593–614.

Fineman, Howard. *The Thirteen American Arguments: Enduring Debates That Define and Inspire Our Country*. New York: Random House, 2008.

Fishback, Price, et al. *Government and the American Economy: A New History*. Chicago, Ill.: University of Chicago Press, 2007.

Fogel, Joshua, ed. *The Nanjing Massacre in History and Historiography*. Berkeley, Calif.: University of California Press, 2000.

Foot, Rosemary. *The Practice of Power: US Relations with China since 1949*. Oxford: Clarendon Press, 1995.

————. "Strategy, Politics, and World Order Perspectives: Comparing the EU and US Approaches to China's Resurgence." In *US-China-EU Relations: Managing the New World Order*, edited by Robert Ross, Øystein Tunsjø, and Zhang Tuosheng, 212–232. London: Routledge, 2010.

Forbes, Robert E. *Personal Reminiscences*. 2nd ed. Boston, Mass.: Little, Brown, 1882.

Friedberg, Aaron L. *A Contest for Supremacy: China, America, and the Struggle for Mastery in Asia.* New York: Norton, 2011.

———. "The Future of U.S.-China Relations: Is Conflict Inevitable?" *International Security* 30, no. 2 (Fall 2005): 7–45.

Friedman, Edward, ed. *China's Rise, Taiwan's Dilemmas and International Peace.* London: Routledge, 2006.

Friedman, Edward, and Mark Selden, eds. *America's Asia: Dissenting Essays on Asian-American Relations.* New York: Vintage, 1971.

Fritz, Christian G. "A Nineteenth Century 'Habeas Corpus Mill': The Chinese before the Federal Courts in California." *American Journal of Legal History* 32, no. 4 (October 1988): 347–372.

Gaddis, John Lewis. *Strategies of Containment: A Critical Appraisal of American National Security Policy during the Cold War.* Revised and expanded ed. Oxford: Oxford University Press, 2005.

Garrison, Jean A. *Making China Policy: From Nixon to G. W. Bush.* Boulder, Colo.: Lynne Rienner Publishers, 2005.

Garver, John W. *Chinese-Soviet Relations, 1937–1945: The Diplomacy of Chinese Nationalism.* New York: Oxford University Press, 1988.

———. *Foreign Relations of the People's Republic of China.* Upper Saddle River, N.J.: Prentice Hall, 1993.

———. *The Sino-American Alliance: Nationalist China and American Cold War Strategy in Asia.* Armonk, N.Y.: M. E. Sharpe, 1997.

Gittings, John. *The World and China, 1922–1972.* London: Eyre Methuen, 1974.

Goh, Evelyn. "Competing Images and American Official Reconsiderations of China Policy, 1961–1968." *Journal of American-East Asian Relations* 10, nos. 1–2 (Spring–Summer 2001): 53–92.

———. *Constructing the U.S. Rapprochement with China, 1961–1974: From "Red Menace" to "Tacit Ally."* Cambridge: Cambridge University Press, 2005.

Goldberg, Jeffrey. "Washington Discovers Christian Persecution." *New York Times,* December 21, 1997.

Goldstein, Jonathan. *Stephen Girard's Trade with China, 1787–1824: The Norms Versus the Profits of Trade.* Portland, Maine: MerwinAsia, 2011.

Goldstein, Steven. "Dialogue of the Deaf? The Sino-American Ambassadorial-Level Talks, 1955–1970." In *Re-Examining the Cold War: U.S.-China Diplomacy, 1954–1973,* edited by Robert S. Ross and Jiang Changbin, 200–237. Cambridge, Mass.: Harvard University Asia Center, 2001.

Gong, Li (宫力). *Deng Xiaoping yu Meiguo* [邓小平与美国 Deng Xiaoping and the United States]. Beijing: Zhonggong dangshi chubanshe, 2004.

———. *Kuayue honggou: 1969–1979 nian Zhongmei guanxi de yanbian* [跨越鸿沟: 1969–1979年中美关系的演变 Overcoming the chasm: The evolution of U.S.-China relations, 1969–79]. Zhengzhou: Henan renmin chubanshe, 1992.

Gordon, David M. "Historiographical Essay: The China-Japan War, 1931–1945." *Journal of Military History* 70, no. 1 (January 2006): 137–182.

Gries, Peter Hays, H. Michael Crowson, and Todd Sandel. "The Olympic Effect on American Attitudes towards China: Beyond Personality, Ideology, and Media Exposure." *Journal of Contemporary China* 19, no. 64 (2010): 213–231.

Griswold, Alfred Whitney. *The Far Eastern Policy of the United States.* 2nd ed., 1st ed. in 1938 by Harcourt, Brace. New Haven, Conn.: Yale University Press, 1966.

Gu Weimin (顾为民). *Jidujiao yu jindai Zhongguao shehui* [基督教与近代中国社会 Christianity and modern Chinese society]. Shanghai: Shanghai renmin chubanshe, 1996.

Gu, Yunshen (顾云深), Shi Yuanhua (石源华), and Jin Guangyao (金光耀) eds. *Jianzhi wanglai: Bainian Zhongmei jingji guanxi de huigu yu qianzhan* [鉴知往来: 百年来中美经济关系的回顾与前瞻 Looking back and forward: A century of Sino-American economic relations]. Shanghai: Fuda daxue chubanshe, 1999.

Guarneri, Carl. *America in the World: United States History in Global Context.* New York: McGraw-Hill, 2007.

Haddad, John Rogers. *The Romance of China: Excursions to China in U.S. Culture, 1776–1876.* New York: Columbia University Press, 2008.

Halpern, A. M., ed. *Policies toward China: Views from Six Continents.* New York: McGraw-Hill, 1965.

Hamashita, Takeshi, Mark Selden, and Linda Grove. *China, East Asia and the Global Economy: Regional and Historical Perspectives.* New York: Routledge, 2008.

Hamilton, John Maxwell. *Edgar Snow: A Biography.* Bloomington, Ind.: Indiana University Press, 1988.

Han, Minzhu, ed. *Cries for Democracy: Writings and Speeches from the 1989 Chinese Democracy Movement.* Princeton, N.J.: Princeton University Press, 1990.

Han, Yugui (韩玉贵). *Lengzhan hou de Zhongmei guanxi* [冷战后的中美关系 Sino-American relations in the post–Cold War era]. Beijing: Shehui kexue wenxian chubanshe, 2007.

Harcourt, Freda. "Black Gold: P&O and the Opium Trade, 1847–1914." *International Journal of Maritime History* 6, no. 1 (June 1994): 1–83.

Harding, Harry. *China's Second Revolution: Reform after Mao.* Washington, D.C.: Brookings Institution, 1987.

———. *A Fragile Relationship: The United States and China since 1972.* Washington, D.C.: Brookings Institution, 1992.

Harding, Harry, and Yuan Ming, eds. *Sino-American Relations, 1945–1955: A Joint Assessment of a Critical Decade.* Wilmington, Del.: Scholarly Research Inc., 1989.

Hardt, Michael, and Antonio Negri. *Empire.* Cambridge, Mass.: Harvard University Press, 2000.

Hayford, Charles W. "American China Missions: An Introductory Bibliography." http://www.library.yale.edu/div/ChinaMissionsBibliog.pdf (accessed August 22, 2012).

———. *Draft Bibliography of American-East Asian Relations.* Chicago, Ill.: Imprint Publications and *Journal of American-East Asian Relations*, 2002.

———. *To the People: James Yen and Village China.* New York: Columbia University Press, 1990.

Henkin, Louis. "The Constitution and United States Sovereignty: A Century of 'Chinese Exclusion' and Its Progeny." *Harvard Law Review* 100, no. 4 (February 1987): 853–886.

Herzstein, Robert Edwin. *Henry R. Luce, Time, and the American Crusade in Asia.* Cambridge: Cambridge University Press, 2005.

Hoe, Susanna, and Derek Roebuck. *The Taking of Hong Kong: Charles and Clara Elliot in China Waters.* Surrey: Curzon Press, 1999.

Hoffman, Bruce. "From the War on Terror to Global Counterinsurgency." *Current History: A Journal of Contemporary Trends* 105, no. 695 (December 2006): 423–429.

Hoffman, Elizabeth Cobbs, and Jon Gjerde, eds. *Major Problems in American History: Documents and Essays.* 2 vols. Boston, Mass.: Houghton Mifflin, 2007.

Hogan, Michael J., and Thomas G. Paterson, eds. *Explaining the History of American Foreign Relations*. 2nd ed. Cambridge: Cambridge University Press, 2004.

Hollander, Paul. *Political Pilgrims: Travels of Western Intellectuals to the Soviet Union, China, and Cuba, 1928–1978*. Oxford: Oxford University Press, 1981.

Hong, Pingfan. "China's Economic Prospects and Sino-US Economic Relations." *China & World Economy* 14, no. 2 (2006): 45–55.

Howse, Robert. "Comment: China—Measures Affecting the Protection and Enforcement of Intellectual Property Rights." *World Trade Review* 10, no. 1 (2011): 87–93.

Hsu, Madeline Y. *Dreaming of Gold, Dreaming of Home: Transnationalism and Migration between the United States and South China, 1882–1943*. Stanford, Calif.: Stanford University Press, 2000.

Huang, Guoxin (黄国信), Huang Qichen (黄启臣), and Huang Haiyan (黄海妍). *Huozh huayang de yueshang* [货殖华洋的粤商 The Cantonese merchants—Trading goods in China and overseas]. Hangzhou: Zhejiang renmin chubanshe, 1997.

Huang, Hua (黄华). *Qinli yu Jianwen: Huang Hua huiyi lu* [亲历与见闻: 黄华回忆录 Witnessing and experiencing at firsthand: The memoirs of Huang Hua]. Beijing: Shijie zhishi chubanshe, 2007.

Hudson, Michael. *Super Imperialism: The Origin and Fundamentals of U.S. World Dominance*. 1st ed. in 1972. London: Pluto Press, 2003.

———. *Trade, Development and Foreign Debt: How Trade and Development Concentrate Economic Power in the Hands of Dominant Nations*. Unknown: ISLET, 2009. 1st ed. in 1992 by Pluto Press.

Hunt, Michael H. *The American Ascendancy: How the United States Gained and Wielded Global Dominance*. Chapel Hill, N.C.: University of North Carolina Press, 2007.

———. "The American Remission of the Boxer Indemnity: A Reappraisal." *Journal of Asian Studies* 31, no. 3 (May 1972): 539–559.

———. "Americans in the China Market: Economic Opportunities and Economic Nationalism, 1890s–1931." *Business History Review* 51, no. 3 (Autumn 1977): 277–307.

———. "The Forgotten Occupation: Peking, 1900–1901." *Pacific Historical Review* 48, no. 4 (1979): 501–529.

———. *Frontier Defense and the Open Door: Manchuria in Chinese-American Relations, 1895–1911*. New Haven, Conn.: Yale University Press, 1973.

———. *The Genesis of Chinese Communist Foreign Policy*. New York: Columbia University Press, 1996.

———. *Ideology and U.S. Foreign Policy*. New Haven, Conn.: Yale University Press, 1987.

———. *The Making of a Special Relationship: The United States and China to 1914*. New York: Columbia University Press, 1983.

Hunt, Michael H., and Steven I. Levine. *Arc of Empire: America's Wars in Asia from the Philippines to Vietnam*. Chapel Hill, N.C.: University of North Carolina Press, 2012.

Hunter, Alan, and Kim-kwong Chan. *Protestantism in Contemporary China*. Cambridge: Cambridge University Press, 1993.

Hunter, William C. *The "Fan Kwae" at Canton before Treaty Days: 1825–1844*. Taipei: Ch'eng-wen Pub. Co., 1965. Reprint of 1882 ed. by Kegan Paul, Trench & Co. in London.

Huntington, Samuel P. *The Clash of Civilizations and the Remaking of World Order*. New York: Simon & Schuster, 1996.

Ikei, Masaru. "Japan's Response to the Chinese Revolution of 1911." *Journal of Asian Studies* 25, no. 2 (1966): 213–227.

Irick, Robert W. *Ch'ing Policy toward the Coolie Trade, 1847–1878*. Taipei: Chinese Materials Center, 1982.

Iriye, Akira. *Across the Pacific: An Inner History of American-East Asian Relations*. Revised ed. Chicago, Ill.: Imprint Publications, 1992. 1st ed. in 1967 by Harcourt, Brace & World.

———. *After Imperialism: The Search for a New Order in the Far East,1921–1931*. Reprint. Chicago, Ill.: Imprint Publications, 1990. 1st ed. in 1965 by Harvard University Press.

———. *The Cambridge History of American Foreign Relations*. Vol. 3, *The Globalizing of America, 1913–1945*. Cambridge: Cambridge University Press, 1993.

———. "Japanese Aggression and China's International Position, 1931–1949." In *The Cambridge History of China*, edited by John King Fairbank and Albert Feuerwerker, 492–546. Cambridge: Cambridge University Press, 1986.

Iriye, Akira, and Warren Cohen, eds. *American, Chinese, and Japanese Perspectives on Wartime Asia, 1931–1949*. Wilmington, Del.: SR Books, 1990.

Isaacs, Harold R. *Scratches on Our Minds: American Images of China and India*. New York: John Day Company, 1958.

Israel, Jerry. *Progressivism and the Open Door: America and China, 1905–1921*. Pittsburgh, Pa.: University of Pittsburgh Press, 1971.

Jacobs, Daniel N. *Borodin: Stalin's Man in China*. Cambridge, Mass.: Harvard University Press, 1981.

Jeans, Roger B., ed. *The Marshall Mission to China, 1945–1947: The Letters and Diary of Colonel John Hart Caughey*. Lanham, Md.: Rowman & Littlefield, 2011.

Jia, Shi. "Future Prospects for Broadening US-China Economic and Trade Cooperation." *Columbia Journal of World Business* 20, no. 4 (Winter 1985): 57–58.

Jin, Chongji (金冲及), ed. *Zhou Enlai zhuan* [周恩来传 A biography of Zhou Enlai]. Beijing: Zhonggong zhongyang wenxian yanjiushi, 1998.

Johnston, Alastair Iain. "Is China a Status Quo Power?" *International Security* 27, no. 4 (2003): 5–56.

Joiner, Lynne. *The Honorable Survivor: Mao's China, McCarthy's America, and the Persecution of John S. Service*. Annapolis, Md.: Naval Institute Press, 2009.

Kaplinsky, Raphael, and Dirk Messner. "Introduction: The Impact of Asian Drivers on the Developing World." *World Development* 36, no. 2 (February 2008): 197–209.

Kaufman, Victor S. "'Chirep': The Anglo-American Dispute over Chinese Representation in the United Nations, 1950–71." *English Historical Review* 115, no. 461 (April 2000): 354–377.

———. "A Response to Chaos: The United States, the Great Leap Forward, and the Cultural Revolution, 1961–1968." *Journal of American-East Asian Relations* 7, no. 1–2 (Spring–Summer 1998): 73–92.

Keliher, Macabe. "Anglo-American Rivalry and the Origins of U.S. China Policy." *Diplomatic History* 31, no. 2 (April 2007): 227–257.

Kennedy, John F. "A Democrat Looks at Foreign Policy." *Foreign Affairs* 36, no. 1 (October 1957): 44–59.

Kennedy, Scott. *China Cross Talk: The American Debate over China Policy since Normalization: A Reader*. Lanham, Md.: Rowman & Littlefield, 2003.

Keohane, Robert O., and Joseph S. Nye. *Power and Interdependence*. 4th ed. Boston, Mass.: Longman, 2011.

Keylor, William R. *A World of Nations: The International Order since 1945*. Oxford: Oxford University Press, 2003.

Kim, Samuel S, ed. *China and the World: Chinese Foreign Policy Faces the New Millennium.* Boulder, Colo.: Westview Press, 1998.

Kirby, James E., Jr. "The Foochow Anti-Missionary Riot—August 30, 1878." *Journal of Asian Studies* 25, no. 4 (August 1966): 665–678.

Kirby, William C. "The Internationalization of China: Foreign Relations at Home and Abroad in the Republican Era." *China Quarterly* 150 (June 1997): 433–458.

———. "Chinese-American Relations in Comparative Perspective, 1900–1949." In *Pacific Passage: The Study of American-East Asian Relations on the Eve of the Twenty-First Century,* edited by Warren I. Cohen, 163–189. New York: Columbia University Press, 1996.

———. "Engineering China: Birth of the Developmental State, 1928–1937." In *Becoming Chinese: Passages to Modernity and Beyond,* edited by Wen-Hsin Yeh, 137–160. Berkeley, Calif.: University of California Press, 2000.

———. *Germany and Republican China.* Stanford, Calif.: Stanford University Press, 1984.

Kirby, William C., Robert S. Ross, and Gong Li, eds. *Normalization of U.S.-China Relations: An International History.* Cambridge, Mass.: Harvard University Asia Center, 2006.

Kissinger, Henry. "The Future of U.S.-Chinese Relations." *Foreign Affairs* 91, no. 2 (March 2012): no page number, Web ed. http://www.foreignaffairs. com/articles/137245/henry-a-kissinger/the-future-of-us-chinese-relations (accessed July 23, 2012).

———. *On China.* New York: Penguin, 2011.

Kluver, Randolph. "Rhetorical Trajectories of Tiananmen Square." *Diplomatic History* 34, no. 1 (January 2010): 71–94.

Kochavi, Noam. *A Conflict Perpetuated: China Policy during the Kennedy Years.* Westport, Conn.: Praeger, 2002.

Koshiro, Yukiko. "Eurasian Eclipse: Japan's End Game in World War II." *American Historical Review* 109, no. 2 (April 2004): 417–444.

Kuhn, Philip A. *Chinese among Others: Emigration in Modern Times.* Lanham, Md.: Rowman & Littlefield, 2008.

Kusnitz, Leonard A. *Public Opinion and Foreign Policy: America's China Policy, 1949–1979.* Westport, Conn.: Greenwood Press, 1984.

LaFeber, Walter. *The Clash: U.S.-Japanese Relations throughout History.* New York: Norton, 1997.

Lai, Him Mark. *Becoming Chinese American: A History of Communities and Institutions.* Walnut Creek, Calif.: AltaMira, 2004.

———. *Chinese American Transnational Politics.* Urbana, Ill.: University of Illinois Press, 2010.

———. *A History Reclaimed: An Annotated Bibliography of Chinese Language Materials on the Chinese in America.* Los Angeles, Calif.: Asian American Studies Center, University of California at Los Angeles, 1986.

Lampton, David M. "The China Fantasy, Fantasy." *China Quarterly* 191 (September 2007): 745–749.

———. *The Making of Chinese Foreign and Security Policy in the Era of Reform, 1978–2000.* Stanford, Calif.: Stanford University Press, 2001.

———. *Same Bed, Different Dreams: Managing U.S.-China Relations, 1989–2000.* Berkeley, Calif.: University of California Press, 2001.

———. *The Three Faces of Chinese Power: Might, Money, and Minds.* Berkeley, Calif.: University of California Press, 2008.

Lang, Xianping (郎咸平). Lang Xianping shuo: Xin Diguo zhuyi zai Zhongguo [郎咸平 说:新帝国主义在中国 Lang Xianping on New Imperialism in China]. 8th printing, 1st ed. in January 2010. Beijing: Dongfang chubanshe, 2011.

———. *Lang Xianping shuo: Xin Diguo zhuyi zai Zhongguo 2* [郎咸平说:新帝国主义在中 国 2 Lang Xianping on new imperialism in China 2]. Beijing: Dongfang chubanshe, 2010.

Latourette, Kenneth Scott. *The History of Early Relations between the United States and China, 1784–1844.* New Haven, Conn.: Yale University Press, 1917.

Lazich, Michael C. "American Missionaries and the Opium Trade in Nineteenth-Century China." *Journal of World History* 17, no. 2 (June 2006): 197–223.

———. *E. C. Bridgman (1801–1861): America's First Missionary to China.* Lewiston, N.Y.: Edwin Mellen Press, 2000.

Lee, Joseph Tse-Hei. "The Lord of Heaven versus Jesus Christ: Christian Sectarian Violence in Late-Nineteenth-Century South China." *Positions* 8, no. 1 (Spring 2000): 77–99.

Leng, Tse-Kang. "State and Business in the Era of Globalization: The Case of Cross-Strait Linkages in the Computer Industry." *China Journal*, no. 53 (January 2005): 63–79.

Levi, Werner. *Modern China's Foreign Policy.* Minneapolis, Minn.: University of Minnesota Press, 1953.

Li, Cheng, ed. *Bridging Minds across the Pacific: U.S.-China Educational Exchange.* Lanham, Md.: Lexington Books, 2005.

Li, Hongshan, and Zhaohui Hong, eds. *Image, Perception, and the Making of U.S.-China Relations.* Lanham, Md.: University Press of America, 1998.

Li, Jing. *China's America: The Chinese View the United States, 1900–2000.* New York: State University of New York Press, 2011.

Li, Laura Tyson. *Madame Chiang Kai-shek: China's Eternal First Lady.* New York: Atlantic Monthly Press, 2006.

Li, Qingsi (李庆四). *Meiguo guohui yu Meiguo duihua zhengce* [美国国会与美国对华政策 The American Congress and American China policy]. Beijing: Dangdai shijie chubanshe, 2002.

Li, Tiecheng (李铁城), and Qian Wenrong (钱文荣), eds. *Lianheguo kuangjia xia de Zhongmei guanxi* [联合国框架下的中美关系 U.S.-China relations within the framework of the United Nations]. Beijing: Renmin chubanshe, 2006.

Liang, Chin-tung. *General Stilwell in China, 1942–1945: The Full Story.* New York: St. John's University Press, 1972.

Liang, Kang. *Pearl S. Buck: A Cultural Bridge across the Pacific.* Westport, Conn.: Greenwood Press, 1997.

Lieberthal, Kenneth. *Governing China: From Revolution through Reform.* 2nd ed. New York: Norton, 2004. 1st ed. in 1995.

Lilley, James, with Jeffrey Lilley. *China Hands: Nine Decades of Adventure, Espionage, and Diplomacy in Asia.* New York: Public Affairs, 2004.

Ling, Jinzhu (凌金铸). *Zhishi Chanquan yu Zhongme guanxi: 1989–1996* [知识产权与中美 关系 Intellectual property rights and Sino-American relations: 1989–1996]. Shanghai: Shanghai renmin chubanshe, 2007.

Link, Perry. *Evening Chats in Beijing: Probing China's Predicament.* New York: Norton, 1992.

Littell, John B. "Missionaries and Politics in China—the Taiping Rebellion." *Political Science Quarterly* 43, no. 4 (December 1928): 566–599.

Liu, Liandi (刘连第), comp. and ed. *Zhongmei guanxi de guiji: 1993–2000 nian dashi zonglan* [中美关系的轨迹: 1993年–2000年大事纵览 The contours of U.S.-China relations: An overview of major events from 1993 to 2000]. Beijing: Shishi chubanshe, 2001.

Liu, Liandi (刘连第), and Wang Dawei (汪大为), eds. *Zhongmei guanxi de guiji: jianjiao yilai dashi zonglan* [中美关系的轨迹: 建交以来大事纵览 The trajectory of U.S.-China relations: An overview of major events since the establishment of diplomatic relations]. Beijing: Shishi chubanshe, 1995.

Liu, Xiao (刘晓). *Chushi Sulian banian* [出使苏联八年 Eight years as Ambassador to the Soviet Union]. Beijing: Zhonggong dangshi ziliao, 1986.

Liu, Xiaoyuan. *A Partnership for Disorder: China, the United States, and Their Policies for the Postwar Disposition of the Japanese Empire, 1941–1945.* Cambridge: Cambridge University Press, 1996.

Lodwick, Kathleen. *The Chinese Recorder Index: A Guide to Christian Missions in Asia, 1867–1941.* Wilmington, Del.: Scholarly Resources, 1986.

Lovell, Julia. *The Opium War: Drugs, Dreams and the Making of China.* London: Picador, 2011.

Lüthi, Lorenz M. *The Sino-Soviet Split: Cold War in the Communist World.* Princeton, N.J.: Princeton University Press, 2008.

MacFarquhar, Roderick, ed. *Sino-American Relations, 1949–71: Documented and Introduced by Roderick Macfarquhar.* New York: Praeger, 1972.

MacFarquhar, Roderick, and Michael Schoenhals. *Mao's Last Revolution.* Cambridge, Mass.: Harvard University Press, 2006.

MacMillan, Margaret. *Paris 1919: Six Months That Changed the World.* New York: Random House, 2002.

Madsen, Richard. *China and the American Dream: A Moral Inquiry.* Berkeley, Calif.: University of California Press, 1995.

Mahoney, Rosemary. *The Early Arrival of Dreams: A Year in China.* New York: Fawcett Columbine, 1990.

Mann, James. *About Face: A History of America's Curious Relationship with China, from Nixon to Clinton.* New York: Knopf, 1999.

Manthorpe, Jonathan. *Forbidden Nation: A History of Taiwan.* New York: Palgrave Macmillan, 2002.

Manuel, Paul Christopher, Lawrence C. Reardon, and Clyde Wilcox, eds. *The Catholic Church and the Nation-State: Comparative Perspectives.* Washington, D.C.: Georgetown University Press, 2006.

Marsh, Christopher, and June Teufel Dreyer, eds. *U.S.-China Relations in the Twenty-First Century: Policies, Prospects, and Possibilities.* Lanham, Md.: Lexington Books, 2003.

Marshall, Joshua Micah. "Remaking the World: Bush and the Neoconservatives." *Foreign Affairs* 82, no. 6 (November/December 2003): 142–146.

Martellaro, Joseph A. "Some Aspects of Sino-American Economic Relations: Post-1950." *China Report* 18 (July–August 1982): 19–33.

May, Ernest R., and John K. Fairbank, eds. *America's China Trade in Historical Perspective: The Chinese and American Performance.* Cambridge, Mass.: Committee on American-East Asian Relations, Harvard University, 1986.

May, Ernest R., and James C. Thomson Jr., eds. *American-East Asian Relations: A Survey.* Cambridge, Mass.: Harvard University Press, 1972.

May, Gary. *China Scapegoat: The Diplomatic Ordeal of John Carter Vincent.* Washington, D.C.: New Republic Books, 1979.

McClain, Charles J., Jr. "The Chinese Struggle for Civil Rights in Nineteenth Century America: The First Phase, 1850–1870." *California Law Review* 72, no. 4 (1984): 529–568.

———. *In Search of Equality: The Chinese Struggle against Discrimination in Nineteenth-Century America.* Berkeley, Calif.: University of California Press, 1994.

McCord, Edward. *The Power of the Gun: The Emergence of Modern Chinese Warlords.* Berkeley, Calif.: University of California Press, 1993.

McDougall, Derek. *Asia Pacific in World Politics.* Boulder, Colo.: Lynne Rienner, 2007.

McDougall, Walter A. *Promised Land, Crusader State: The American Encounter with the World since 1776.* Boston, Mass.: Houghton Mifflin, 1998.

McGregor, James. *One Billion Customers: Lessons from the Front Lines of Doing Business in China.* New York: Free Press, 2005.

McKee, Delber L. *Chinese Exclusion versus the Open Door Policy, 1900–1906: Clashes over China Policy in the Roosevelt Era.* Detroit, Mich.: Wayne State University Press, 1977.

McKeown, Adam. "Ritualization of Regulation: The Enforcement of Chinese Exclusion in the United States and China." *American Historical Review* 108, no. 2 (April 2003): 377–403.

Menegon, Eugenio. *Ancestors, Virgins, and Friars: Christianity as a Local Religion in Late Imperial China.* Cambridge, Mass.: Harvard University Asia Center, 2010.

Mertha, Andrew C. *The Politics of Piracy: Intellectual Property in Contemporary China.* Ithaca, N.Y.: Cornell University Press, 2005.

Miller, Stewart. *Unwelcome Immigrant: American Images of the Chinese, 1875–1882.* Berkeley, Calif.: University of California, 1969.

Mitter, Rana. *The Manchurian Myth: Nationalism, Resistance, and Collaboration in Modern China.* Berkeley, Calif.: University of California Press, 2000.

Morse, Hosea Ballou. *The Chronicles of the East India Company Trading to China, 1634 to 1833.* 5 vols. Oxford: Oxford University Press, 1926–29.

———. *The International Relations of the Chinese Empire.* 3 vols. New York: Longmans, Green, 1918. Reprint by University of Hawaii Press, 2004.

Mun, K. C., and T. S. Chan. "The Role of Hong Kong in United States-China Trade." *Columbia Journal of World Business* 21, no. 1 (Spring 1986): 67–73.

Myers, Ramon H., Michel C. Oksenberg, and David Shambaugh. *Making China Policy: Lessons from the Bush and Clinton Administrations.* Lanham, Md.: Rowman & Littlefield, 2001.

Nash, Gary B., et al., ed. *The American People: Creating a Nation and a Society.* New York: Pearson Education, 2004.

Nass, Matthias. Interview with Henry Kissinger, "Der Anfang Einer Neuen Zeit [The beginning of a new age]." *Die Zeit,* May 26, 2011, 23.

Nathan, Andrew, and Robert S. Ross. *The Great Wall and the Empty Fortress.* New York: Norton, 1997.

Nathan, Andrew J., and Perry Link. *The Tiananmen Papers.* New York: PublicAffairs, 2001.

Naughton, Barry. *The Chinese Economy: Transitions and Growth.* Cambridge, Mass.: MIT Press, 2007.

Newman, Robert P. *Owen Lattimore and the "Loss" of China.* Berkeley, Calif.: University of California Press, 1992.

Ni, Shixiong (倪世雄). *Jiejiao yiyan zhong, xiangqi qianli zhi: Yige Zhongguo xuezhe yan-zhong de Zhongmei jianjiao sanshi nian* [结交一言重,相期千里至: 一个中国学者眼中的中美建交三十年 Keeping one's word regardless of the obstacles: The thirtieth anniversary of U.S.-China diplomatic relations as seen through the eyes of a Chinese scholar]. Shanghai: Fudan daxue chubanshe, 2009.

Nie, Rongzhen (聂荣臻). *Nie Rongzhen huiyilu* [聂荣臻回忆录 Memoirs of Nie Rongzhen]. Beijing: Jiefangjun chubanshe, 2007.

Niu, Dayong (牛大勇). "Yingguo yu duihua Menhu Kaifang zhengce de qiyuan" [英国与对华门户开放政策的起源 Great Britain and the origins of the Open Door policy]. *Lishi yanjiu*, no. 4 (1990): 21–35.

Niu, Jun. "1962: The Eve of the Left Turn in China's Foreign Policy." Cold War International History Project, Woodrow Wilson International Center for Scholars, working paper no. 48, October 2005.

Niu, Jun (牛军). "1969 nian Zhongsu bianjie chongtu yu Zhongguo waijiao zhanlue de tiaozheng" [1969 年中苏边界冲突与中国外交战略的调整 The Sino-Russian border conflict in 1969 and the adjustment of China's diplomatic strategy]. *Dangdai Zhongguo yanjiu*, no. 1 (1999): 66–77.

Nixon, Richard M. "Asia after Viet Nam."*Foreign Affairs* 46, no. 1 (October 1967): 111–125.

Nokes, Gregory R. *Massacred for Gold: The Chinese in Hells Canyon*. Corvallis, Oreg.: Oregon State University Press, 2009.

Novak, William. "The Myth of the 'Weak' American State." *American Historical Review* 113, no. 3 (June 2008): 752–772.

Nye, Joseph S., Jr. *The Paradox of American Power: Why the World's Only Superpower Can't Go It Alone*. New York: Oxford University Press, 2002.

Oksenberg, Michel, and Elizabeth Economy. *Shaping U.S.-China Relations: A Long-Term Strategy*. New York: Council on Foreign Relations, 1997.

O'Neill, William L. *American High: The Years of Confidence, 1945–1960*. New York: Free Press, 1989.

Osterhammel, Jürgen. "'Technical Co-Operation' between the League of Nations and China." *Modern Asian Studies* 13, no. 4 (1979): 661–680.

Ostermann, Christian F., ed. *Inside China's Cold War*. Vol. 16, *Cold War International History Project Bulletin*, Fall 2007/Winter 2008.

Pantsov, Alexander. *The Bolsheviks and the Chinese Revolution, 1919–1927*. Honolulu, Hawaii: University of Hawaii Press, 2000.

Paterson, Thomas, et al. *American Foreign Relations: A History*. 7th ed. Florence, Ky.: Wadsworth Publishing, 2009.

Paulsen, George E. "The Szechwan Riots of 1895 and American 'Missionary Diplomacy.'" *Journal of Asian Studies* 28, no. 2 (February 1969): 285–298.

Pearson, Margaret M. "The Case of China's Accession to GATT/WTO." In *The Making of Chinese Foreign and Security Policy in the Era of Reform, 1978–2000*, edited by David M. Lampton, 337–370. Stanford, Calif.: Stanford University Press, 2001.

Peng Dehuai zhuan bianxie zu (彭德怀传编写组). *Peng Dehuai zhuan* [彭德怀传 The biography of Peng Dehuai]. Beijing: Dangdai Zhongguo chubanshe, 2006.

Pepper, Suzanne. "The KMT-CCP Conflict, 1945–1949." In *The Cambridge History of China: Republican China, 1912–1949*, vol. 13, edited by John K. Fairbank and Albert Feuerwerker, 723–788. Cambridge: Cambridge University Press, 1986.

Perkins, Bradford. *The Cambridge History of American Foreign Relations.* Vol. 1, *The Creation of a Republican Empire, 1776–1865.* Cambridge: Cambridge University Press, 1995.

Perlmutter, David. *Picturing China in the American Press: The Visual Portrayal of Sino-American Relations in Time Magazine, 1949–1973.* Lanham, Md.: Rowman & Littlefield, 2007.

Pfaelzer, Jean. *Driven Out: The Forgotten War against Chinese Americans.* New York: Random House, 2007.

Philip A. Kuhn. *Chinese among Others: Emigration in Modern Times.* Lanham, Md.: Rowman & Littlefield, 2008.

Platt, Nicholas. *China Boys: How U.S. Relations with the PRC Began and Grew. A Personal Memoir.* Round Top, N.Y.: Vellum, 2010.

Pollard, Robert T. *China's Foreign Relations, 1917–1931.* New York: Macmillan, 1933.

Pomfret, John. "John Pomfret Interview (2007): Conversations with History; Institute of International Studies, UC Berkeley." http://globetrotter.berkeley.edu/people7/Pomfret/pomfret07-con0.html (accessed September 2, 2012).

Powell, Robert. *In the Shadow of Power: States and Strategies in International Politics.* Princeton, N.J.: Princeton University Press, 1999.

Price, Eva Jane. *China Journal 1889–1900: An American Missionary Family during the Boxer Rebellion; with the Letters and Diaries of Eva Jane Price and Her Family.* New York: Scribner, 1989.

Prime, Penelope B. "Studies of China's Economy in the United States." In *China Watching: Perspectives from Europe, Japan and the United States,* edited by Robert Ash, David Shambaugh, and Seiichiro Takagi, 80–96. London: Routledge, 2007.

Qi, Zhou. "Conflicts over Human Rights between China and the US." *Human Rights Quarterly* 27, no. 1 (February 2005): 105–124.

Qian, Qichen (钱其琛). *Waijiao shiji* [外交十记 Ten diplomatic episodes]. Beijing: Shijie zhishi chubanshe, 2003.

Qin, Julia Ya. "Trade, Investment and Beyond: The Impact of WTO Accession on China's Legal System." *China Quarterly,* special issue, 191 (2007): 720–744.

Qin, Yucheng. *The Diplomacy of Nationalism: The Six Companies and China's Policy toward Exclusion.* Honolulu, Hawaii: University of Hawai'i Press, 2009.

Qing, Simei. *Visions of Modernity, Identity, and U.S.-China Diplomacy, 1945–1960.* Cambridge, Mass.: Harvard University Press, 2007.

Rea, Kenneth W., and John C. Brewer, eds. *The Forgotten Ambassador: The Reports of John Leighton Stuart, 1946–1949.* Boulder, Colo.: Westview Press, 1981.

Reilly, Thomas H. *The Taiping Heavenly Kingdom: Rebellion and the Blasphemy of Empire.* Seattle, Wash.: University of Washington Press, 2004.

Reynold, Douglas R. *China, 1898–1912: The Xinzheng Revolution and Japan.* Cambridge, Mass.: Harvard University Press, 1993.

Roberts, Priscilla. "William L. Clayton and the Recognition of China, 1945–1966: More Speculations on the 'Lost Chances in China.'" *Journal of American-East Asian Relations* 7, nos. 1–2 (Spring–Summer 1998): 5–37.

Ross, Robert S. "International Bargaining and Domestic Politics: U.S.-China Relations since 1972." *World Politics* 38, no. 2 (1986): 255–287.

———. *Negotiating Cooperation: The United States and China, 1969–1989.* Stanford, Calif.: Stanford University Press, 1997.

Ross, Robert S., and Jiang Changbin, eds. *Re-Examining the Cold War: U.S.-China Diplomacy, 1954–1973.* Cambridge, Mass.: Harvard University Asia Center, 2001.

Ross, Robert S., Øystein Tunsjø, and Zhang Tuosheng, eds. *US-China-EU Relations: Managing the New World Order*. London: Routledge, 2010.

"Roundtable: Turning to the Pacific: U.S. Strategic Rebalancing toward Asia." *Asia Policy*, no. 14 (July 2012): 21–49.

Rubinstein, Murray A. "The Wars They Wanted: American Missionaries' Use of the *Chinese Repository* before the Opium War." *American Neptune* 48, no. 4 (Fall 1988): 271–282.

Rule, James B. "The Military State of America and the Democratic Left. George Packer Responds. Michael Walzer Responds. James B. Rule Replies." *Dissent* 57, no. 1 (Winter 2010): 81–90.

Ruskola, Teemu. "Canton Is Not Boston: The Invention of American Imperial Sovereignty." *American Quarterly* 57, no. 3 (September 2005): 859–884.

Sang, Ye. *China Candid: The People on the People's Republic*. Berkeley, Calif.: University of California Press, 2006.

Saxton, Alexander. *The Indispensable Enemy: Labor and the Anti-Chinese Movement in California*. Berkeley, Calif.: University of California Press, 1971.

Schaefer, Donald D. A. "U.S. Foreign Policies of Presidents Bush and Clinton: The Influence of China's Most Favored Nation Status upon Human Rights Issues." *Social Science Journal* 35, no. 3 (July 1998): 407–415.

Schaller, Michael. *The United States and China: Into the Twenty-First Century*. 3rd ed., 1st ed. in 1979. Oxford: Oxford University Press, 2002.

Schlesinger, Arthur M., Jr., ed. *The Dynamics of World Power: A Documentary History of United States Foreign Policy 1945–1973*. 4 vols. New York: Chelsea House Publishers, 1973.

———. "Origins of the Cold War." *Foreign Affairs* 46, no. 1 (October 1967): 22–52.

Schmidt, Hans. "Democracy for China: American Propaganda and the May Fourth Movement." *Diplomatic History* 22, no. 1 (December 1998): 1–28.

Schoppa, R. Keith. *Revolution and Its Past: Identities and Change in Modern Chinese History*. 2nd ed. Upper Saddle River, N.J.: Pearson, Prentice Hall, 2005.

Schrecker, John. "'For the Equality of Men—for the Equality of Nations': Anson Burlingame and China's First Embassy to the United States, 1868." *Journal of American-East Asian Relations* 17, no. 1 (2010): 9–34.

Schulzinger, Robert D. *The Making of the Diplomatic Mind: The Training, Outlook, and Style of United States Foreign Service Officers, 1908–1931*. Middletown, Conn.: Wesleyan University Press, 1975.

Schwar, Harriet Dashiell, ed. *Foreign Relations of the United States, 1964–1968*. Vol. 30, *China*. Washington, D.C.: Government Printing Office, 1998.

Schwarcz, Vera. *Long Road Home: A China Journal*. New Haven, Conn.: Yale University Press, 1984.

Schwartz, Harry. "The Moscow-Peking-Washington Triangle." *Annals of the American Academy of Political and Social Science* 414, issue *USA-USSR: Agenda for Communication* (July 1974): 41–50.

Scobell, Andrew. *China's Use of Military Force: Beyond the Great Wall and the Long March*. Cambridge: Cambridge University Press, 2003.

Scully, Eileen P. *Bargaining with the State from Afar: American Citizenship in Treaty Port China, 1844–1942*. New York: Columbia University Press, 2001.

Service, John S. *The Amerasia Papers: Problems in the History of U.S.-China Relations*. Berkeley, Calif.: Center for Chinese Studies, University of California, 1971.

Shambaugh, David. *Beautiful Imperialist: China Perceives America, 1972–1990*. Princeton, N.J.: Princeton University Press, 1991.

———, ed. *Deng Xiaoping: Portrait of a Chinese Statesman*. Oxford: Clarendon Press, 1995.

———. "A New China Requires a New US Strategy." *Current History* 109, no. 728 (September 2010): 219–226.

———, ed. *Power Shift: China and Asia's New Dynamics*. Berkeley, Calif.: University of California Press, 2005.

Shambaugh, David, Eberhard Sandschneider, and Zhou Hong, eds. *The China-Europe Relations: Perceptions, Policies and Prospects*. London: Routledge, 2007.

Shaw, Samuel. *The Journals of Major Samuel Shaw, the First American Consul at Canton, with a Life of the Author by Josiah Quincy*. Taipei: Ch'eng-wen Pub. Co., 1968. Reprint of Boston Wm. Crosby and H. P. Nichols ed.

Shaw, Yu-ming. *An American Missionary in China: John Leighton Stuart and Chinese-American Relations*. Cambridge, Mass.: Council on East Asian Studies, Harvard University, 1992.

Shen, Yu (沈予). "Lun Kangri Zhanzheng shiqi Rijiang de 'heping' jiaoshe" [论抗日战争时期日蒋的"和平"交涉 On the "peace" negotiations between Japan and Chiang during the War of Resistance]. *Lishi yanjiu*, no. 2 (1993): 108–127.

Sheng, Michael M. "Chinese Communist Policy toward the United States and the Myth of the 'Lost Chance' 1948–1950." *Modern Asian Studies* 28, no. 3 (1994): 475–502.

Shirk, Susan L. *China: Fragile Superpower*. Oxford: Oxford University Press, 2008.

Shiroyama, Tomoko. *China during the Great Depression: Market, State, and the World Economy, 1929–1937*. Cambridge, Mass.: Harvard University Asia Center, 2008.

Simmel, Georg. *Georg Simmel on Individuality and Social Forms*. Chicago, Ill.: University of Chicago Press, 1972.

Singer, Peter Warren. "America, Islam, and the 9–11 War." *Current History: A Journal of Contemporary Trends* 105, no. 695 (December 2006): 415–422.

Skidmore, David, and William Gates. "After Tiananmen: The Struggle over U.S. Policy toward China in the Bush Administration." *Presidential Studies Quarterly* 27, no. 3 (Summer 1997): 514–526.

Smith, Philip Chadwick Foster. *The Empress of China*. Philadelphia, Pa.: Philadelphia Maritime Museum, 1984.

So, Wai Chor. "The Making of the Guomindang's Japan Policy, 1932–1937: The Roles of Chiang Kai-Shek and Wang Jingwei." *Modern China* 28, no. 2 (April 2002): 213–252.

Solow, Robert M. "A Contribution to the Theory of Economic Growth." *Quarterly Journal of Economics* 70, no. 1 (February 1956): 65–94.

Soman, Appu K. "'Who's Daddy' in the Taiwan Strait? The Offshore Islands Crisis of 1958." *Journal of American-East Asian Relations* 3, no. 4 (Winter 1994): 373–398.

Song, Hongbin (宋鸿兵). *Huobi zhanzheng* [货币战争 The currency war]. Beijing: Zhongxin chubanshe, 2007.

Song, Qiang (宋强), Zhang Cangcang (张藏藏), et al. *Zhongguo keyi shuobu: Lengzhan houshidai de zhengzhi yu qinggan jueze* [中国可以说不: 冷战后时代的政治与情感抉择 China can say no: Politics and sentiment in the post–Cold War era]. Beijing: Zhonghua gongshang lianhe chubanshe, 1996.

Song, Xiaojun (宋晓军), Wang Xiaodong (王小东), et al. *Zhongguo bugaoxing: Da shidai, da mubiao ji women de neiyou waihuan* [中国不高兴:大时代、大目标及我们的内忧外患

China is unhappy: Broad picture, grand strategy, domestic concerns and external threats]. Nanjing: Jiangsu renmin chubanshe, 2009.

Spence, Jonathan. *God's Chinese Son: The Taiping Heavenly Kingdom of Hong Xiuquan.* New York: Norton, 1996.

———. *To Change China: Western Advisers in China.* Reprint. New York: Penguin, 2002. 1st ed. in 1969 by Little, Brown.

Steigerwald, David. "The Reclamation of Woodrow Wilson?" *Diplomatic History* 23, no. 1 (Winter 1999): 79–99.

———. *Wilsonian Idealism in America.* Ithaca, N.Y.: Cornell University Press, 1994.

Storti, Craig. *Incident at Bitter Creek: The Story of the Rock Springs Massacre.* Ames, Iowa: Iowa State University Press, 1991.

Stromquist, Shelton. *Re-Inventing 'the People': The Progressive Movement, the Class Problem, and the Origins of Modern Liberalism.* Champaign, Ill.: University of Illinois Press, 2006.

Stross, Randall E. *Bulls in the China Shop and Other Sino-American Business Encounters.* New York: Pantheon Books, 1990.

———. *The Stubborn Earth: American Agriculturalists on Chinese Soil, 1898–1937.* Berkeley, Calif.: University of California Press, 1986.

Su, Ge (苏格). *Meiguo duihua zhengce yu Taiwan wenti* [美国对华政策与台湾问题 America's China policy and the Taiwan question]. Beijing: Shijie zhishi chubanshe, 1998.

Su, Weizhi (苏位智), and Liu Tianlu (刘天路), eds. *Yihetuan yanjiu yibainian* [义和团研究一百年 One hundred years of Boxer studies]. Jinan: Qilu shushe, 2000.

Suettinger, Robert. *Beyond Tiananmen: The Politics of U.S.-China Relations.* Washington, D.C.: Brookings Institution Press, 2003.

Sullivan, Michael P. *Theories of International Relations: Transition and Persistence.* New York: Palgrave, 2001.

Sun, Youli. *China and the Origins of the Pacific War, 1931–1941.* New York: St. Martin's, 1993.

Sun, Zhe (孙哲). *Meiguo Guohui yu Zhongmei guanxi: Anli yu fenxi* [美国国会与中美关系: 案例与分析 The American Congress and U.S.-Chinese relations: Case studies and analysis]. Beijing: Shishi chubanshe, 2004.

———. *Meiguo xue: Zhongguo dui Meiguo zhengzhi waijiao yanjiu, 1979–2006* [美国学: 中国对美国政治外交研究 American studies: Chinese writings on American politics and foreign relations]. Shanghai: Shanghai renmin chubanshe, 2008.

Sutter, Robert. "Asia in the Balance: America and China's 'Peaceful Rise.'" *Current History* 103, no. 674 (2004): 284–289.

Swaine, Michael D. "Chinese Decision-Making Regarding Taiwan, 1979–2000." In *The Making of Chinese Foreign and Security Policy in the Era of Reform*, edited by David M. Lampton, 289–336. Stanford, Calif.: Stanford University Press, 2001.

Swaine, Michael D., and Zhang Tuosheng, with Danielle F. S. Cohen. *Managing Sino-American Crises: Case Studies and Analysis.* Washington, D.C.: Carnegie Endowment for International Peace, 2007.

Swan, Trevor W. "Economic Growth and Capital Accumulation." *Economic Record* 32, no. 63 (November 1956): 334–361.

Szuprowicz, Bohdan O. "China Fever: Scrambling for Shares in a $600 Million Buying Spree." *Management Review* 68, no. 5 (May 1979): 8–16.

Tai, Paul H., ed. *United States, China and Taiwan: Bridges for a New Millennium.* Carbondale, Ill.: Public Policy Institute, 1999.

Tamarin, Alfred, and Shirley Glubok. *Voyaging to Cathay: Americans in the China Trade.* New York: Viking, 1976.

Tang, Chi-hua (唐启华). *Bei "Feichu Bupingdeng Tiaoyue" zhebi de Beiyang xiuyue shi (1912–1928)* [被"废除不平等条约"遮蔽的北洋修约史 A history of the Beijing Government's treaty revision efforts that was overshadowed by the "Abolition of the Unequal Treaties"]. Beijing: Shehui kexue chubanshe, 2010.

Tang, Tsou. *America's Failure in China, 1941–50.* Chicago, Ill.: University of Chicago Press, 1963.

Tanner, Harold M. "Guerrilla, Mobile, and Base Warfare in Communist Military Operations in Manchuria, 1945–1947." *Journal of Military History* 67, no. 4 (October 2003): 1177–1222.

Tao, Wenzhao (陶文钊). *Zhongmei guanxi shi* [中美关系史 A history of Sino-American relations]. 3 vols. (vol. 2 edited). Shanghai: Shanghai renmin chubanshe, 2004.

Taylor, Jay. *The Generalissimo: Chiang Kai-Shek and the Struggle for Modern China.* Cambridge, Mass.: Belknap Press, 2009.

Teitler, Ger, and Kurt W. Radtke, eds. *A Dutch Spy in China: Reports on the First Phase of the Sino-Japanese War (1937–1939).* Leiden: Brill, 1999.

Teng, Ssu-yu, and John King Fairbank. *China's Response to the West: A Documentary Survey, 1839–1923.* Reprint of 1954 ed. with a new preface. Cambridge, Mass.: Harvard University Press, 1982.

———. *Research Guide for China's Response to the West: A Documentary Survey, 1839–1923.* Cambridge, Mass.: Harvard University Press, 1954.

Terrill, Ross. *The New Chinese Empire: And What It Means for the United States.* New York: Basic Books, 2003.

Teufel Dreyer, June. "The Shifting Triangle: Sino–Japanese–American Relations in Stressful Times." *Journal of Contemporary China* 21, no. 75 (2012): 409–426.

Thomas, S. Bernard. *Season of High Adventure: Edgar Snow in China.* Berkeley, Calif.: University of California Press, 1996.

Thomson, James Claude, et al. *Sentimental Imperialists: The American Experience in East Asia.* 2nd ed.. New York: Harper & Row, 1985. 1st ed. in 1981.

Thomson, James C., Jr. *While China Faced West: American Reformers in Nationalist China, 1928–37.* Cambridge, Mass.: Harvard University Press, 1969.

Tiedemann, R. Gary, ed. *Handbook of Christianity in China.* Vol. 2. Leiden: Brill, 2009.

———. "Protestant 'Missionary Cases' (Jiao'an) in Shandong Province, 1860–1900." *Ching Feng* 8, no. 1–2 (2007): 153–195.

Tong, Sarah Y. "The US-China Trade Imbalance: How Big Is It Really?" *China: An International Journal* 3, no. 1 (March 2005): 131–154.

Tuchman, Barbara. *Notes from China.* New York: Collier Books, 1972.

Tuchman, Barbara W. "If Mao Had Come to Washington: An Essay in Alternatives." *Foreign Affairs* 51, no. 1 (October 1972): 44–64.

———. *Stilwell and the American Experience in China, 1911–45.* New York: Bantam Books, 1972. 1st ed. in 1971 by Macmillan.

Tucker, Nancy Bernkopf, ed. *China Confidential: American Diplomats and Sino-American Relations, 1945–1996.* New York: Columbia University Press, 2001.

———. *The China Threat: Memories, Myths, and Realities in the 1950s.* New York: Columbia University Press, 2012.

———, ed. *Dangerous Strait: The U.S.-Taiwan-China Crisis.* New York: Columbia University Press, 2005.

———. *Patterns in the Dust: Chinese-American Relations and the Recognition Controversy, 1949–1950.* New York: Columbia University Press, 1983.

———. *Strait Talk: United States-Taiwan Relations and the Crisis with China.* Cambridge, Mass.: Harvard University Press, 2011.

———. *Taiwan, Hong Kong, and the United States, 1945–1992.* New York: Twayne Publishers, 1994.

Tyler, Patrick. *A Great Wall: Six Presidents and China, an Investigative History.* New York: Public Affairs, 1999.

Unger, David C. *The Emergency State: America's Pursuit of Absolute Security at All Costs.* New York: Penguin, 2012.

Van de Ven, Hans. "Stilwell in the Stocks: The Chinese Nationalists and the Allied Powers in the Second World War." *Asian Affairs* 34, no. 3 (November 2003): 243–259.

Van Dyke, Paul A. *The Canton Trade: Life and Enterprise on the China Coast, 1700–1845.* Hong Kong: Hong Kong University Press, 2005.

Varg, Paul A. *Open Door Diplomat: The Life of W. W. Rockhill.* Urbana, Ill.: University of Illinois Press, 1952.

Ver Steeg, Clarence L. "Financing and Outfitting of the First U.S. Ship to China." *Pacific Historical Review* 22, no. 1 (February 1953): 1–12.

Vogel, Ezra F. *Deng Xiaoping and the Transformation of China.* Cambridge, Mass.: Belknap Press, 2011.

Wachman, Alan. *Why Taiwan? Geostrategic Rationales for China's Territorial Integrity.* Stanford, Calif.: Stanford University Press, 2007.

Wakeman, Frederic, Jr. "The Canton Trade and the Opium War." In *The Cambridge History of China*, vol. 10, edited by Denis Twitchett and John K. Fairbank, 163–212. Cambridge: Cambridge University Press, 1978.

Wallerstein, Immanuel. *Geopolitics and Geoculture: Essays on the Changing World-System.* New York: Columbia University Press, 1991.

Walton, Gary M., and Hugh Rockoff. *History of the American Economy.* 10th ed. Mason, Ohio: South-Western, 2005.

Waltz, Kenneth N. *Theories of International Politics.* New York: McGraw-Hill, 1979.

Wang, Bingnan (王炳南). Zhongmei huitan jiunian huigu [中美会谈九年回顾 Recollections of nine years of Sino-American talks]. Beijing: Shijie zhishi chubanshe, 1985.

Wang, Chaoguang (汪朝光). *1945–1949: Guogong zhengzheng yu Zhongguo mingyun* [1945–1949: 国共战争与中国命运 The political conflict between the GMD and CCP and China's destiny]. Beijing: Shehui kexue wenxian chubanshe, 2010.

Wang, Dong. "China's Trade Relations with the United States in Perspective." *Journal of Current Chinese Affairs* 39, no. 3 (November 2010): 165–210.

———. *China's Unequal Treaties: Narrating National History.* Lanham, Md.: Rowman & Littlefield, 2005.

———. "Circulating American Higher Education: The Case of Lingnan University (1888–1951)." *Journal of American-East Asian Relations* 9, no. 3–4 (delayed 2000 issue, appeared in 2006): 147–167.

———. "The Discourse of the Unequal Treaties in Modern China." *Pacific Affairs* 76, no. 3 (November 2003): 399–425.

———. "Internationalizing Heritage: UNESCO and China's Longmen Grottoes." *China Information* 24, no. 2 (July 2010): 123–147.

———. *Managing God's Higher Learning: U.S.-China Cultural Encounter and Canton Christian College (Lingnan University), 1888–1952.* Lanham, Md.: Rowman & Littlefield, 2007.

———. "Portraying Chinese Christianity: The American Press and U.S.-China Relations since the 1920s." *Journal of American-East Asian Relations* 13 (November 2008): 81–119.

———. "Redeeming 'a Century of National Ignominy': Nationalism and Party Rivalry over the Unequal Treaties, 1928–1947." *Twentieth-Century China* 30, no. 2 (April 2005): 72–100.

———. "Restructuring Governance in Contemporary Urban China: Perspectives on State and Society." *Journal of Contemporary China* 20, no. 72 (November 2011): 723–733.

Wang, Gungwu. *Anglo-Chinese Encounters since 1800: War, Trade, Science, and Governance*. Cambridge: Cambridge University Press, 2003.

Wang, Guo. "The 'Revolution' of 1911 Revisited: A Review of Contemporary Studies in China." *China Information* 25, no. 3 (2011): 257–174.

Wang, Jisi. "China's Search for Stability with America." *Foreign Affairs* 84, no. 5 (September/October 2005): 39–48.

Wang, Jianlang (王建朗). "Xin Zhongguo chengli chunian Yingguo guanyu Zhongguo Lianheguo daibiaoquan wenti de zhengce yanbian" [新中国成立初年英国关于中国联合国代表权问题的政策演变 The evolution of British policy on the Chinese representation question in the UN in the early years of new China]. *Zhongguo shehui kexue*, no. 3 (2000): 179–190.

———. "Xinren de liushi: Cong Jiang Jieshi riji kan Kangzhan houqi de Zhongmei guanxi" [信任的流失: 从蒋介石日记看抗日后期的中美关系 The loss of trust: Sino-American relations in the later phases of the Anti-Japanese War as seen through the diary of Chiang Kai-Shek]. *Jindaishi yanjiu*, no. 3 (2009): 49–62.

Wang, Jingyu (汪敬虞). *Waiguo ziben zai jindai Zhongguo de jinrong huodong* [外国资本在近代中国的金融活动 The financial activity of foreign capital in modern China]. Beijing: Renmin chubanshe, 1999.

Wang, Qingjia Edward. "Guests from the Open Door: The Reception of Chinese Students into the United States, 1900s–1920s." *Journal of American-East Asian Relations* 3, no. 1 (Spring 1994): 55–75.

Wang, Qisheng (王奇生). *Geming yu fan geming: shehui wenhua shiye xia de Minguo zhengzhi* [革命与反革命:社会文化视野下的民国政治 Revolution and counterrevolution: Politics in the First Republic of China from the viewpoint of society and culture]. Beijing: Shehui kexue wenxian chubanshe, 2010.

Wang, Taiping (王泰平). *Zhonghua Renmin Gongheguo waijiaoshi* [中华人民共和国外交史 A diplomatic history of the People's Republic of China]. Beijing: Shijie zhishi chubanshe, 1999.

Wang, Xi (汪熙). "Lüelun Zhongmei guanxishi de jige wenti" [略论中美关系史的几个问题 A brief discussion of several issues in Sino-American relations]. *Shijie lishi*, no. 3 (1979): 12–19.

Wang, Xi (汪熙), and Tajiri Tōru (田尻利), eds. *150 Nian Zhongmei guanxishi lunzhu mulu (1823–1990)* [150 年中美关系史论著目录 A bibliography of works on the history of Sino-American relations over the last 150 years]. Shanghai: Fudan daxue chubanshe, 2005.

Wang, Yongqin (王永钦). "1966–1976 nian Zhong Mei Su guanxi jishi" [1966–76 年的中美苏关系纪事 A chronicle of China-U.S.-USSR relations, 1966–76]. Parts 1–3. *Dangdai Zhongguoshi yanjiu*, nos. 4–6 (1997): 112–26, 110–27, 143–156.

———. "1966–1976 nian Zhong Mei Su guanxi jishi." Part 4. *Dangdai Zhongguoshi yanjiu*, no. 1 (1998): 103–118.

Wang, Yunsheng (王芸生). *Liushi nianlai Zhongguo yu Riben* [六十年来中国与日本 China and Japan over the past sixty years]. Beijing: Sanlian chubanshe, 1981.

Weathersby, Katheryn. "New Findings on the Korean War." *Cold War International History Project Bulletin*, no. 3 (Fall 1993): 1, 14–18.

Wei, Shiyan (魏史言). *Nikesong fanghua* [尼克松访华 Nixon's visit to China]. *Xin Zhongguo waijiao fengyun* [新中国外交风云 New China's diplomatic experience]. 3 vols. Beijing: Shijie zhishi chubanshe, 1994.

Welch, Ian. "'Our Neighbors but Not Our Countrymen': Christianity and the Chinese in Nineteenth-Century Victoria (Australia) and California." *Journal of American-East Asian Relations* 13, a special volume edited by Dong Wang (November 2008): 149–183.

Werking, Richard H. "The Boxer Indemnity Remission and the Hunt Thesis." *Diplomatic History* 2, no. 1 (January 1978): 103–106.

West, Philip, ed. *Remembering the "Forgotten War": The Korean War through Literature and Art*. Armonk, N.Y.: M. E. Sharpe, 2000.

Westad, Odd Arne. *Cold War and Revolution: Soviet-American Rivalry and the Origins of the Chinese Civil War, 1944–1946*. New York: Columbia University Press, 1993.

———. *Restless Empire: China and the World since 1750*. New York: Basic Books, 2012.

White, Donald W. *The American Century: The Rise and Decline of the United States as a World Power*. New Haven, Conn.: Yale University Press, 1996.

White, Theodore H. "An Old China Hand in the New China." *Life*, March 17, 1972.

White, Theodore H., and Annalee Jacoby. *Thunder out of China*. New York: William Sloane Associates, 1946.

Whiting, Allen S. *Soviet Policies in China, 1917–1924*. 2nd ed. New York: Columbia University Press, 1957.

Whyte, Bob. *Unfinished Encounter: China and Christianity*. Harrisburg, Pa.: Morehouse Publishing, 1988.

Wilbur, C. Martin, and Julie Lien-ying How. *Missionaries of Revolution: Soviet Advisers and Nationalist China, 1920–1927*. Cambridge, Mass.: Harvard University Press, 1989.

Wilhelm, Alfred D., Jr. *The Chinese at the Negotiation Table: Style and Characteristics*. Washington, D.C.: National Defense University Press, 1991.

Wingrove, Paul. "Russian Documents on the 1954 Geneva Conference." Introduction. *Cold War International History Project Bulletin*, no. 16 (Fall 2007/Winter 2008): 85–91.

Wong, J. Y. *Deadly Dreams: Opium, Imperialism, and the Arrow War (1856–1860) in China*. Cambridge: Cambridge University Press, 1998.

Wong, R. Bin. "Centennial Perspectives on China's 1911 Revolution." *China Information* 25, no. 3 (2011): 275–282.

Wu, Cheng-tsu, ed. *Chink! A Documentary History of Anti-Chinese Prejudice in America*. New York: World Publishing, 1972.

Wu, Xinbo. "The Promise and Limitations of a Sino-U.S. Partnership." *Washington Quarterly* 27, no. 4 (Autumn 2004): 115–126.

Wu, Yixiong (吴义雄). "Yapian Zhanzheng qian zaihua xiren yu duihua zhanzheng yulun de xingcheng" [鸦片战争前在华西人与对华战争舆论的形成 The moulding of public opinion in support of war with China among Westerners in China prior to the Opium War]. *Jindaishi yanjiu* 179, no. 2 (March 2009): 23–43.

Xi, Xuan (席宣), and Jin Chunming (金春明). *"Wenhua Dageming" jianshi* ["文化大革命" 简史 A brief history of the "Cultural Revolution"]. Expanded ed. Beijing: Zhonggong dangshi chubanshe, 2006.

Xia, Yafeng. *Negotiating with the Enemy: U.S.-China Talks during the Cold War, 1949–1972.* Bloomington, Ind.: Indiana University Press, 2006.

Xiang, Liling (项立岭). *Zhongmei guanxi shi quanbian* [中美关系史全编 A comprehensive history of U.S.-Chinese Relations]. Shanghai: Huadong shifan daxue, 2002.

Xinbo, Wu. "Forging Sino–US Partnership in the Twenty-First Century: Opportunities and Challenges." *Journal of Contemporary China* 21, no. 75 (2012): 391–407.

Xiong, Xianghui (熊向晖). *Lishi de zhujiao: Huiyi Mao Zedong, Zhou Enlai ji si laoshuai* [历史的注脚:回忆毛泽东、周恩来及四老帅 Footnotes of history: Reflections on Mao Zedong, Zhou Enlai, and the four marshals]. Beijing: Zhongyang dangxiao chubanshe, 1995.

———. *Wode qingbao yu waijiao shengya* [我的情报与外交生涯 My careers in espionage and diplomacy]. Expanded ed. Beijing: Zhonggong dangshi chubanshe, 2006. 1st ed. in 1999.

Xiong, Zhiyong (熊志勇). *Bainian Zhongmei guanxi* [百年中美关系 A century of Sino-U.S. relations]. Beijing: Shijie zhishi chubanshe, 2006.

Xu, Guangqiu. *Congress and the U.S.-China Relationship, 1949–1979.* Akron, Ohio: Akron University Press, 2007.

———. "The Issue of U.S. Air Support for China during the Second World War, 1942–1945." *Journal of Contemporary History*, no. 36 (July 2001): 459–484.

———. *War Wings: The United States and Chinese Military Aviation, 1929–1949.* Westport, Conn.: Greenwood Press, 2001.

Xu, Guoqi. *China and the Great War: China's Pursuit of a New National Identity and Internationalization.* New York: Cambridge University Press, 2005.

Xu, Yihua (徐以骅). "Meiguo '1998 nian guoji zongjiao ziyoufa'" [美国1998年国际宗教自由法 The U.S. International Religious Freedom Act of 1998]. In *Zongjiao yu Meiguo shehui* [宗教与美国社会 Religion and American society], edited by Xu Yihua, 515–546. Beijing: Shishi chubanshe, 2004.

———. "'Patriotic' Protestants: The Making of an Official Church." In *God and Caesar in China: Policy Implications of Church-State Tensions*, edited by Jason Kindopp and Carol Lee Hamrin, 107–121. Washington, D.C.: Brookings Institution Press, 2004.

Xu, Yan (徐焰). *Diyi ci jiaoliang: Kangmei Yuanchao Zhanzheng de lishi huigu yu fansi* [第一次较量:抗美援朝战争的历史回顾与反思 The first showdown: Reflections on the Anti-American Korean War]. Beijing: Zhongguo guangbo dianshi chubanshe, 1990.

———. *Kangri Zhanzheng shengli qianxi zhi shengli hou wodang zhanlüe fangzhen de zhuanbian* [抗日战争胜利前夕至胜利后我党战略方针的转变 The transformation of CCP strategy from the eve to the aftermath of victory in the War of Resistance]. *Dangshi yanjiu ziliao*, edited by Zhongguo geming bowuguan dangshi yanjiushi (中国革命博物馆党史研究室). Vol. 7. Chengdu: Sichuan renmin chubanshe, 1987.

Yang, Guohua (杨国华). *Zhongmei Zhishi Chanquan wenti gaiguan* [中美知识产权问题概观 An overview of the U.S.-Chinese intellectual property question]. Beijing: Zhishi chanquan chubanshe, 2008.

Yang, Kuisong (杨奎松). "Huade Shijian yu xin Zhongguo dui Meiguo zhengce de queli" [华德事件与新中国对美国政策的确立 The Ward incident and the formulation of new China's policy toward the U.S.]. *Lishi yanjiu*, no. 5 (1994): 104–118.

———. *Shiqu de jihui? Kangzhan qianhou Guogong tanpan shilu* [失去的机会? 抗战前后国共谈判实录 A lost opportunity? A true account of the negotiations between the GMD and CCP before and after the War of Resistance]. Beijing: Xinxing chubanshe, 2010.

———. *Zhonggong yu Mosike de guanxi (1920–1960)* [中共与莫斯科的关系 The Chinese Communist Party's relations with Moscow]. Hong Kong Haixiao chuban shiye youxian gongsi, 1997.

———. *"Zhongjian Didai" de geming: Guoji da beijing xia kan Zhonggong chenggong zhidao* ["中间地带"的革命: 国际大背景下看中共成功之道 The "Mid-zone" revolution: Tracing the CCP's path to success within a broad international context]. Taiyuan: Shanxi renmin chubanshe, 2010.

Yang, Tianhong (杨天宏). *Jidujiao yu Minguo zhishi fenzi* [基督教与民国知识分子 Christianity and the intelligentsia in the Republic of China]. Beijing: Renmin chubanshe, 2005.

———. "Wanqing 'Junshi' waijiao yu 'Menhu Kaifang.'" [晚清"均势"外交与"门户开放" The diplomacy of "the Balance of Power" in late Qing and the "Open Door"]. *Shehui kexue yanjiu*, no. 6 (2008): 146–153.

Yang, Yunruo (杨云若), and Yang Kuisong (杨奎松). *Gongchan Guoji he Zhongguo geming* [Comintern and the Chinese Revolution 共产国际和中国革命]. Shanghai: Shanghai renmin chubanshe, 1988.

Ye, Weili. *Seeking Modernity in China's Name: Chinese Students in the United States, 1900–1927.* Stanford, Calif.: Stanford University Press, 2001.

Yen, Ching-hwang. *The Chinese in Southeast Asia and Beyond: Socioeconomic and Political Dimensions.* Singapore: World Scientific Publishing Co., 2008.

———. *Coolies and Mandarins: China's Protection of Overseas Chinese during the Late Ch'ing Period (1851–1911).* Singapore: Singapore University Press, 1985.

Young, Ernest P. *The Presidency of Yuan Shih-k'ai.* Ann Arbor, Mich.: University of Michigan Press, 1977.

Young, Kenneth Ray. "The Stilwell Controversy: A Bibliographical Review." *Military Affairs* 39, no. 2 (April 1975): 66–68.

Young, Louis. *Japan's Total Empire: Manchuria and the Culture of Wartime Imperialism.* Berkeley, Calif.: University of California Press, 1998.

Yung, Judy, Gordon H. Chang, and Him Mark Lai, comps. and eds. *Chinese American Voices: From the Gold Rush to the Present.* Berkeley, Calif.: University of California Press, 2006.

Zakaria, Fareed. *The Post-American World.* 1st ed. in 2008. New York: Norton, 2009.

Zarrow, Peter. *China in War and Revolution, 1895–1949.* London: Routledge, 2005.

Zhang, Baijia (章百家). "Cong 'Yibiandao' dao 'Quanfangwei': Dui wushi nian lai Zhongguo waijiao geju yanjin de sikao" [从"一边倒"到"全方位":对50年来中国外交格局演进的思考 From "Leaning to One Side" to "Multidirectional": Thoughts on the evolution of China's diplomatic framework over the last 50 years]. *Zhonggong dangshi yanjiu*, no. 1 (2000): 21–37.

Zhang, Baijia (章百家), and Jia Qingguo (贾庆国). "Cong Zhongguo jiaodu kan Zhongmei dashiji huitan" [从中国角度看中美大使级会谈 Sino-American ambassadorial talks seen from the Chinese perspective]. *Dangdai Zhongguoshi yanjiu*, no. 1 (2000): 40–51.

Zhang, Kaiyuan (章开沅), and Zhu Ying (朱英), eds. *Jindai jingji guanxi yu Zhongguo jindaihua* [近代经济关系与中国近代化 Modern economic relations and the modernization of China]. Wuhan: Huazhong chubanshe, 1990.

Zhang, Shu Guang. *Deterrence and Strategic Culture: Chinese-American Confrontations, 1949–58.* Ithaca, N.Y.: Cornell University Press, 1992.

———. *Economic Cold War: America's Embargo against China and the Sino-Soviet Alliance, 1949–1963.* Stanford, Calif.: Stanford University Press, 2001.

Zhang, Wenqin (章文钦). "Cong fengjian guanshang dao maiban shangren: Qingdai Guangdong hangshang Wu Yihe jiazu pouxi" [从封建官商到买办商人:清代广东行商伍怡和家族剖析 From feudal official merchant to comprador: An analysis of Guangdong's Hong merchant Yihe Wu Clan in the Qing Dynasty]. *Jindaishi yanjiu*, nos. 3 and 4 (1984): 167–97, 231–253.

———. *Guangdong Shisanhang yu zaoqi Zhongxi guanxi* [广东十三行与早期中西关系 Guangdong's Thirteen Hongs and early Sino-Foreign relations]. Guangzhou: Guangdong jingji chubanshe, 2009.

Zhang, Xiaojing. "Rebalancing the Global Economy." In *Global Power Revisited: The United States in a Changing World Order*, edited by Foresight. Berlin: Foresight, 2009.

Zhao, Suisheng, ed. *China and the United States: Cooperation and Competition in Northeast Asia*. New York: Palgrave Macmillan, 2008.

———. "Shaping the Regional Context of China's Rise: How the Obama Administration Brought Back Hedge in Its Engagement with China." *Journal of Contemporary China* 21, no. 75 (2012): 369–389.

Zheng, Bijian. "China's 'Peaceful Rise' to Great-Power Status." *Foreign Affairs* 84, no. 5 (September/October 2005): 18–24.

Zheng, Huixin (郑会欣). *Guomin Zhengfu zhanshi tongzhi jingji yu maoyi yanjiu (1937–1945)* [国民政府战时统制经济与贸易研究 A study of the Nationalist government's controlled wartime economy and trade regime]. Shanghai: Shanghai shehui kexueyuan chubanshe, 2009.

Zhonggong zhongyang wenxian yanjiushi (中共中央文献编辑委员会), ed. *Zhou Enlai xuanji* [周恩来选集 Selected works of Zhou Enlai]. Beijing: Renmin chubanshe, 1980.

Zhongguo guoji wenti yanjiu suo (中国国际问题研究所). *Guoji xingshi he Zhongguo waijiao lanpishu (2009/2010)* [国际形势和中国外交蓝皮书 The bluebook of the international situation and China's foreign affairs (2009/2010)] Beijing: Shijie zhishi chubanshe, 2010.

Zhu, Zhiqun. *US-China Relations in the 21st Century: Power Transition and Peace*. New York: Routledge, 2006.

Zi, Zhongyun (资中筠). Meiguo duihua zhengce de yuanqi he fazhan (1945–1950) [美国对华政策的缘起和发展 The origins and development of American policy toward China]. Chongqing: Chongqing chubanshe, 1987.

Zweig, David. *Internationalizing China: Domestic Interest and Global Linkages*. Ithaca, N.Y.: Cornell University Press, 2002.

Zweig, David, Chen Changgui, and Stanley Rosen. "Globalization and Transnational Human Capital: Overseas and Returnee Scholars to China." *China Quarterly* 179 (September 2004): 735–757.

# About the Author

Dong Wang is professor of contemporary Chinese history and director of the Centre for East Asian Studies at the University of Turku in Finland. As research associate, she is also affiliated with the Fairbank Center for Chinese Studies at Harvard University. Among other publications to her credit, she is the author of *China's Unequal Treaties: Narrating National History* (2005) and *Managing God's Higher Learning: U.S.-China Cultural Encounter and Canton Christian College (Lingnan University), 1888–1952* (2007). Her ongoing book projects include China's Longmen Grottoes in a changing world and global cooperation through the lens of intellectual property rights.

# Index

Yuan Shikai, 14, 124, 126, 175
Yung Wing, 88, 174, 188n1

Zakaria, Fareed, 295
Zeng Guofan, 105, 111
Zhang Jinfu, 251
Zhang Xueliang, 136, 154
Zhang Zhidong, 9, 63
Zhang Zuolin, 134
Zhao Ziyang, 259
Zheng Bijian, 291
Zhigang, 78
Zhili clique, 133

Zhou Enlai, 161, 164, 195, 199, 203;
    bilateral talks willingness of, 204;
    Far East tensions announcement of,
    214n6; Nixon conversations with,
    230; Romanian delegation meeting
    with, 228; U.S. and Soviet relations
    concerns of, 233; U.S. imperialism
    comments of, 226
Zhu De, 181
Zhu Rongji, 277, 280, 311, 312
Zongli Yamen (foreign office), 74
Zuo Zongtang, 111